Digests of Great American Plays

DIGESTS OF
GREAT AMERICAN PLAYS

COMPLETE SUMMARIES OF
MORE THAN 100 PLAYS FROM
THE BEGINNINGS TO THE PRESENT

By John Lovell, Jr.
Professor of English, Howard University

A CROWELL REFERENCE BOOK

THOMAS Y. CROWELL COMPANY
New York · Established 1834

To Marian

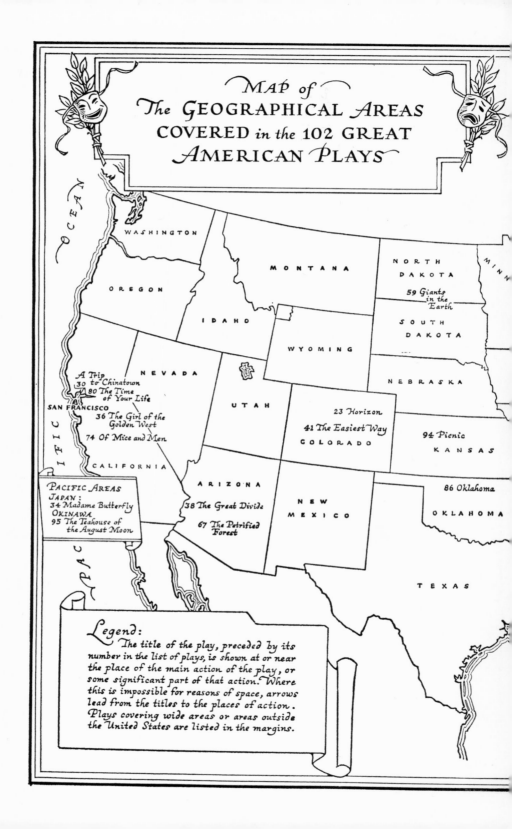

MAP of
The GEOGRAPHICAL AREAS
COVERED in the 102 GREAT
AMERICAN PLAYS

OCEAN

WASHINGTON

OREGON

IDAHO

MONTANA

NORTH
DAKOTA

59 Giants
in the
Earth

SOUTH
DAKOTA

MINN

WYOMING

NEBRASKA

NEVADA

A Trip
30 to Chinatown
80 The Time
of Your Life
SAN FRANCISCO

36 The Girl of the
Golden West

74 Of Mice and Men

UTAH

23 Horizon

41 The Easiest Way

COLORADO

94 Picnic

KANSAS

PACIFIC

CALIFORNIA

PACIFIC AREAS
JAPAN:
34 Madame Butterfly
OKINAWA:
95 The Teahouse of
the August Moon

ARIZONA

38 The Great Divide

67 The Petrified
Forest

NEW
MEXICO

86 Oklahoma

OKLAHOMA

TEXAS

Legend:
    The title of the play, preceded by its
number in the list of plays, is shown at or near
the place of the main action of the play, or
some significant part of that action. Where
this is impossible for reasons of space, arrows
lead from the titles to the places of action.
Plays covering wide areas or areas outside
the United States are listed in the margins.

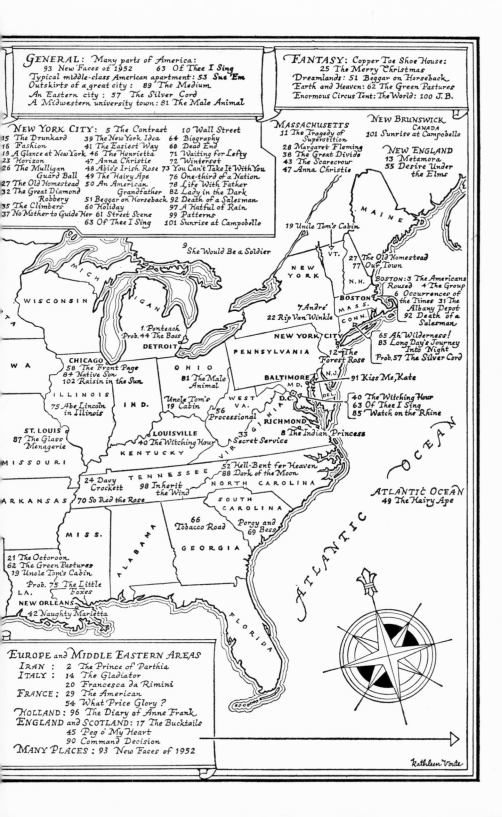

Preface

Although *Digests of Great American Plays* is a book of synopses, it contains more than a mere series of plot outlines. First, it attempts to reproduce not only the story but the flavor, the mood, and the dramatic essence of each play and its characters, so that the reader who lacks the time or the opportunity to see or read the original play may receive a clear impression of its characteristic qualities. Secondly, the book analyzes the basic components of each play: its principal theme, its plot and characters, the probable goals of the author in writing it, the social and cultural characteristics of the period and milieu in which it was written. Thirdly, this collection offers a comprehensive sampling of a dramatic literature that has been unjustly neglected.

The plays summarized date from 1766 to 1959. They represent works by every major writer and many minor writers, every significant theatrical trend, every phase of American life treated in the drama. For purposes of study or reference, each synopsis is provided with certain useful information: dates of writing or first performance and author's dates; identification of kind of play, theme, and main characters; a list of musical highlights; and historical notes on the play, its author, main performances, and prominent actors who have appeared in it. Usually one paragraph has been devoted to each act or scene, whichever is basic to the structure of the play. This rule is not followed when a scene is purely transitional or otherwise not dramatically significant. It is also not followed when a logical development of the dramatic action requires more than one paragraph to an act or scene.

A series of convenient appendixes list themes, periods, settings, actors, and musical selections, in addition to basic identifying information.

In the preparation of this volume, more than seven hundred plays have been assembled and classified.* The chief criterion of selection used in reducing that number to the present one hundred and two was that each play should represent a significant aspect of American drama. All the playwrights whose works appear in this collection were Americans by birth or adoption. At least one major work by every outstanding American dramatist will be found here. So will plays like *Uncle Tom's Cabin* that have made a strong impact on the nation's social or political thinking. A comedy that has achieved the popularity of *Abie's Irish Rose* reveals more about the temper of its times than many a drama of greater intrinsic merit. Occasionally a play is included that was little known in its own day, but nevertheless exemplifies a specific type of drama or portrays a particular element of American life. Examples are also given of plays for the musical stage, the motion pictures, television, and radio.

For too long it has been widely assumed that significant American dramatic writing began only in the twentieth century. On the contrary, over a period of two hundred years Americans have tried their hands successfully at every form of writing for the theater. It is hoped that this volume will reveal some of the splendid variety and vitality of their achievement—and that the reader will be encouraged to turn for further evidence to the plays themselves.

* This task was made possible by a grant from the Evening Star Foundation, Washington, D.C.

Contents

LIST OF PLAYS

TYPE	TIME COVERED	LOCALE
Blank verse historical drama: 5 acts	1760's	Area near Detroit
Blank verse romantic tragedy: 5 acts	First century B.C.	Northeast Iran
Dramatic dialogue	1775	Boston
Sardonic farce: 2 acts	1775	Boston
Manners and folk comedy: 5 acts	1785	New York City
Satirical farce: 2 acts	1789	Boston
Blank verse tragedy: 5 acts	1780	New York
Operatic blank verse drama (melodrama): 3 acts	1607–1610	Jamestown, Virginia
Semi-historical drama: 3 acts	1814	Upper New York and Canada
Farce with realistic and allegorical touches: 3 acts	1819	New York City
Blank verse tragedy: 5 acts	1675	Massachusetts
Pastoral opera: 2 acts	1820's	New Jersey farmland
Blank verse tragedy: 5 acts	Late 17th century	New England
Blank verse romantic tragedy: 5 acts	B.C. 73	Rome and other parts of Italy
Temperance melodrama	1843	New York City and nearby rural area
Manners comedy	1845	New York City
Manners comedy: 5 acts	1815	Bath, England
Local drama: 2 acts	1848	New York City
All-purpose drama: 6 acts	1850	Ky., Ohio, La., Vt.
Blank verse romantic tragedy: 5 acts	1300 A.D.	Rimini and Ravenna, Italy

List of Plays

TYPE	TIME COVERED	LOCALE
Southern problem drama	1850	Louisiana
Legendary and folk drama: 4 acts	1763; 1783	Hudson River village, New York
Frontier drama: 5 acts	Late 1860's	New York City; Far West
Frontier melodrama: 5 acts	Early 19th century	Backwoods section in Tennessee
Community entertainment drama: 1 act	Christmas night	Copper Toe Shoe House
Vaudeville-drama: 1 act	About 1878	New York City
Vaudeville-type Yankee melodrama: 4 acts	1880's	New Hampshire; New York City
Realistic drama: 4 acts	1890	Canton, Mass.
Drama of international contrasts: 4 acts	1875	Paris and environs, France
Farcical musical melodrama: 3 acts	1890	San Francisco
Literary farce: 1 act	Early 1890's	Boston
Melodrama: 6 acts	1895	New York City
War and espionage drama: 4 acts	1864–1865	Richmond
Oriental-American tragedy: 1 act	1900	Japanese harbor city
High society drama: 4 acts	1900	New York City and environs
Frontier drama: 4 acts	1849–1850	Manzanita County, California
Pure melodrama: 4 acts	Early 1900's	New York City and nearby rural area
Drama of American contrasts: 3 acts	End of 19th century	Arizona; Milford Corners, Massachusetts
Manners comedy, emphasizing divorce: 4 acts	1906	New York City
Realistic drama of mental telepathy: 4 acts	1907	Louisville, Ky.; Washington, D.C.

TYPE	TIME COVERED	LOCALE
Naturalistic drama: 4 acts	1907	Colorado; New York City
Operetta: 2 acts	1750	New Orleans
Symbolical drama: 4 acts	Late 17th century	Massachusetts
Impressionistic drama: 4 acts	1910	Eastern lake port (probably Detroit)
Irish-American comedy: 3 acts	Early 1900's	England
Business and society drama	1900	New York City
Drama: 4 acts	1920	New York City; Provincetown; Boston
Vaudeville-type sentimental-and-comic drama: 3 acts	1920	New York City
Expressionistic tragic drama: 8 scenes	1920	Atlantic Ocean; island near N.Y.; New York City
Immigrant-Americanization drama: 1 act	1924	Ellis Island, New York
Part-realistic, part-expressionistic, psychoanalytic fantasy: 2 parts	Early 1920's	New York City; dreamlands
Folk drama: 3 acts	1920	Western Carolina mountains
Radio farce: 1 act	1924	Typical middle-class American apartment
Realistic war drama	World War I	France
Freudian realistic tragedy: 3 parts	1850	New England
Musical drama: 4 acts	1920	West Virginia
Psychological drama	Mid 1920's	Eastern city
Photographic drama and satire: 3 acts	1927	Chicago
Frontier tragedy: 3 acts	1873–1880	Dakota prairie

TYPE	TIME COVERED	LOCALE
High society drama: 3 acts	1928	New York City
Melting pot drama: 3 acts	1920's	New York City
Religious fable: 2 parts	Sunday School time	Lower Louisiana town; Earth; Heaven
Musical comedy and drama of political satire	Early 1930's	All over the country; New York City; Washington, D.C.
Manners comedy: 3 acts	1930	New York City
Comedy: 3 acts	July 4 and 5, 1906	New London, Connecticut
Tragedy of the soil: 3 acts	1930	Back country, Georgia
Realistic Western drama: 2 acts	1934	Arizona
Naturalistic drama: 3 acts	Early 1930's	Lower Manhattan
Folk opera: 3 acts	1920's	Charleston, S. C.
Motion picture play: 9 reels	1860–1865	Tennessee
Agitprop, expressionistic drama: 7 scenes	1935	New York City
Blank verse tragedy: 3 acts	Early 1930's	New York City
Comedy drama: 3 acts	About 1935	New York City
Naturalistic tragedy: 3 acts	1937	Salinas Valley, California
Biographical drama: 3 acts	1830's to 1861	New Salem and Springfield, Illinois
Living newspaper style of agitprop drama: 2 acts—11 scenes	1705 to 1930's	New York City
Presentational drama	1901–1913	Grover's Corners, N.H.
Comedy: 3 acts	Late 1880's	New York City
Drama: 3 acts	1900	Southern town, probably in Louisiana

List of Plays

TYPE	TIME COVERED	LOCALE
Drama: 5 acts	1939	San Francisco
Comedy with social emphasis: 3 acts	1939	Midwest university town, probably Ohio
Musical psychological drama: 2 acts	1904–1940	New York City; Mapleton
Psychological drama: 4 acts	1912	New London, Connecticut
Expressionistic sociological drama: 10 scenes	Late 1930's	Chicago
Drama: 3 acts	1940	Near Washington, D.C.
Musical drama: 2 acts	About 1900	Oklahoma
Expressionistic-type drama, semifantasy: 8 scenes	1944, 1935, and the past	St. Louis
Folk drama and fantasy: 2 acts	Indefinite	Great Smoky Mountains— Tenn.–N.C. border
Opera: 2 acts	1945	Outskirts of a great city
Military drama: 3 acts	1944	England
Musical comedy: 2 acts	1940's	Baltimore
Naturalistic drama: 2 acts	1900's to 1940's	New York City; Boston
Musical revue: 2 acts	1950's	Many parts of England and America, esp. New England, N.Y. &theSouth
Midwestern domestic drama	1953	Kansas
Satirical dramatic tale: 3 acts	1953	Okinawa
Drama: 2 acts	1943 to 1945	Amsterdam, Holland

List of Plays

TYPE	TIME COVERED	LOCALE
Realistic drama: 3 acts	1950's	New York City
Semihistorical drama: 3 acts	1925	Tennessee
Television drama: 3 acts	1954	New York City
Verse drama and philosophical allegory: 11 scenes	Any time and always	Enormous circus tent: the world
Biographical drama: 3 acts	1921 to 1924	New Brunswick, Canada; New York City
Realistic drama: 3 acts	Sometime between 1945 and 1959	Chicago

Digests of Great American Plays

MAJOR ROBERT ROGERS (1731–1795)

Ponteach; Or, The Savages of America (written 1766)

*Elizabethan-style blank-verse
historical drama in five acts*

MAIN CHARACTER AND THEME: Strenuous efforts of the great Indian chief *Ponteach* (also spelled Pontiac), Emperor of the Great Lakes, to overthrow the British just after they had conquered the French.

OTHER CHARACTERS:

Philip and *Chekitan*, Ponteach's sons

Tenesco, his chief counselor and generalissimo

Astinaco, The Bear, and *The Wolf*, Indian Kings who join Ponteach

Torax and *Monelia*, son and daughter of Hendrick, *Emperor of the Mohawks*

Indian conjurer

French priest

Sharp, Gripe, and *Catchum*, three English governors

Colonel Cockum and *Captain Frisk*, commanders of a garrison in Ponteach's country

McDole and *Murphey*, two Indian traders

Jack, McDole's servant

Honnyman and *Orsbourn*, two English hunters

Mrs. Honnyman, wife of Honnyman

Warriors

Messengers

TIME: 1760's.

PLACE: Area near Detroit.

MUSICAL HIGHLIGHT: "War Song" to tune of "Over the Hills and Far Away."

1

HISTORICAL NOTE: Francis Parkman has stated that the drama opens with an authentic picture and analysis of the reasons for Ponteach's campaign against the British. As the drama continues, however, it accompanies history only partly through the massacres of 1763 in the Detroit area, and departs from history entirely to tell a story of inter-Indian rivalries and of love affairs and ambitious schemings within Ponteach's own household. Its author was in command of the English fort at Detroit in 1760, met Ponteach personally, and shows himself fully conversant with the political and human issues surrounding the great chief and his destiny. As a colorful ranger and Indian fighter, Rogers became the hero of Kenneth Roberts' *Northwest Passage* (1937). Parkman and Moses Coit Tyler refer to Rogers and his drama as important and reliable historical source material. The drama was printed by J. Millan in London, 1766, and again by the Caxton Club, Chicago, edited by Allan Nevins, 1914. It has, undeservedly, not been produced.

ACT I (*four scenes*)

The trader, McDole, in an Indian trading house, shows Murphey how to cheat Indians. He gives them drugged rum, to befuddle them, and uses trick scales. The British, he says, are better than the French, who give no rum. For six quarts of watered rum, McDole gets ninety pounds of "sterling beaver." Although aware that if Indians detect the fraud they will take revenge on innocent whites, McDole persists.

In a desert, Orsbourn and Honnyman, whose relatives have been killed by Indians, defy the law that makes it death to kill an Indian; they ambush two approaching Indians, kill both, steal their packs of abundant furs, and scalp the braves (for the 200 crowns that will be paid when the next Indian war starts). Honnyman says he has killed a dozen. The two hunters plan to turn their furs to gold, their gold to wine.

Colonel Cockum and Captain Frisk give a cool and insolent reception to Indian chiefs who have come to the English fort to ask that the whites stop giving rum to braves and stop cheating them. The chiefs remind them that the French always listened to the Indian. Ponteach warns the English commanders not to let their victory over the French delude them. Agreeing among themselves that the Indians are dangerous, the commanders are glad for the strong walls, the shot, and the cannon that surround them.

2

"*Ponteach; or, The Savages of America*" (written 1766)

Governors Sharp, Gripe, and Catchum gather in an apartment in the fort to present to the chiefs the gifts from the English king. Ironically quoting Holy Writ, they say their religion teaches them to look out for themselves first. Thus they send to their own apartments the greater part of what the king had sent for distribution. When given the gifts, Ponteach, speaking for the other chiefs and remarking on the skimpiness—a very few blankets, hatchets, pans, knives, kettles, and very little wampum—hints at venality. On the other hand, the belts and furs that the chiefs leave for the king are valuable indeed. The governors appropriate these gifts to themselves on the ground that the king would be insulted to receive them.

ACT II (*two scenes*)

On the Indian side, the sons of Ponteach note his dour appearance. Chekitan, having watched him in secret, has heard him say: "'Tis fix'd, I'll be reveng'd; I will make War; I'll drown this Land in Blood." Chekitan fears that the Emperor Hendrick will stand with the English rather than with Ponteach and his allies—Fox, Bear, Eagle, Otter, Wolf, all strong Indian chiefs.

To his sons, whom he swears to secrecy, Ponteach says that he cannot bow to the English any longer and still be Ponteach. He wonders why the English differ so much from the French, who studied the Indian tongue and manners, wore Indian dress, and even intermarried. He has foreseen all risks and knows he can win. After hearing their father, Chekitan urges caution and deliberate wisdom; Philip calls his brother a coward. Ponteach quiets them and departs. Chekitan admits that his caution is based on his fear of losing Monelia, daughter of Hendrick. Pretending to help him keep Monelia, Philip devises a plan, to which Chekitan joyfully agrees. Alone, Philip cries out: "Oh! what a wretched thing is a man in love!" Actually, Philip's plan is to kill both Monelia and Torax, Hendrick's son, out of vengeance for Chekitan's refusing him the captive Ionanta in the past and to the end of accusing the English and thus forcing Hendrick into the war. He also hopes to eliminate Chekitan and leave himself the heir apparent.

ACT III (*three scenes*)

In the forest, Chekitan meets Monelia and declares his love with great oaths. She asks him to forbear, because he reminds her of false Christians who

3

aim at seduction. He cannot believe she would compare him to a Christian. Soon they are immersed in mutual admiration. Chekitan tells her and Torax of the impending war. Monelia wants to go home; Torax wants to stay and fight; both finally agree to accept Chekitan's sponsorship and to stay.

Appearing before the Indian conjurer and the French priest, Ponteach asks his prospects. After he has told them what he intends to do, they consult their oracles and promise him success. Later, the French priest reveals his scheme to pass the news to France and Rome and to capitalize on it politically. But he intends, before going away, to revel with Monelia.

Before an assembly of chiefs in the Indian Senate House, Ponteach eloquently pleads that they all die rather than be slaves to cowards, and that they swear to keep the liberty and land their fathers left them. Tenesco, Ponteach's counselor, says that the British, through pride, insult, encroachment, knavery, and fraud, have earned this war. The French priest promises that every Indian who dies in this war will merit heaven. Eventually the chiefs rise one by one and sink their hatchets into a block, signifying agreement and union. They go out singing their "War Song."

ACT IV (*four scenes*)

The war has started. But Chekitan is delayed because he must rescue Monelia from the libidinous grasp of the French priest. After much begging, the French priest is granted his life. He tells Chekitan that he has a dispensation from St. Peter to quench the fire of love when it grows painful. Chekitan curses him for lying, and the French priest angrily departs. Chekitan tells Monelia she is now eternally his. Leaving her in Torax' care, Chekitan sets forth for the war.

From messengers it is learned that three English forts have fallen and that all the English therein have been destroyed by fire, except some few who escaped to die of hunger. Warriors show the scalps of Colonel Cockum and Captain Frisk and say the dogs have eaten their brains. Orsbourn has been scalped, but Honnyman, his wife, and two children—one a sucking babe—have been brought in.

As Mrs. Honnyman prays for her children, Honnyman, now touched, confesses the guilt (murdering the two braves with Orsbourn) that helped condemn all whites. Mrs. Honnyman, hearing the shouts for death outside, fears their punishment is just. Honnyman asks to receive all the torture,

4

begging that the innocent go free: Ponteach so orders. Mrs. Honnyman leaves. The braves fall upon Honnyman with various instruments of torture. After he escapes in death, they brush the walls to dislodge and drive out his spirit. Philip strikes the dead body and spits upon its face.

ACT V (*five scenes*)

Philip stabs Monelia with his knife and hews Torax with his hatchet. Then he calls out that he has been attacked by an English band, showing a self-inflicted wound. As Philip goes to have his wound dressed, Ponteach declares the murderers blind not to have trembled before majesty and worth.

As Ponteach arranges proper funeral rites, Chekitan returns in glory although without a big victory. He is stupefied at the loss of Monelia. "Oh wretched, wretched, wretched Chekitan!" he cries out. Later he says of Monelia:

> You've all been cruel; she died to torment me;
> To raise my pain, and blot out every joy.

He says he will kill everything he sees; he'll even kill the earth that dared to drink her blood. As Chekitan embraces Monelia, Torax arises and begs Philip not to kill him, not to be so cruel. Revived, Torax tells the full story of Philip's bloody deed. Finding Philip, Chekitan challenges and kills him. Chekitan, desolate, stabs himself.

Now Ponteach is destroyed by the loss of his sons—"more than murder'd, more than lost by death." They did not die for their country's cause, but by way of guilt, treason, murder, falsehood, deceit, unbridled passion, cowardice, revenge, and other infamous things, which bring upon man the just contempt of all. But he must return to public duty. Tenesco goes to excite the troops. Ponteach says:

> I'll rise above this hurricane of fate,
> And show my courage to the Gods themselves.

Tenesco returns to say that Ponteach's troops are defeated and routed. Standing fast, Ponteach does not fear—he will obey his stars. He says good-by to field, streams, groves, and hills, of which he is no more owner and king. He will go where there is no British foe, beget more sons, arm fresh troops, and plot new schemes of future greatness:

> Britons may boast, the Gods may have their Will,
> Ponteach I am, and shall be Ponteach still.

THOMAS GODFREY (1736–1763)

The Prince of Parthia (1767)

Blank-verse romantic tragedy in five acts

MAIN CHARACTER AND THEME: Struggles of *Arsaces*, favored son of the king of Parthia, to free his nation from foreign domination and vicious domestic influences and to be united happily with his sweetheart.

OTHER CHARACTERS:

Artabanus, King of Parthia
Vardanes and *Gotarzes*,
  his other sons
Barzaphernes, lieutenant general
  under Arsaces
Lysias and *Phraates*,
  officers of the court

Bethas, a noble Arabian captive
Thermusa, the queen
Evanthe, beloved of Arsaces
Cleone, her confidante
Edessa, attendant on the queen
Guards
Attendants

TIME: Probably first century B.C.

PLACE: Ctesiphon on Tigris River (near Baghdad), in what is today northeast Iran.

MUSICAL HIGHLIGHTS: Hymn to the sun, "Parent of Light"; "Tell me Phillis; tell me why."

HISTORICAL NOTE: *First drama by an American to be professionally produced.* First performed March 24, 1767, at Southwark Theatre, Philadelphia. Written to promulgate the noble ideals of the cultural community in which Godfrey was educated, that of Provost William Smith of the College of Philadelphia (later the University of Pennsylvania), whose other pupils included Benjamin West and Francis Hopkinson.

ACT I (*six scenes*)

Before the Temple of the Sun, people shouting and throwing flowers glorify Arsaces, their savior. He has routed the Arabian enemy. Since childhood he has led a model life. But Vardanes works against his brother because Arsaces is heir apparent and is beloved by Evanthe, whom Vardanes covets. Queen Thermusa hates Arsaces for having killed Vonones, her son by a former marriage, who had plotted to usurp the Parthian crown. Expecting advancement from Vardanes, the officer Lysias is also Arsaces' enemy. Besides Arsaces, Thermusa hates her husband, King Artabanus, who neglects her. In the grand victory celebration, Artabanus praises Arsaces and commutes the death sentence of Bethas, the Arabian captive, to life imprisonment.

ACT II (*eight scenes*)

When Arsaces comes to visit Bethas, Lysias and Vardanes watch nearby, hoping to prove him a traitor. Bethas declares Arsaces' generosity a rare thing for Parthians. Then Bethas welcomes Evanthe, his long-lost daughter. Arsaces promises to beg the king for Bethas' freedom. Though touched by the scene, Lysias still condemns Arsaces. Vardanes swears to gain the crown, or else a glorious tomb.

ACT III (*nine scenes*)

En route to Evanthe's chamber, Artabanus is intercepted by Thermusa. He tells her that marriage palls and that he is not ashamed of his passions. Calling him "Traitor! Villain!" she vows revenge. When Bethas is ordered freed, Evanthe abases herself before the king, to offer thanks. He elevates her most graciously. In his generous mood, he grants, unasked, a boon to Arsaces: it is permission to marry Evanthe. In pain the king is led away by Vardanes, to whom he confesses his disappointed love. This is Vardanes' cue to show the king a paper describing Arsaces' plot to seize the throne. The king orders Vardanes to seize Evanthe and hide her for him. Vardanes, in soliloquy, swears to hold Evanthe for himself, saying it would be a sin to give her to an old man.

ACT IV (*seven scenes*)

The courtier Phraates reports to Gotarzes that the preceding night his father Artabanus was murdered and Arsaces imprisoned; at Lysias' instigation,

7

Vardanes has been declared king. Gotarzes flees to Barzaphernes. Thermusa comes to stab Arsaces but she finds that she cannot because Artabanus' ghost tells her three times to forbear. She runs out distracted, pursued by guilt and fears. Later, she is found dead. Barzaphernes and Gotarzes force the palace and rescue Arsaces, who will not permit himself to be crowned king until he avenges his father.

ACT V (*nine scenes*)

To Evanthe sleeping amidst slow music enters a sex-mad Vardanes. He assures her that only her "kindness" to him will save Arsaces' life. Ignoring her pleas to think on her innocence and to protect her from becoming a flower robbed of its sweetness and universally spurned, he prepares to ravish her. At the moment, Lysias rushes in to tell him to arm and face Barzaphernes and Arsaces, who, though thrice repulsed, have returned with increased fury. At Evanthe's request, her confidante Cleone observes the battle from the turret; cursing Vardanes, Cleone reports Arsaces' fall. On the contrary, Arsaces is conqueror. He orders Lysias, Artabanus' actual killer, hurled from the highest tower. Dying also, Vardanes is sorry that only Phraates' sword prevented his killing Arsaces. He is ready for cold death to let him "forget Ambition's mighty toil." Having drunk poison on Cleone's report, Evanthe is brought in. She asks Arsaces for one tear to celebrate her impending death; Arsaces promises fountains. With her dying breath, she asks Arsaces to protect her father (not knowing he is already dead from despair). Ignoring the salutes of "Royal Sir," Arsaces stabs himself with Barzaphernes' sword. He wills the crown to Gotarzes and asks to be laid by Evanthe's side. Offering to stab himself, Barzaphernes is persuaded to "dare to live" by Gotarzes. The new king orders everyone to the Temple to appease the angry powers.

8

3

JONATHAN SEWALL (1728–1796)

The Americans Roused, in a Cure for the Spleen; Or, Amusement for a Winter's Evening; Being the Substance of a Conversation on the Times, over a Friendly Tankard and Pipe (printed 1775)

Dramatic dialogue

MAIN CHARACTER AND THEME: As the country gets more and more deeply involved in dangerous revolutionary matters, *Sharp*, a country parson, discusses the issues with six good companions in an old New England "taproom."

OTHER CHARACTERS:

Bumper, a country justice	*Trim*, a barber
Fillpot, an innkeeper	*Brim*, a Quaker
Graveairs, a deacon	*Puff*, a recent representative

TIME: 1775.

PLACE: Boston or environs.

HISTORICAL NOTE: A dramatic piece presenting in troublous times both the revolutionary and the Tory arguments, with emphasis on the latter. The author was a Harvard graduate and a Boston lawyer who inclined

9

to the patriotic side until chagrined by the refusal of the state of Massachusetts to pay the debts left by his uncle (Chief Justice Stephen Sewall) and by the opposition of the Otises to his petition. He had an excellent reputation for eloquence and acuteness. After service with Tory newspapers, Sewall was rewarded by the British government with lucrative appointments. In 1775 he was forced to leave America for England; in 1779 his American estate was confiscated. Present dramatic dialogue was printed in Boston in 1775 and printed and sold in Tarrytown, New York, the same year.

ACTION

At the outset Sharp is willing to leave affairs of state to wiser heads, but as a good barber Trim objects. He says that to take away his privilege of denouncing politics, Lord North, the East India Company, the constitution, charter rights, duties, taxes, and the like, is equivalent to stripping him of his razors, soap, combs, and all, and setting fire to his shop. Moreover, Trim would like to trim Lord North, the East India Company, Lords and Commons (excepting the dissentients), Governor Bernard, and Governor Hutchinson— he would have them all head over ears in suds if he could get at them. In spite of his feelings, Trim concedes that there is little difference between a true Whig and an honest Tory, and further that Americans cannot withhold obedience to King and Parliament.

With this last statement Brim and Fillpot agree. But Puff says they are mistaken. It is Chatham and Pitt and Camden who are right, and not North and Hilsboro, who have stripped us of our birthright as Englishmen. Then Graveairs agrees with Puff.

At this point, Sharp reminds Graveairs and Puff that we *do* have freedom of conscience in religion, we *do* reap the fruits of our own labors, and we are *not* overburdened with taxes. Trim now bursts into Latin: *O fortunates, nimium, sua si bona norint Americanos!* (How happy are Americans, if they did but know it!) Sharp seconds this declaration, saying that Americans, like Dryden's Jews, talk foolishly of their privileges. When Fillpot says it is true he does not like the idea of taking up arms, Sharp continues by objecting to the doctrine that the tea tax is taxation without our consent. He says, further, that it is silly to talk of fighting the best military machine in Europe.

Opposing Sharp, Puff speaks complimentarily of the Suffolk Resolves of

10

the Continental Congress. Devastatingly, Sharp deplores such ill-advised resolutions and shows them to be founded on very shaky logic. Brim joins him by demonstrating that popular uprisings have all been bad. Bumper also supports Sharp and calls the talk about "redress of grievances" a "decoy set up to catch the ignorant and unwary."

After further argument, Puff and Graveairs are won over from their revolutionary positions. All seven companions now agree to stand against treason and to support King and Parliament.

MERCY WARREN (1728–1814)

The Group (printed 1775)

Blank-verse sardonic farce in two acts

MAIN CHARACTER AND THEME: Astringent patriotic drama condemning with excessive contempt "The Group" of Americans who became tools of the British King and Parliament during the perilous days following the Regulating Act, effective June, 1774, when the King and his chief agents —Lord North and General Gage—substituted their own for the popular electees. Although not in the cast, the head of "The Group" is Governor (formerly Chief Justice) Hutchinson, native of Massachusetts, called Rapatio.

OTHER CHARACTERS (their real names in parentheses):

Lord Chief Justice Hazlerod
    (Oliver, Stamp Act officer, hanged in effigy, August 14, 1765)
Judge Meagre (E. Hutchinson)
Brigadier Hateall (Ruggles)
Hum Humbug, Esquire
    (John Erving)
Sir Sparrow Spendall
    (Sir William Pepperell)
Col. Hector Mushroom
    (Col. Murray)
Beau Trumps (John Vassall)

Dick, the Publican (Lechmere)
Simple Sapling, Esquire
Monsieur de François
    (N. R. Thomas)
Crusty Crowbar, Esquire
    (J. Boutineau)
Dupe, Secretary of State
    (T. Flucker)
Scriblerius Fribble
    (Daniel Leonard, Tory journalist, called Massachusettensis)
Commodore Bateau (Loring)
Collateralis, a new-made judge

12

The style of the drama is to have the members of "The Group," through revealing their deeds and motives, condemn themselves.

TIME: 1775.

PLACE: Boston—first a little dark parlour; later, a large dining room.

HISTORICAL NOTE: Printed in Jamaica and Philadelphia, 1775. The author was the wife of General Joseph Warren and sister of James Otis, both outstanding leaders of the American Revolution in Massachusetts. The drama is a sample of dozens condemning British warmongers and American traitors, commending and upholding the justice and heroism of the American cause. It contrasts with the light, frivolous plays produced by the English occupiers of New York during much of the Revolution, such as General Burgoyne's *The Blockade of Boston.*

ACT I

Sapling speaks of the sad times and of the people resolved to die rather than submit. Hateall says let them die: as long as he has the friendship of North and Gage, he would not recede to save from swift perdition his wife, country, family, or friends. Crowbar, however, begins to sicken at the parade of honors purchased at the price of peace. Hazlerod claims to have followed his conscience even though the result has destroyed careers in commerce, mechanics, and ironmongering throughout the country. He later gives his tears and conscience to the winds. Mushroom wonders if their British friends will support them when the whole continent, from Hampshire through the wide western plains to southern shores, is united in arms. Hateall assures them of English support; as proof, he has sent "his new-born brat" abroad to avoid the impending destruction, misery, death, confiscated estates, slavery, despair, wrecks, halters, orphans, and starving babes. Hazlerod will feel no pity since the Americans have been warned of what will happen to them if they refuse to accept the badge of slaves. Hateall agrees, saying he would send all these dissenters "murm'ring to the shades of hell."

ACT II

François recalls his father's escape from oppression in France and his command to his son to resist oppression at all costs. Fribble tells him, then, to go begging to Freedom's Sons. He says he never can—he has too great

13

an itch for titled place, even should it mean flame and fagot blazing in every street. Trumps can understand; he once walked and worked with decent men in fair virtue, but he found the patriotic path unprofitable. The Arch Traitor (Rapatio) persuaded him to persevere in spite of wounded friendships, a goaded mind, and the sacred ties of truth and honor. Even now Rapatio weeps crocodile tears for "his people." Before dawn, says Trump, ships will come, laden with troops from Hannover and Hesse. He believes that the Americans will greatly resist and show themselves descended from freedom-fighters like Hampden, Fairfax, and Pym. He hopes, however, that the carnage will bring victory to "The Group" and will invigorate their sinking souls.

14

ROYALL TYLER (1757–1826)

The Contrast (1787)

Manners and folk comedy in five acts

MAIN CHARACTER AND THEME: Dramatic demonstration by *Colonel Henry Manly* of the superiority of the social ideals of the new American nation over those of the most brilliant European societies.

OTHER CHARACTERS:

Billy Dimple, American-born but English-educated—an ardent Chesterfieldian

Vanrough, strong American father who minds the main chance

Jessamy, Dimple's man and imitator

Jonathan, Manly's attendant but his own man—a Yankee

Charlotte, Manly's sister

Maria, Vanrough's daughter, affianced in childhood to Dimple

Letitia, an heiress, a ward to Charlotte's uncle

Jenny, maid

Servants

TIME: About 1785.

PLACE: New York City.

MUSICAL HIGHLIGHT: "Yankee Doodle"; "The sun sets in night."

HISTORICAL NOTE: First performed April 16, 1787, John Street Theatre, New York, then in principal American cities. Author later chief justice of Vermont Supreme Court. *Second drama by an American to be professionally produced; first native American drama.* Also introduces into American drama the European-American social contrast, later a prime force in American literature, especially in the emerging American realism as developed by Howells and James.

ACT I (*two scenes*)

In conversation, Charlotte reveals herself to Letitia as reckless, society-struck, and antisentimental, but charming. The two discuss the activities of society, —promenading on the mall, shopping tours, new styles of dress and hair, and the prevalence of scandal. They also discuss the incongruity of the "romance" between Billy Dimple and Maria, the latter spending all her time reading Richardson and growing daily more staid and sentimental, the former a racy gentleman with foreign airs. Charlotte is proud, in aside, that Dimple is also paying court to her.

In Vanrough's house, Maria soliloquizes on the outrage done to her affections by her "solemn engagement." When Vanrough reminds her of the fortune she is acquiring by marriage, she says that one hundredth of that plus the heart of the man she could love would be better. Ignoring her unbusiness-like talk, he plans to open an expensive pipe of Madeira on her wedding day. When he goes, Maria again pities herself, especially because her husband-to-be is a depraved wretch whose only virtue is a polished exterior, one who breaks families by pursuing women, and one "whom, though my lips may solemnly promise to honor, I find my heart must ever despise."

ACT II (*two scenes*)

As Charlotte announces her firm adherence to the laws of fashion and scandal, she receives a letter from her brother, Colonel Manly, stating that he, who has never been closer to the city than Harlem Heights, will soon pay her a visit. She describes her brother as her exact opposite, a *penseroso* like Maria. Manly arrives. In his self-revealing conversation, he speaks with due respect for his parents, General George Washington, and his country (he will not cash his commutation notes for fear of embarrassing the national treasury); he does not drink or game; he fears he lacks the proper appreciation for the society into which Charlotte would like to introduce him.

On the mall, Dimple's man, Jessamy, speaks of the inferiority of things to those in London. Accosting Jonathan as a servant, he is corrected: Jonathan advertises himself as the colonel's waiter and a true-blue son of liberty;

16

his father's farm is as good as the colonel's. By referring to General Shays and the Order of the Cincinnatus, Jonathan demonstrates the lack of distinction between quality and other folk in America. Jonathan is impressed by New York sights—marble monuments, Holy Ground, a prostitute (with sailors). When Jessamy offers to teach him gallantry and Chesterfieldian ways, Jonathan declares himself as good as married to Tabitha Wyman, the deacon's daughter back home. Jessamy's plan is to send Jonathan to "attack" Jenny, the maid, and fill her with disgust, thereby making easier Jessamy's conquest of her.

ACT III (*two scenes*)

Dimple, always reading Chesterfield, lets it be known that he is swamped with bills. Consequently, he plans to break with Maria and marry Letitia because of her fortune, but meanwhile to command the person of Charlotte, whom he says he loves. He sends Jessamy with private letters for Charlotte and Letitia.

On being introduced to Jenny, Jonathan is asked how he liked the play the previous evening. Jonathan says he would never be caught in "the devil's drawing-room" (the playhouse). Whether he knew it or not, says Jenny, he was at the theater. His description is most naive (including a note on Darby Wignell, who played Jonathan in production). When he went to demand his money back, says Jonathan, he was told he had seen *The School for Scandalization* (Sheridan's *The School for Scandal*).

Jessamy gone, Jenny queries Jonathan. She wants all information about Manly, who visited the Vanrough home that morning and made a fine impression on Maria. When asked if he can sing, Jonathan says yes, church songs; when Jenny inquires about his mastery of popular songs ("Roslin Castle," "The Maid of the Mill"), he counters with "Yankee Doodle," and proceeds to sing a few verses. He says he can sing only 190 verses, unlike Tabitha at home, who knows them all. Following Jessamy's instructions, Jonathan proceeds to seize Jenny and kiss her; she slaps his face and flees.

Manly soliloquizes on the speed with which luxury, dissipation, and foreign imitation can undermine our country. On the mall, Dimple accosts him and wins his immediate favor, which is tempered by Dimple's talk of the Chesterfieldian conquest of women. Dimple is flabbergasted to learn that Manly is Charlotte's brother.

17

ACT IV (*two scenes*)

To Charlotte, Maria confesses her distress at having to go forward with her marriage, the impossibility of breaking off (she'd be called capricious), and her meeting accidentally a man she could love. When Dimple and Manly arrive, Maria is shocked to learn that the man she had met accidentally is Charlotte's brother. Manly counters Dimple's praise of Europe with a declaration of great partiality for his native land; recognizing his country's faults, he proclaims her virtues. Maria anxiously determines that Manly is not married. At Charlotte's insistence, Manly takes Maria home, the latter begging Charlotte not to betray her feelings. Dimple makes an appointment with Charlotte for six, and with Letitia for eight.

Vanrough has learned that Dimple is £17,000 in debt, largely as a result of gaming; he is now ready to listen to Maria. Eavesdropping, he hears Manly make his plea and Maria deny him because she is engaged. When Manly chides her at allowing him to go so far, Maria confesses that she gives her hand without her heart. Since they are both unhappy, says Manly, they must do the right thing and at least deserve to be happy.

ACT V (*two scenes*)

Assuring Jonathan that he lost out with Jenny because he lacks the graces, Jessamy (using a passage from Ben Jonson) tries to teach Jonathan to smile and laugh by rule.

In Charlotte's apartment, an unhappy Manly withdraws to the consolation of books in a nearby closet. Dimple leads Letitia in, assuring her he cannot marry Maria and is waiting only for her to break off the match. As to Charlotte, says Dimple—why, she is beneath his contempt, "trifling, gay, flighty coquette, disagreeable." Charlotte comes in as he talks and Dimple immediately changes his tune. A few minutes later the situation is reversed: Dimple is telling Charlotte of "that insipid, wry-mouthed ugly creature!" (Letitia), as Letitia eavesdrops. Kissing Charlotte, Dimple tries to overwhelm her on the spot. Manly comes forward, sword in hand, and demands that Dimple defend himself. Vanrough beats down their swords. Letitia tells all and condemns Dimple. Thus thwarted, Dimple challenges Manly, who refuses to treat Dimple as a man of honor or to notice his accusation of cowardice. Dimple leaves, reminding one and all of the superiority of the

18

man with European polish over "an unpolished, untravelled American." Begging Maria's hand, Manly is accepted by her and her father, who is assured that Manly minds the main chance. Charlotte is converted to propriety in behavior. Manly's benediction is that probity, virtue, and honor will secure to an honest American—even without the polish of Europe—the good graces of his fair countrymen and, he hopes, "the applause of THE PUBLIC."

6

ANONYMOUS

Occurrences of the Times;
Or, The Transactions of
Four Days (printed 1789)

Satirical farce in two acts

MAIN CHARACTER, THEME, AND HISTORICAL NOTE: Satire on the author of *The Power of Sympathy* (probably the first or second American novel published; it dealt with the subject of seduction in the raciest Richardsonian manner). First publication carried the author's name as Sarah Wentworth Morton (the author has since been determined to be William Hill Brown), but in the drama "Mr." Morton is identified with the main character Mr. Sidney; other characters are identified with actual persons, as given below in parentheses. Drama concentrates upon ridiculous weaknesses of the characters rather than upon plot situation.

OTHER CHARACTERS:

Quaker (Joseph Rujel)	*Turncoat* (Dr. Phipps)
Dr. Harangue (Dr. Jarvis)	*Steady* and *Firm* (Printers)
Worthy (Sheriff Anderson)	*Impartialist*
Positive (Lovell)	*Debauchee* (Negro servant)
Friendly (Johannek)	*Mrs. Sidney* (Mrs. Morton)
Peep (Hughes)	*Mrs. Turncoat* (Mrs. Phipps)
Dupe (Warren)	*Martha* and *Tipsy* (servants)
Harcourt (Apthorp)	

TIME: Friday, January 16, to Monday, January 19, 1789.
PLACE: Boston; a neighboring town.

20

"Occurrences of the Times; or, The Transactions of Four Days" (printed 1789)

ACT I (*five scenes*)

In their home, Mr. and Mrs. Sidney discuss Sidney's impending duel with Harcourt. Sidney has challenged Harcourt apparently because of the latter's gossip about Sidney's conduct with women. Mrs. Sidney thinks he will have no trouble. Sidney says that Dupe and Debauchee have promised to help him. He has learned, however, that his servants do not generally support him.

Sidney's world seems to be nothing but duels and novels. Positive tells Dupe that Steady and Firm are expected during the following week to publish a novel that will brand Sidney as a villain for centuries to come. Debauchee visits Peep. He passes along the rumor that Sidney and Harcourt met that morning, that Sidney would not fight and that Harcourt disgustedly departed.

ACT II (*five scenes*)

Sidney comes to Impartialist to discuss measures to take if the scurrilous book comes out. He has already sharply warned the printers, but he believes to no avail. Sidney is held back by extreme delicacy: the young lady with whom Sidney is associated in the book is not angel-pure as the world believes.

Around the town things are in a hubbub. At Worthy's house, Worthy and Friendly seem to believe that Sidney acted like a frightened coward while Harcourt honorably attempted defense of his name. In Sidney's kitchen, Debauchee has returned, fatigued, from much scouting in Sidney's service. Part of his fatigue is associated with his burden of gossip concerning his employer, but he has added to his load a story of Peep's discomfiture. Peep, it seems, while peeping, fell into suds, was pushed into a gutter, and tumbled down a chimney.

At Turncoat's house, Turncoat tries to relate to his wife his version of the "duel," which has Worthy saving Sidney from Harcourt. For some secret reason Mrs. Turncoat is quite disappointed that Sidney did not get his head shot off. She takes her husband's story away from him and proceeds to roast him about his covering up for Sidney's libidinous conduct. Mrs. Turncoat leaves a suggestion that she might be the woman in Sidney's life.

Mrs. Sidney is forlorn over her husband's behavior and reputation: *The horrid book is out*! Quaker and Dr. Harangue console her. Sidney is near distraction. He wants Positive to go to Planting Grove next morning to see what can be done about the publishing company; he says he will blow out

21

the author's brains, if he can find the author. Mrs. Sidney tells him he will only make matters worse. Positive and Dupe leave for Planting Grove. Dr. Harangue advises taciturnity, but Sidney says it is strange that *he* never practices it. Sidney aloofly brushes aside Quaker's questions about the duel. Quaker assures Sidney of needed help, but Sidney, in pitiful melancholy, awaits the news from Planting Grove.

7

WILLIAM DUNLAP (1766–1839)

André (1798)

Blank-verse tragedy in five acts

MAIN CHARACTER AND THEME: The momentous campaign to win reduction of sentence for *André*, young British officer who cooperated with Benedict Arnold, was captured, and condemned as a spy.

OTHER CHARACTERS:

General (George Washington)	*Children*, one male, one female
M'Donald, forty	*American Sergeant*
Seward, thirty	*American Officers* and *Soldiers*
Bland, captain of Horse	*Servants*
Melville, middle-aged, grave	*Mrs. Bland*, Captain Bland's
British Officer	mother
American Officer	*Honora*, André's sweetheart

TIME: Ten hours of October 1 and 2, 1780.

PLACE: Village of Tappan, New York, Encampment, and adjoining country.

HISTORICAL NOTE: Performed in New York, March 30, 1798, by the Old American Company, with Mr. Hallam as General and Mr. Cooper as Bland. Sample of the early patriotic drama and of the output of Dunlap, playwright-producer, often called the father of American drama.

PROLOGUE

Proclaims native bard and native scene; poet's right to embellish true events; need for impartiality in treating this issue.

ACT I (*two scenes*)

Following Melville's condemnation of war as folly, guilt, and madness which shows "man the murderer . . . in all the gaiety of festive pomp," Bland and Melville join in praise of General, who never sleeps past sunrise because he is always "planning the welfare of our war-worn land." Melville is proud, also, of the nearby farmers who refused the bribes of the British spy. Hearing that André is the spy, Bland is incredulous, recalling André's kindness when he was on a prison ship. He vows to save his friend.

General emphasizes the invulnerability of free men and the fine example Americans are setting by breaking the shackles of slavery. Seward, more interested in André, calls him a victim of misfortune; M'Donald condemns him as a vicious man.

ACT II (*three scenes*)

Bland visits in prison a disheveled, despairing André, who recounts the steps in his downfall: (1) the "advantageous deal" with Arnold; (2) the drawn-out talks until dawn, bringing necessity of concealment until night; (3) the departure of the vessel that guaranteed his return; (4) his being forced to use disguise—civilian clothes; (5) his treating with traitors, encouraging treason, and offering bribes. Bland says he has influence enough with General to save André. André wants only one thing: to be shot instead of hanged. Bland reiterates that André shall not die at all, and that he will desert to the British and work against his country ("with fire, / And word, and every instrument of death / Or devastation") if America sacrifices such worth as his.

M'Donald and Seward turn their thoughts from André to England and the war. The former wishes barriers to rise up and separate the two countries to insure America against tyranny and the extremes of poverty and riches; the latter predicts that, after America has won the war, from Europe will come "enriching commerce" and "blest science."

Meanwhile, Captain Bland's mother and her young children expect her husband, also a British prisoner, to be freed momentarily. A message arrives, however, stating that if André dies, so will Bland senior. Mrs. Bland seeks out General to save her husband.

ACT III (*four scenes*)

General tells Bland the country is greatly in his debt. But he suddenly grows indignant over maltreatment of American prisoners and the failure of the

English to recognize the nation. General says they must be taught to respect rude, simple men as men; and, having started the war, they must abide by its laws. Bland pleads that André should not be held responsible for Britain's errors. When General promises Bland promotion but tells him firmly the André matter is closed, Bland hotly tears from his helmet the cockade symbolic of the American arms, replaces his helmet, and marches out. General is glad there was no witness to this outburst.

A message from Bland senior tells General: "Do *your* duty." Notified of the bloody retaliation, André writes his general, earnestly requesting Bland senior's release.

ACT IV (*three scenes*)

Debating André's case with M'Donald, Bland calls him liar and coward, but M'Donald refuses to be badgered. Simultaneously, Mrs. Bland entreats General in vain. Bland tells André it is ironical that the doomed smiles while his friend writhes in remorse and shame. André gives Bland some verses to deliver to Honora. As they talk, Honora comes. She swears to save him, but promptly faints. Later Honora begs the guard coming to take André to execution for time to show her dispatches to General.

ACT V (*four scenes*)

Bland apologizes to M'Donald. General, deploring his power of life-and-death, receives Honora on her knees, and is touched; but when a messenger reports the drumhead court-martial and hanging of Hastings, a gallant American fighter, General no longer hesitates.

Bland, still indignant, promises his friend to care for Honora. The guard remorselessly returns. Mrs. Bland reports that her husband has been released. Honora is almost mad with anguish. Mrs. Bland comforts her.

In his final speech, André declares that he has acted in the honest belief that the American cause is mistaken. The cannon signaling André's death is at last heard. M'Donald implores future generations of Columbia's children to learn the true significance of the event: namely, to ward off oppression, foreign force, and European influence.

8

JAMES NELSON BARKER (1784–1858)

The Indian Princess; Or, La Belle Sauvage (1808)

Operatic blank-verse drama (called poetic melo-drama)
in three acts

MAIN CHARACTER AND THEME: How *Pocahontas* fell in love with a European and how her love made life dangerous for her as the contest between Europeans and entrenched Indians grew more and more intense.

OTHER CHARACTERS:

Europeans:

Delawar, English lord who brings new settlers to Virginia

Captain Smith, adventurer, leader of the Jamestown colony

Lieutenants Rolfe and *Percy*, Smith's chief officers

Walter, *Larry*, *Robin*, and *Talman*, Smith's helpers

Geraldine, separated from Percy through misunderstanding

Kate, Larry's sweetheart, from Ballinamone, Ireland

Alice, Walter's wife

Soldiers

Adventurers

Virginians:

Powhatan, Indian king

Nantaquas, his son

Miami, Susquehannock prince, who has been promised Pocahontas for his wife

Grimosco, a priest

Nima, attendant of Pocahontas who falls in love with Robin

Warriors

Indian Girls

"The Indian Princess; or, La Belle Sauvage" (1808)

TIME: From the arrival of Smith in March, 1607, to the arrival of Lord Delawar on June 9, 1610.

PLACE: The neighborhood of Jamestown.

MUSICAL HIGHLIGHTS: "Jolly Comrades, raise the glee"; "In the wild wood will I range"; "Och, dismal and dark was the day, to be sure"; "Fair Geraldine"; "We three, adventurers be"; "Song to Aresqui" (Indian god of war); "Captain Smith is a man of might."

HISTORICAL NOTE: Drama derives its significance from its dramatic handling of the Pocahontas story in both action and song. Author declares that he follows history as far as drama will permit, and most of the way his declaration holds. His story of Pocahontas' saving of Smith's life is more historical than that found in most dramatic versions, and his semihistorical scene when Pocahontas prevents an English massacre by warning Smith of her father's intentions is well developed. Author deviates from history by having Pocahontas meet Rolfe in 1607, thus providing time for a romance to grow. Actually Pocahontas did not meet Rolfe until after her capture in 1612. Smith's prediction at the end of the play that the Rolfe-Pocahontas marriage would bring peace can be compared to the historical fact that a period of eight years of peace and expansion actually did follow the marriage. Play first performed at New Theatre, Philadelphia, April 6, 1808, where its reception was ruined by a riot.

ACT I (*five scenes*)

In their settlement on the Powhatan River, the English are quite pleased with their New World. At first blush it is a great improvement over the fogs and dank vapors of home. Smith feels his comrades will be worthy of the future fame the expedition will bring and Smith's helpers are proud of his reputation for heroism, garnered in Turkey and Tartary. But Robin tells Larry how foolish they are to come to a place where they are surrounded by savages.

At Werocomoco, Powhatan's royal village, preparations for a wedding are far advanced—the expected nuptials of Pocahontas and Miami. Pocahontas, however, listens unimpressed to Miami's boastings of his prowess as hunter and warrior.

Smith, bemazed, enters from the forest. Surrounded by Indians, he fights singlehandedly so well that Nantaquas, Powhatan's son, compares him to

Aresqui, their god of war. Nantaquas claims him as brother and asks him to be Powhatan's friend. At Nantaquas' request, Smith tells of the world beyond the wide water (where Nantaquas thought the sun slept) and of the shipbuilding arts of the Europeans. Smith says he came over to teach these arts to the Indian. In a burst of savage music and in spite of Nantaquas, Smith is seized and borne off.

Back at the English settlement, Smith is reported lost after a battle with three hundred fiends. Lieutenant Rolfe plans the expedition to rescue him. En route, Rolfe teases Percy about still being in love with Geraldine in England. He urges Percy to forget false women and be free, as he is. He is sure that Smith is alive, since he was obviously not born to perish in this fashion. If Smith is gone, says Rolfe, the colony will perish.

ACT II (three scenes)

Before Powhatan, Smith is described as having come from the bosom of the waters in thunder and fire. Pocahontas asks if he is not a god. Miami demands his immediate execution so that the spirits of the six men he killed may lie at rest beyond the mountains. The priest, Grimosco, says Smith must die because the whites are not God's children; Nantaquas, that he must live to help the Indian. Hearing all, Powhatan finally decrees Smith's death. Pocahontas saves him, crying, "White man, thou shalt not die; or I will die with thee!" As Miami and Grimosco grow angrier every moment, Powhatan permits Nantaquas to accompany Smith back, and Pocahontas to follow part of the way.

Rolfe's party meets Smith's party, and Rolfe is immediately smitten by Pocahontas. Saying unhesitatingly that he loves her, he still calls her princess. He kisses her; she calls him lover and tells him he has made her cheek burn and her heart beat. When they have parted and Rolfe has returned with Smith to the English settlement, Miami tells Pocahontas that he has observed the love scene. He assures her he will not yield to anyone, least of all to the hated white man. She leaves him, consumed by great anger and loss of pride. At Powhatan's palace, Pocahontas begs her father not to send her to Miami. Miami's tribe has sent a red hatchet, accusing Powhatan of having broken his promise. Powhatan swears to fight Miami and gain the help of the English in the fight. He commands a reluctant Grimosco to call his chiefs together.

28

"The Indian Princess; or, La Belle Sauvage" (1808)

ACT III (*four scenes*)

Jamestown is now built. Walter tells Alice how the English assisted Powhatan to defeat his enemies and of the phenomenal spoils of war, including robes of raccoon, crowns of feather, and thirty kings as tributaries.

In a grove, Robin meets Nima, the Indian girl, whom he calls his dusky divinity. Rolfe and Pocahontas continue their song of love, she swearing that love has changed her from a savage child of savage Nature. But very soon, when the English are gone, she and Nima see Miami and Grimosco conspiring. Later, Grimosco, speaking as priest (rather than as military leader), threatens Powhatan with spiritual agonies after death if he does not agree to invite all the white leaders to a banquet and there to order their extermination. Powhatan yields. Pocahontas rushes to warn her white friends.

Lord Delawar arrives, and has scarcely landed before he is compelled to order a hasty expedition to rescue Smith, Percy, Rolfe, and other leaders. At the Werocomoco banquet, the Indians prepare to strike with tomahawks upon Grimosco's signal, but the English, breaking through, seize their uplifted arms. Powhatan is transfixed with confusion; he confesses his crime, and Smith deplores crimes committed in religion's name. Miami stabs himself. Smith prevents Powhatan's destroying himself and introduces Lord Delawar, who praises Pocahontas. Geraldine finally convinces Percy that she was never false. Pocahontas comes to Rolfe's arms. Smith predicts for the land civilized society, flourishing arts and industry, peace and prosperity. He says the country will be enviable when "disjoin'd from old licentious Europe" to become "a great, yet virtuous, empire in the west!" The banquet ends in dance and song.

9

MORDECAI MANUEL NOAH (1785–1851)

She Would Be A Soldier; Or, The Plains of Chippewa (1819)

Historical drama in three acts

MAIN CHARACTER AND THEME: Trials of *Christine*, trained by her father in military skills, when she seeks solace from unrequited love with the American Army in upper Canada, during the War of 1812.

OTHER CHARACTERS:

General (probably Winfield Scott)	*Corporal Flash*, soldier
Jasper, French-American farmer, Revolutionary veteran, and Christine's father	*Walter*
	Jailor
Lenox, a wounded lieutenant	*Soldiers*
Pendragon and *LaRole*, British officers	*Peasants*
	Indians
Jerry, wealthy farmer	*Christine*
Jenkins	*Adela*
Indian chief	*Maid*
First officer	*Peasant Women*

TIME: About 1814.

PLACE: Upper New York and upper Canada (neighborhood of York and Chippewa).

MUSICAL HIGHLIGHTS: Pastoral; "The Knight Errant by the late Queen of Holland"; "Robin Adair"; "Shall the pleasures of life unknown fade away"; "Hail, Columbia" (Band).

"She Would be a Soldier; or, The Plains of Chippewa (1819)

HISTORICAL NOTE: Author's father was a Revolutionary veteran and a friend of George Washington. A newspaper editor, Noah strongly advocated principles which led America into the War of 1812; during the war period, he received diplomatic appointment from President Monroe. He wrote several semihistorical melodramas, including one called *The Siege of Tripoli*, significant because Noah was American consul at Tunis in 1813 when Algerian piracy was a problem.

ACT I (*three scenes*)

Through conversation with Jenkins, Jasper gives his background in full and revealing detail: born a French farming peasant; came to America with Lafayette; wounded at Yorktown; promoted to sergeancy by Washington in person; saw independence acknowledged; purchased piece of land near Great Lakes, and himself leveled the oaks, cleared the meadows, burnt out wolves and bears, built a cottage; married the miller's daughter; acted as both father and mother to Christine since her mother's death shortly after her birth. He is now acting as host to Lieutenant Lenox, wounded in battle at Niagara but awaiting his orders to return. Christine does not encourage Lenox's suit, although quite fond of him, saying, "No, I won't love a soldier—that's certain," but she does want him ever as a faithful friend. Meanwhile, Jerry, a boorish but rich farmer, has come to claim Christine. Jasper places Christine's hand in Jerry's when Christine and Lenox return from a walk down the mountain, and the latter two are both shocked. Although decidedly no fighting man, Jerry is (by his own admission) outstanding at racing, opossum hunting, partridge snaring, and electioneering; to top things off, he is squire, county judge, and "brevet ossifer" in the militia. He is not impressed by Jasper's praise of Christine's military skills—she can crack a bottle at twelve paces with a pistol and bring down a buck at any distance—; he wants only to know of her domestic skills—milking, knitting gaiters, making apple butter and maple sugar, dancing a reel at midnight—and of the superior talents she possesses which will brighten his status—parley-vooing, dancing, singing, and such elegant things.

Lenox receives his orders and leaves, obviously confused. In spite of her father and the giant wedding celebration which the neighbors are preparing, Christine rejects Jerry outright. Knowing her father's determination, she puts on a disguise—frock coat, pantaloons, and hat—and secretly departs.

After a search Jasper finds a note from her telling him he has driven his daughter away by not consulting her happiness. Reaching camp, where she expects to be with Lenox again, she finds him in close converse with Adela, the General's daughter. Not knowing that they are just old friends rather than sweethearts, she declares Lenox and his vows false and decides to enlist, not as drummer or fifer, but in the ranks. She passes the musket tests, shouldering and presenting arms, and promises, though small, to be capable.

ACT II (*four scenes*)

In the British camp at York, upper Canada, an Indian chief in a comic scene reduces LaRole and Pendragon from aristocratic fighters to simple Indian warriors: they must get moccasins, a blanket, rings through nose and ears, feathers in head, and the proper paint on their faces, or the Indian chief will not let them fight. After failing to impress the chief with their pedigrees, their having fought under Wellington and their other elegant qualifications, LaRole and Pendragon prepare to obey, especially when the former is threatened with roasting over a slow fire before being able to report the matter to the commander in chief.

In the American camp, Christine, on guard in her disguise as a male soldier, cannot bear hearing Lenox inside sing to the General and Adela of a warrior who won the battle and his love. She throws down her gun and is about to enter the General's tent when a soldier seizes her. She draws her sword, fights a little, and escapes, but is pursued and captured. General orders her held for court-martial.

In another part of the camp, Jasper, Jerry, and peasants search for Christine. Jerry sees Corporal Flash, whom he knew at the Battle of Queenstown, where Jerry had marched and marched and camped and camped his "village sogers" but had never fought. Jerry and Flash sit down to a whiskey punch.

Christine is charged with mutiny and with trying to force her way into the tent of the commanding general. She pleads guilty and is convicted. Told by officers to prepare to die, she says she is ready. She tells herself death is the best way out. In another part of the prison, Jerry is being incarcerated for starting a riot. Jerry says it stemmed from some soldiers' accusing him of running away from the Battle of Queenstown. He tries to bribe the jailor with a pig to secure his release, and is placed on black bread and water. News comes that the Battle of Chippewa has begun.

ACT III (*four scenes*)

General announces victory, the enemy having abandoned the field, lost more than five hundred in killed and wounded, and left several principal officers as prisoners. Lenox describes the battle, giving in detail the exploits of Scott, Towson, Porter, Jessup, Ketchum, Leavenworth, and Harrison, the last of whom lost a leg in the battle and fought on a stump.

LaRole and Pendragon are among the captives, claiming to be in masquerade: LaRole is amazed that the bullets of common soldiers sometimes reach men of fashion. The Indian chief, also captured, insists he is ready for the flames. When General tells him Americans want him for a friend, he demands that they remember the old times with their white man treachery. His rage cools when General gives him a bag of wampum.

In prison, Christine laments her fate, kisses the miniature Lenox gave her, and throws it away. General confirms Christine's death sentence. Finding the miniature, an officer seeks to restore it to Lenox.

Drums roll for Christine's execution. Her coat is off and the stock unloosened from her neck. Lenox rushes in, miniature in hand, and pushes up the soldiers' guns. Christine cries out: "Traitor, begone! let me die at once! Is she not your bride?" Lenox wonders how she could ever have doubted his love. They embrace. Jasper forgives his daughter and approves her marriage to Lenox. Even Jerry concurs, since Christine had worn the breeches before marriage. General is glad for victory and love. He tells Lenox that in his old age he will recall the Plains of Chippewa, and feel toward Britain as freemen should feel toward all the world: "Enemies in war—in peace, friends!"

MEAD (probably RICHARD W. MEAD)

Wall Street; Or, Ten Minutes Before Three (1819)

Farce with strong realistic and allegorical touches in three acts

MAIN CHARACTER AND THEME: Intensive experiences of a merchant, *Mr. Hardrun,* and his associates on the New York Stock Exchange, during a typical business day in the early nineteenth century.

OTHER CHARACTERS (identified by their surnames):

Mr. Easy, another merchant	*President*
Mr. Oldtimes	*Directors*
Mr. Shinner	*Cashier* and *Clerk* of a bank
Mr. Shaver	*Mrs. Hardrun,* the merchant's wife
Mr. Broker	*Miss Julia Hardrun,* the daughter
Mr. Merchant	*Brokers*
Mr. Borrower	*Boys*
Mr. Bankrupt	

TIME: From ten to three on a day in 1819.

PLACE: Wall and Pearl Streets, New York City.

HISTORICAL NOTE: Mead wrote at least two plays about Wall Street, a favorite subject of later playwrights, such as Bronson Howard, Clyde Fitch, and Philip Barry in the present list. So sober and precise is Mead's analysis of the stock exchange at this early period in its life that much of the farcical effect is lost. It is replaced by an implication of needed change in ethical principles underlying the exchange.

"Wall Street; or, Ten Minutes Before Three" (1819)

ACT I (*two scenes*)

In the bubbling center of Wall Street—between William Street and the post office—Hardrun and Easy talk of hard times during the peace following the War of 1812. High prices brought by cotton, tobacco, and rice have lured many to the Southern trade, but also have induced many to overstretch themselves. From a letter just received, Hardrun reads that the eminent Baltimore firm of James Littlecash and Company is refusing remittances, partly because of investigations which have caused the United States Bank to stop discounting. It is impossible to raise money on the best paper, even at 4 per cent.

Oldtimes appears contrastingly, speaking of the busy, merry place Wall Street has become, especially in recent years. Thirty years ago, he says, there were no banks, brokers, shavers (tricky, sharp dealers), or money borrowing. Later, listening to the gloomy talk, Oldtimes comments that these people are all shavers but Saunders, the barber: "He only cuts hair."

Almost in confirmation of Oldtimes, Shaver and Broker appear very well off, except that now and then, they confess, they also "get bit." Merchant frantically offers Shaver his insurance policy on a valuable coffee ship due from St. Domingo, for immediate cash; Shaver casually agrees to meet him at one o'clock.

For his debt, Bankrupt offers Hardrun ten shillings on the pound (about 50 per cent); he says his other creditors are agreeable except "one or two hardhearted old Scotchmen." Loaded with boxes and bundles, their latest purchases, Mrs. Hardrun and daughter Julia visit the merchant and hear him complain of their extravagance in these perilous times. Mrs. Hardrun replies that even the parson gives a more splendid party than she. "Ah," says Hardrun, "he is a salary man—he can afford it." Even so, says Mrs. Hardrun, Julia must have a new dress in which to meet young Mr. Auctioneer, who has a rich father. Hardrun, still swearing they will bankrupt him, skimpily authorizes them to use sixty to seventy dollars.

ACT II (*three scenes*)

The bank directors receive much bad news: the usury laws operate against them (they must be repealed); bank patrons have demanded $80,000, more than the funds in the bank. When they find that a remedy which will

MEAD (probably RICHARD W. MEAD)

help one will hurt another, everyone begins brutally to protect his own interests. In spite of the crisis, the directors adjourn without doing anything.

At the bank discount desk, the cashier refuses to honor notes of Hardrun and Merchant. A shaver's note is accepted.

In Brokers' Hall, around a table holding decanters and glasses, there is an air of troubled festivity. Shaving goes "damn'd well" for some, and "damn'd ill" for others. Another broker drinks "to the glorious uncertainty of bank accommodations!" which helps shavers. Shaver announces blowup in Mechanics' Bank—cashier and first teller resigned; $140,000 missing. The bank obviously is "not worth a damn." Other stocks fluctuate.

ACT III (*three scenes*)

At Hardrun and Company's Pearl Street store, Hardrun finds himself dangerously short. Beleaguered, he wishes all banks were in hell. When Julia comes to tell him that her purchases are only $83, he is too busy to listen. Boy from the store (Broadway and Company) presents the bill, for a dress, thread lace, an ornamental comb, a pair of "corsetts," elastic garters. Haggard, Hardrun tells the boy to return next day.

At Broker's office, at *ten minutes to three*—three is the fatal closing hour on the street—Hardrun tells Broker that he must have money. After refusing, delaying, haggling, and insisting he is unsure of his own financial status, Broker lends him $800 on his promise to return $803 next day (lending rate: 137 per cent per annum).

Oldtimes comments on the noisy crowd devouring the bank with a run. He is down to cash a check for the sale of his house on William Street, but prospects for completing the transaction are obviously very poor. Waiting in doubt, he reviews the picture on the Street before him, particularly the young upstarts with their ruffled shirts, billiard playing, carousing in hotels and theaters, cards, brandy, whiskey punches. Hardrun tells Oldtimes that this being short of cash is worse than being short of breath. The clock strikes three, leaving Hardrun, Oldtimes, and all the frantic and cool people around them in the bank for whatever comes.

36

JAMES NELSON BARKER (1784–1858)

The Tragedy of Superstition (1824)

Blank-verse tragedy in five acts

MAIN CHARACTER AND THEME: *Isabella Fitzroy* and her son *Charles*, nineteen, are victims of bigoted Puritan persecution in a time of Indian war and social crisis.

OTHER CHARACTERS:

Sir Reginald Egerton,	*Edward,* Isabella's servant
Charles II's ambassador	*Boy*
George Egerton, his nephew	*Second Judge*
Ravensworth and *Walford,*	*Officer*
Puritan leaders	*Villagers*
The Unknown	*Indians*
Judge	*Supernumeraries*
First Villager	*Mary,* daughter of Ravensworth
Second Villager	*Alice,* daughter of Walford
Messenger	*Lucy*
First Officer	*Female Villagers*
Second Officer	

TIME: About 1675.

PLACE: Massachusetts.

HISTORICAL NOTE: The political and social hysteria of this play is intended as overt criticism of the Salem witchcraft trials and of all similar hysteria. The play, therefore, falls in the same category as Arthur Miller's *The Crucible* (1953), which, though set in seventeenth-century Massachusetts, was directed against McCarthyism and similar public arousals. The Indian uprising is a phase of King Philip's War. Drama first performed March 12, 1824, at Chestnut Street Theatre, Philadelphia.

ACT I

Though forbidden by her father to associate in any way with the Fitzroys, Mary confesses to Alice her close friendship with Isabella and her plighted troth to Charles. Pointing toward the Fitzroy mansion, Ravensworth urges upon Walford special punishment for those who scorn the church discipline and engage in bold infidelity and dark sorcery. Ravensworth also advocates extermination of King Philip, the Indian chief, and all his people. Walford speaks of the arrival of couriers from King Charles II. The couriers, Sir Reginald and George, get a glimpse of Mary. The uncle warns the nephew that these Puritans burn their old women for witches and will instantly execute anyone who lays hands on a maid. George vows to himself, nevertheless, to pursue Mary though they hang him.

ACT II (*three scenes*)

Unknown, dressed in skins, but of dignified manner, reveals that for nineteen years he has been an outlaw and wanderer. After a quick misunderstanding with Charles Fitzroy, Unknown gets news from him about his mother and is visibly upset. He swears Charles to secrecy about him.

George, making little headway talking to Mary, finally seizes her. Charles, en route home, comes to Mary's rescue and throws him off; George challenges him for two hours hence in the east grove.

Isabella tells her son she can bear the persecutions but wants to shield him from them, especially from such insults as his recent unjust expulsion from school. Secretly, Charles has the servant, Edward, get his rapier and he speeds to the east grove.

ACT III (*two scenes*)

Charles pinks George, and goes for aid, leaving his handkerchief in George's wound. To Sir Reginald, George says the duel was fair and that if he dies, Sir Reginald must so testify.

Walford is distressed that the Indians have got past the guarding troops, but Ravensworth blames all afflictions on bad people in their midst. He

38

tells Walford of George's being carried along, dying or dead, from Charles's criminal act.

As the Indians come closer, alarm bells ring, houses begin to blaze, and Mary is brought in on Charles's arms. Villagers retreat in panic and disorder. Unknown comes forth and rallies the routed villagers, first with brave words, then with deeds. As Isabella silently prays for Charles, Ravensworth accuses her of muttering incantations. Victory shouts eventually rise, and Indian prisoners are taken. Crowd gazes on Unknown with awe, but he declines their praise, turning it up to God. When he has gone, debate arises as to his being mortal or immortal, of good or evil origin. Ravensworth notes that Charles does not bleed.

ACT IV (*four scenes*) [not in acting version]

Ravensworth now demands summary action against both Fitzroys. Walford says:

> Ah, my friend
> If reason in a mind like yours, so form'd,
> So fortified by knowledge, can bow down
> Before the popular breath, what shall protect
> From the all-with'ring blasts of superstition
> The unthinking crowd, in whom credulity,
> Is ever the first born of ignorance.

Charles and his mother decide to move because of intolerance throughout the country. Charles begs to know why they left England, and who his father is, but Isabella can tell him only that she came to the New World to find her father who was banished when she was fifteen because of his activities against the existing order, and that his father is of high rank. Officers enter to put the Fitzroys under house arrest. Escaping them, Charles steals away to visit Mary and to beg her to come with him. Seeing her father approaching, Mary tells Charles "to unhand her." She faints in Charles's arms, but reviving, calls for him. Ravensworth orders Walford to hold Charles for trial.

ACT V (*two scenes*)

In the church, arranged as a hall of justice, judges tell the prisoners that confession will help them, but Isabella pleads not guilty. Charles refuses to plead, to save Mary. When Charles confesses to Ravensworth's charge of trying to force Mary, Mary collapses. A storm has arisen, with thunder and lightning. Officers drag Charles away; Mary, awaking, absolves him, but Ravensworth will not let her be heard. Unknown identifies himself as Isabella's father, but Charles, executed, is brought back on a bier. Sir Reginald presents papers from King Charles II, seeking a lady named Isabella, whom he espoused in secret, and her son. Over Charles's body, Mary delivers a mad speech, declaring her love; in a few moments, she dies of shock. Ravensworth is utterly crushed. The curtain comes down under a roaring storm.

12

SAMUEL WOODWORTH (1784–1842)
MUSIC BY JOHN DAVIES

The Forest Rose; Or,
American Farmers (1825)

Pastoral opera in two acts

MAIN CHARACTER AND THEME: Story of *Lydia* and *Harriet*, two "forest roses" of New Jersey farmland, and their adventures with lovers both rural and city bred.

OTHER CHARACTERS:

Farmer Miller, a farm owner, father of Harriet

Blandford, member of an elegant city family

Bellamy, English-born beau living in the city, close friend of Blandford

William, an eligible country boy

Jonathan Ploughboy, Yankee storekeeper transformed into a farmer

Waiter

First Farmer

Second Farmer

Caesar, a black fiddler

Villagers

Laborers and *others*

Sally, a pretty country lass

Rose, a Negro servant

Village Maidens

TIME: One day in the 1820's.

PLACE: A village in New Jersey, near New York City.

MUSICAL HIGHLIGHTS: "Here in scenes of sweet seclusion"; "When bashful Lubin sought my hand"; "The morn awakes"; "A smile from thee

41

would banish pain"; "The heart sustained by Hope alone"; "Is there a light. . . ."

HISTORICAL NOTE. First produced at Chatham Garden Theatre, New York, October 7, 1825, with Mrs. Wallack as Lydia, Mrs. Burke as Harriet, and Mr. Simpson as Jonathan. Reproduced many times as an audience favorite. The role of Jonathan, one of the most popular in the stage-Yankee tradition before the Civil War, was afterward played by G. H. Hill (1832), Danforth Marble (1838), and Joshua Silsbee (1843), all distinguished comedians.

ACT I (*four scenes*)

Overture: sounds of the country at dawn, including birdsong, shepherd's pipe, hunter's horn. Clock strikes four, starting villagers on their day. Then Lydia and Harriet, carrying their milk pail, join William in singing "Here in scenes of sweet seclusion," which tells about the superiority of country over city joys. But Harriet yearns for city life in spite of Lydia's disappointment with Blandford, Lydia's secret city lover. Harriet would like to spend at least a year in the city—to see the fashions, the Park, the Battery, Castle Garden, Museum, theatres, circuses, gaslights, waterworks, fireworks, stepping-mill, and other amusement places. But William spoils her dream a little by reporting that from Whitehall to the Hospital city houses are joined together. Harriet, nevertheless, deliberately seeks the Englishman Bellamy's attention by singing "When bashful Lubin sought my hand," which concludes by saying that sprightly girls of gay sixteen ne'er spurn a saucy lover. In return, Bellamy satirically describes city life. When asked where "the creatures" (animals) are kept, he replies that the geese stay in the Park, as in his native London; the donkeys (dandies) line Broadway; the pigs have the freedom of the city. As for the sheep, says Bellamy, the clergymen take the fleeces and leave the flock to shift for themselves. When Bellamy invites her to the city, Harriet asks permission of her father, Farmer Miller, who reproves her for being naive and for neglecting a fine farmer like William. After reassuring William, Harriet sings "The morn awakes."

The scene turns to Sally and Jonathan Ploughboy. Jonathan is complaining about Sally's "two-timing": he saw her kissing Tom Clover. Sally reminds him that he fell asleep when she last sat on his knee. This time, Sally begs a kiss of him. When he closes his eyes, she substitutes the servant

Rose who smells of onions and garlic. Jonathan, thoroughly exasperated, vows to marry Harriet instead of Sally.

The scene shifts to a nearby wood where the city man Blandford, who has lost his way, thinks of Lydia and sings "A smile from thee would banish pain." Blandford is found by Jonathan, who talks of his past: he was formerly a shopkeeper in Taunton, Massachusetts, and he sold whiskey, molasses, calicoes, spelling books and patent gridirons. Jonathan is proud now of being a farmer. He invites Blandford to the shindig that Squire Miller is holding that very evening. All the girls will be there.

Before the guests arrive for Squire Miller's party, Lydia, saddened by the obstacles placed in the way of her marriage to Blandford, sings "The heart sustained by Hope alone." Bellamy arrives and, mistaking Lydia for Harriet (they dress exactly alike), seizes her. Struggling to escape, Lydia drops a locket given to her by Blandford as a token of love. Bellamy, still thinking he has "courted" Harriet, the girl who would never spurn a saucy lover, pockets the locket as evidence of his conquest. Now Jonathan arrives to court Harriet because she can milk a cow, make a cheese, and boil a pudding with the best. Harriet, however, rejects Jonathan because he refuses to live in town. Finally, the guests—the stalk cutters, apple pickers, and cider grinders, among others—begin to gather for dinner. There is Caesar with his fiddle, and Jonathan with his jew's harp. Soon all are dancing and singing.

ACT II (*five scenes*)

In his apartment, Blandford, grieving for his lost Lydia, sings "Is there a light whose effulgence can dry? The tear of affliction and rapture restore?" Blandford's roommate, Bellamy, bragging of his conquest, reveals he expects to keep his "forest rose" for a whole month, an improvement over the London swains who take a new conquest every two weeks. Blandford, upbraiding him for his immorality, is overwhelmed when he sees the locket that Bellamy has taken. He makes Bellamy promise to take him to the girl who supplied it. The two confront Harriet, who, naturally, cannot remember the encounter with Bellamy. In the meantime, Lydia, missing her locket, becomes extremely upset.

A little later, Bellamy decides to bribe Jonathan to commit a crime. By accepting twenty-three dollars from Bellamy, Jonathan apparently agrees to cooperate, but later he reveals Bellamy's plot to Sally: Jonathan is to assist

43

in kidnapping Harriet, who will then be conveyed to a waiting sloop and carried off by Bellamy. Sally arranges a counter trick.

Lydia now receives a letter from Blandford saying that all obstacles to their happiness are removed since his haughty father is dead and his mother and sister await her. Blandford and Lydia embrace. Then Bellamy, finally dubbed a virgin-stealer, is properly squelched when he opens his prize and discovers Rose the servant. Farmer Miller gives Harriet to William, and all ends in song.

44

13

JOHN AUGUSTUS STONE (1800–1834)

Metamora; Or, The Last of the Wampanoags (1829)

Blank-verse Indian tragedy in five acts,
prologue, and epilogue

MAIN CHARACTER AND THEME: The efforts of *Metamora* (great son of the great chief Massasoit), who was the King Philip from New England that settlers fought decisively in 1675—1676, to maintain his lands and dignity, with the clear understanding that should he fail, the Indians' influence in this sector would be forever dead.

OTHER CHARACTERS:

Indians:

Kaneshine [sometimes spelled Kaweshine], a prophet

Annawandah, the traitor

Otah, a boy

Child of Metamora

Nahmeokee, wife of Metamora

Other Indians

Warriors

English:

Lord Fitzarnold, well-born but dissolute young adventurer

Sir Arthur Vaughan and *Captain Church*, political and military leaders in the New England colony

Mordaunt, leading settler, who carries a guilty secret

Errington, Puritan Chief of Council

Walter (also Horatio), an orphan, in love with Oceana

Wolfe, friend of Walter

Goodenough, Puritan adherent

Tramp, a messenger

Oceana, daughter of Mordaunt

Soldiers   Sailors   Peasants

45

TIME: Late seventeenth century.

PLACE: Adjacent Indian and English settlements in New England.

MUSIC: Varied and comprehensive, including flutes, drums, trumpets, and Indian conch shells.

HISTORICAL NOTE: First produced December 15, 1829, Park Theatre, New York, with Edwin Forrest as Metamora. Won five hundred dollar prize offered by Forrest (in 1828) for the best five-act tragedy of which the "hero, or principal character, shall be an aboriginal of this country." Play remained in Forrest's repertory for forty years, was acted hundreds of times, and made him a fortune. Completely disillusioned by the poor living for playwrights, Stone, the author, committed suicide at age thirty-three.

PROLOGUE

Elizabethan-style prologue proclaims the dramatic possibilities of the native scene to be as full as those in Shakespeare—"subject, and bard, and actor, all are ours...."

ACT I *(three scenes)*

Learning of the approach of a ship, the settler Mordaunt sends word to his daughter, Oceana, that the man she must marry, Lord Fitzarnold, is arriving. Before the message arrives at her isolated home, Oceana tells Walter how she was just saved from a fierce panther by an Indian, "grandest model of a mighty man." Her savior, Metamora, wounded by the panther, appears. He accepts Oceana's scarf to staunch his wound, predicts the impending final contest between red man and white, and gives Oceana an eagle plume that will protect her from any red invader. When Tramp brings Oceana her father's message about marrying Fitzarnold, Walter begs her never to forget his love for her.

In Sir Arthur's house, Walter complains to Sir Arthur, his benefactor since the day Walter was rescued from shipwreck, that Fitzarnold has outstripped him for Oceana's hand purely because of his rank. Sir Arthur urges him to hold steady; Walter determines to fight for Oceana.

Tramp brings news that the Indian tribes "conspire from east to west" and have already killed Sasamond, an Indian friend of the English.

"*Metamora; or, The Last of the Wampanoags*" (1829)

ACT II (*three scenes*)

In his wigwam, Metamora tells his wife Nahmeokee that in his dreams his knife is red in his hands and the scalp of the white man is streaming. When Nahmeokee reminds him that the white man is "our brother," he reminds her that white men will stop killing their people only when the Indian bows are unstrung and the war whoop is hushed. The boy Otah brings news that an armed English party approaches. Calling for Annawandah, Metamora learns his counselor has defected to the English. The English party, led by Sir Arthur, insists that Metamora come with them at once to a council of peace. He promises to come later; in spite of implied threats, he will not accompany them. The English go. Metamora swears that his son shall never be a white man's slave. About to leave for the council, he declares that "Manito [God] is with me."

Mordaunt abjectly begs Oceana to marry Fitzarnold because Fitzarnold shares a secret that can take Mordaunt's life and blight his honor eternally. As Oceana is about to agree, Walter enters with a message to Mordaunt from the council; Oceana prevents a deadly fight between Walter and Mordaunt. Later, Mordaunt again assures Fitzarnold that Oceana will marry him.

At the peace meeting, the great chief baits the English because of their obvious fear of him. Answering the charge that he gave shelter to a man banished by their holy synod, Metamora twits them about practicing the same tyranny that drove them from their fathers' hearths in England. He also says that he follows the dictates of their great book—"to give good gifts to the stranger and deal kindly with him whose heart is sad"—because the Great Spirit has written the dictum upon his heart. If they want to be just, he says, they will return the lands received from Massasoit fifty years before. When they confront him with Annawandah to prove his faithlessness to the Indian-English agreements, Metamora stabs Annawandah, defies their threats and power, and, departing, threatens them in turn with the mighty wrath of the wronged Indian. The soldiers, firing after him, seriously wound Mordaunt, who has accidentally got in the way.

ACT III (*four scenes*)

Fearing Mordaunt will die before he can marry Oceana, Fitzarnold decides to kidnap her, put her on his ship, and sail the next day. He orders Walter's friend, Wolfe, to bring a surgeon for Mordaunt and a priest to perform the marriage. Wolfe, aside, says Fitzarnold will be surprised at who the priest will be.

Metamora tells his advisers that his father's ghost has ordered him to abandon peace and to fight for freedom—"revenge or death!" He sends his wife Nahmeokee to get help from the Narragansett and orders the old and infirm transferred to Narragansett territory.

Fitzarnold attempts to take Oceana by storm, but the priest Wolfe has sent turns out to be Walter. Again Oceana prevents a bloody fight. Tramp announces the approaching yell of the Wampanoag chieftain and his crew.

ACT IV (*three scenes*)

Nahmeokee is a captive in the house of Errington. Walter has been taken by the Indians and is about to be dispatched when Metamora gets the news of his wife's capture. He orders Walter held as a hostage.

Into the lair of the white men Metamora boldly comes to rescue his wife. Indian and white sign a temporary treaty providing for exchange of captives. When Nahmeokee is released to carry news of the treaty, she is treacherously surrounded by soldiers. Metamora disperses the soldiers, and refuses to surrender his gun to them, saying that when his land is threatened, the *gun can talk*. Once again, the land is shown to be Metamora's primary concern— the land of his people's food and homes, the fair hunting ground, the land encompassing the bones of his fathers.

ACT V (*five scenes*)

Oceana, alone and helpless, is about to fall into the defiling arms of Fitzarnold when Metamora appears. Oceana faints. Accusing Fitzarnold of being the one who "smote the red cheek of Nahmeokee," Metamora disarms and kills him. He then bears Oceana away.

Metamora has escaped the English. Mordaunt, now dead, has been revealed as Hammond of Harrington, who gave up the royal martyr Charles I to his death; and Walter, through Wolfe's confession, is discovered as Sir Arthur's son. Wolfe reveals also that Oceana's kindness to Nahmeokee (during Oceana's captivity) has purchased her and Walter's freedom.

Urging his warriors to new attack, Metamora shouts: "Our lands!

"*Metamora; or, The Last of the Wampanoags*" (1829)

Our nation's freedom! Or the grave!" But the prophet Kaweshine prophesies against further battle because Manito no longer loves the Wampanoag. Metamora is about to stab him—calling him a half-Mohigan, of tainted blood—but banishes him instead when Nahmeokee says Kaweshine saved their son's life. Then Metamora urges his braves forward in spite of Manito's hatred.

At a rocky pass, the English hold the field. Errington, the Chief of Council, proclaims that "the red man's power is broken forever." The task now is to bribe Kaweshine to show them Metamora's place of safety.

In the secret stronghold, characterized by rocks, bridges, and waterfall, Nahmeokee tells the weary Metamora how his child died from English bullets though she tried to save him. Nahmeokee asks if their nation is dead and if they are alone in the land of their fathers. Metamora admits that they are destroyed, but not vanquished: "We are no more, yet we are forever." Looking upon her husband's last knife (which once belonged to her brother), Nahmeokee rejoices in the thought of what is in his heart. Stabbing her, Metamora sends her to join the spirit of her murdered father. At last, he kisses her. The approaching English, directed by Kaweshine, declare Metamora their prisoner. Defying them, he begs them to come up to him singly. The English fire: Metamora falls, but dying, he curses them fully and deeply with a variety of curses. One says: "And may the wolf and panther howl o'er your fleshless bones, fit banquet for the destroyers!" His very last words, however, are directed to "his wife, his queen, his Nahmeokee."

EPILOGUE

Epilogue inquires if this native picture is acceptable: it sees approval from a maid, a beau, and a confirmed theatregoer; when a salty critic is mute, epilogue claims victory.

14

ROBERT MONTGOMERY BIRD (1806–1854)

The Gladiator (1831)

Blank-verse romantic tragedy in five acts

MAIN CHARACTER AND THEME: Historical story of the revolt of gladiator-slaves in ancient Rome, led by *Spartacus*, a Thracian superman, and, incidentally, of the fight against slavery in America being prosecuted in the 1830's.

OTHER CHARACTERS:

Marcus Licinius Crassus, Roman Praetor
Lucius Gellius, Consul
Scropha, Quaestor
Jovius, a Centurion
Mummius, lieutenant to Crassus
Batiatus Lentulus, a Capuan lanista, or master of gladiators
Bracchius, a Roman lanista
Florus, son of Lentulus

Gladiators:
Phasarius, brother of **Spartacus**
Aenomaiis, a Gaul
Crixus, a German
A crowd of others
A Boy, son of Spartacus
Julia, niece of Crassus
Senona, wife of Spartacus
Citizens
Soldiers
Others

TIME: 73 B.C.

PLACE: Rome; other parts of Italy.

HISTORICAL NOTE: Example of the product of Bird, historically important among early American playwrights, and of effective antislavery propaganda in the theatre. Produced in the same year as the first issue of Garrison's *Liberator*, it is preoccupied with the universal slavery question

50

and with the fear that the subjugation of everything to a lust for money might destroy America. It is, nevertheless, a highly dramatic play, with rousing poetic speeches and good theatricality. Like *Metamora*, it was one of Edwin Forrest's greatest theatrical vehicles and was acted by him and others for seventy-five years after its first production. It echoes Shakespeare, Marlowe, and even Homer. It was first produced on September 26, 1831, at the Park Theatre, New York, with Forrest as Spartacus.

ACT I

The gladiators, Phasarius and Aenomaiis, discuss the folly of Roman conquest, which leaves no protection to the homeland and which is shot through with corruption. They wonder if thirty gladiators, by setting their dens afire and forcing the armory, could not lead a revolt. Ignoring the valuable Phasarius's taunts, Bracchius, a master of gladiators, warns him that a new gladiator owned by Lentulus will annihilate him. Lentulus, however, complains that the gladiator, captured through trickery, has refused to take the gladiatorial oath. Brought forth, Spartacus expresses in sweeping words his misery at being enchained, his love of Thrace, his contempt for the Romans. By accident, his wife, Senona, and his son are brought in as captives. When Bracchius discovers the relationship, he doubles the price for them. Lentulus buys them, but only after Spartacus promises to fight as a gladiator. Then Senona and Spartacus talk together of their sorrows, Spartacus vowing that his son shall be free.

ACT II *(three scenes)*

In the house of Crassus, the praetor, the Romans' worship of the money god is discussed, and the caprice of the populace in advancing men to office and power in return for great shows and feasts. Though acknowledging the basic truth, Crassus is resentful that his public service has been overlooked in the accusation of corruption. Florus, requesting the hand of Crassus's niece, is told to gain glory and wealth by whatever means: he is descended from a German slave, while Julia is of noble blood. To prevent further converse between Florus and Julia, Crassus sends her to the country (Campania), denying even her request to see Phasarius fight just once more. He comments on the worthlessness of barbarian lives.

Florus instructs Spartacus that only the people, by turning thumbs up, may spare a disabled opponent; otherwise, the gladiator must kill. But

Spartacus learns that in the arena there will be four hundred armed slaves who hate their masters. He is encouraged by this fact until he is told that there will also be four legions of Praetorian Guards, five thousand to the legion.

In the arena of an amphitheatre, before going forth to fight, Spartacus fearlessly reminds Crassus that each possible foe—Spaniard, Carthaginian, Gaul—represents a nation that has defied Rome and even been momentarily successful. Spartacus goes forth and kills a Gaul; he is promised freedom for himself and family if he kills one more gladiator. Against his will, he is matched with a Thracian, who turns out to be his own brother, Phasarius. Instead of fighting each other, they give the signal to the other gladiators and lead the revolt. "Kill and spare not—" they shout; "for wrath and liberty!—/ Freedom for bondmen—freedom and revenge."

ACT III (*four scenes*)

Spartacus has already defeated three Roman praetors in pitched battles and his army grows. Ordered by the senate to stop him, Crassus martials six legions: he is jealous of Pompey's glory and wants to defeat the gladiators before Pompey can intervene.

The gladiators fight among themselves: in anger, Crixus and his German troops pull away from Spartacus. The rash Phasarius urges Spartacus immediately to turn upon Rome itself.

In Crassus' villa, Florus tells Julia of a Roman victory and of the rumored death of Spartacus. He grieves that the price of victory has been the loss of the consul, Creus Lentulus, and his army. As Florus talks, Spartacus bursts in and captures all the Romans in the villa. He holds Julia hostage for his own wife. To his lieutenants, charged with closing the trap on the nearby Roman army, he orders: "Let none 'scape, / And let none live."

Next, Spartacus storms the camp of the Consul Gellius, who thinks that in Crixus he has defeated the main army of gladiators and who expects to win glory at the expense of Crassus. In the storming, Spartacus rescues Senona and their child.

ACT IV (*three scenes*)

Senona assures Julia that Spartacus is decent and fair, not a madman killer. When Spartacus refuses to give Julia to Phasarius as a prize of war or to

52

march immediately upon Rome, Phasarius deserts, taking fifty thousand men with him to attack the city.

Only seven thousand true soldiers are left with Spartacus. He plans to invade Sicily as a diversionary move, regretfully rejecting the idea of helping Phasarius by falling upon the Roman rear. When the centurion Jovius, unaware that Senona is rescued, proposes to exchange her for Julia, Spartacus sends him back empty-handed, refusing all ransom.

ACT V (*seven scenes*)

On the peninsula of Rhegium, Phasarius returns wretched, having lost his whole army. Spartacus tells him:

> Thou hast murder'd fifty thousand men, destroyed
> Thy brother and thy country, and all hope
> Of the earth's disenthralment.

Phasarius reports that six thousand of his men, who had surrendered, were crucified along the Roman highways:

> Some howled, and prayed for death, and cursed the gods;
> Some turned to lunatics, and laughed at horror;
> And some with fierce and hellish strength, had torn
> Their arms free from the beams, and so had died,
> Grasping, headlong, at air.

Meanwhile Spartacus's retreat is cut off by the desertion of his pirate allies. Leaving Phasarius to rescue his wife and child, Spartacus attacks Crassus and Jovius as they discuss bribing him with Roman citizenship to release Julia. In the battle, Spartacus escapes with his army. Crassus orders him pursued, to prevent his falling into Pompey's hands.

Among the hills, Spartacus, blocked by the sea, faces three Roman armies led by Pompey, Lucullus, and Crassus—seven thousand men against one hundred thousand. Crassus's offer of his own life and citizenship Spartacus indignantly refuses. He tries to play the glory-seeking generals against one another. But he loses heart for fighting when Phasarius arrives to tell him that his wife and child are dead. He curses Rome now and forever, calling down upon her civil war, anarchy, imperial torturers, and hosts of Northern savages. He then commands his men to kill and die, and to be utterly merciless. His grief is blackened into a mad thirst for vengeance.

Crying, "Kill, kill, kill all," and condemning especially the band that slew his helpless wife, Spartacus reaches and kills Lentulus. Nearing Crassus, he is wounded by several intervening swords. Julia asks that he be spared because he saved her life, but he dies, saying:

> There are green valleys in our mountains yet.—
> Set forth the sails.—We'll be in Thrace anon.—

Crassus orders him buried like a noble hero.

15

WILLIAM H. SMITH (born Sedley) (1806–1872)

The Drunkard; Or,
The Fallen Saved (1844)

Temperance melodrama in five acts originally written and produced as "a moral domestic drama," based on a novel by an undesignated author and written to aid the cause of temperance

MAIN CHARACTER AND THEME: The downward flight of *Edward Middleton*, twenty-three, promising son of a respectable, rich, and recently deceased father, and his bitter struggle with the demon rum.

OTHER CHARACTERS:

Lawyer Cribbs

William Dowton, Edward's foster brother

Farmer Gates

Farmer Stevens

Old Johnson, a friend of Edward's father

Sam Evans, a friend of Edward and Mary

First Loafer

Second Loafer

Mr. Arden Rencelaw, a noble philanthropist

Landlord

Bar Keeper

Watchman (policeman)

Mary Wilson, a sweet girl in financial straits

Agnes Dowton, William's mentally deranged sister

Mrs. Wilson, Mary's mother

Patience Brayton, a kindly villager

Miss Spindle, a dwelling-house keeper who is desperate for a husband

Julia, child of Edward and Mary

Villagers

Loafers

Others

TIME: About 1843.

PLACE: New York City; village and rural areas nearby.

MUSICAL HIGHLIGHTS: "I am a rich widow, I live all alone" (ring-game song); "Brake and fern and cypress dell"; "Upon the heather, when the weather, is as wild as May"; "Dan Tucker" and "Boatman Dance" (barroom songs); "Home, Sweet Home."

HISTORICAL NOTE: Though lacking in high literary distinction, this play mirrors its time physically and sentimentally. Its depiction of the alcoholic is at times almost clinical. It is one of a host of plays and novels (e.g., Walt Whitman's *Franklin Evans*, 1845) which were integral parts of the temperance movement. First produced at the Boston Museum, February 12, 1844, by its adapter, who was then manager of that famous theatre, it was later picked up by Phineas T. Barnum and played in Philadelphia, New York City, and all over the land. In a time when frivolous amusement was the keynote of the theatre, this drama aiming unabashedly at the moral salvation of its audience (and one of the first of a long series of dramas dealing with temperance and other moral subjects), was a tremendous stage hit and, reportedly, effective propaganda. Nearly a century later, it was replayed as burlesque melodrama to audiences who found its original purposes most laughable: in Hollywood, California, from 1933 to 1953, it became a theatrical phenomenon by attracting two million people—playing every night for nearly seven thousand consecutive performances—an olio, accompanied by beer and pretzels.

ACT I (*five scenes*)

In a pretty rural cottage, Mrs. Wilson and Mary, recently bereaved of husband and father, face the future most uncertainly. Lawyer Cribbs, agent for the house on behalf of Edward, son of the deceased owner, plans to evict the Wilsons; in his soliloquies, he is a self-declared villain. The Wilsons decide that their only hope is to go to Edward and offer him the thirty dollars they had saved up for winter fuel. While talking to Edward, Mary must face the bitter opposition of Cribbs, who accuses the Wilsons of letting the place run down. Edward rebuffs Cribbs, refuses Mary's money while granting her request to remain in the house, and almost proposes to Mary on the spot. Cribbs swears vengeance.

At her dwelling house, Miss Spindle soliloquizes on the way she keeps "maidenly soft" by reading affecting novels at the modest cost of fifty dollars a year. Edward's foster brother William appears and is bluntly discouraging to her schemes to get Edward to marry her. Edward proposes to Mary, and their wedding is soon planned, to the delight of the villagers. Cribbs vainly tries to corrupt William with drink. When Cribbs attempts to cane Agnes, William's deranged sister, who knows a secret Cribbs fears, William reappears to defend her. The wedding of Edward and Mary takes place amid "vines, entwined roses, etc."

ACT II (*five scenes*)

After the wedding, Miss Spindle hires Cribbs to file a breach-of-promise suit against Edward. Disappointedly, Cribbs finds that the affection was all on Miss Spindle's side. The villagers, however, are not without anxiety about Edward, who, although generous and seemingly respectable, is "spending his Sabbaths going from one tavern to another." In one of these, Cribbs lures Edward to take the fateful step from brandy to Irish whiskey; before long, Edward is screamingly drunk and disorderly. William rescues Edward, who is later ashamed of himself and in "agony! agony!" over his wife and child. He persuades himself, however, that "a very little will revive and strengthen" him to face his family; soon he is boasting of "the arch cunning" of the drunkard. Cribbs, realizing his partial victory, tries to get Edward to sell his house for five hundred dollars to supply his thirst. This offer Edward rejects, but consents to drink one more brandy with Cribbs.

At the cottage, Mary's mother is dying. Mary's child by Edward, Julia, notices her father's recurrent illnesses. Edward returns drunk as his mother-in-law dies; he blames himself and rushes out, crying, "Farewell forever!" Julia, running to catch him, falls on the threshold.

ACT III (*six scenes*)

On Broadway, in New York City, Edward drinks with loafers and stoops so low as to take pittances from Cribbs. Cribbs tells him his wife is sewing for gentlefolk to supply herself and his child. Although needing brandy, Edward refuses to join Cribbs in forging a check for five thousand dollars in the name of Mr. Rencelaw, a philanthropist. He returns to the barroom, drinks, raucously sings low songs, and becomes involved in a brawl.

Mary and Julia live in a wretched garret, but Mary wants her husband back. Telling Mary that Edward has been unfaithful with prostitutes, Cribbs tries to overcome her scruples. When Julia screams, William enters and drives Cribbs out. He promises Mary he will find Edward. At that moment, however, Edward is being led to jail for disorderly conduct. In a general brawl, William manages to rescue Edward and turn Cribbs over to the police.

ACT IV (*four scenes*)

Some time later, living in a wretched shed, Edward dreams horrid dreams and, waking, imagines himself dead. When the landlord of an inn arrives, Edward chokes him, demanding drink. William rescues the landlord. Edward collapses in *delirium tremens*, then tries suicide. In the nick of time, Mr. Rencelaw appears and persuades Edward to take the temperance pledge. The philanthropist's arguments are strong because he was himself ridden by the demon rum for twenty years, made an about-face, and now is rich and respectable.

Out of jail, Cribbs plans to go through with his forgery scheme and to use the money to go abroad. William observes him send a boy to the bank with the check. The garrulous Miss Spindle appears, to Cribbs' confusion. Meanwhile Rencelaw learns that the check has been cashed and sends for a policeman. William visits Rencelaw, learns that Edward will soon rejoin his family, and tells Rencelaw about Cribbs and his suspicious maneuvers. Edward, now reformed and well, is reunited with Mary and little Julia.

ACT V (*three scenes*)

While aiding the search for Cribbs in the village, Farmers Stevens and Gates reveal that Agnes' mind has been restored and that she carries a happy secret. Agnes meets William and relates how, recalling vaguely that she has long ago seen something buried, she has unearthed the senior Middleton's will, which confirms Edward in full possession of his grandfather's property and proves Cribbs' authority a forgery.

Cribbs returns to try to find the will. Agnes feigns madness and is attacked by Cribbs. He is captured. Before he is led away, he confesses seeking revenge on Edward's father, who, instead of betraying him when he had committed an act of vile atrocity, had "pardoned, pitied, and despised" him.

A tableau in the final scene shows the happy home of Edward, Mary, and Julia, with Edward playing "Home, Sweet Home" on the flute and Julia singing the first verse.

16

ANNA CORA MOWATT RITCHIE (1819–1870)

Fashion; Or, Life in
New York (1845)

Manners comedy in five acts

MAIN CHARACTER AND THEME: Conflict between two dynamic Americans—
Adam Trueman, seventy-two, robust, rich farmer of Catteraugus county,
proud to be a plain man, and *Mrs. Elizabeth Tiffany*, a lady of New York
City, who imagines herself fashionable.

OTHER CHARACTERS:

Count Jolimaitre, a fashionable European importation

Colonel Howard, officer in the United States Army

Mr. Tiffany, New York merchant

T. Tennyson Twinkle, a modern poet

Augustus Fogg, a drawing room appendage

Snobson, rare species of confidential clerk

Zeke, colored servant

Prudence, maiden lady of a certain age

Millinette, a French lady's maid

Gertrude, governess

Seraphina Tiffany, a belle

TIME: About 1845.

PLACE: New York City.

HISTORICAL NOTE: Pursuing the theme of European-American contrasts
originally broached in *The Contrast* (see #5, above), and adding the
emphasis upon the American parvenu, *Fashion* is distinguished because
its author was a woman and an actress born and nurtured in the midst of

high society, both American and European. Turning to playwriting because her rich merchant husband had failed in business, she quickly recouped the family fortunes; *Fashion* was an immediate success after its introduction at the Park Theatre, New York, on March 24, 1845, running for twenty consecutive nights—phenomenal for the time. It had equal success in Philadelphia and other American cities. As Anna Cora Mowatt, the author wrote *Autobiography of an Actress, or Eight Years on the Stage* (1854), a most valuable document in American theatrical history.

ACT I

Mrs. Tiffany is determined to climb to the highest rung of society. She has hired a colored butler-footman (Zeke, renamed Adolph) in dashing livery and scarlet coat. For a whole week she studied *French Without a Master* and now interlards her conversation with such elegant phrases as *jenny-says-quoi*, *ee-light*, and *fo-tool*. Because it is despicably American to introduce people to one another (all fashions are foreign), she does not do so in her home. From Paris she has acquired her maid, Millinette, to teach her the French mode; she orders her friend Prudence to concentrate on belonging to the "upper ten thousand" and to forget entirely the days of their humble hat-making. Her daughter, Seraphina, is being courted by Twinkle, a poet, and Fogg, member of one of the oldest families, who is indifferent to everything —except food. But Mrs. Tiffany clears them all away so that Seraphina may be fully occupied with Count Jolimaitre, who knows like the back of his hand Tortoni's and the Café Royale in Paris and St. James's and Hyde Park in London, and who is so abashed by American deficiency in fashion that he finds it difficult to exist here. When Adam Trueman, wearing boots covered with dust and carrying a stout cane, invades her sacred premises, Mrs. Tiffany treats this old friend of her husband's with great disdain. A moment later, she is not there to see the count startled when he recognizes Millinette, or to notice Millinette start and scream when she sees the count.

ACT II (*two scenes*)

In Mr. Tiffany's countinghouse, Snobson, the confidential clerk, has just received another one hundred dollar raise, his fourth in a year. He also demands that Tiffany tell his daughter that Snobson is to marry her. Adam

60

tells Tiffany that he is shocked at the disgustingly materialistic atmosphere of both his business and his home, and he dislikes intensely the hangdog face and ill-sounding laugh of the confidential clerk. Adam and Tiffany gone, Snobson soliloquizes that six months from now, he expects to be driving down Broadway in a tandem with two footmen.

The entrance of the count prevents a declaration of love by Colonel Howard to the governess Gertrude. Later, however, the count tells Gertrude that after his marriage to Seraphina, she must remain in a certain capacity (as they delicately arrange things in France). When he tries to embrace her, he is brusquely prevented by Adam with his hickory stick. Mrs. Tiffany accepts the count's explanations and apologizes for Adam's lack of "how ton!" Gertrude thanks Adam, who warns her never to tell a lie. In his heart he feels her to be "true." Obviously attempting to attract Adam, Prudence makes little headway.

ACT III *(two scenes)*

An unpleasant scene arises between Mrs. Tiffany and her husband when the latter declares, first, that her extravagance will ruin him; second, that Seraphina will not marry the count; and third, that Snobson must be allowed to call that morning, reception day or no, and that he must receive an invitation to her ball on Friday evening. Snobson arrives almost too quickly; he is very coolly received. Reception day or not, Mrs. Tiffany arranges an audience for the count with Seraphina. The count proposes to Seraphina but insists that they be married in private. Snobson swears to Tiffany that he will not accept such insults. Millinette whispers to the count that she must speak to him that day, or she will tell all.

In the housekeeper's room, Millinette charges the count with deserting her in Paris and taking all her money. The count promises to explain after the ball on Friday night. Guessing the tenor of their conversation, Gertrude confronts the count and agrees not to betray him if he will follow her instructions. She has decided to entrap him; he believes that she has fallen for his charms.

ACT IV *(two scenes)*

During the cotillion of Mrs. Tiffany's great ball, the count whispers to Seraphina that they will be married tomorrow. Again Snobson is by-passed. After Mrs. Tiffany takes Adam off, the count leads Gertrude into a polka.

Gertrude knows of Millinette's appointment with the count in the house-keeper's room—to unmask him—and gets Mrs. Tiffany to keep Millinette busy meanwhile. Millinette is deeply chagrined. Prudence has been eaves-dropping on Gertrude's activities.

Posting the servant Zeke at the door of the housekeeper's room, Gertrude prepares to keep Millinette's appointment with the count. When the count arrives, he calls for Millinette and tries to kiss her. He hears someone trying to push pass Zeke at the door and rushes to the closet to avoid disgrace. Carrying a light, Prudence leads Adam, Mrs. Tiffany, and Colonel Howard into the room. No count is in evidence, but Prudence searches until she finds him in the closet. Howard is dismayed; Mrs. Tiffany calls Gertrude "a depraved little minx" and orders her to leave next day; even Adam, at last, believes Gertrude guilty, a victim of fashion. Not allowed to explain, Gertrude is heavy of heart against a background of lively music.

ACT V

Next day, Gertrude, preparing to leave, convinces Adam that the count is an impostor and that she has nothing to be ashamed of. Adam is most happy: he has found one true woman at last. She likewise convinces Howard, who begs forgiveness. Prudence enters with a note from Seraphina, saying she has eloped with the count. Tiffany says he is ruined. Adam identifies Gertrude as his long lost grandchild, whom he claims, now that she has proved herself and found a man willing to take her for herself alone—the man being Colonel Howard. When Mrs. Tiffany brags of her daughter's being a countess and visiting the fashionable folk in Washington, D.C., both Gertrude and Millinette brand the count as an impostor; Millinette identifies him as Gustave Treadmill, head cook, of Paris. Revealing his hold over Tiffany, Snobson says he will send his employer to prison for forgery; Adam then informs him that if he does, he will go also as an accessory. Snobson promptly leaves for California and tries to get Tiffany to go with him. Seraphina, returning at the count's instance for her jewels, learns the awful truth about her betrothed, but she is not married because the clergyman was not at home. Adam promises help to Tiffany, providing he sells his house and bundles his wife and daughter off to the country to learn economy, true independence, and home virtues in place of foreign follies. Tiffany agrees. The count, coming in to see what has detained Seraphina, is nailed by

"Fashion; or, Life in New York" (1845)

Adam as an impostor, and confesses. Accepting Adam's promise to set him up in business if he will visit his society acquaintances in his cook's attire, the count also accepts Millinette's proposal of marriage. In benediction, Adam declares Nature's the only nobility.

17

JAMES KIRKE PAULDING (1778–1860)

The Bucktails; Or, Americans in England (written 1847)

Manners comedy in five acts

MAIN CHARACTERS AND THEME: The disturbance created by the appearance in English society of *Henry* and *Frank Tudor*, brothers and young Americans of wealth, just after the War of 1812.

OTHER CHARACTERS:

Obsolete, an antiquary

Noland, a profligate lord

Sir Christopher, a physician

Admiral Gunwale, always bragging of England's exploits at sea

Major Longbow, retired on half pay

Threadneedle, a banker

Paddy Whack, servant to Noland

Rust, servant to Obsolete

Jonathan Peabody, a Yankee, servant to the Tudors

Bamfylde Moore Carew, King of the Gipsy Beggars and Crows

Fortune Teller

Potluck, the King's man

Little Billy

Beggars

Rogues

Mrs. Carlton, wife of a young American merchant in London

Jane Warfield, her sister, an heiress to $500,000

Miss Obsolete, sister of Obsolete

Mary, Obsolete's daughter

TIME: About 1815.

PLACE: Bath, in England.

HISTORICAL NOTE: A bold society drama in which international rivalry is

64

"The Bucktails; or, Americans in England" (written 1847)

stressed (especially that between the English and Americans) and in which the independence of America as a place of high society is declared. Though never acted, it is upheld by literary variety and robust dialogue. Its author had been successful in 1831 with *Lion of the West*, the first American drama to introduce a raw frontiersman (named Wildfire).

ACT I *(two scenes)*

After the manner of Portia and Nerissa in *The Merchant of Venice*, Jane and her sister, Mrs. Carlton, review Jane's suitors: the admiral, old and blustery and showing his age; the major, who drinks gunpowder tea for breakfast and was made a Knight-companion of the Bath, but who does not qualify for a lifelong companion; the banker, who should have been a tailor because he invents the fashions he wears; the antiquary and the physician, who as husbands would make their wives unsuccessful rivals to dry parchment manuscripts; Lord Noland, who is a nuisance and an outlaw. Mrs. Carlton agrees that in England the distinctions in society rest upon other considerations than education, morals, and manners.

In his antiquary's room, Obsolete learns that his Egyptian mummy and the Americans coming to visit will arrive at virtually the same time; hating young men and new worlds, he hopes the mummy will compensate for the visitors. His sister, Miss Obsolete, cares little for people who are not hopeless cripples, deep in jail, or otherwise sadly incommoded. Moreover, she has heard (and believes) that Americans generally wear copper rings in their noses, eat raw meat, paint their faces red and black, are half-naked, and need interpreters. She is dismayed that neither of the Tudors, whom she calls aboriginals, is a cripple. She chides Mary for expressing interest in the young Americans, telling her that she might be making for herself a future in which she would carry a papoose on her back while her husband hunted beaver or took scalps. Mary replies that her present boredom might welcome even that.

ACT II *(three scenes)*

The rivals for Jane's hand assemble for dinner; each is trying to gain a selfish advantage. It is obvious that each considers Jane's fortune imperative to his happiness. Obsolete invites them to his home to meet the American bucktails. They all accept. In the midst of wooing Jane, they are introduced

65

to Henry and Frank. Confusion reigns, especially when Miss Obsolete declares that it is necessary to converse in Choctaw, Chickasaw, or Pota-wottomy in order to understand the Americans clearly. Henry and Jane are part of the confusion, but Mary and Frank seem to be immediately, though quietly, smitten with each other. When Obsolete tries to get Henry to trace back his ancestry, Henry informs him that Americans long ago forgot their pedigrees through toils and dangers. Noland and Sir Christopher are shocked at this radicalism. Sir Christopher calls Frank a bucktail, but Rust, walking behind Frank, can see no convincing evidence that the title is justified.

ACT III (two scenes)

Meanwhile, there is considerable ridicule being passed among the servants—Rust, the Englishman, Paddy, the Irishman, and Jonathan, the Yankee. The latter two almost come to blows. Their differences of opinion parallel those of their masters.

In the drawing room after dinner, Henry offers to accompany Mary on a stroll in the country; Miss Obsolete dubs him a rake for making such a suggestion. Henry defends himself by referring to the customs of America where such behavior results in happy marriages and where girls do not marry to come into gay society but to retire from it. The other rivals have been drinking heavily: when the admiral, in his cups, bustles up to Jane to request her hand, she says she will marry him if he gets command of a British ship and brings in an American ship of equal force. She makes the same test a condition for the success of each of her English suitors. Eventually Jane asks Henry to see her to her carriage, and Mary permits Frank to stay and read to her until her father or aunt returns. Noting Jane's attraction to "the bucktail," and knowing that his financial affairs will stand no long delay in settlement, Lord Noland plans to make Jane a Lady, and his Lady, against her will.

ACT IV (four scenes)

With his servant Paddy's help, Noland prepares a forced elopement. His method is to send a letter to Miss Obsolete, signed Elizabeth Dumps, in which Mrs. Dumps says she is a widow, with five children, unable to work, and in need of a visit. The widow wants souchong tea and wants Miss Obsolete to bring Jane along. Jane agrees to go. Not far along the route, ruffians appear; they carry Jane with them and leave "the old Tabby" (Miss Obsolete) to find her own way home. Miss Obsolete calls them unmannerly for preferring one lady to another; soon, however, she screams and runs.

ACT V (nine scenes)

In a garden, Mary and Frank declare their love. When Frank asks Mary's father for permission to marry her, Obsolete refuses because he hates an America with no mystery, no hieroglyphical obscurity, no mark of antiquity. Since Mary will not go with him unless they can take her father along, Frank disconsolately leaves.

Through persistence and threats, Jonathan, the Tudors' servant, worms out of Paddy the story of the kidnapping. Jonathan tells Paddy he is half-horse and half-alligator (like the legendary Mike Fink), and will plan the rescue of Jane. At his instigation, all the rivals, but especially Frank and Henry, search for Jane through the forest at night. Pale and fatigued, Jane gets away from the ruffians but is lost in the wood. Her experiences include being lost in a graveyard during a thunderstorm, meeting the King of the Beggars and his men, and finally being reunited with Henry, who with the other searchers has had equally hair-raising experiences. Lord Noland is not punished after he begs pardon. Jane and Henry decide to be lifelong partners, and Frank wins Mary when Obsolete says he is willing to search in America for the nation of pigmy skeletons, three feet high, and other unexplored antiquities. It is hey for the New World, to Jane—land of free maids and happy wives; to Paddy—land of exiles, foster home of poor Irishmen; to Henry—land of the free, and home of the brave!

18

BENJAMIN A. BAKER (1818–1890)

A Glance at New York (1848)

Local drama in two acts

MAIN CHARACTER AND THEME: The vivid street life of New York City in the late 1840's as it radiates within the circle of acquaintance of *Mose*, a New York fire boy (fireman).

OTHER CHARACTERS:

Harry Gordon, a city boy who has just returned from a visit in the country (village near Newburgh)

Jake and *Mike*, city slickers

George Parsells, a country boy, whom Harry recently visited

Major Gates, an oratorical bum

Sykesee, Mose's fire pal

Joe, who lives in the streets

Eliza Stebbins, shopgirl, who reads sentimental books and who is Mose's best girl

Mrs. Morton, a society lady

Mr. Morton, her husband, an old friend of George's father

Mary Morton, their daughter

Jane, their niece from the country, a cousin of George

Jenny Bogart, Eliza's friend at the shop

Bill Waters and *Johnny Stokes*, loafers

City types:

Woman with baby, Boat passengers, Boys, Ladies bowling, Loafers, Street sweepers, Dancers, Several Peter Funks (come-ons at an auction), *Newsboys, Porters, Apple-women, Others*

TIME: 1848.

PLACE: New York City.

MUSICAL HIGHLIGHTS: "The folks are all waiting" (air, "Jolly young waterman"); "For pleasure, there's no denying" (air, "Fra Diavolo"); "I'm sure the world can't blame a man" (air, "Bow-wow-wow"); "Here we are, a precious crew, that's always on hand" (Irish air); "Go, Major, go, for half the night's past" (air, "Canadian Boat Song"); "Lovely Mae"; "Here we are, as you diskivir" (air, "Oh Lud, Gals").

HISTORICAL NOTE: In dramatic history, this play is set down as a new departure in that it uses realistic city life as background for sensational action and characterization. Lacking formal plot, the drama nevertheless possesses humor and insight into city life and the peculiarities of city people. Written by an actor and manager, who was later associated with the Actors' Fund and affectionately known as "Uncle Ben Baker."

ACT I (*six scenes*)

Returning with his country friend George Parsells from a visit to a small village, Harry Gordon speaks proudly—as they step off the boat—of the wonders and delights of the city, despite extremes of wealth and poverty. Every time Harry leaves George alone in the street, however, George is victimized by various city tricks, chiefly by two city slickers, Jake and Mike. First, he is taken for the "watch-stuffer" (whereby his fine silver watch is exchanged for a worthless gilt one); then, for the ancient "pocketbook-drop"; and then, for guide service—to see a nonexistent elephant, to have the privilege of walking in the Park (free to all), to be shown the Battery (utterly wide open). Besides his watch, he loses over fifty dollars in cash.

Unknown to George, his cousin Jane has also come to the city to visit the Mortons, friends of George's father—and privately hoping to see more of Harry.

Harry introduces George to Mose, a fire boy, disgusted because he has been mistreated by the chief engineer. Mose helps Harry show George the town. The three of them disguise themselves as women and go bowling at a ladies' bowling saloon, where Mrs. Morton, her daughter Mary, and Jane are bowling with other fine, exclusive ladies. Pretending not to see through their disguises, the Mortons tease them. George finds Mary as attractive as Harry does Jane. This escapade ends in flight when Mose cannot resist kissing Mrs. Morton; accused of being "a man," Mose declares: "Yes, sir-ree, I am a man, and no mistake—and one of de b-hoys at dat!" Harry and George pull Mose away.

69

On the street again, Mose suggests they go to the Bowery Theatre to see old Jack Scott "take" Don Keyser de Bassoon. When Harry thinks it is too late for the theater, Mose insists on the "Loafer's Paradise," to which the other two agree. It is only a dirty barroom, but there is plenty of action among the town's choice grifters and foo-foos (defined by Mose as an outsider "who can't come de big figure . . . three cents for a glass of grog and a night's lodging"). Mose is looking for a fight, but no one will fight him. There is, however, some colorful speechmaking by Major Gates and Jake; the general tenor of remarks is "Up with no work, up with no watch-house [jail]!" For this latter declaration, there is much applause. Later Mose has his fight, with two fellows who follow him. He knocks them both down, and they get up fighting each other, while Mose slips away.

ACT II (*six scenes*)

In the fight, George, not smart the way Mose is, has got his hat smashed and his eye blackened. This, plus his losses, makes him disgusted with city life and ready to return home at once. Meanwhile, Mose's sophistication in city ways is dented by his being given a baby in a basket by a passing woman. He tries to walk away from the crying baby, but then he reminds himself of the honor of the fire boys. "It never shall be said," weeps Mose, "dat one of de New York boys deserted a baby in distress." Mose takes the baby to an almshouse.

Later, dressed as a butcher, Mose encounters his best girl, Lize, who, though a shopgirl, is an incessant reader. This time she is pondering *Matilda, the Disconsolate*. In the course of making a date for the evening, Mose and Lize treat the audience to a lively sampling of the latest city argot, such as Lize telling Mose to pick her up at her shanty any time after tea, and Mose praising Lize by calling her "a gallus gal" (meaning, an exciting woman). Returning to his job, Mose tells the driver: "Drive up Chrystie Street till you smell blood, and dere stop." Major Gates's advice is colorful also: "Change your money as much as you like, but still adhere to your mind."

George is taken one more time by the slickers, but in a fake auction in which he bids for false gems, George is rescued by Mose, who knocks down the cheaters and tears up the counter. When Mose tells George he is going to pick up his "prize lamb" (his best girl), George says he understands that, he was always good at judging cattle.

70

"A Glance at New York" (1848)

At the Vauxhall Garden, with arches of variegated lamps and refreshment tables, and groups dancing gallopades, Mose's crowd and the upper-class Mortons come together on Harry's invitation. Mose asks his girl: "Say, Lizey, ain't this high?" Lize answers: "Well, it ain't nothin' else." When time comes to order food, Lize orders coffee and nine doughnuts while Mose orders pork and beans with a "skin" of brandy.

Before the evening is over, Mr. Morton abruptly suggests a double wedding. Jane and Harry, Mary and George are more than willing to oblige. Harry proudly introduces his pal Mose to his new family.

19

GEORGE L. AIKEN (1830–1876)

Uncle Tom's Cabin; Or, Life Among the Lowly (1852)

*All-purpose drama in six acts based on the world-famous novel
(1852) by Harriet Beecher Stowe*

MAIN CHARACTER AND THEME: The story of slavery and freedom, South and North, as seen through the poignant experiences of an old, wise, religious slave, *Uncle Tom*, and his associates, black and white.

OTHER CHARACTERS:

George Harris, fiery, young mulatto slave

George Shelby, son of Tom's original owner

Augustine St. Clare, Tom's later owner

Phineas Fletcher, former slave owner being remade by his Quaker sweetheart Ruth

Gumption Cute, man of many occupations, distant relative of Ophelia

Mr. Wilson, owner of a bagging factory, who used to employ George Harris

Deacon Abraham Perry, recent widower in Vermont, suitor of Ophelia

Shelby, original owner of Tom, Eliza, and Harry

Haley, a slave dealer and hunter

Simon Legree, a Northern-born slave owner

Tom Loker, a slave hunter

Marks, lawyer and slave hunter

Sambo and *Quimbo*, Legree's beastly Negro guards

Doctor

Waiter

Harry, child of the slaves George Harris and Eliza

Three more slave hunters

Skeggs, a slave auctioneer

Mann, a spectator at slave auctions

Other spectators and potential buyers at slave auctions

Adolf, a valet, one of St. Clare's slaves

Eva, St. Clare's daughter

Eliza, pretty, near-white mulatto, owned by Shelby, married to George, mother of little Harry

Cassy, Legree's slave

Marie, St. Clare's wife

Ophelia, St. Clare's cousin and housekeeper, from Vermont

Aunt Chloe, Tom's wife in Kentucky

Topsy (also Topsey), a grotesque slave

Emmeline, a young quadroon slave, originally belonging to St. Clare

TIME: About 1850.

PLACE: Kentucky, Ohio, Louisiana, Vermont.

MUSICAL HIGHLIGHTS: There is music everywhere, to fit the deep moods of the scenes and to mask and guide scene transitions. In addition, Tom sings Methodist hymns and Topsy sings as she dances her breakdowns. Two of Tom's favorites are "Oh, had I the wings of morning" and "I see a band of spirits bright." "Old Folks at Home" is sung in Act V, scene 3.

HISTORICAL NOTE: Though far from a literary masterpiece, *Uncle Tom's Cabin* is without question the most significant theatrical phenomenon in America, and perhaps in world theatrical history. Down to the present, it has been overwhelmingly influential as a sociological and a stage force. This drama of thirty scenes, lasting three and a half hours in its original production, encompasses nearly all the major devices of popular effect: straight drama, agitprop drama, minstrel play, melodrama, sentimental drama, farce, and tragedy. Its great variety of appeal is probably due to the following outstanding factors: the indestructible will of George and Eliza to be free, the overpowering desire of Uncle Tom to be free, and the spirit of helping those who want to be free, demonstrated by Phineas; the fascinating character of thorough villains, like Haley and Marks, who work imaginatively to enslave others or who live as gloating parasites; the pleasant atmosphere of broad acres tended by a happy-go-lucky master; the uplifting character of genuine goodness and sweetness (Eva), coupled with the deep and delicious sorrow felt when observing the apparently useless demise of such personified goodness; the contrasting excitement of crude but

73

charming badness (Topsy); the gripping vision of human flesh actually being bought, sold, and paid for—of families torn apart as though by some unseen hurricane; the tortured soul torn between good and evil, enclosed in a completely evil body (Legree); the constant efforts of careless good to recover its mastery over always efficient evil (George Shelby); the terror of real tragedy at the end of the story; and the soothing hand of fantastic benediction in an environment that really looks like heaven.

Uncle Tom's Cabin—based on Mrs. Stowe's book (which Aiken follows faithfully), in turn based on Theodore D. Weld's *Slavery As It Is* and the autobiographies of Frederick Douglass, Lewis Clark, and Josiah Henson (the original Uncle Tom)—began its phenomenal career at the Troy Museum, Troy, New York, September 27, 1852. It is still often revived throughout the world. Aiken, who wrote the first version of the play at twenty-two, was commissioned by his cousin, G. C. Howard, and was paid forty dollars and a gold watch above his regular wages. Mrs. Stowe never had anything to do with the multitude of dramatizations of her book, nor did she ever receive a penny of royalties. Against her religious scruples, she saw the play from backstage once in New York.

The drama played one hundred nights in Troy and was witnessed by twenty-five thousand people, in a town of thirty thousand. Its New York City opening, at the National Theatre, was on July 18, 1853: it made theatrical history by constituting for the first time the entire evening's entertainment. Thereafter it played everywhere, and everywhere it continued a phenomenon. According to Elizabeth Corbett, it was 1930, seventy-seven years, before it missed being performed at least once a year. Once during the 1860's, forty-nine "Tom companies" were reported; at one time in the late 1890's, over five hundred. Considering the number of companies that have played it, often simultaneously, and the fact that in the 1880's America boasted more than four thousand theatres and opera houses—all of which offered it at least a few times each season—and the fact that European and Asiatic companies have performed it countless times, *Uncle Tom's Cabin* may well claim the distinction of being the only drama written that has been performed millions of times.

Perhaps more even than the novel, the drama has affected American and international thinking on such subjects as the character of Afro-Americans, the nature of life in the South, and the melodramatic struggle between good and evil. It was not essentially anti-South. As propaganda for abolition, however, the drama probably equaled the novel in power: both helped to galvanize majority opinion against slavery—dormant, apologetic, and compromising for years—into a crusading force that demanded immediate action (note Lincoln's famous comment to Mrs. Stowe: "So you are the little woman who brought on the great war"). In public domain from the start, its dozens of versions have often reflected private and group attitudes, or reactions to contemporary social and dramatic issues, or theories and experiments in theatrical expression. Hundreds of American actors and actresses received their basic training in various "Tom" parts. Otis Skinner as Uncle Tom and Fay Bainter as Topsy—both of whom had made their theatrical debuts in the drama—starred in a notable revival, produced by The Players and based on an adaptation of the Aiken version by A. E. Thomas, at the Alvin Theatre, New York, opening May 29, 1933.

ACT I (*six scenes*)

In consultation with his wife, George Harris, a slave, expresses his anger about losing his place in the factory and about having a hard master. Being told by his master that he must give up Eliza and "marry" and settle down on his own place, George is determined to run away to Canada and later to buy Eliza and little Harry. He cannot hear Eliza's counsel of patience and religious obedience. "I'll be free or die," he says again and again.

As the slave dealer Haley tells Shelby he must have more than Uncle Tom to satisfy the debt Shelby owes, little Harry runs in, followed by Eliza. Because of his wife, Shelby absolutely refuses to consider selling Eliza: he will let Haley know that evening if little Harry can be thrown into the Uncle Tom deal.

Having overheard the Shelby-Haley conversation, Eliza comes to tell Tom that she is running away with her child. Tom's wife Chloe asks Tom to run away also, rather than wait to be sold, but Tom says no. Eliza asks her to get word to George about her leaving. Tom urges Eliza to believe in and trust God.

In a tavern by the riverside, Phineas is waiting to cross the icy Ohio to see Ruth, the Quaker girl, who has transformed him from slave owner to Quaker. In the same tavern, Eliza overhears the plans of the hunters who search for her and her son to sell her in New Orleans and to return Harry to Shelby. Eliza decides she must try to cross the river on the ice floes before she is caught.

Eliza runs toward the river, the slave hunters in pursuit. "Courage, my child!" says Eliza to Harry; "we will be free—or perish!" Haley offers one hundred dollars for a ferryboat.

On a cake of ice, Eliza and Harry are seen floating across the river (in some versions, she is pursued by trained bloodhounds). On the southern bank, the slave hunters watch in frustration. On the opposite shore, Phineas stands.

ACT II (*four scenes*)

St. Clare brings his cousin Ophelia and Tom to his Lake Pontchartrain estate in Louisiana. St. Clare had purchased Tom after Eva had insisted— Tom had saved Eva's life once when she was pushed into the water. Ophelia calls the whole business "shiftless." Marie, St. Clare's wife, is also not pleasant to her husband.

On a water bank, Eva sits on Tom's knee. Tom sings; Eva reads the Bible, as Tom explains. St. Clare reproves Ophelia for being a Northerner who condemns the wrongs to Negroes but feels abhorrence when she gets close to them. To correct her poor understanding, he gives Topsy to Ophelia to bring up. When asked of her origin, Topsy says: "I 'spect I growed."

Back in Ohio, a placard offers four hundred dollars reward for the runaway George Harris. Phineas' Ruth insists that Phineas must find George, upon pain of losing her. Phineas finds George, who shows his pistol and makes it clear that he may die but will not return to the South: "All men are free and equal in the grave," contends George. Shortly thereafter, Phineas protects George from the slave hunters Haley, Marks, and Loker.

Back in Louisiana, Eva and Topsy are seen in sharp contrast. "I's so wicked," confesses Topsy, who despises the "cream-colored" of her race who behave as fine ladies. When Topsy reiterates that she is bad because she is unloved, Eva says she loves her. Topsy promises to be good for Eva's sake.

In Ohio again, George and Eliza are united. Phineas, now a Quaker even to his *thees* and *thous,* helps them plan to escape to Canada, since under

76

the new Fugitive Slave Law, they are unsafe anywhere in the United States. Although George does not like to be obligated, he accepts Phineas' vehicle and Phineas' offer to go as driver.

In a bloody battle at a rocky pass, George shoots Loker, and Phineas throws him over a large rock, reciting: "Friend, thee is not wanted here." The other slave hunters retreat and run off. As George and Eliza kneel in thanksgiving, Phineas stands over them exulting.

ACT III (*four scenes*)

Following the pattern of the 1850's, Tom preaches a temperance sermon to St. Clare, who drinks too often. Ophelia is ready to give up on Topsy, but St. Clare wonders about her Christianity, if she cannot tolerate *one* little heathen. On the other hand, Ophelia worries about Eva's cough.

From her Bible, Eva reads to Tom of the "sea of glass mingled with fire." As Tom sings, Eva can see "the spirits bright" he sings of. Eva knows her end is near and makes her father promise to free Tom as soon as she is gone.

Tom tells Ophelia that someone must constantly watch near Eva: angels are not far away.

Eva is dying. Feebly smiling, she cries, "Oh! love! joy! peace!" and passes to a new world of bliss. St. Clare kneels by her side and prays over her.

ACT IV (*four scenes*)

Refusing Marks's offer to become a slave hunter, Gumption Cute searches for his relative, Ophelia.

Speaking of firsthand experience with the Lord, Tom again tries to save St. Clare's soul. Telling Tom to pack, St. Clare promises to free him and take him back to Kentucky. Tom is joyful; admitting that no one could have a better master, he nevertheless tells St. Clare that he would rather be a poor freeman than a rich slave; freedom is what he yearns for most. Meanwhile, Ophelia takes a lock of Eva's hair from Topsy, who had received it from Eva. Topsy, remarkably, sobs when deprived of the precious lock: obviously she is improving. St. Clare goes to town to hear the news.

In a mysterious way to be revealed later, St. Clare dies without signing Tom's freedom papers.

ACT V (*four scenes*)

In a bitter, heart-rending scene at the auction mart, St. Clare's former slave Emmeline is sold for one thousand dollars and Tom for one thousand two hundred dollars to Simon Legree, a Red River planter.

The scene shifts to Vermont. Ophelia has returned home with Topsy and made her an adopted daughter. When Cute arrives, searching for Ophelia, he and Topsy don't agree and are very sharp with each other.

Down in his dismal new setting, Tom lives in a vale of shadows, comforted only by a curl of Eva's hair. When Emmeline resists becoming Legree's mistress, Legree orders Tom to flog her. Tom refuses; though badly whipped, Tom tells his brutal master that only his body is marketable, not his soul. Legree turns Tom over to the unconscionable pair, Sambo and Quimbo, the Negro guards.

In Vermont, Cute wins his way into Ophelia's household. But when the widowed Deacon Perry comes proposing marriage to Ophelia, Cute, fearful he will lose a fortune, forbids the wedding. Ophelia banishes Cute, who makes a dash for the Deacon, but runs instead into Topsy's lively broom.

ACT VI (*six scenes*)

Back in Louisiana, Legree's slave Cassy begs Tom not to struggle against the devil (Legree). She has lived in hell with Legree for five years and cursed each moment. Tom says he will not submit to wrong. In spite of her despair, Cassy begs Tom to pray for her.

Also in Louisiana, George Shelby has come looking for Tom—to take him back to Kentucky. Learning from the slave hunter Marks that St. Clare is dead and Tom sold to Legree, George contracts with Marks (for a handsome sum) to be guided to where Tom is.

In beating him, Sambo has taken "a witch thing" from Tom—Eva's curl of hair. Seeing it, Legree stamps and writhes as though burned. The curl reminds him of his mother in Connecticut, who struggled to pull him from sin, and who, just before she died, sent him a lock of her hair. Simon burned her letter and the lock, but has often been reminded of the event, and his soul has writhed in horror. This time, he calls Sambo and Quimbo to sing gay songs to him. But Cassy warns him that the golden tress was charmed.

"Uncle Tom's Cabin; or, Life among the Lowly" (1852)

Cute agrees to go with Marks when he guides George Shelby to Legree's plantation: it was Legree who drew a bowie knife on Cute the night St. Clare was stabbed by Legree. Cute wants revenge, but Marks wants money— he has a warrant for Legree's arrest for murdering St. Clare but intends to use it to blackmail Legree of one thousand dollars, of which Cute will receive half for helping.

Because he cannot find Cassy or Emmeline, Legree blames Tom. Tom says he knows where the girls are but cannot tell: "I can die!" Legree beats Tom almost to death. When George Shelby and the others arrive, Marks and Cute show Legree the warrant. Upon his resistance, Marks shoots Legree and kills him. Having forgiven Legree, and claiming victory, Tom dies in George Shelby's arms.

Final scene: gorgeous clouds, tinted with sunlight. Eva, robed in white, soars upward on a milk-white dove. Hands extended, she blesses St. Clare and Tom, who, kneeling, gaze up to her. Expressive music. Slow curtain.

20

GEORGE HENRY BOKER (1823–1890)

Francesca Da Rimini (1855)

Blank-verse romantic tragedy in five acts

MAIN CHARACTERS AND THEME: Love triangle involving the two sons of the Lord of Rimini—*Lanciotto*, the warlike son, and *Paolo*, the graceful, artistic son—and *Francesca*, daughter of the rival Lord of Ravenna, who married Lanciotto but loved Paolo.

OTHER CHARACTERS:

Malatesta, Lord of Rimini, a Guelf, bitter, feuding enemy of the Ghibelins

Guido da Polenta, a Ghibelin, Lord of Ravenna

Pepe, Malatesta's jester

Cardinal, friend of Guido

Rene, a troubadour

Ritta, maid to Francesca

Lords, Ladies, Knights, Priests, Soldiers, Pages, Attendants

TIME: About 1300 A.D.

PLACE: Rimini; Ravenna; and the neighborhood.

MUSICAL HIGHLIGHTS: "The babe's confession" (Pepe); "Ring high, ring high!" (Ritta); "'Tis jolly to walk in the shady greenwood/With a damsel by your side."

HISTORICAL NOTE: This play is the high point of the early romantic drama in the United States. Based on a story found in Dante's *Inferno* and retold hundreds of times in many languages, the present drama affects the style of Shakespeare and the lesser Elizabethans and tends to stress the idealistic values precious to the culturally advanced Americans of its day. Instead of concentrating on the love of Paolo and Francesca in his plot, as most writers have done, Boker emphasized the love of the two brothers and the family honor, and the unbearable impact thereupon of Francesca's love and loveliness. It was first performed in 1855 by E. L. Davenport and Mme. Ponisi; it was memorably revived by Lawrence Barrett in 1882 and by Otis Skinner in 1901. This last revival was roughly contemporary with three other famous *Francesca* productions: a version of Stephen Phillips by Beerbohm Tree in London; an F. Marion Crawford version by Sarah Bernhardt in Paris; and a Gabriele d'Annunzio version by Eleonora Duse in Rome.

ACT I (*three scenes*)

When news comes to the troubadours that Lanciotto is to be married, several of them laugh, remembering his homely appearance. Paolo angrily challenges them, saying they make fun of the man whose strong arm and sword have given them security and the privilege of sitting around in satin. At about the same time, Lanciotto tells his father that he wants their hated rival city, Ravenna, leveled and burned. He recalls the prophecy of his old nurse: "May this spot stand till Guido's dearest blood/Be mingled with my own!" Malatesta, to calm his son and to keep the political peace, tells Lanciotto that he should marry the legendarily beautiful Francesca. After some resistance, Lanciotto agrees to obey his father. In solitude, he curses the destiny by which he, spindle-shanked, wry-hipped, and hunchbacked, should have so fair a wife. The jester Pepe comes to announce that the deaf bell ringer, by Pepe's order, is *tolling* the bells instead of ringing them normally to announce the wedding. When Lanciotto strikes him, Pepe says he has a foolish honor and will have Lanciotto's life.

Paolo rushes in and prevents Lanciotto's suicide. Lanciotto tells his brother:

> Thus are we all
> Mere slaves and alms-men to a scornful world,
> That takes us at our seeming.

Declaring that although he will marry he will never agree to go to Ravenna and get his bride, Lanciotto talks Paolo into being his messenger, and is grateful for Paolo's love. Paolo in turn convinces Malatesta that it would be unwise to trust Lanciotto, Rimini's best soldier, inside Ravenna's walls. Pepe says that to send Paolo is like sending a thief to carry home a jewel. Lanciotto himself is homesick for the army camp.

ACT II (*three scenes*)

In Ravenna, Guido warns Ritta, Francesca's maid, that if she tells Francesca of Lanciotto's looks, she will be boiled in oil. Word is received from Rimini that Paolo will accompany the bride to Rimini and that to hold him for ransom will result only in the payment of cold steel. Dutiful as she is, Francesca finds being given away like a horse or falcon very hard to take, and meeting a solemn, head-shaking Dante in the hall has not helped her morale. Cardinal tells Guido that Francesca might have been given the chance to choose—she would have chosen rightly, but Guido cannot take the chance. Seeing Paolo at a distance, Francesca takes him for Lanciotto, and no one corrects her; she is delighted. When Ritta, taking her life in her hands, finally tells her the truth, Francesca pitifully says:

> Ha! ha! I'm glad it went no further, girl;
> I'm glad I kept my heart safe, after all.

Going to her father, she tells him he might have trusted her—suppose she had fallen in love with this messenger? Her father tells her the two brothers are much alike. But Francesca is wounded because she has found her father untrustworthy, and because she has no mother to guide her. Paolo nearly declares himself to her, but checks himself. When she begs to know what Lanciotto looks like, Paolo praises Lanciotto's mind. Francesca senses another deceit. Later, Paolo is ashamed of his implicit lying.

ACT III (*two scenes*)

Waiting for his bride, Lanciotto discusses his times: he is proud of belonging to an era of great advancement in mechanics and science. Pepe mockingly speaks of his own plans for political reform, calling himself a "wrongs-of-man" man.

With banners waving and citizens, in holiday dress, shouting, the bridal parade approaches. Malatesta has his men create deceptions for the military-minded among the visitors. Guido and his knights, nevertheless, make note of weaknesses in the fortifications. Francesca, seeing Lanciotto, starts, turns away, and grows pale. Lanciotto can see that Francesca has not been told the truth; when they come together, he offers to release her without penalty, but Guido, standing behind her, whispers that she must not accept this trick. When Francesca chooses to marry Lanciotto rather than accept his offered release, Lanciotto believes that she mysteriously loves him. In turn, he pours forth to her his love which he had previously withheld. Francesca is ashamed of practicing this necessary deceit upon a noble heart. Lanciotto is all exuberance.

ACT IV (*three scenes*)

Although he can get no outright declaration of love from Francesca, Lanciotto is still happy. Constantly tormented by Pepe who hints of an understanding between Francesca and Paolo, his mood changes. But he asks Paolo to instruct him in the arts of love. A little while later, Ritta can see that Francesca is ensnared by love of Paolo. The marriage proceeds. Lanciotto feels that Francesca shrinks from his nuptial kiss. Examining Paolo, Lanciotto tells him he looks like "a full-convicted thief." He begs Paolo not to betray a brother who loves him. Paolo tells him to stop talking nonsense and to join his bride. Gladly hearing that the Ghibelins have started a new war, Lanciotto prepares for it, rejecting Paolo's offer to go in his stead. Lanciotto exclaims, "O! accursed day,/That I was mated to an empty heart!", and then pushes by Paolo with "Out of my way, thou juggler!"

ACT V (*three scenes*)

Paolo and Francesca walk into a garden followed by Ritta. Pepe hides in the bushes to observe. Francesca must command Ritta before she will leave, and then only with a warning to her mistress to beware. Taking off his dagger, Paolo reads to her of Guenevra and Sir Lancelot. When he comes to the part where these two lovers kissed, he kisses Francesca, who throws herself into his arms, declaring:

> Take me all,
> Body and soul. The women of our clime
> Do never give away but half a heart:

She justifies herself by saying that she has followed her father's orders and loved the man given her. She gives his kisses back, and "like a spendthrift, only ask of thee/To take while I can give." They decide to take their love now and fully, in all its bloom of sweetness and in all its peril. She leads him into her room. Pepe, stopping only long enough to mimic their behavior, rushes to carry the news to Lanciotto.

For Pepe's pains, Lanciotto, in camp, stabs the jester. Before he dies, Pepe shows him Paolo's dagger he had taken from the scene of love and tells him that Paolo had sent him to kill Lanciotto. Lanciotto arrives in time to hear Francesca request a kiss of Paolo. Stepping forth, he says: "Take it: 't will be the last." Francesca replies: "The last! so be it." Paolo admits his love-guilt, denies Pepe's story, and begs for release for Francesca who was entrapped. Lanciotto stabs first Francesca, then Paolo; looking upon their bodies, he observes that the nurse's prophecy has come true. He tells Malatesta and Guido that they began in tragedy; he has ended it. Then he says he killed for the honor of the house. But falling upon his brother's body, he asserts:

> I loved him more than honor—more than life—
> Here let me rest, till God awake us all!

21

DION BOUCICAULT (1820–1890)

The Octoroon (1859)

Southern problem drama in five acts based on The Quadroon (1856), *a novel by Mayne Reid, British writer*

MAIN CHARACTER AND THEME: The story of *Zoe*, a Louisiana mulatto beauty, much beloved in her plantation high society, who becomes a most tragic figure through being loved by one white lover and coveted by another.

OTHER CHARACTERS:

George Peyton, English-born nephew of Judge Peyton

Salem Scudder, a Yankee overseer

Mr. Sunnyside, who holds a mortgage on the Peyton's Terrebonne Plantation

Jacob M'Closky, a Connecticut-born overseer

Wahnotee, Indian friend of Paul

Captain Ratts, captain of the *Magnolia*, a steamer

La Fouche, Jules Thibodeaux, Judge Caillou, and *Jackson*, prospective buyers at the auction

Colonel Pointdexter, the auctioneer

Old Pete, seventy-two, a lame slave who tries to pass for forty-six

Paul, his grandson

Solon, Paul's father

Mrs. Peyton, widow of Judge Peyton, George's aunt

Dora Sunnyside, an heiress, in love with George

Grace, wife of Solon, a yellow girl with two children

Minnie and *Dido*, slaves

Slave children

TIME: About 1850.

PLACE: Terrebonne Plantation in Louisiana, on the Mississippi River.

HISTORICAL NOTE: *The Octoroon* is more than a drama of the tragic mulatto: it also delineates the peculiar relationships of the Southern plantation. Inclined toward melodrama and oversimplification, and unwilling to enter on either side of the great debate on the merits of slavery as an institution, it nevertheless shows the interlocking connections of master-family and slave-groups, of Northern investment in Southern establishments, and of the various levels of racial acceptance and prejudice. In a different version from the present one, the drama ends when the steamer *Magnolia* blows up in a turpentine explosion that carries all characters with it. In still another version, played in England, Zoe and George are allowed to marry, showing the tolerance of English audiences at the time. The present version was popular and accepted in America, South as well as North. Opening at the Winter Garden, New York, on December 12, 1859, it boasted the following stars: A. H. Davenport as George, Joseph Jefferson as Scudder, Dion Boucicault as Wahnotee, and Agnes Robertson (Mrs. Boucicault) as Zoe. It was successfully revived at the Phoenix Theatre, New York, January 27, 1961.

ACT I

George is impressed by the friendly feeling between master and slaves on the plantation. A month ago he came from Paris to help settle business affairs. When the old judge died two years ago, he left the property to George, subject to Mrs. Peyton's life interest and an annuity for Zoe. But the judge was a careless businessman and a free spender, and M'Closky has come into control of the richest half of Terrebonne and Scudder in control of the rest. Interested in such inventions as photographic apparatus, new cotton gins, and steam sugar mills, Scudder exhausted his share. Now things are at a crisis, and must be settled.

Zoe, unmindful of the crisis, has been out riding horseback with George, whom Dora unashamedly likes. On the other hand, M'Closky, who covets possession of the whole of Terrebonne, covets even more ownership of Zoe. Expecting an important letter from Liverpool which might give her hope of recovering Terrebonne, Mrs. Peyton urges the slave Paul to bring the mailbags securely to her, but Paul is afraid to take Wahnotee, who loves him dearly, because of the Indian's irresponsibility about rum. Mrs. Peyton's peace of mind is not helped by having M'Closky show her an advertisement in the New Orleans *Picayune* stating that her banker, Lafouche, is dead, and in the windup of his affairs, Terrebonne is up for sale. Even so, if she receives an expected $50,000 from Mason Brothers of Liverpool, she will be in an excellent position to make settlement. Away from Mrs. Peyton, M'Closky curses these old families and their pride; he determines to intercept the Liverpool dispatch and take over the plantation. Moreover, he has learned, by perusing the judge's papers, that Zoe's freedom papers were issued in 1841 at a time when a lien, dated 1838, was on the property. This gives him evidence that Zoe is an octoroon slave who was never legally freed. If, then, he can head off the mailbags, he intends to sink every dollar he has into buying the property and owning Zoe.

ACT II

With fascination Paul and Wahnotee watch the workings of the camera as Scudder photographs Dora. Old Pete, the slave, reports that the sheriff is putting up "for sale" signs on the property. In the house, Dora requests Zoe's help in getting George to propose to her: with her fortune she can save his plantation, and he is so slow. When George sets Zoe down to talk, Zoe thinks he is going to talk about Dora, but she is soon set right. George makes clear that he wants *her* as his wife; he is not worried about the property. Although reciprocating his love, she tells him that they are separated by a gulf "as wide as your love, as deep as my despair." On her fingers and in her eyes she points out the faint blue marks that she calls the ineffaceable curse of Cain. George is not overwhelmed by her declarations, nor by the problem it presents to him with respect to his family. As they go off, M'Closky rises from behind a rock, having overheard the whole conversation and been much impressed by the octoroon's capacity for love. He says he will have her now even if it should cost him his life.

Sitting on the mailbags, Paul tries to get Wahnotee to snap his picture. As Wahnotee runs off, Paul, right in camera focus, is hit on the head and killed by M'Closky, who then steals the letter from Liverpool which gives Mrs. Peyton the relief she needs. Wahnotee, returning, shakes Paul and finds him dead. Thinking the camera has killed Paul, Wahnotee smashes it to pieces with his tomahawk. Before the dead Paul he expresses in pantomime his grief, sorrow, and fondness; then he takes him in his arms and carries him away.

ACT III

As preparations for the auction proceed, Mrs. Peyton learns that George is in love with Zoe. Since by law he cannot marry her, he allows his aunt to persuade him to marry Dora, to save the plantation and the slaves. To be honorable, he confesses to Dora that he loves another, and when Dora asks who it is, Zoe says "Me." Dora leaves, saying she hates them both. Zoe, willing to be sold, is in great agony at feeling herself a slave. At Dora's insistence, Sunnyside buys Terrebonne in the auction for $120,000. But when the slaves are put up, neither Scudder nor Dora can match M'Closky's high bids, and Zoe goes to M'Closky for $25,000. George wants to fight him; M'Closky waves a knife and wins the octoroon.

ACT IV

At the wharf, the steamer *Magnolia* swings alongside a bluff rock. When Wahnotee is found, M'Closky accuses him of Paul's murder and demands that he be lynched. The lost mailbags are also found. But at Scudder's insistence, Wahnotee gets a trial—lynching, says Scudder, would "bring disgrace upon our Western life." On the basis of evidence on the photographic plate, M'Closky is discovered to be Paul's murderer. The jury then decides to try M'Closky. Defending himself, he whips out a knife, but he is disarmed. When they search him, they find the Liverpool letter and a draft for $85,000. Now, they have M'Closky's motive. The jury votes M'Closky guilty and sets his punishment at death. But because the turpentine barrels catch fire and the steamer must move, M'Closky escapes, swimming. He is trailed by Wahnotee, who knowns from Pete that M'Closky is Paul's murderer.

ACT V (*four scenes*)

By a ruse, Zoe gets Dido to make up a strong poisonous drink. When Dido learns that Zoe plans to kill herself rather than be taken off by M'Closky, Dido tries, in vain, to get the drink back.

In a canebrake bayou, with a canoe nearby, M'Closky sleeps. He awakes screaming about flames, choking, and murder. In soliloquy, he reveals his plan to run away to Galveston and Matagorda until the business about Paul blows over. Wahnotee still trails him as he paddles off in his canoe.

In a cedar swamp, M'Closky rushes in upon Scudder and Pete, declaring that he is being pursued by unnatural forces. Wahnotee follows and attacks him. M'Closky begs Scudder to give him over to the white law and not let him be butchered by a redskin. Not allowing his sense of justice to be affected by racial matters, Scudder will not interfere; he throws M'Closky a bowie knife and tells him to defend himself. M'Closky leaves, pursued by Wahnotee.

In a Terrebonne parlor, Zoe comes to say good-by to George and to ask Dora's forgiveness. Before them both, she drinks the poison, calling it a restorative. When Dora says she would buy Zoe if she had the money, Zoe answers that she is already free. Dying, she tells George he may without blushing now confess his love for the octoroon. George kneels beside her.

22

JOSEPH JEFFERSON (1829–1905)
DION BOUCICAULT (1820–1890)
CHARLES BURKE (1822–1854)
AND OTHERS

Rip Van Winkle (1865)

*Legendary and folk drama in four acts of composite authorship,
based on the story by Washington Irving, published in*
The Sketch Book (*1819-1820*)

MAIN CHARACTER AND THEME: The adventures of the Dutch-American
legendary figure, *Rip Van Winkle*, who went to sleep in one generation
and awoke in another (twenty years later), but who, in the drama,
though a drunkard, is a sensitive person and a canny businessman.

OTHER CHARACTERS:

Derrick Von Beekman, village capitalist

Nicholas Vedder, keeper of the inn

Hendrick, Nicholas' son

Cockles, Derrick's nephew

Jacob Stein, Rip's drinking companion

Seth Slough, villager in the new Falling Waters

Gretchen, Rip's wife

Meenie, Rip's daughter

Katchen, a woman of the new village

Schneider, Rip's faithful dog

Demons (dwarfs), including one representing *Hendrick Hudson*

Villagers

TIME: 1763 and 1783.

90

PLACE: The village of Falling Waters on the Hudson River in the foothills of the Catskill Mountains.

HISTORICAL NOTE: Though lacking the prime literary quality of the Irving story—the incisive description, the rich characterization, and the genial humor—this drama has many appealing qualities, such as Rip's pleasant alcoholism (in an era of temperance propaganda), his magnetic simplicity, his awareness of the clash of the poetic and the realistic in life, and one big scene in the mountains in which Rip, the only speaker, behaves most revealingly. His wife is a far larger character in the drama than she is in the Irving story. The play was first acted in London on September 4, 1865, for 172 performances, and became a memorable vehicle for Joseph Jefferson, who belonged to the third of four generations of famous actor-producers of the same name. First produced in America at the Olympic Theatre, New York, September 3, 1866, it was carried by Jefferson throughout the country for nearly forty years.

ACT I

In Nicholas' inn, where Rip has drunk away his wealth—ten years ago he owned most of the village—Gretchen severely scolds Derrick for lending him the money on which to drink and Nicholas for giving him the drinks. Derrick reminds her that ten years ago she might have had him but took the vagabond Rip instead; he says that she can still have him if she will turn away from Rip. Unhesitatingly she replies that she can love Rip if he mends his ways, but that no one could love Derrick. When she has gone, Derrick lays the foundation for getting the remainder of Rip's estate and Gretchen also eventually. Cockles, Derrick's nephew, brings news from Derrick's lawyer that the papers Rip has signed are but mortgages upon the estate; if Derrick wants to be secure, he must get Rip's signature upon a full conveyance. Since Rip cannot read, only his cross is needed.

Rip enters, running and skipping, surrounded by children, one of whom carries his gun. Rip's dog Schneider follows. For Rip, Derrick orders the best liquor. Rip takes a drink or two but says his score for schnapps (strong Holland gin) is already too high. But Derrick is standing the bill. He gives Rip a bag of money, to compensate for his empty hunting bag. Rip is somehow suspicious: "It don't clink like good money," he says. "It rattles like a snake in the hole." Outside, Gretchen is heard beating Schneider with a broom and telling all who will listen that Rip has nothing left of his vast estate except one bull. Rip says that Gretchen had better not try to use the broom on the bull. When Derrick returns with a document which presumably covers the loan Rip has just received, Rip wants to hear the document read— bill, claws, and feathers. Derrick reads ad lib, but leaves out the main element of the conveyance. Rip will not sign at once: "W-e-l-l, I'll yust think about it," he says, assuring Derrick he never signs anything the day after Friday. A few minutes later, he has the young Hendrick, the innkeeper's son, read the document to him; it says that for £16, Rip conveys to Derrick all his estate, houses, lands, and whatsoever is covered by mortgaged deeds. Rip decides he must stop drinking to avoid such calamities as signing papers. At a feast that evening, however, he is king; he has sworn off, but takes just one drink, which doesn't count. When Gretchen sees him dancing, he drops his dancing partner at Gretchen's feet and points to her, blaming her for his conduct.

ACT II

For two days, Rip has been away and Gretchen alternates between worrying about him and swearing that she will never let him show his face in the house again. The children, Hendrick Vedder and Meenie, also worry about him, but very devotedly. With a great storm rising, Hendrick tells Meenie that the ghosts of Hendrick Hudson and his pirate crew are due on the mountain tonight; they have been seen up there smoking, drinking, and playing at tenpins (bowling). The lightning is Hudson lighting his pipe; the thunder is his rolling the balls. Not seeing Gretchen, Rip sticks his head through the window and asks: "Has the wildcat come home?" Hearing him, Gretchen seizes and holds him by his hair. He asks if she wants a bald-headed husband. She takes his flask, and he stirs up quite a rumpus in getting it back, although it has but one drink, which he drinks (but does not count). In hunting, he says, he missed the rabbit he shot at and killed—alas! the old bull. Telling him the house is hers, she orders him out. The children object; he begs her not to turn him out like a dog into the storm; but he says that if he goes, he will never darken her door again. Eventually Gretchen relents. By now, however, Rip has reached the point where he says: "Well, see, then, I wipe the disgrace from your door." He staggers out into the storm. Gretchen cries: "No, Rip! Husband, come back." She faints.

92

ACT III

Up in the mountains, Rip fights his way through the storm. He sees a strange dwarfish figure clad in gray like a Dutch seaman of the seventeenth century, and he refuses to help the dwarf carry his keg of schnapps up the hill. Blown up to the topmost peak of the Catskills, through feeble and watery moonlight, he sees the bowling game. "Donner and Blitzen!" Rip says, "I'm a dead man to a certainty." Eventually, Hudson himself offers Rip a cup; he accepts, and since it is the first time, he won't count it. At Hudson's offering, he drinks one cup after another. Finally, his exhilaration dies, and he loses his grip on reality. He reels and falls heavily to the ground. Though Rip asks them not to leave, the demons begin to disappear. With a last effort he tries to drink their health and their families', but instead falls back heavily, asleep.

ACT IV (*five scenes*)

When he wakes, his hair and beard are white, and his voice betrays lapse of time. Gretchen, he is sure, will lambaste him good now. He picks up his gun, only to have it fall to pieces. Down below, he sees Falling Waters, twice as large as before. He decides to go to Gretchen to get straightened out.

Down in the village, Gretchen has been Derrick's wife for fifteen years now, and he treats her like a menial. Meenie, now twenty-six, warns Derrick not to mistreat her mother or she will tell Hendrick when he returns from sea. Derrick tells her that, according to the *Shipping Gazette*, Hendrick is dead, and she had better marry Cockles, his nephew, or she will be driven out.

In the village proper, the portrait of George Washington has replaced that of King George. Viewing the site of his cottage, Rip sees only blackened and crumbling walls. The villager Seth tells Rip that Rip Van Winkle, the laziest of drunken vagabonds, has been dead for twenty years, and Nicholas Vedder for fifteen. Meanwhile, Hendrick has arrived in the village and searches for Meenie. Not recognizing the old man as Rip, he nevertheless defends him from the attacking villagers. Derrick and Gretchen pass by Rip; she does not recognize him, but she gives the old man a penny and leads him to a warm fire.

Cockles tells Derrick that Meenie must marry him at once, or as Rip's heiress she can overthrow the applecart at any time.

Gretchen leads Rip into Derrick's house. After some time, it is Meenie who recognizes him. Gretchen will not allow Meenie to sign the papers Derrick brings, and Hendrick breaks in to refute the lie that he is dead. Derrick orders all of them—Gretchen, Meenie, and Hendrick—from his house. But Rip comes forward, takes the old paper he had refused to sign twenty years ago from his gamebag, establishes his claim, and banishes Derrick and Cockles. Gretchen begs to be forgiven: she tells Rip he can fight as often as he pleases. Although once again a sworn teetotaler, Rip must drink the health of all in a single drink that does not count.

23

AUGUSTIN DALY (1838–1899)

Horizon (1871)

Frontier drama in five acts, with melodramatic touches

MAIN CHARACTER AND THEME: Adventures of *Sundown Rowse*, a gigantic collector, through shady Congressional deals, of land grants in the Western territories, and his efforts to occupy his legally granted lands.

OTHER CHARACTERS:

Captain Alleyn Van Dorp, Mrs. Van Dorp's adopted son, Rowse's military aide, for whose commission Rowse was responsible

Coke Ballou, a realistic lawyer

The Honorable Arthur Wellesby Vere de Vere Smith, attached to the British Legation at Washington

John Loder, alias Panther Loder, alias White Panther, a disreputable Western character

Wolf Van Dorp, who disappeared from New York, abandoned his wife, and took their daughter to the West

Rocks of Tennessee, mayor of Rogue's Rest, and landlord of the hotel there

"Uncle Billy" Blakely, a proud citizen of Rogue's Rest and member of its Vigilance Committee

Mr. Mackenzie, also known as Sandy Mac, another proud citizen and vigilante

Judge Scott, chairman of the Vigilance Committee

Saleratus Bill and *Gopher Joe*, other members of the Committee

Cephas, a Negro, called "a Fifteenth Amendment"

A heathen Chinee

Sergeant Crockett of the United States Police

Wannemucka, a troublesome Indian

Wahcotah, a friendly Indian who lives at Fort Jackson

A guide

Med, also known as White Flower of the Plains, Van Dorp's daughter

Miss Columbia Rowse, Sundown's daughter, who accompanies her father westward

Mrs. Van Dorp, the abandoned wife, a New York society woman

The Widow Mullins, an immigrant

Rhoda, her daughter

Onata, an Indian girl

Notah, another Indian girl

Alice, who works for Mrs. Van Dorp

Citizens of Rogue's Rest, Indians, Soldiers, Servants

TIME: The late 1860's.

PLACE: New York City; Fort Jackson in the Far West (Colorado); other Western places.

MUSICAL HIGHLIGHTS: "I'm proud to be in the service of the Lord"; "Little Indians"; "Song by Boatmen"; Indian chant: "Let us speak of her."

HISTORICAL NOTE: One of the earliest efforts to depict the broad western frontier with appropriate dramatic quality. Daly had already distinguished himself by taking steps toward realism in drama with *Under the Gaslight* (1867). Though not having the high ideals of literary drama, *Horizon* unveils the colorful frontier in its true atmosphere, especially in such matters as the supremacy of local law over national law. He also portrays the interactive influences of Eastern civilization and Western frontier, and, like Twain-Warner's *The Gilded Age*, points up the alliances between big business, speculators, and venal congressmen.

ACT I

At the Van Dorp city house on Waverly Place, the lawyer Ballou gives Alleyn some background about his family (the Van Dorps). Both parents were aristocrats, the father poor and proud, the mother rich and proud. Because Van Dorp would not bow down to his wife, she kept him on short rations. After he had failed in business, she locked him out of her house. In retaliation, he later broke into the house, stole their daughter, and disappeared. He has not been heard of since.

Mrs. Van Dorp, however, has been more generous with her son. Hearing that he had acquired a military commission as captain and a job in the West, she orders his allowance sent wherever he indicates and invites the man responsible for his good luck to her home. Mr. Rowse, Alleyn's good angel, tells Mrs. Van Dorp of his determination to go west and occupy some of the lands Congress has voted him in grants. He is taking with him, besides Captain Van Dorp, his daughter Columbia and her latest sweetheart, a British diplomat named Smith. Although he speaks of hair-raising differences between the "civilization" where he is going and that with which they are acquainted in the East, he seems not the least bit frightened. He intends to carry the blessings of Eastern ways to the Far West where savage Indians and crude white men abound.

ACT II

In Rogue's Rest, sixty miles from Fort Jackson (one of the private forts of the fur traders), the vigilantes discuss the cleaning job before them—the removal from their village of a drunken sot called Whiskey Wolf, a gambler named Loder, an Indian named Wannemucka, and a heathen Chinee. Rowse arrives and hears of their determined plan. Since the citizens they are about to expel are no worse than many others, Rowse says the condemned may remain: this is his land; he shows them his grant. They draw knives and pistols and order Rowse and his friend Smith to clear out. Only the news that Loder and the "Chinee" are nearby prevents more drastic action. Meanwhile Alleyn has noticed a "backwoods Venus" whom he wishes to see again. A short while later he finds her—her name is Med. Columbia, Rowse's daughter, discovers them embracing. But there is hardly time for romance because the mob is closing in on its quarry. At a meeting of the Vigilance Committee, Loder, Wolf, Wannemucka, and the "Chinee" are given "thirty calendar minutes" to leave the settlement. Wolf announces that he will refuse to go: he gives Loder a packet of letters and charge of his daughter Med, and steps up to be hanged. When Rowse arrives in time to stop the hanging, Wolf changes his mind and decides to go on to Fort Jackson with Rowse and his company. But Wannemucka shoots Wolf in order to have Med for himself. Loder defies Wannemucka and holds Med.

ACT III *(three scenes)*

The stage now represents the head of a flatboat on Big Run, near Fort Jackson. In a series of episodes, Rowse and his party are exploring his

97

Western properties. First, an Irish widow and her child attach themselves to the exploration boat. Then, a little Indian girl (Notah) "adopts" Rowse because he was kind to her. Third, there are signs in the background of the treacherous Wannemucka. Taking care of Med, Loder hopes to marry her off to Alleyn, and then to relieve her of further worries about himself by blowing out his brains. Eventually, Wannemucka and his braves raid the boat in an attempt to capture Med. Just before the nearby soldiers arrive, Loder shoots Wannemucka, who staggers front and falls.

ACT IV

But Wannemucka is not dead. At a stockade in the prairie, Alleyn courts Med, and Loder has a secret for Alleyn, about Med, if he is really in love with her. Loder shows Alleyn the packet Wolf left, and the two go on a foraging expedition. Med tells Columbia that she loves Alleyn, but Columbia can hardly appreciate the news: she has loved too often. With the men gone, the women experience another attack from Wannemucka. By a trick, Wannemucka captures Med, as the other Indians overpower the rest of the women.

ACT V

The Indians camp in a ravine surrounded by mountains. An Indian girl, Onata, tells Wannemucka that the Indian women resent the white captives: Wannemucka replies that the white maidens will not see the sun rise. Meanwhile, Rowse has been captured; he is told by Wannemucka that his daughter will make a bride for one of the braves. With grim humor he replies that if he gets back to Washington, he intends to turn his attention to Indian affairs. When Wannemucka asks him what battles he has fought, Rowse can only reply that he has killed a great many—bills on the floor of Congress: his battleground is the lobby. Little by little the soldiers close in at the back, but in the foreground things seem quite dark for the white captives. Even Smith is captured by Indians; he calls their attention to the necessity of honoring the British flag. Learning that Loder has escaped and will probably bring help, Wannemucka prepares to remove his captives to a safer area. Before he can do so, Loder and Alleyn rescue Med from Onata's knife, Loder shoots Wannemucka with his rifle, and the ravine is filled with soldiers.

98

24

FRANK HITCHCOCK MURDOCH (1843–1872)

Davy Crockett; Or, Be Sure You're Right, Then Go Ahead (1872)

Frontier melodrama in five acts

MAIN CHARACTER AND THEME: Events in the life and legend of Davy Crockett (1786–1836), as superman but very human person, pitting the plain American backwoods way against the ways of foreign or cultured-American sophistication.

OTHER CHARACTERS:

Oscar Crampton

Neil, Oscar's nephew, engaged to Eleanor

Major Royston, formerly of the Continental Army, guardian of Eleanor

Big Dan, *Briggs*, and *Yonkers*, hunters, friends of Davy

Little Bob, Davy's nephew

Quickwith

Watson, Major Royston's servant

Parson

Eleanor (also Little Nell), Squire Vaughn's daughter, returning home after education

Dame (also Dame Crockett), Davy's mother

Little Sal, Davy's niece

Tot

TIME: Early nineteenth century.

PLACE: A backwoods section, probably in Tennessee.

MUSICAL HIGHLIGHTS: Familiar tunes: Hunter's song; "Auld Lang Syne"; "Annie Laurie"; "Home Sweet Home."

HISTORICAL NOTE: First produced (unsuccessfully) at the Opera House, Rochester, New York, December 23, 1872, with Frank Mayo in the lead; played on February 24, 1873, at Park Theatre, Brooklyn, and on June 2, 1873, at Wood's Museum, New York. From 1873, a great hit in the United States and England, until Mayo's death in 1896.

ACT I

At Dame Crockett's cottage, set in a clearing in the forest, the hunters are told that supper will consist of bear steaks—from the bear which they all had missed, but Davy had killed. Davy's nephew, little Bob, shoots a nearby squirrel; Davy, arriving, tells him that for being a good inch off the squirrel's eye, the Crocketts will disown him. A sophisticated company arrive, including Neil, Eleanor (very pretty), and Major Royston, her guardian. Eleanor reveals herself as Nelly Vaughn, who had been brought up with Davy in the backwoods. Reading aloud a letter, Eleanor learns that her engagement to Neil is part of a plot. But Eleanor enlists Davy's future assistance, which Davy enthusiastically guarantees. Davy's mother enjoins him to go ahead if he is sure he is right.

ACT II

Inside his hut, Davy watches the snow fall. Neil stumbles in; Eleanor is outside, fainting and freezing. Davy bears her inside in his arms, barely saving her life. Revived, she tells how she was blocked by the snow while searching for holly berries. Davy appropriates for firewood the huge bar which secures the door. After taking a drink, Neil falls asleep. Davy hands Eleanor the book she had left at his mother's house; it is Scott's *Marmion*. Eleanor reads to him of Lochinvar, boldly rescuing his sweetheart from her prospective bridegroom. The story causes Davy to declare his love, but to denounce himself as entirely unworthy. Davy alone hears the "one howl" which indicates the approach of wolves, attracted by drops of Eleanor's blood. As wolf after wolf hurls himself against the door, Davy bars them with his arm, the stout door-bar being gone.

ACT III

All night long Davy holds against the wolves. Awaking and praising Davy, Eleanor deplores the fate that separates them. Relief arrives with Oscar and the Major, whose rifle disposes of the wolves. His arm monstrously

100

"Davy Crockett; or, Be Sure You're Right, Then Go Ahead" (1872)

swollen, Davy groans and falls on the couch. Neil is discovered to be seriously ill. Only Davy can save him, since only Davy can get through the snow "to the nighest settlement—a short ten miles" away. Eleanor tries to stop him because of his own condition, but he argues that he must not shirk his duty. She agrees he is right. Davy says: "Then let me 'go ahead.' "

ACT IV

At Major Royston's mansion, Oscar Crampton, Neil's uncle, discloses the plot: the Major, who is Eleanor's guardian, is releasing her to Neil so that Oscar can command her fortune, in exchange for the Major's forged notes, which Oscar holds. Although he has promised not to see Eleanor again, Davy enters on her wedding night—"to get one more look at the sweet face, and then to go away forever." Explosively, she declares her love, but asserts herself entrapped by honor and duty. Davy swears to win her in spite of the odds; then he remembers that she is greatness itself and he only an ignorant backwoodsman. She replies that if he saves her from the disgusting marriage, she is his. Davy next talks the Major into giving him Devilskin, a fast black stallion. As the ceremony starts, Davy, quoting Lochinvar, runs off with Eleanor. The others cry "Stop him! Stop him!"

ACT V

At Dame Crockett's, the Dame and the Parson are discussing the reckless behavior of Davy, who has been away for a month. Davy rushes in with Eleanor and asks the Parson to marry them. The Parson is in the midst of the ceremony when Neil, the Major, and Oscar break down the door. The Major begs Eleanor not to ruin him by marrying Davy; she replies that Davy is already her husband. When Oscar threatens to tear Eleanor away from him, Davy presents his rifle. Turning to Eleanor, Davy tells her she can still renounce him and the backwoods; she insists her heart is completely his. The Major, conscience-stricken, defies Oscar and impending ruin. Oscar brings forth the damaging papers only to have them seized by Davy. Burning the papers, Eleanor promises to pay the money they represent. Oscar menaces Eleanor, but Davy easily drives him away. Eleanor is happy to be brought at last to "the heart and home of Davy Crockett." The music rising above her speech is "Home Sweet Home."

101

25

GEORGE MELVILLE BAKER (1832–1890)

The Merry Christmas of the Old Woman Who Lived in a Shoe (1875)

Community entertainment drama in one act

MAIN CHARACTER AND THEME: What happens when *Santa Claus* pays an unexpected visit to the famous lady from Mother Goose, the *Old Woman Who Lived in a Shoe*, and her large family.

OTHER CHARACTERS: Ten or twelve children, boys and girls, of various ages.

TIME: Christmas night.

PLACE: Exterior of Copper Toe Shoe House (design for which is enclosed in playscript), set on rear of platform with tree set back of house, well covered. The Copper Toe Shoe House has four insert positions from which children pop out: one each from "Split in the Heel," "Patch in the Corn" on left side, and "Copper Toe" on right side; and three from "Lookout, or Observatory" at top of house.

MUSICAL HIGHLIGHTS: "There was an old woman," sung to air of "Revolutionary Tea"; "Old woman," air, "Comin' Through the Rye"; "My name's Johnny Schmoker," air, "Them Blessed Roomatics"; "Oh, dear, what can the matter be?" (parody by the children); "Oh, you shan't be hungry now," air, "Balm of Gilead"; "We'll gather round the Christmas Tree."

HISTORICAL NOTE: This play represents the nonprofessional community drama, important in all periods of American theatrical history. At present, it is estimated that there are more than twenty-five thousand amateur theatrical groups in this country; most of them perform community drama regularly. In the late nineteenth century, their influence was beginning to be deeply felt because of the increase in the number of towns and cities. George M. Baker and his publishers, Lee and Shepard of Boston, were among the first to satisfy the needs of community drama on a large scale. Among Baker's hundreds of plays of all lengths were comedies, farces, school entertainments, plays for Christmas, Easter, Independence Day, and other holiday celebrations, dialect pieces (Irish, Yankee, Negro, among others), temperance dramas, gold-rush dramas, fairy plays, women's suffrage dramas, character sketches, dramas to inspire bravery and other desirable traits, allegories, extravaganzas, burlesques, mimic stage plays, separate plays for boys and girls, and an "Artemus Ward wax figger show." The present play is taken from *The Exhibition Drama.*

ACTION

The children of the proverbial Old Woman sing of being happy only when their mother does *not* spare the rod. The Old Woman complains because children's heads pop out everywhere; since they have no food, they must thrive on air and sleep. Christmas, the Old Woman notes, has come again, and she cannot join in "the triumphant strain which moves all hearts." At #1 position, a child wants a drum; at #2 position, a doll; at #3 position, a sword. At #4 position, three children ask if there are presents for all. The Old Woman sings her sorrow at having nothing; she wishes Santa would visit. Tucking the children away, she tries to make them warm.

Santa appears, his fabled dress hidden by a long domino, or coat. Using the tin kitchen swung about his neck, he grinds imaginary accompaniment to his song, which announces a mystic project in this "mansion"

> Where dwells a dame, with children great and small,
> Enough to stock a school, or crowd a hall.

If these children are found worthy, they will get a rich reward; if rude, Santa will vanish and return no more.

Putting on his best beggar's manner, Santa sings "My name's Johnny Schmoker," grinds his organ, and talks of having "lumbager, dyspepsy, and ager." Children come out and crowd around him. Old Woman tells him to go away: there is no money here for music. Santa asks, if nothing more, for just a crust of bread. Singing that no beggar shall go hungry, the children scamper inside and return with food on sticks—apples, potatoes, bread crusts, a turnip, and a carrot. They pitch the food into Santa's tin bowl.

Throwing off his disguise Santa says he is theirs to command. Muttering cabalistic words ("Ene, meni, moni, suti, sutter"), he splits the Shoe and discloses a giant tree. As he and the Old Woman distribute the presents, children sing "We'll gather round the Christmas Tree."

26

EDWARD HARRIGAN (1845–1911)

The Mulligan Guard Ball (1879)

Vaudeville-type local drama
in one act and seven scenes

MAIN CHARACTER AND THEME: How *Daniel Mulligan*, usually called Dan, leader of the Mulligan Guard, an ultra-chauvinistic Irish military organization, plans for and conducts the organization ball in spite of interferences from the German and Negro elements and even from his own family.

OTHER CHARACTERS:

Cordelia Mulligan, Dan's wife
Tommy Mulligan, his son
Gustavus Lochmuller, the butcher, a German
Tommy Lochmuller, his son
Katrine Lochmuller, usually called Katy, Gus's daughter but Tommy Mulligan's girl in spite of the constant German-Irish feuding
Sim Primrose, the colored barber
Brother Palestine Puter, chaplain of the Skidmore Guards
Walsingham McSweeney, the Swiss warbler

Maggie Kierney, the hair dresser
Bridget Lochmuller, Gus's wife
Gustavus Lochmuller, Jr.
August Sneider, the tailor
Rosenfelt, the dealer in cutaways
Mr. Garlic, the renter of the Harp and Shamrock Hall
Other Members of the Mulligan Guards
Other Members of the Skidmore Guards
Two Negro Girls
Caroline Williams, a guest of the Skidmores
Six butchers

TIME: About 1878.

PLACE: New York City.

MUSICAL HIGHLIGHTS: "We Shouldered Guns"; "Skidmore's Fancy Ball"; "Babies on Our Block"; "The Hallway Door"; Puter's Hymn.

HISTORICAL NOTE: The Mulligan Guard series was the brainchild of a famous playwright and actor, Edward Harrigan, who collaborated with another actor named Anthony Cannon but known on the stage as Tony Hart. The Harrigan-Hart sketches, growing out of brisk and imaginative vaudeville, began about 1872 and were supremely popular. The first of the Mulligan Guard series, *The Mulligan Guard* (1873), was presented in Chicago and transported to New York. It was a burlesque upon the excursions of military organizations which sprang up in New York City as tributes to local politicians and which sometimes led to riots because of their intense national or racial chauvinism. The chauvinism was usually shared by the audiences. Nevertheless, these dramas were an accurate portrayal of the crude melting pot atmosphere during a burgeoning era of New York City, in spite of their vaudeville and burlesque characteristics. In the same series were *The Mulligan Guard Chowder* (1879) and *The Mulligan Guard Picnic* (1880); an interesting Harrigan contribution outside the series was *McSorley's Inflation* (1882), a comedy in three acts. Accompanying the present play, a set of black and white pictures, depicting the 14 most striking scenes, was published (New York: Dick and Sullivan, 1879) under the title, *Harrigan and Hart's Pictorial History of the Mulligan Guard Ball*.

Scene 1—Dan's house

Dan quarrels with his wife because she buys bread at the wrong bakery. Supporting him, Tommy says he would rather have a mahogany sandwich than the wrong bread. Speaking of food and drink, Dan recalls the time his distillery blew up because the sun set the barrels of whiskey on fire (they were so strong): when a man drank two drinks of the whiskey, Dan would have to turn the hose on him. Tommy has sold twenty tickets for the Mulligan Guard Ball the next night, and there is talk of uniforms and fancy dress: Dan expects to wear his double-breasted frock coat. During the conversation, Tommy tricks his father with an explosive cigar, and Dan seems rather proud of his son. His pride quickly turns to anger when Tommy speaks of

106

marrying Katy, daughter of a despised German. Dan tells Tommy he must marry Mary O'Brien, who loves the ground he walks on. Issuing an ultimatum, Dan declares: "The name of Mulligan will never be varnished with the name of Lochmuller. The divil a Dutch drop of blood will ever enter this family." Gus Lochmuller overhears: he enters, swears he is no Dutchman, and demands the $35 Dan owes him for back food bills. He also challenges Dan "to put up his dukes." Tommy succeeds in separating the two old gentlemen until after the ball. Gus insists, however, that he is of the finest German extraction (his father fought in the Franco-Prussian War), and he is not afraid. Making up with Dan, he recalls that they are both lodge brothers and "Dimocrats." Gus promises to furnish all the meat for the supper after the ball, but must rush out when his son Tommy arrives to report that two boys are stealing the drawer out of the butcher shop.

Scene 2—Local street

Katy tells Tommy that her father Gus wants her to marry a Swiss warbler (a Lieder-krantzer) named Walsingham McSweeney; her mother agrees because McSweeney is from the same part of Ireland: she promises Tommy that she will be a French nurse at $15 a month before she does. Pleased, Tommy tells her he will open a saloon when they are married and will make a lady of her. Katy says they must operate secretly: Maggie Kierney, the hair dresser on the other side of the partition from Sim Primrose, the colored barber, will help them and keep their secrets. Tom gets her to promise not to wear spitlocks; she agrees to go pompadour. Tom says Maggie can go with them to Judge Duffy's where the ceremony can be performed just before the Ball (to be married by a judge gives a young fellow popularity). Katy agrees—for 7:30 the next night. Tom says that once married they can rent a room and bedroom in Batavia Street.

Once they go, Sim and Puter come in. Puter tells how he won the position of Chaplain over four Baptists and three "Prespeterians" by advocating dancing and pleasures. Sim has spent the day cleaning his uniform for the Skidmore Ball, the colored function that rivals the Mulligan Ball and that is held on the same night. From all indications, Sim says, the Ball will be gorgeous—for instance, Lieutenant Newlimber's sister Ruth will represent the Goddess of Liberty. Puter suggests that for supper the Skidmore Guards march to his friend's grocery and munch a few crackers; Sim says this would be scandalous. Puter says he knows proper social behavior since he's the Grand Dispenser of the colored secret society, the Ancient Order of Full Moons. By promising to propose Sim at the next meeting, Puter wins the argument. Puter announces the band for the Ball—"De El Dorado Reed Striding Military, Cotillion Brass Band." For his services to the Ball, Sim will take Puter's bunion out with glycerine and a match. When Sim has gone, Puter learns that Lyric Hall, the place of the Skidmore Ball, has been seized; the Skidmores must change to The Harp and Shamrock where the Irish will be. When Puter sees the Irish, Dan and McSweeney, approaching, he wonders why the government cannot quarantine and fumigate more, and he walks indignantly away.

Dan is instructing McSweeney on the decorations for the Harp and Shamrock Hall—American flags with Irish flags between them; rows of wax candles on the balcony with the sign, "Look out for the drip"; 33 canaries and blackbirds in cages hung from the chandeliers. The band leader is to be told that if he plays a single Dutch tune, he'll not get a cent. Loudly singing "We Shouldered Guns," the two planners leave for McQuade's to play handball.

Scene 3—Barber Shop with two chairs, next to Hair Dresser's

In his shop, Sim is cleaning kerosene off his Skidmore uniform. It is the night of the Balls. Dan and Gus, both in evening dress, enter almost simultaneously: they argue vehemently about who will be shaved first. Sim says that if he were a "Simese twin," he could shave both. He finally arranges to shave half of one and half of the other together, beginning on Germany if Ireland will allow. As the shaving continues, the conversation turns to boxing. When Gus makes a disparaging remark about a colored boxer in the ring with a German, Sim menaces him with his razor. Gus apologizes.

On the hair dresser side of the partition, Maggie "fixes" Katy's hair as Tom waits. Katy's laughter is vaguely recognized by Gus (beyond the partition), but he dismisses the thought of his daughter's being there. When Sim leaves Gus and Dan alone, those two argue the relative merits of German and Irish in the neighborhood: Gus, for instance, declares that there are more German babies in Avenue A than tombstones in Greenwood Cemetry. Eventually, Gus and Dan overhear the conversation beyond the partition and suffer deep distress as they learn of the planned elopement. They then face each other and warmly demand to know why their children associate together. When

108

"The Mulligan Guard Ball" (1879)

Maggie comes to get Sim to watch her store as she goes off with Tommy and Katy, the two fathers seize her and bring her into the barber shop. Gus is on his knees begging Maggie to assure him that the girl in her shop was not his daughter when Bridget, his wife, comes in. Bridget demands to know if she, "a decent Irish girl," left $12 a week in a feather factory to marry a bologna pudding butcher and raise a family, for this! Also getting on his knees, Dan begs Bridget to keep Katy away from his Tommy. Cordelia, Dan's wife, finds him there and proceeds to beat him with her fists. Bridget declares herself a lady and dares Cordelia to pull her hair. Cordelia says, "Let me at her." Bridget says, "Let her come." Gus begs Dan to take his wife away, but Dan says, "If you interfere, I'll pulverize you." From next door, Sneider, the tailor, comes and begs to be allowed to get back to sleep.

Scene 4—Local street

Still raving, Bridget is in the street with her husband. Gus manages finally to get her to understand what he was doing. Bridget says that of course Katy will not marry a Dutchman, throwing herself away as her mother did, when Bridget herself could have had an Irish lawyer.

Although knowing nothing of the row, Katy is fearful to complete the marriage plans; Tom quiets her.

Dan and Cordelia come along, the latter apologetic. She assures Tom that two whole pigs are cooking, enough for a post-Ball party of 50 people. Rosenfelt gets Dan's word that he will pay the rental on the 33 cutaways ordered for the Ball. Looking forward to the Ball, Dan announces he will do Yankee dances he has learned from a book. He has also put kerosene on his head to cure his baldness.

Sim announces the change of place to the Skidmores. If there is trouble at The Harp and Shamrock, he tells them to have their muskets in the hat rack and their razors sharpened—no one must interfere with their pleasures. Although Puter decries the shedding of blood, the Skidmore Company take note of Sim's injunction. They all sing lustily "Skidmore's Fancy Ball" and praise the colored coterie.

Scene 5—Interior of Ballroom, Harp and Shamrock

Tommy and Katy, their plan now to elope during intermission, enjoy the dance nervously. Surreptitiously, Dan and Gus try to prevent Tommy and

109

Katy from dancing together. Near intermission time, Tommy whispers to Katy in hog Latin to be ready to "give her old man the slip."

The Skidmores arrive; their music clashes with the music of the Irish. Tommy asks the colored guardsmen what they want in the Harp and Shamrock. In reply, Sim says, "What are you Irish trespassing here for?" Sim also tells his men to look to their arms. When Dan orders the Mulligans to rush the intruders, the Skidmores draw their razors. Sim tells his boys to hold—"I'll tell you when to cut." Garlic, the hall manager, explains the error: he had rented the hall to the Mulligans and his clerk had rented it to the Skidmores for the same time. Garlic offers the Skidmores the Red Men's Hall upstairs, for $10 less. Sim leads the Skidmores in three cheers for the Mulligans, and Dan leads the Mulligans in a similar three cheers for the Skidmores. From upstairs a short while later the Skidmore band—bones, fiddle, banjo—is heard playing. As Dan calls for the Virginny Reel, the Skidmores come through the ceiling upon the Mulligans. There is a "Grand Crash."

Scene 6—Street

After the crash, Tommy takes Katy and Maggie off, in accordance with the plan: Tommy will get the cop on the beat to stand up for him.

Somewhat scratched up, Sim tells Puter that much plaster will be required to put the Skidmores back together; he says that one ice wagon took 10 Skidmores to the hospital. Puter promises revenge on the Mulligans for beating the Skidmores. Puter is nevertheless to wait on table at the Mulligan Guard Supper for $15—says he, color and enmity do not matter where money is concerned. He invites Sim to close up shop, go over to Jamaica, and roll in gin and sugar for a month.

Dan brags of the licking he gave the colored society people and of hiring them thereafter. In the course of a conciliatory meeting, Dan and Gus fall out again. Gus pulls out a sausage disguised as a gun and offers to fire on Dan. Dan yells for the police and runs off; Gus eats the sausage. Garlic and Rosenfelt come to collect their money from Dan; they have little success.

Scene 7—Interior of Mulligan cottage

Tom introduces his new wife. Dan, reconciled to the newlyweds, leads the drinks for the Mulligan Guard. All laugh when Dan announces that the

110

"The Mulligan Guard Ball" (1879)

Captain of the Skidmore Guards (Sim) is his waiter. Sim tells them not to laugh, for when he sees a dollar, he will grab it. A rat crosses—the guests pet it; a pig gets down from the table and goes off. Cordelia announces partners for the Cotillion. Again Garlic and Rosenfelt, this time joined by Sneider, come forth and demand their money. A big fight (scrimmage) ensues, in which Puter joins. Gus and six of his butchers, armed with cleavers, join the general melee as the final curtain falls.

27

DENMAN THOMPSON (1833-1911)
GEORGE W. RYER

The Old Homestead (1886)

Vaudeville-type Yankee melodrama in four acts

MAIN CHARACTER AND THEME: Story of *Joshua Whitcomb*, undergoing the normal shocks of everyday life on his New England farm homestead, including the entertainment of city guests, and journeying to the city to find and support his erring son.

OTHER CHARACTERS:

Cy Prime, who loves Aunt Matilda

Seth Perkins, his rival

Happy Jack Hazard, a tramp ripe for transformation

Frank Hopkins, son of Henry, a rich city boy visiting in the country

Eb Granzey, a neighbor of Joshua

John Freeman, friend of Frank

Henry Hopkins, formerly of Joshua's village but now a rich New Yorker

Judge Patterson, one of Frank's high society friends

Reuben Whitcomb, Joshua's son, who fell into disgrace in New Hampshire and went to New York City and became lost

Len Holbrook, a village fiddler

Pat Clancey, a "Yankified" Irish villager

François Fogarty, the Hopkins' very elite servant, dressed in livery

Aunt Matilda Whitcomb, Josh's sister

Mary Ann Maynard (Rickety Ann), a vivacious young villager who loves to tease city folk

Annie Hopkins, Henry's daughter

Nellie Freeman, Annie's friend

"The Old Homestead" (1886)

Maggie O'Flaherty, who works on the Whitcomb place

Mrs. Maguire, the apple woman

Mrs. Henry Hopkins, Henry's wife, very elegant

Mrs. Murdock, a village singer and dancer

Mrs. Nellie Patterson, the Judge's wife

Elinor Stratton, a pretty village girl

Two other Stratton girls

Hoboken Terror, a proud boxing man

Quartette, Dude, Policeman, Salvation Army Group, Postman

TIME: 1800's.

PLACE: New Hampshire, a few miles from Keene; New York City.

MUSICAL HIGHLIGHTS: "Lawn Tennis"; "Devil's Dream"; "Old Oaken Bucket"; "Hard Times Come Again No More"; "White Wings"; "Sixteen Dollars in My Inside Pocket"; "Oh, Where Is My Boy Tonight"; "Fire! Fire! Fire!"; "After the Opera Is Over"; "Wedding March"; "I'll Meet Her When the Sun Goes Down"; "Grandfather's Clock."

HISTORICAL NOTE: The drama began as a vaudeville sketch for Thompson; grew into a full-length drama through its thirteen years of success. First performed in its finished state in Boston; then at the Grand Opera House, Brooklyn, April 26, 1886; and finally at 14th Street Theatre, New York, for twenty weeks, beginning January 10, 1887. Above and beyond its huge drawing power, its popularity was further attested to by the numerous burlesques upon it. Acted by the author as a homely theatrical favorite until his death in 1911 (twenty-five years).

ACT I

Rickety Ann is having fun with the city folk, who are playing tennis: first, she tells them that they will be charged for the broken windows; later she frightens the girls by saying there are snakes around. Joshua is happy to have these city youngsters around: Frank and Annie are children of Henry Hopkins, who was brought up with Joshua right here in New Hampshire (they both sat on the same bench in district school) and who is now rated as worth over a million in New York City. Though he has "never sot foot" in New York, Joshua often thinks of the place because his son, whom he has not heard from in four to five months, is there. His son had been cashier

113

of a bank in Keene, was tried for a theft and proved innocent, but decided his usefulness thereabouts was over; thus, he went to New York. Across the conversation is heard Rickety Ann's sharp voice calling the cows, "Co boss, co boss, co boss."

For a long time now, Cy Prime has been trying to propose to Aunt Matilda. He begins by offering her "a little mess o' rassberries"; he circles the conversation around to weather, cucumbers, and tomatoes; by the time he reaches his proposal, with his head turned, he looks around to find that Rickety Ann has carried Matilda off to look after a burning cake. On three occasions, there are similar interruptions.

Happy Jack, whom Rickety Ann had called the "awfullest looking tramp," asks for food. To Joshua he confesses that his being a tramp is the natural result of drink. Last night he had slept in Widow Green's haystack, but he had slept in similar places from the Florida Everglades to the snowy ranges of the Sierras. Impressed by his sad story, Josua gives him ten dollars if he will go to New Haven on the train and catch the boat for New York. Happy Jack accepts the money and promises "to give John Barleycorn the toughest scuffle he ever had for the underhold." As Joshua gazes meditatively at the departing hobo, a quartette offstage sings, "Oh, Where Is My Boy Tonight," first pianissimo, then gradually very loudly.

ACT II

In the Parlor of the Hopkins mansion in New York City, Joshua is introduced to the family by the Hopkins children, his recent guests. Joshua identifies Hopkins as "Redheaded Hank" and his society-minded wife as "Betsy Richardson," "Bets" for short, who "druv down to the store" with her father on a load of wood in calico frock, sunbonnet and new yard stockings. Gazing at the statue of Venus of Melos, flanked by palms, Joshua wants to know if Venus had been a New York lady before she died. Mrs. Hopkins tells her husband to take Joshua off, anywhere, to the stables. Happy to go there, Joshua is delighted at the beautiful barn, although disappointed that the coachman will not let him unharness and fodder. Asked about the old homestead by Hopkins, Joshua tells of poor yield, dry season, two circuses, the balloon ascension, and the wrestling match. Joshua and Hopkins talk of old times; then of Joshua's son, Reuben, whom Hopkins promises to help him find. When Hopkins strikes the gong for the servant, Joshua decides

114

it's one o'clock; when François brings in a card on the tray, Joshua dives into his pocket for collection, saying, "There's the plate! Meetin's commenced." Talking politics with François, Joshua tells him that from the neck down he looks like a Republican, but from the neck up like a Democrat. Gazing upon the figure of alabaster marble, Joshua tells François that if he put that figure in his cornfield, he'd be arrested before night. Before he retires, Joshua asks for "a sasser o' taller" with which to grease his boots when he gets up in the morning. Once Joshua has retired, Judge Patterson asks Mrs. Hopkins to sing his favorite song. As she shouts the refrain at the top of her voice, "Fire! Fire! Fire!" Joshua enters in nightdress, boots in right hand, dragging his trunk with his left, shouting "Fire!" himself at the top of his voice. Frank and his father manage to stop him.

ACT III

At the corner of Broadway and Tenth Street in New York, Joshua and Hopkins search for Reuben. Joshua characteristically becomes involved with the various city folk. Reuben appears when Joshua is searching elsewhere. Happy Jack sees Reuben shaking and gives him a dollar to get a good strong milk punch as bracer, a shave, a head rub, and something to eat. After Joshua has returned and attempted to arrest the postman for looting the mailbox, Happy Jack comes up to him and, with thanks, returns his ten dollars. Joshua says he has not found Reuben, but has found much wickedness and misery. Reuben returns; of him, Happy Jack says, "Here comes my dollar investment and about as drunk as they make them." Promptly Joshua recognizes his boy.

ACT IV

Back at The Old Homestead, Cy and Seth compete for the love of Matilda. They nearly come to blows. Matilda wonders if Reuben will come home that night. Joshua says he has so promised, after he had begged his father to let him stick things out a while longer, in order that his failure be not too noticeable. In the midst of other gay activities, bells are heard and a shout goes up: "Reub is here!" Joshua excitedly orders someone to put the shed under the hoss, and throw a blanket over the barn. Happy Jack is still grateful for his reformation, begun by Joshua. Much in evidence is Len Holbrook's fiddle. Cy and Seth, brought together partly by Joshua's

intervention, are on the same side of a broom-handle pull; the stick breaks—
they fall over backwards together. Secretly Joshua assures Reuben that no
one has heard of his New York episode. On the sleigh ride just planned,
Elinor chooses Reuben as her escort. Joshua talks of the healthiness of a
good old-fashioned New England winter, which builds appetites so that instead
of one's saying, "What hev you got for dinner?" one says, "How much hev
you got?" Rickety Ann wants Eb Ganzey to help her put red pepper on the
popcorn because she is not allowed to ride on the sleigh. Joshua announces
that he and Reuben have agreed to work the farm on shares: Reuben takes
possession next day, New Year's Day. When Happy Jack whispers that he
likes Elinor, Joshua tells him to "shin up to her." Joshua orders the chairs
cleared away that dancing may start. He asks fathers with wild boys to go
easy—the boys may have inherited their wildness. He invites one and all to
come to The Old Homestead in June "and let the scarlet runners chase you
back to childhood."

28

JAMES A. HERNE (1839–1901)

Margaret Fleming (1890)

Realistic drama in four acts

MAIN CHARACTER AND THEME: Story of a devoted young wife, *Margaret Fleming*, afflicted by a philandering husband and threatened by glaucoma.

OTHER CHARACTERS:

Philip Fleming, mill owner	*Maria Bindley*, middle-aged German woman, a nurse
Dr. Larkin	
Joe Fletcher	*Mrs. Burton*
Mr. Foster, manager of the mill	*Hannah*, the cook
Williams, foreman	*Jane*, a maid
Bobby, office boy	*Lucy*, a tiny baby
Charlie Burton	*Another Tiny Baby*

TIME: About 1890.

PLACE: Canton, Massachusetts.

HISTORICAL NOTE: *Margaret Fleming* is a definite part of the beginnings of the realistic movement in American literature. Although earlier plays had evidenced realistic method and materials, the author of this play was striving to develop character according to the impact of precise environmental forces rather than through conventional devices. He was encouraged to produce this play as a pioneering act by such leaders in the realistic movement as William Dean Howells and Hamlin Garland. He also stated his principles clearly in such articles as his "Art for Truth's Sake in the Drama," which appeared in *Arena* for February, 1897. Other plays for which he is respected are *Hearts of Oak*

(1880), *The Minute Men of 1774-75* (1886), *Shore Acres* (1892), and *The Reverend Griffith Davenport* (1899). *Margaret Fleming* was first performed in Lynn, Massachusetts, on July 4, 1890, with the playwright's wife as Margaret; it had difficulty gaining a full hearing because of the boldness of its realistic approach.

ACT I (*two scenes*)

On an ordinary business day, Philip reflects anxiety over pinched conditions in his business and entertains Joe Fletcher, a peddler and corn doctor, who was foreman in the plant during the time of Philip's father, but who met his downfall through liquor and immorality. Philip sends him to his home to sell goods to Margaret. Dr. Larkin, remembering Joe well, deplores his example; but, he tells Philip, he deplores even more men who do not even use tippling as an excuse. In this way, he tells Philip that last night he delivered Lena Schmidt's illegitimate baby and left her near death. Philip is incensed since he is the father and has tried to get Lena to go away. Having discovered this connection, Dr. Larkin forces Philip to visit Lena and console her. Even though it is the birthday of his young daughter, Lucy, Philip fakes a previous engagement to his wife and obeys the doctor.

At home, Margaret complains to Lucy about Philip's nonappearance all day. Maria weeps furtively, having driven off her thieving ex-husband that morning (it was Joe, the peddler) and knowing that her sister Lena is dying after giving birth to a child by a rich man whom, out of mistaken love, she refuses to identify. Maria swears to find the man and choke the confession from his throat. Margaret sends Maria to her sister, telling her to stay all night. Soon Philip comes in, a drenched, pitiful figure. He shows Margaret a bankbook in her name with five thousand dollars in it, and a certificate for twenty thousand dollars in United States bonds, maturing in 1930, for "Margaret Fleming, guardian of Lucy Fleming." When he tells her he has done all this "just in case," she urges him to sell the house if he is financially troubled, since nothing can destroy their home so long as they three stay together.

ACT II

Dr. Larkin treats Margaret for an eye condition, suggesting that she wear glasses—which suggestion Margaret gaily rejects. Reluctantly, the doctor
118

gives her medicine for her husband, who has caught a cold from being drenched. In Margaret's absence, Philip informs Dr. Larkin that after he and Margaret have grown closer together—and they are on the way—he will confess about Lena, and obtain forgiveness. For this, Dr. Larkin thinks him all the more a cad. He instructs Philip to take Margaret away because, with her tendency toward glaucoma, any great shock may drive her blind. Without telling her husband, Margaret promises Maria to go with her to visit Lena, who has heard of her. Margaret speaks touchingly of the beautiful picture Philip and Lucy make and orders him to keep taking his medicine, and to give up smoking until he is "well."

ACT III

At Mrs. Burton's cottage, Mrs. Burton describes to Dr. Larkin Lena's sleeping, writing a letter, sighing, and calmly dying. Dr. Larkin nearly succeeds in pushing Margaret out before she is well inside the cottage, but Mrs. Burton's bringing in the baby interferes. Maria comes in, letter in hand, swearing to send the baby to Philip. Maria threatens Dr. Larkin when he attempts to destroy Lena's letter; she reads it to Margaret. Drawing a pistol, Maria swears she will lay Margaret stiff and cold beside Lena, if Margaret attempts to halt her revenge upon Lena's seducer. Margaret overawes Maria, pistol and all, telling her that in five minutes she has suffered a thousand times more than Lena did in her whole life. She sends a peremptory summons to Philip, which reads: "I am waiting for you, here. That *girl* is *dead*." Dr. Larkin warns her that if she continues in this excited manner her eyesight and life are in danger. On her knees, Maria begs forgiveness, but Margaret, insisting there is nothing to forgive, sends Maria away. Lena's baby, deprived of mother's milk, continues to fret. Philip arrives in time to see Margaret in the sunshine begin to unbutton her dress to give nourishment to the child.

ACT IV

At the entrance to the Fleming garden, Maria keeps guard. Philip has been gone for seven days; Margaret, bright and cheerful despite her breaking heart, unseeingly tends blossoms and babies. Lucy's first tooth has come through; she plays with the other baby in the crib beside her. Philip returns, declaring he went away because he could not face Margaret or his problem. He learns she is blind, but Margaret assures him she will be cured. She tells him not to worry, reiterating his chances with the sentence: "Oh, you are a man—people will soon forget." She says she has nothing to forgive him, and she wants to forget. She will let him come back, but rejects his note of affection, saying the wife's heart has gone out of her. Again she implies double standards when she asks him how he would feel had *she* proved unfaithful. She has brought Lena's baby to their home and charges Philip with giving him a name, parental care, education, and respect for his mother's memory. Philip finally confesses to trying to drown himself in the Charles River, and to being revived in the hospital. When he speaks of making her respect him again, she says: "Ah, dreams! Philip! And we must get to work." Philip swears to start at once reviving her respect and asks for his daughter. With serene joy, Margaret answers: "They are both out there."

29

HENRY JAMES (1843–1916)

The American (1891)

*Drama of international contrasts
in four acts*

MAIN CHARACTER AND THEME: A rich Californian, *Christopher Newman*, determines by the merit of sheer money to establish himself in the highest society of France.

OTHER CHARACTERS:

Valentin de Bellegarde, a French count

Marquis Urbain de Bellegarde, his older brother

Lord Deepmere

M. Nioche, Noémie's father, who teaches Newman French

M. Gaston de Marignac, one of Valentin's close friends

The Doctor (a physician)

Madame de Bellegarde, English-born mother of Valentin, the Marquis, and Claire

Madame de Cintré, née Claire de Bellegarde

Noémie Nioche, who does portraits of the well-to-do

Mrs. Bread, housekeeper and secret-keeper for the Bellegardes

A Sister of Charity

A Servant

TIME: About 1875.

PLACE: Paris; the Château de Fleurières.

MUSICAL HIGHLIGHTS: A waltz and a mazurka as background at appropriate times.

HISTORICAL NOTE: James's dramatization of his great novel (1877). A sample of the sophisticated treatment of the European-American society contrast, which formed one of the significant bases of American realistic literature in the 1870's and 1880's and which had been the theme of the first American drama, *The Contrast* (1787) (see #5, above). It opened at the Opéra Comique, London, July 26, 1891, and ran for seventy performances.

ACT I

At the Nioche place in a small Parisian establishment, Deepmere, Valentin, and Newman cross paths. The two noble gentlemen are there presumably to be painted by Noémie, but actually to flirt with her; the American, to be taught French by M. Nioche, to invest three thousand francs in art objects, and to hear an accurate account of French high society. Nioche introduces Newman to Valentin while Deepmere is in hiding, placed there by Noémie, who knows that conflicts are not good for her business. In conversation, Valentin learns that Newman, though somewhat crude, is likable and frank and wears his great wealth warmly. Newman, meanwhile, announces that he is looking for a suitable lady—"I don't care what she is, so long as she's only perfect: beautiful, amiable, clever, good, the product of a long civilization and a great cultivation!" For these qualities—what else has he toiled for, Newman asks—he is willing to pave the lady's future with pure gold. When Valentin has gone, Nioche tells him of Valentin's sister who, although having suffered a ghastly marriage, probably meets all of Newman's qualifications. Newman says that if she is what Nioche describes—"as beautiful as an old picture—some delicate pastel—and a saint into the bargain . . . " he is ready to marry her on the spot.

ACT II

Having wangled an invitation from Valentin, Newman appears at the Hotel de Bellegarde, at a reception. One of the first persons he sees is Deepmere, of whom he had caught a very slight glimpse at the Nioche's. Deepmere has been sent back to England by Madame de Bellegarde to make a thorough examination of the state of his property to support his offer for Claire's hand. Before Deepmere can do more than speak informally with Claire, Newman has advanced his case. He is entirely pleased with Claire, and tells her so. She seems more pleased with him than she is with Deepmere. But Madame and the Marquis are more concerned about the state of his wealth and what he is willing to settle upon them than about romantic qualifications. When he tells them of the new huge house he has *purchased*—not rented—in Paris, they seem mildly satisfied. But Madame is still fearful that his low beginnings and crudity will overmatch even his astounding great wealth. Even Claire tells him: " . . . when I used to think, as a girl, of what I would do if I were to marry freely and by my own choice, I thought of a man different from you." It is agreed that the Bellegardes will visit next day at Newman's big house and settle things.

Meanwhile, however, Deepmere, after putting himself out, has received no encouragement; to Valentin he accuses the family of gross and shameless duplicity. Valentin accepts his accusation as a challenge: they plan a duel for the next day. Ironically, after this exchange, Madame tells the Marquis that she has decided to give Claire to Deepmere rather than to the American. He can leave it to her to find the necessary excuse when they visit Newman the next day.

ACT III

Valentin arrives first at the large Newman place and borrows a key to a garden, which is set in "virgin forest"; then he disappears. When the Bellegardes arrive, minus Claire, Madame sees Noémie in a place of prominence. Using this as an opening excuse, she tells Newman that their whole agreement has been cancelled. She assures him that she speaks for Claire, but Newman is not satisfied with this assurance. A while later, Valentin is brought in by Deepmere's doctor; he has been severely wounded in the duel. Claire is sent for since Valentin seems to be fading rapidly. When she comes, she tells Newman that matters were not precisely as her mother had painted them. Privately, Valentin tells Newman that there are family secrets he should know—he tells Newman to inquire of Mrs. Bread. Before very long, Valentin is dead, and Claire, inconsolable, quickly departs. So deeply hurt is Newman that he gives his new house to Nioche and his valuable pearls to Noémie.

ACT IV

At the old Chateau de Fleurières, Claire tells Marignac that she intends to enter a convent at once. Marignac says he will try to prevent her by calling her mother and older brother. Newman arrives; he has the sympathy of

Marignac and Mrs. Bread. In close conversation with Claire he is unable to convince her that she is not ill-fated. Although expressing her deep respect and admiration for him, she swears she will be a nun within the hour. The Marquis and Madame interrupt their conversation; they deplore Newman's presence and go within. Later, Mrs. Bread tells Newman the secret of which Valentin spoke: it is that the Marquis and Madame were accused by Madame's husband of killing him. Just before Madame's husband died, he wrote a note which declared that Madame had deprived him of his medicine in the midst of his last attack. Mrs. Bread has the damaging note and gives it to Newman. Realizing from Newman's destruction of the paper—to save the Bellegardes from annihilation—that Newman is "perfect," Claire agrees to marry him in spite of her mother.

30

CHARLES H. HOYT (1860–1900)

A Trip to Chinatown; Or, An Idyl of San Francisco (1891)

Farcical musical melodrama in three acts

MAIN CHARACTER AND THEME: Although lacking a main character, drama revolves around *Welland Strong*, proud of being a man with one foot in the grave and using his approaching "death" as a means to live off his friends.

OTHER CHARACTERS:

Ben Gay, wealthy San Francisco bachelor, of the Union Club

Rasleigh Gay, his nephew

Tony Gay, his niece

Wilder Daly, young society man, friend of Ben

Willie Grow, proposed at the Bohemian Club

Norman Blood, chum of Rasleigh

Noah Heap, waiter at the Riche Restaurant

Hoffman Price, landlord at Cliff House

Turner Swift, who works for Price

Slavin Payne, servant of Ben Gay

Waiters

Isabelle Dame

Cora Fay

May Wing

Flirt, apparently a vivacious society girl

Mrs. Guyer, widow from Chicago ("not too strenuous on culture but makes up for it with a 'biff' ")

Young Men Singers

TIME: 1890.

PLACE: San Francisco.

MUSICAL HIGHLIGHTS: "The Widow"; "Push Dem Clouds Away" (minstrel piece containing famous line—"Just push! Don't shove!"); "Out for a Racket"; "A Crisp Young Chaperone"; "In Me, a Modest Maid You See"; "Never to Know"; "Reuben, Reuben, I've Been Thinking"; "The Bowery" (a witty dig at New York). Harris' famous "After the Ball" was reputedly sung for the first time during a road production of the play.

HISTORICAL NOTE: First performed November 9, 1891, at Hoyt's Madison Square Theatre, New York, for 657 performances, a record of continuous performances sustained until Smith-Bacon's *Lightning*, which reached 1,291 performances, 1918–1920. The songs—"Reuben, Reuben," "The Bowery," and "After the Ball"—achieved tremendous popularity and influence, which they still hold to some degree.

ACT I

In Ben Gay's house, the servant Slavin Payne decides to misdirect a letter addressed to Rasleigh, and give it to his austere uncle. Wilder Daly and Rasleigh plot how to get the girls Tony and Flirt out for a masquerade ball that night. Their plan is to get permission to go on a night tour of Chinatown, but to go instead to the Riche for supper, and thence to the ball. Mrs. Guyer's consent to act as chaperone has smoothed the way for Flirt, but Ben refuses permission for both Flirt and Tony to go to Chinatown in spite of the chaperonage. Receiving the letter from Slavin (it actually consisted of Mrs. Guyer's instructions to Rasleigh concerning the steps in the plot), Ben considers himself especially invited and now approves the trip for all. He assumes Mrs. Guyer has confirmed her date with him. A telegram from Welland Strong says he has reached Oakland en route to San Francisco. To the others Ben introduces him as his boyhood's dearest friend, coming west with the hope that the climate will prolong his existence. Earlier than expected, Strong enters, with cat and parrot. He knows he is dying, but he still does harmful things like taking a bit of wine. He trusts only the horse doctor. He has come out especially because of the earthquakes, which he considers invigorating. If they will take him, he will make the sacrifice to go with the young people to Chinatown: it will take ten days off his life. He consults a book which gives him the time loss for each occasion—e.g., a cat fight that develops takes off a week. The young people are now stymied until Mrs. Guyer arrives and tells them to take Strong along without telling

126

him where he is going. Strong meets Mrs. Guyer and demonstrates to her how he may explode any minute. She faints at the demonstration. When he orders a horse doctor for her, she springs up and glares at him.

ACT II

For the Riche Restaurant, stage is divided into three compartments: private supper rooms center and left; office with desk on right. Rasleigh's party of six comes into the center supper room after Strong fails to settle the hackman's five dollar fee for two dollars. Strong orders whale's milk and suffers when the waiter Noah pulls off his porous plaster. Ben enters office and is shown to left supper room to await his lady. Wearing a Hamlet dress, Mrs. Guyer comes into center room and frisks about considerably, singing among other things "A Crisp Young Chaperone." Ben is impatient; he drinks heavily. When Noah drops a tray, Strong thinks his lung has gone. Even the youngest girls envy the Widow Guyer. Still drinking, Ben gets angrier and angrier at being "stood up." He finally accepts the newspaper Noah has been offering him (to while away the time) and progressively tears it to bits. The group in center sing "Reuben, Reuben, I've Been Thinking." When Ben cannot settle his bill, now one hundred dollars, a hubbub develops in which Ben catches Strong in the adjacent room and forces him to pay the one hundred dollars to prevent Ben's going to jail.

It is the balcony of Cliff House, with a view of Seal Rocks at the back, a notable spot in San Francisco. Swift is running the ice crusher. Flirt has been flirting with Mrs. Guyer's beaux all evening, in various disguises. The party waits for Strong: he has "run" from the Riche in a nighthawk coupe, which lost its bottom after the driver obeyed his instruction to "drive like the devil!" Flirt is finally unveiled as Mrs. Guyer's maid. In reminiscent mood Strong is carried back to New York: he sings "The Bowery." At the end of the song he has forgotten that he is a sick man. Mrs. Guyer extracts a proposal from Strong. Now engaged, she plans to entertain Ben at breakfast. Slavin, although discharged from Ben's service, searches for his employer to try to prevent his suicide, presumably the result of his deep shame. Behind a screen, Ben is heard stealing a kiss from Mrs. Guyer. She gaily extricates herself from the seeming embarrassment. When they all prepare to celebrate with champagne, they open up the ice crusher to find Strong inside, all crumpled up. He comes up reminding Ben that the clothes he has on belong to Ben.

31

WILLIAM DEAN HOWELLS (1837–1920)

The Albany Depot (1892)

Literary farce in one act

MAIN CHARACTER AND THEME: Uproarious experiences of *Edward Roberts*, upper-middle-class gentleman, left by his wife in a big Boston station to greet and hold the attention of a new cook, whom he has never seen.

OTHER CHARACTERS:

Mrs. Edward Roberts (Agnes)
Willis Campbell, Agnes' brother
Mrs. Willis Campbell (Amy)
Michael McIlheny, a thorough Irish-American and city councilor

Mrs. Michael McIlheny, (Mary)
Chorewoman
Colored train caller
Two or three old ladies in rocking chairs
Maggie, the cook being sought

TIME: A Saturday afternoon of the early 1890's.

PLACE: Ladies' room of the great Albany railroad station in Boston.

HISTORICAL NOTE: A sample of the farces of William Dean Howells, little masterpieces of literary polish and humor, although not written precisely for production. Howells' skill in characterization and his use of background and atmosphere in this piece are quite on a par with the prose fiction and criticism which gave him his enormous reputation.

Scene 1

Finding her husband in the spacious depot, Agnes interrupts his avid reading of the *Popular Science Monthly* to dump upon him innumerable packages she has acquired through shopping and to tell him she must go back to Stearns's

128

(department store) where she left her plush bag with her purse in it. Also, she has found "a perfect treasure" of a cook. Her name is Bridget, or Norah, or something like that. Only one thing: Edward will have to meet her here at the station. Agnes is so much in a hurry that she has no time to describe the cook. Leaving, Agnes instructs Edward positively not to tell their sister-in-law Amy that they had to get a new cook since Amy and Willis are to accompany them to their summer home in Weston and since Amy and Agnes are perpetually in competition on home management.

Scene 2

Coming up suddenly, Willis teases Edward about being much absorbed in his magazine. When Edward explains his problem of waiting for the cook, Willis teases him further, saying that all he needs is to locate a butterball the right size for cooks, whose name is Bridget or Norah or possibly even Maggie, and to strike up, very delicately of course, a conversation about the weather, the last novel, or society gossip. At that moment, the train caller announces a new train. Pursuant to his call, a woman—a butterball—moves toward the train just called. At Willis's suggestion, Edward intercepts her and asks her if she is the cook he is to meet. She replies in a savage negative, much insulted at being taken for a cook. A few moments later, the woman returns, accompanied by a small, wiry Irishman, a little more vivacious for refreshment recently taken, and obviously pugnacious.

Scene 3

The little Irishman, who later identifies himself as Michael McIlheny, a city councilman, asks Edward point-blank if he took Mrs. McIlheny for a cook, and he asks Willis equally pointedly if he put Edward up to it. Not satisfied with Edward's explanation, Michael advances "with a saltatory briskness." When he gets the full import of the incident, he says it is just like a woman to do what Agnes has done. He roars with laughter. Before taking his wife off, he invites both gentlemen to City Hall when Council is meeting.

Scene 4

Amidst his laughter, Willis tells a very serious Edward that he must be more diplomatic next time he advances to an unknown butterball: he must lead up gently, in fact, must let the lady take the lead. There is, admonishes Willis, "all the difference in the world between asking a lady whether she *is* a cook and whether she's *seen* a cook." Michael is suddenly back wanting to know why his wife even looked like "a cuke." He explains that his wife's family is the best in County Mayo—her father kept six cows, she never put her hands in water. This time Willis explains and Michael accepts the explanation. Michael wants them both to join him in a glass of wine "on the corner across the way . . . and domn the thrain!" As Michael goes back to tell his wife he will be late, Willis and Edward discuss how they will escape. When Michael returns, he is again angry—his wife insists it was all a put-up job, accompanied by laughing and winking; but he is again won over by Willis. Michael, however, makes his regrets about the wine, glances at the clock, and rushes out. When Edward says he may have to call the police to get rid of Michael, Willis reminds him that since both police and councilman are Irish, it is Edward who would wind up in jail.

Scene 5

Agnes returns, with Amy, and with the bag she went for. Willis, through great laughter, describes the events that have taken place. Amy accuses her husband of having played another of his "vile practical jokes," but Willis declares, "I couldn't invent anything equal to *this*." Meanwhile, the cook, named Maggie, has found her employers. In the midst of Willis' rehash, Michael once more returns. Accosting Edward alone, he asks if his wife looked like *lady* or *cuke*. At this point, Maggie breaks in and thrashes Michael with a sharp tongue. She calls him "ye drunken blaggurd" and recalls quite definitely that Mary Malloy McIlheny's family had no cows— only one pig under the bed. As Michael's cousin, she says she's every bit as good as Mary Malloy. "Be off wid ye," she concludes, "or I'll say something ye'll not like to hear!"

Michael insists he was only joking; he actually came back, he says, to try to get the cook's job for her because he recognized Edward as a perfect gentleman. Hearing the train caller announce their train, all rush away except Michael, who says: "Sure, I wonder what Mary'll be wantun' me to ask um next."

130

32

EDWARD M. ALFRIEND (b. 1843)
A. C. WHEELER (1835–1903)

The Great Diamond Robbery (1895)

*Melodrama in six acts (typical of
the Ten-Twenty-Thirty Theatre)*

MAIN CHARACTER AND THEME: Monumental efforts of *Dick Brummage*, incorruptible detective, to solve a robbery by international jewel thieves, in spite of interference from the clever criminals and from venal politicians.

OTHER CHARACTERS:

Frank Kennet, a wronged clerk

Clinton Bulford, businessman

Grandfather Lavelot, an ancient citizen

Mario Marino, Mrs. Bulford's brother

Dr. Livingstone, a physician

Senator McSorker, a crooked but powerful politician

Count Garbiadoff, owner of fabulous jewels

Sheeney Ike, Jack Clancy, Mickey Brannigan, members of McSorker's gang

Jimmy McCune, one of Mother Rosenbaum's boys

Phillip, servant of the Bulfords

Policeman

Mrs. Mary Bulford, wife of Clinton, but with a mysterious past

Mary Lavelot, who wants to marry Frank

Mother (Frau) *Rosenbaum*, a gang leader

Mrs. O'Geogan, old friend of McSorker's

Peggy Daly, one of Mother Rosenbaum's girls

Mme. Mervaine, friend of Dick's who escorts the count *Heelers, Clubman, Salvation*   *Army Lass, Messenger Boy, Barkeepers, Waiters, Street Gamin, Blind Musician, Guests*

TIME: 1895.

PLACE: New York City, in places as indicated.

HISTORICAL NOTE: A melodrama, mixed with crime and detective story. It resulted from the combined efforts of Alfriend, a Confederate colonel who had organized and commanded a company in the Civil War, and A. C. Wheeler, a New York newspaperman who had gained a considerable reputation as critic, essayist, and novelist, partly under the pseudonym of Nym Crinkle. The Ten-Twenty-Thirty Theatre, which this play epitomizes, took its name from its comfortable admission prices (10¢, 20¢, 30¢) and its catering to the tastes of those who could not afford higher prices. By experimenting with all types of unsophisticated drama, it made a contribution to theatrical and dramatic history. The present play, after opening at the American Theatre, New York, on September 4, 1895, was extremely popular. As late as 1905, it was listed by a theatrical journal as one of the most popular plays throughout the nation.

ACT I

In the Bulford home on Lexington Avenue, as a bitter storm rages outside, the butler enters with a sealed letter. Mrs. Bulford and her brother (Mario) compare Europe and America: the brains, finesse, and diplomacy of the former versus the crooked politicians who can be manipulated by clever women of the latter. Mario warns her against Senator McSorker, but she wishes for the chance of six months to let him think she would marry him. Bulford comes in with a sealed case to show that he has gained possession of the Garbiadoff diamonds, stolen in Europe by the infamous Don Plon and his woman accomplice. Frank comes in to beg Bulford for two or three days to prove his innocence of embezzlement charges, and thereby to save his impending marriage to Mary Lavelot. Bulford refuses. Surreptitiously, Mrs. Bulford reads the letter accompanying the diamonds and learns that she is therein revealed as Don Plon's accomplice. She thereupon puts poison in a wineglass and pours it down her husband's throat, killing him instantly. Then she has her brother call a doctor, reporting that her husband had accused Frank of poisoning him, but she thinks he died of apoplexy.

132

Commanding the poison glass and the sealed jewel case, she stares wildly into space.

ACT II

Three days later, in Grandfather Lavelot's house on Houston Street, Dr. Livingstone instructs Mrs. O'Geogan on medicine for old Lavelot. Mary is red-eyed over Frank's disappearance, and Dick is snooping around in various disguises to get the truth. Frank comes in, telling how he was shanghaied on a South American ship, and escaped; he begs Mary to believe him innocent of the robbery and murder of which he is charged. He came only to see her, and then to surrender. Looking for the answer to the murder, also, is Mario; Mary hides Frank while talking to Mario and later to Dick, who persuades her to apply for the advertised job of maid in Mrs. Bulford's home. Later, Mario brings back an officer to arrest Grandfather Lavelot as Frank in disguise (he had been confused by Dick who used a Lavelot disguise). Dick assures Frank that he and Mary are his true friends; that the superintendent of police is on their side, but that they must fight the commissioners and the crooked politicians. "We've got a big fight," says Dick, "but if you'll be steered by Dick Brummage, we will run the real culprit to earth."

ACT III

Mary is the new Bulford maid, called Susanne. Dick, disguised as an Irish flower boy, has brought two bouquets of flowers and leaves the wrong one so he can come back. Mary is to put a note in the small bouquet if she wants to communicate with him. Dr. Livingstone tells Mrs. Bulford he has retrieved the poisonous sherry glass, and had seen her drop it, but that no one else knows. Upon his departure, the senator (McSorker) comes to invite Mrs. Bulford to be his "Goddess of Liberty" when his election victory is celebrated at his house the next day. According to Mario, Dr. Livingstone has just been killed by a fire truck which ran into his carriage. To Mother Rosenbaum, who hates Don Plon for causing the execution of her son, Mrs. Bulford reports that Susanne is Don Plon's woman; but Mother Rosenbaum will not kill Susanne unless she is promised a famous jewel called "Heart of Fire." Before Mother Rosenbaum shepherds Mary out on a rigged errand, Mary leaves a note in the small bouquet, which Dick promptly collects. With Mary (Susanne) gone, Mrs. Bulford believes herself safe.

133

ACT IV

At the Hoffman House Cafe on 24th Street, at 8 P.M., Dick instructs Count Garbiadoff to be at 1360 Madison Avenue (McSorker's home) to identify his jewels, but to make no other moves. Dick tells Frank that the two of them must cover the two Rosenbaum hideouts (Rivington and Canal) to rescue Mary who has been kidnapped. Although surrounded by McSorker's men, Frank escapes and Dick brazens his way through.

ACT V

At the Rosenbaum Canal hideout, at 9 P.M., Ike, who has overheard the Dick-Frank plans, warns Mother Rosenbaum, who has her henchman, Jimmy, dress like the policeman Dick arranged to cooperate with him. Jimmy drags Frank in.

At the Rivington den, Mother Rosenbaum reveals that her coldness, brutality, and alliances with politicians (resulting in her ill-gotten gains) are all the result of the loss of her son; now that she has Don Plon's woman, who was responsible, she will surely have revenge. Dick has managed to substitute for Jimmy in bringing Frank before Mother Rosenbaum. Frank and Mary hungrily greet each other. They struggle with Mother Rosenbaum and her minions and would be destroyed but for Dick's coming out of his apparent drunken stupor and brandishing his pistol. The curtain shows Frank and Mary embracing.

ACT VI

It is 11 P.M. at McSorker's Madison Avenue house. The senator's party is a "triumph." Clancy talks of how McSorker has promised to "spring" his brother from Sing Sing (for services Clancy has rendered) and make him a sheriff. Flirting with McSorker, Mrs. O'Geogan wants to know if he recalls the days he wore a buttoned-up coat as he tended bar, while she washed his shirt. The count asks Mme. Mervaine if all American mansions are filled with such canaille. When Mrs. Bulford arrives, dressed to the ears and dripping with jewels, she is surprised first to see Mary, who tells her she has come back from the grave to see justice done, and then to see the count. Trying to escape up the steps, she falls backward into the count's arms. Dick tells her the police are waiting and seizes her by the left wrist. On the

134

platform on top of the steps, she cries, "My God! This is the end!" drinks from a small vial she has carried in her bosom, falls, and dies. Dick identifies the drink as Para poison, which killed Mr. Bulford. When McSorker tries to interfere, Dick commands: "Stand back! The lady belongs to the law— her diamonds to the Count Garbiadoff! . . . senator, it is twelve o'clock!" Mary is in Frank's arms as the curtain falls.

33

WILLIAM GILLETTE (1855–1937)

Secret Service (1895)

War and espionage drama in four acts

MAIN CHARACTER AND THEME: The official and unofficial activities of *Lewis Dumont* of the United States Secret Service, known in Richmond as Captain Thorne, one of the host of Union spies who infested the Confederate capital during its final siege.

OTHER CHARACTERS:

General Nelson Randolph, Confederate commander in Richmond

Mrs. General Varney, wife of a Confederate officer of high rank

Edith Varney, her daughter

Wilfred Varney, her youngest son

Caroline Mitford, from across the street

Henry Dumont, United States Secret Service, Lewis' brother

Benton Arrelsford, Confederate Secret Service

Miss Kittridge, serving for hospitals

Martha and *Jonas*, Negro servants in the Varney home

Lieutenant Maxwell of the President's detail

Lieutenant Foray, first operator in military telegraph lines

Lieutenant Allison, second operator in military telegraph lines

Lieutenants Tyree and *Ensing* of the artillery

Sergeant Wilson

Sergeant Ellington

Corporal Matson

Cavalry Orderly

Artillery Orderly

Hospital Messenger

Four War Department Messengers

Two Telegraph Office Messengers

Eddinger, an aide

TIME: Late 1864 and early 1865.

136

"Secret Service" (1895)

PLACE: Richmond.

HISTORICAL NOTE: Although many dramas were written of operations in the Civil War, only a few were reasonably successful, as theatre or as dramatic literature: Gillette wrote two of the successful ones, *Held by the Enemy* and *Secret Service*, in which Gillette played the leading role of Captain Thorne. As an outstanding actor and a deep student of Civil War records, he had good background. *Secret Service* was produced at the Broad Street Theatre in Philadelphia on May 13, 1895, and then by Charles Frohman at the Garrick Theatre, New York, for 176 performances. It was played abroad successfully until 1897.

ACT I

In the excitement and confusion of besieged Richmond, "starvation parties" are being given by the younger set to keep up morale. But in Mrs. Varney's home, much serious activity, such as bandage-making, goes on. Her youngest son Wilfred begs to be allowed to enlist before the draft call gets down to age sixteen and he is drafted. His mother hesitates since her older son, Howard, is upstairs dying of his wounds. She promises to write her husband for advice on Wilfred. The daughter Edith, meanwhile, has wangled from the President himself a commission for Captain Thorne to head the Telegraph Service, so that he may stay nearby. This action places her in the black books of Arrelsford, whom Edith recently rejected romantically. When Thorne hears the news, he refuses the new commission; he even prevents himself from telling Edith of his love, saying, "You shan't have this against me, too." As Edith goes to get the commission papers as final proof for Thorne, the latter is ordered by Caroline to attend her "starvation party." An ex-sweetheart, Caroline makes up with Wilfred when the latter brings her a uniform, taken from a dead soldier, to cut down to his size.

Meanwhile, Arrelsford arrives at the Varney home and tells Mrs. Varney that he is about to liquidate a plot in which her servant Jonas and Thorne are participants. Arrelsford has captured a paper which he says is intended for Thorne, containing Union instructions reading: "Attack Tonight—Plan 3—Use Telegraph." The idea, says Arrelsford, is to weaken Confederate lines at the point of attack. Although Edith is sure this is Arrelsford's means of showing pique, she decides she must go along with him to be sure that there is no plot.

137

ACT II

At nine that night, Wilfred is sent for by his father, the general; almost at once, Caroline calls off her party and goes to the telegraph office to send Wilfred a congratulatory telegram. Suspecting Caroline's implication in the plot he is investigating, Arrelsford orders her followed. Because Thorne has professed his love for her, Edith tries to withdraw from the investigation, but Arrelsford and Mrs. Varney push her on. At Arrelsford's instigation, Edith shows Thorne the supposed spy paper. The only result is that Thorne tries earnestly to solve the mystery. Bringing Thorne's suspected brother into the house, Arrelsford arranges for him and Thorne to come together where they can be observed. The brother, Henry Dumont, begs Thorne to shoot him, but Thorne refuses. To protect his brother from suspicion, Henry shoots himself and Thorne picks up his gun. "There's your prisoner, corporal," Thorne says, "—look out for him!"

ACT III

In the telegraph office, the indignant Caroline has her message taken and read by Arrelsford: it is merely a sweet note to Wilfred, begging his forgiveness for being unkind and pledging her support. When Thorne arrives, he arranges for the other operators to be relieved so that he may take over the board. When all have gone, he pastes his message over one carrying a War Department signature. With Edith in hiding, Arrelsford indicates what Thorne is doing: the strong moonlight etches Thorne sharply. At what he considers the strategic moment, Arrelsford breaks in, shoots Thorne in the hand, and disarms him. A few moments later, Thorne orders the guard to arrest Arrelsford; despite the latter's plea, Edith will not help him. He is about to be carried away struggling when General Randolph arrives. Thorne continues to send his message. At Arrelsford's insistence that it is an espionage signal, Randolph stops Thorne; in fact, he starts and stops him several times. Thorne suggests that the disputed message be verified at the War Department. He angrily opposes the general, who asks for his authority. Edith produces his commission signed by the President. At this, Randolph has Arrelsford removed and tells Major Thorne (his commission carried a promotion) he should have identified himself at once. When the general has gone, Edith tells Thorne she saved his life only long enough for him to get away. As he

138

goes on with the message, she hides her head in her hands and then leaves. Thorne is caught in a desperate self-struggle as the clicking key demands completion of the order. Finally, with his commission crumpled in his hand, he revokes the order and unsteadily exits.

ACT IV

Throughout this act is heard the thunder and flashes of cannonading and musketry and the ringing of church bells. In conversation Mrs. Varney and Caroline reveal that the Confederates are resisting a terrible attack on Cemetery Hill. Arrelsford comes in with a guard and demands to see Edith whom he blames for the success of the Yankee attack; he says Thorne has escaped. Wilfred returns wounded; Caroline cares for him. He tells Caroline how deeply shocked he is to hear that Edith has betrayed her country. Behaving like his father, he orders Edith sent to him. And when Thorne backs into the room from the veranda side, Wilfred "captures" him.

Thorne confesses his role as espionage agent to Edith and says he is not ashamed. When Arrelsford sees Thorne, he orders him shot at once; Wilfred, however, demands a trial for Thorne. In the process of a drumhead trial, the servant Jonas goes through the stacked guns and bites off the heads of the musket balls, asking Edith to tell Thorne what he has done. Edith does so. But when Thorne asks if she is concerned about him, and she says no, Thorne tells the sergeant of the firing squad that his muskets have been tampered with. The muskets are reloaded.

Meanwhile, though, General Randolph comes in and informs Arrelsford that Thorne never sent any message; thus, he has been wrongly convicted. Randolph relieves Arrelsford of further responsibility and dismisses him. Since the President has disapproved Thorne's execution, General Randolph holds him as a prisoner of war. Edith, Wilfred, and Caroline greet Thorne warmly. General Randolph invites him to work for the Confederate side— Thorne respectfully declines. Generously, Randolph promises him prison until the Confederate Army marches into Washington. Thorne says this will be forever; Edith sweetly agrees with Thorne. As the soldiers take Thorne off, Edith declares her love and no good-by until they meet again.

34

DAVID BELASCO (1854–1931)
JOHN LUTHER LONG (1861–1927)

Madame Butterfly (1900)

Oriental-American tragedy in one act

MAIN CHARACTER AND THEME: How *Cho-Cho-San* (Madame Butterfly), seventeen, awaiting the return of her American husband, faced the supreme challenge of her Japanese concept of honor.

OTHER CHARACTERS:

Suzuki, servant of Madame Butterfly

Mr. Sharpless, American consul

Lieutenant B. F. Pinkerton of the warship *Connecticut*

Yamadori, a citizen of New York

The Nakodo, a marriage broker

Kate, Pinkerton's American wife

"Trouble," the child of Madame Butterfly and Pinkerton

Two Male Attendants

TIME: About 1895.

PLACE: Madame Butterfly's house at the foot of Higashi Hill, facing the harbor of a Japanese city, probably Nagasaki.

MUSICAL HIGHLIGHTS: "I Call Her The Belle of Japan"; "Rog' a Bye Bebby, Off in Japan. . . ."

HISTORICAL NOTE: Based on a short story by John Luther Long. First performed at the Herald Square Theatre, New York, March 5, 1900, with Blanche Bates as Madame Butterfly and Claude Gillingwater as Mr. Sharpless. Opera by Giacomo Puccini based on this play, performed in English in New York, December 12, 1906; then, memorably, on February 11, 1907, with Geraldine Farrar as Cio-Cio-San, Louise

Homer as Suzuki, and Enrico Caruso as Pinkerton. First of a long line of Oriental-American plays, still very popular on stage, screen, and television, usually concentrating on romantic exploits of military personnel since the opening of Japan to the West by Commodore Matthew Perry in 1853.

ACTION

Surrounded by cherry blossoms, Madame Butterfly prays to Shaka (god) for the early return of "Lef-ten-ant B. F. Pinkerton." Suzuki reports that only two dollars of the Lieutenant's money remains, and he has been gone almost two years. Madame Butterfly replies: did he not sign Japanese lease for 999 years and put 'Merican locks on doors and windows? But, says Suzuki, Pinkerton has not written. She is burningly told: "Speak concerning marriage once more, you die!" Her husband swore to return "we'n robins nes' again!" Madame Butterfly has already seen a robin, and wonders only if Japanese and American robins are on the same schedule. She thinks of his farewell ("Goon-by, sayonara, Butterfly"), of their many hours of gayety, and of her dancing for him as she formerly did when a geisha girl. She dances reminiscently as Sharpless and Nakodo enter. Sharpless notes the mementoes of Pinkerton: his tobacco jar decorated with the American flag; sawdust in the cigarettes; his infernal jokes which Madame Butterfly pitifully retells; his slang; and the way Madame Butterfly winks from behind her fan. Nakodo says that her family has "outcasted" her. Madame Butterfly reviews her background, beginning with her father who killed himself after suffering defeat in battle because he followed the inscription on his sword, which Madame Butterfly reads aloud: "To die with honor, when one can no longer live with honor." She recalls her first meeting with Pinkerton whom she did not at first like; her soon believing him "jus' a god! gold button—lace on his unicorn"; her liking his kisses in spite of abhorrence of Japanese girls to kisses.

Yamadori returns for the third time to get Madame Butterfly to "make smash" with him, offering her a thousand servants. Once more she refuses. But when Sharpless assures him that Pinkerton's American wife is already in the city, Yamadori goes out with a contented smile. "Trouble" comes in; Sharpless wants to know if Pinkerton knows of his child; he is told no. When Sharpless tells her flatly that she is not Pinkerton's wife, she abruptly dismisses him.

A ship's gun is heard. Believing this the signal for Pinkerton's immediate return, Madame Butterfly gets all in order. She waits. Night comes, with stars. Pinkerton comes after dawn. Sharpless and Pinkerton chide Nakodo for having told Kate (Mrs. Pinkerton) about the child, but Nakodo still hopes for the big marriage fee from Yamadori. Without seeing Madame Butterfly, Pinkerton gives Sharpless money for her and goes. Kate comes, calling Madame Butterfly "you pretty little plaything" and wanting to adopt the child; Madame Butterfly tells her she can look at "Trouble" but not touch. Kate reluctantly goes.

Madame Butterfly says "goon' bye" to Suzuki. Bolting the door, she lights fresh incense before the shrine, takes down her father's sword, and again reads the inscription aloud. She draws her finger across the blade, puts on more rouge, bows to shrine, and is pressing the blade to her neck when Suzuki pushes the child in. Madame Butterfly drops the sword, sets the child, with an American flag, on the mat, and goes behind the screen with sword. When sword drops, Madame Butterfly reappears with deathly face, and scarf around her neck. Kate brings Pinkerton back to embrace Madame Butterfly and her child. Madame Butterfly says to Pinkerton, "Too bad those robins didn' nes' again," and dies.

142

35

CLYDE FITCH (1865–1909)

The Climbers (1901)

High-society drama in four acts

MAIN CHARACTER AND THEME: The self-imposed tortures of a New York City lawyer, *Richard Sterling*, thirty-eight, to become so financially secure as to be free of worries in maintaining his place in a society that was always moving out of his reach.

OTHER CHARACTERS:

Edward Warden, about Sterling's age, his college pal and friend of his family

Frederick Mason, elderly, solid New Yorker

Johnny Trotter, foolish, young, wealthy, and fearful of being someone's "Dodo bird"

Dr. Steinhart, a society physician

Howard Godesby, frivolous brother of Miss Godesby

Ryder, one of those who entrusted his money to Sterling

Servant at the Hermitage

Servants at the Hunters':

Jordan, Leonard, A Footman

Richard Sterling, Jr., five-year-old son of Richard and Blanche

Mrs. Florence Hunter, widow of the recently deceased George Hunter

Mrs. Blanche Sterling, Mrs. Hunter's oldest daughter

Jessica Hunter, her middle sister

Clara Hunter, her youngest sister, ready to be brought out into society

Miss Ruth Hunter, George Hunter's sister, in her thirties, an unpretentious aristocrat

Miss Godesby, intelligent and sincere under a cynical mask

Miss Sillerton, attractive but thoroughly conventional

Maids at the Hunters':

Tompson, Mrs. Hunters' maid

Marie, Clara's French maid

143

TIME: About 1900.

PLACE: New York City; The Hermitage on the Bronx River.

MUSICAL HIGHLIGHTS: "Follow the Man from Cook's"; "Once in Royal David's City" (a Christmas carol).

HISTORICAL NOTE; Significant drama by an American playwright of great theatrical skill and the knowledge and power to penetrate the roots of American society, who refused to carry his analyses to their logical outcomes for fear of jeopardizing his popularity and financial status. This play is historically important because the very nature of the American promise of prosperity for all induces climbing and status-seeking of all degrees of intensity and brings about tragic results through the inevitable impact of shifting standards of value. Fitch also demonstrated power in analytical drama with plays about women with basic faults: abnormal jealousy in *The Girl with the Green Eyes* (1902); congenital lying in *The Truth* (1907). His drama, *The City* (1909), shows keen understanding of the impact of urbanization upon American standards of value.

ACT I

Returning from the funeral of her husband, who had always been a fully accepted member of society, Mrs. Hunter, whose high position had often been questioned, has been more concerned about the funeral as a social success than anything else. She notes to her daughters that everyone of importance in society was there, and that even her original set was present— some of whom had failed of acceptance because they were Presbyterians. She deplores the burdens of mourning including such "social pushers" as the Witherspoons who used the funeral to make people think they were on the Hunters' visiting list. In selecting their stationery, the Hunters choose that with the blackest possible border.

Mrs. Hunter's sister-in-law, Ruth, calls the funeral a show spectacle, and therefore a disgrace, and says it represents the main reason why Mrs. Hunter was always a failure in society. She openly accuses Mrs. Hunter of loving social status better than she did her late husband. On the other hand, she tells Blanche that she has forgiven Sterling and will put her business into his hands.

Frederick Mason then informs the Hunters that the deceased has left no money. Just before he died, Mr. Hunter had gambled everything on

144

Continental Copper, and had lost. Horrifying her mother, the middle sister Jessica comes out with the obviously truthful statement that the extravagance of his family had ruined Mr. Hunter. The girls talk of possible ways to retrieve their fortune—Clara, the youngest sister, speaks of the stage, Jessica of becoming a "typewriter" (stenographer), teacher, or companion. Mrs. Hunter suggests marriage as the most profitable, and probably the only dignified, possibility. When Ruth suggests that they take in boarders to make the big house pay, Clara and Mrs. Hunter indignantly leave. They do not hesitate later, however, to bargain with Miss Sillerton and Miss Godesby in selling their gowns created by Worth, Doucet, and Paquin for exorbitant sums in view of the fact that they cannot wear them in mourning. During this session, Johnny Trotter is introduced, and he can talk of nothing but his money—his Newport lot, his house on Long Island, his building plots on Fifth Avenue; in the talking, he commits many social faux pas. He has come, however, to meet Clara because he needs a woman of approved social position to develop his social career.

In the interim, Sterling also arrives, somewhat intoxicated, and really disappointed when he learns that Mr. Hunter has left nothing. He was depending upon his wife's share of the Hunter fortune to prevent his disgrace and poverty, since he has been speculating with other people's money. Sterling's friend Warden now accuses him of misusing funds and stocks, of immoral behavior, and of being a moral coward. Sterling, however, is extremely grateful to Ruth for her trust in him and for the several hundred thousand dollars' worth of bonds she has placed in his care. Privately, Blanche tries to get her husband to promise to be honest with his trust, but he brushes aside her implications. After Warden assures Blanche of his deep friendship as always, Blanche learns from a letter case left by Mr. Hunter that her father had found her husband irregular in his business.

ACT II

Fourteen months later, at a Christmas Eve party in the Hunter home, now shared with the Sterlings, Sterling is discovered by Mason and Warden to be deeply involved in Hudson Electric stocks, and they know that the complete failure of Hudson Electric will be announced next day. Warden and Mason discuss possible outcomes; learning that Sterling is preparing to abscond that night, they use a trick to stop him. Blanche tells her husband her love and respect for him are gone, but that she wants him to confess his involvement to save his son. The lights turned out on his demand, Sterling tells his story. He admits being a climber after wealth. In the first week he had Ruth's money, he gambled and made $100,000 clear profit. Since then, in an effort to make a real killing, he has used Ruth's bonds repeatedly; now, not only Ruth's securities but those of Miss Godesby and Ryder, another of Sterling's clients, are sunk in Hudson Electric. Ruth promptly declares that she will not prosecute, but Warden and Mason expect trouble from the other two, especially since they cannot get Sterling to promise to talk to them. Later, Warden and Mason must prevent Sterling from stealing away in the dark.

ACT III

Mrs. Hunter, not Clara, has married Trotter, and they are now living at his home, The Hermitage, on the Bronx River. Appealing to his membership in the family, Warden and Mason get Trotter to agree to back Sterling's note to Ryder; Ryder accepts the note and promises to keep the transaction a secret. Miss Godesby is harder to handle: she finally agrees to secrecy if Warden will sign a guarantee. In the course of negotiating with Warden, she deduces his love for Blanche, and admires him for it. A short while later, Blanche becomes aware of the fact that all along Warden has protected and loved her; she returns his love. Intoxicated again, Sterling breaks in on them, accuses them of cheating him, and tries to shoot himself in their presence. They prevent his suicide, although Blanche confesses to him her love for Warden, and guide him home. As the Sterlings leave, Warden kisses Blanche's hand.

ACT IV

In the Sterlings' library next morning, Ruth tries desperately to stop Blanche from divorcing Sterling. Confessing her own case—she has loved Mason for twenty years, during which time his wife has been hopelessly insane—she assures Blanche that heartbreak comes from the sorrow of doing wrong, not from the pain of doing right. Sterling has managed to get Dr. Steinhart to prescribe two morphine pills for his persistent headache; after the doctor leaves, he alters the prescription to raise it to twelve pills. When Blanche promises not to leave him, he promises her to earn her love and respect anew: she remembers tenderly the days of their early love but urges him not to believe he can infuse life into a dead thing; she will live with him and keep up appearances, but that is all.

After throwing away the additional ten pills, Sterling retrieves them and takes six pills in a glass of champagne. While Warden is out, winning Ruth over to his plan to take Blanche away from Sterling and give her the happiness she deserves, Sterling is in the library gradually falling asleep—an eternal sleep. He decides to write a note saying he is going away for good. In his dying moment, he remembers that he has once again failed everybody because the whole structure preventing the family from disgrace rests upon his redeeming the notes. He is actually dead when Blanche and Warden return, but they do not know it, and they do not quite understand what he means to do. Warden, standing by, concludes the play with the remark: "We will know when he wakes."

36

DAVID BELASCO (1854–1931)

The Girl of the Golden West (1905)

Frontier drama in four acts

MAIN CHARACTER AND THEME: The exciting life of *Minnie Falconer*, always known as The Girl, a rare woman in the man's world of gold mining, owner of the Polka Saloon, schoolteacher, moral guide, and sentimental first citizen; especially, The Girl's first adventure in love.

OTHER CHARACTERS:

Wowkle, an Indian squaw, Billy Jackrabbit's girl

Dick Johnson, thirty, a stranger (actually Ramerrez, the road-agent)

Jack Rance, gambler and sheriff

Sonora Slim, a miner

Trinidad Joe, his partner

Nick, bartender of the Polka

The Sidney Duck, an Australian faro dealer

Jim Larkens, a shabby and despondent miner

Happy Halliday, a long-legged miner

Handsome Charlie, a big, picturesque miner

Deputy Sheriff

Billy Jackrabbit, an Indian

Ashby, the Wells-Fargo agent

José Castro, ex-padroña of the bullfights and horse-breaker, now with Ramerrez' band

Rider of the Pony Express

Jake Wallace, a traveling-camp minstrel

Bucking Billy, from Watson's, a neighboring mining community

The Lookout

A Faro Dealer

The Boy from the Ridge

Joe, a gambler

Concertina players

Citizens of the Camp

Boys of the Ridge

148

"The Girl of the Golden West" (1905)

TIME: Days of the gold fever, 1849–1850.

PLACE: Cloudy Mountain, California, a mining camp in Manzanita County, and the boundless prairies of the West.

MUSICAL HIGHLIGHTS: "The Camptown Races"; "Wait for the Wagon"; "Old Dog Tray"; "America."

HISTORICAL NOTE: Though not distinguished for dramatic and literary integrity, this drama reflects the true atmosphere of the California gold rush, based as it is on an incident in the life of the playwright's father. It is distinguished for its authentic language, characterization, folk tradition, and sentimentality; its Far Western morality reflects both the Eastern foundation and the demands of survival in a precarious, acquisitive, dangerous settlement. This play is the ancestor of the contemporary "Western." Written especially for Blanche Bates, it opened in Pittsburgh on May 3, 1905, and ran for 224 performances after opening at the Belasco Theatre in New York, November 14, 1905.

ACT I

Vigorous gambling goes on in the Polka Saloon and vigorous folk dancing in the dance hall beyond. A poster on the back of the door of the Polka, signed by Wells-Fargo, offers five thousand dollars for Ramerrez, the highwayman. As the minstrel Jake Wallace sings to the accompaniment of his banjo, many gamblers stop to weep. When the Sidney Duck is caught cheating, the sheriff Rance gives him the supreme punishment, worse even than a stringing-up: a deuce of spades over his heart, to signify him as a cheater, and an order not to leave the camp, or ever to play cards again.

Later, Rance announces that he intends to marry The Girl; when he broaches the subject to her, she tells him to go back to his wife in New Orleans. The Pony Express rider reports a big holdup at the Forks. Very shortly, there enters an unexpected guest, Mr. Johnson, smooth-faced, tall, wearing Sacramento clothes. Although Rance tells Johnson that strangers are not welcome, The Girl remembers meeting him on the road when she went to Monterey: she orders a special bottle for him. When Johnson asks her to waltz, The Girl accepts with only the proviso that she cannot waltz, but she can "polky."

Too obligingly, Castro leads the Wells Fargo agent Ashby and his men to where Ramerrez is allegedly hiding in spite of Rance sniffing a heavy snow-fall in the air. When the men are decoyed away, Castro secretly tells Johnson to hurry and rob the place as they planned. Instead of robbing, Johnson chats with The Girl, who informs him that "keepin' saloon is a great educator." After an interesting talk, Johnson accepts The Girl's offer for a rare visit to her cabin. Promptly The Girl sends Nick, the bartender, to get "two charlotte rusks an' a lemming turnover"—for supper.

ACT II

It is 1 A.M. at the home of The Girl on Cloudy Mountain. In spite of having borne him a papoose, Wowkle is not sure she wants to marry Billy. Wowkle's talk of romance, though, is swept away by The Girl's frantic preparations. In a few minutes, Johnson arrives. After The Girl praises the beautiful peaks by which she is surrounded, Johnson gets down to his major purpose: to tell her that he loves her and to ask her for a kiss. After some romantic negotiation, The Girl gives him a kiss, her very first one. In a little while, two shots are heard on the mountain below, and The Girl suggests that possibly Ramerrez has been captured. Also, the snow is beginning to fall heavily.

Breaking into The Girl's bliss come Rance and other members of a posse. Johnson begs her not to admit them, but she must because of the snow. Hiding Johnson, she admits the group. They tell her that Johnson is certainly Ramerrez; he has been identified by Nina, his girl, who also supplied his autographed picture. Getting rid of the search party, The Girl turns upon Johnson, most angry because of Nina, less angry because she has given her first kiss to a road agent. She finally says she loves him and will stand by him. Refusing to hide behind a woman, Johnson starts out of the door, is shot, and falls back. Rance and his men return: The Girl hides Johnson in the loft, opens the door, and asks Rance to search the place. Cajoling Rance, she gets him to start away again. As Rance holds out his hand to say good night, a drop of blood from the loft falls upon it. Rance orders Johnson down; he comes down, lurching. Girl then offers to play Rance poker: if he wins, he gets both of them; if he loses, he shuts up and loses like a gentleman. On the third hand, by pretending to faint when she sees her losing cards and by getting five new cards when Rance turns to get her a drink, The Girl manages to win.

150

"The Girl of the Golden West" (1905)

ACT III

In the "Academy" where The Girl teaches the miners, everything seems different from what it was before. Rance can think only of The Girl nursing Johnson for a whole week in her cabin. The others believe Johnson lying dead at the foot of the canyon. The only book left for teaching is "Old Joe Miller's Jokes." When The Girl, now more pitying, admits the cheater Sidney to school, the miner Trinidad wants to know if honesty is no longer the best policy. Only the two Indians can sing "My Country 'Tis." Gloom settles down over all when The Girl says she must leave Cloudy Mountain soon. In the girl's absence, Rance tells them that Johnson is The Girl's man and the reason for her leaving.

Ashby brings Johnson in, and Johnson swears he is ready to die, but he doesn't want The Girl to know his end. He wants her to think he escaped to the East. At length, the boys allow Johnson to see The Girl alone before he dies. Their farewell talk is cheerful—she looking to the future, he trying to say good-by without giving away his imminent death. Johnson finally says "God bless you . . . good-by, Girl!" and leaves. When The Girl realizes the boys are about to hang Johnson, she begs them not to. The boys decide that if The Girl thinks that way then "maybe God's back of this here game." They then force Rance to free Johnson. Nick says the Polka will never be the same without The Girl.

ACT IV

On the boundless prairies of the West, The Girl and Johnson are headed East. The Girl grieves over losing more and more of the hills, red and shining, which were her promised land. Johnson says that through her his old bad life is gone. He calls for the new life and for her to trust him. Assuring him of her trust, she says she still grieves to leave the California mountains—her home.

37

LILLIAN MORTIMER

No Mother to Guide Her (1905)

Pure melodrama in four acts

MAIN CHARACTERS AND THEME: The search for happiness by a secretly married couple—*Rose Day* (the heroine), a sweet country girl, and *Ralph Carlton* (the hero), a young man of good instincts who has sown a generous crop of wild oats—in the face of the enterprising opposition of *John Livingstone* (the villain), an ingenious criminal.

OTHER CHARACTERS:

Silas Waterbury, the town constable

Jake Jordan, an escaped convict

Farmer Day, Rose's father

Lindy Jane Smithers, Rose's aunt, in love with Silas but afraid to marry him

Bess Sinclair, a shopgirl

Mother Tagger, a tool of Livingstone's

Bunco, Bess's friend, a former shopgirl

Harry Patent, Tommy Fischer, Walter Perkins, Frank Caldwell, Parson Thomas—the sweet-singing gypsies (off stage)

Officer Keough

Policeman Todd

Captain Hennessy

TIME: Early 1900's.

PLACE: Rural district in New York State; New York City.

MUSICAL HIGHLIGHTS: "Blow, blow, winds/While the pot bubbles on"; "When the robins nest again"; weird music; gypsy quintette.

HISTORICAL NOTE: Miss Mortimer, author, actress, and producer won outstanding popularity with this play from 1905 to 1913, following its

152

opening at the Whitney Theatre in Detroit on August 6, 1905. She wrote at least seven other plays in the same vein, that is, the vein of unadulterated melodrama.

Although melodrama is hard to define because it is usually interlocked with other forms, basic American melodrama possesses the following characteristics: (1) It concerns itself with the activities of homely folk with simple, direct goals rather than long-range, philosophical goals. (2) It has plenty of action, though this is often deliberately inconclusive (e.g., many are shot, but few die) to suggest the parade of troubles and heartaches that plague every life, but can be overcome by the individual by persistent drive. Note that this type of action is consonant with the simple, direct goals, and that in the welter of activity the hunger is always for something stable. (3) Most of the characters are solidly good or solidly bad; but a few of the good characters inadvertently help the bad through lack of foresight, and a few of the bad help the good because they realize that goodness is a superior way of life. Selfishness is always bad, unselfishness always good. (4) Every character or action is a moral example. (5) Country life is better than city life for the affirmation of virtue. (6) Having a mother to guide one is essential to the assurance of virtue for both male and female. (7) Romantic love is the great desideratum, marriage the great end. (8) Hero, heroine, and villain are clearly distinguished, never ambiguous. (9) Whatever troubles heroic characters have and whatever successes or advantages villains have are always temporary: truth and villainy will unquestionably receive just rewards. (10) The language of the drama has a minimum of irony; frankness is the keyword. (11) Insight and foresight are kept to a minimum and the player in Life's game plays as well as he can with the cards immediately before him.

Although melodrama is generally denigrated or despised, historically, in its pure form, it has not been frivolous or easy to write; it requires proficiency in a very definite kind of artistry.

ACT I: The Murder

At the farm of Farmer Day, Livingstone is in hiding from a city robbery (which netted him ten thousand dollars) and has just held up Stebbins' bank nearby for five hundred dollars. Secretly, Mother Tagger tells him she has choked to death the baby he consigned to her care—the illegitimate child of Livingstone and Bess, the shopgirl.

Livingstone tells her to hold herself in readiness for other villainy; meanwhile, he expects to marry Rose and settle down. In another private meeting, Ralph and Rose reveal that they have recently and secretly married. Although Rose refuses to listen, Ralph indicates that he has sown some rather strong wild oats and hopes that his past will not plague them. Unseen by Livingstone, Bunco brings Bess to the farm and bargains with Lindy, Rose's aunt, to work in exchange for food for the two of them: they are both near starvation. Another of Livingstone's former partners, an ex-convict named Jake, has also appeared at the farm. He seeks to blackmail Livingstone since he was present at the city robbery where Livingstone murdered a man. Jake accepts a mere twenty dollars to keep silent for the present, but indicates that he will return again and again.

In the rapid movement of persons around the farm, Bess has seen Livingstone and has thrown herself into his arms: she still expects him to marry her. But Bunco knows that Livingstone is treacherous; when he tries to take Bess away under a false promise to marry her, Bunco draws a gun from her boot and prevents him. Somewhat later, though, Bunco's attempt to snatch Bess from Livingstone's arms is foiled by Mother Tagger who comes up from behind and hits Bunco on the head.

Ralph, meanwhile, has met Livingstone and told him that he and Rose are married. Holding a secret of Ralph's past which can put him in Sing Sing, Livingstone tells Ralph openly that, married or not, Rose must come to him. Livingstone, however, pretends to be ready to release Ralph if Ralph will help him rob Farmer Day, who, distrusting banks, keeps all his money in his house. Seeing this maneuver as the only way to avoid trouble and save his marriage, Ralph consents to stand guard as Livingstone does the robbery. Actually, Ralph plans to have Livingstone discovered in the act. In the mix-up of the burglary, Farmer Day is reported (by Rose's aunt Lindy) to be murdered, and Ralph is shot by Rose, who cannot see him clearly as he tries to run away. (Farmer Day is in fact only injured, and later recovers.)

ACT II: The Gypsy Camp

At the gypsy camp three months later, Bess is held by the cruel Mother Tagger. Believing Ralph dead, Rose has promised to marry Livingstone to give her unborn son (by Ralph) a home. Ralph, alive and well, comes to the camp, looking for Rose and determined to punish Livingstone. The sounds of a storm approaching are heard from time to time. Silas, the town constable, and Lindy come to the gypsies to have their fortunes told. When Silas is given information by "gypsy" Mother Tagger that Sally Tomkins loves him, he uses the information to make Lindy marry him—she has put him off for ten years. Ralph and Livingstone come face to face; in the struggle, Ralph is hit with a billy. As Ralph lies unconscious, Livingstone shoots Jake, the blackmailer, with Ralph's pistol and later makes Ralph believe he is responsible. But Jake is not seriously hurt—the bullet only grazed his head. He swears vengeance on Livingstone.

Meanwhile, a double marriage is planned: Livingstone-Rose and Silas-Lindy. When the imported Parson gets to the request for anyone objecting to the marriage to speak or forever hold his peace, Bess comes down and points to Livingstone, declaring that, in Heaven's eyes, he is her husband. Livingstone says she is Mother Tagger's crazy grandchild: Mother Tagger carries her off. Parson completes the two ceremonies in one operation with Rose and Lindy meekly saying, "We do." As Parson makes his final pronouncement, Rose swoons and faints. A terrible tornado strikes at that moment. In spite of the storm, Jake comes up to settle with Livingstone. They fight. Gaining the advantage, Livingstone is about to dispatch Jake with his knife when Bunco shoots Livingstone.

ACT III: In the Big City

A year later, Rose has realized the terrible mistake she has made in her second "marriage." Livingstone avows frankly that he is a thief and house-breaker; Bunco corrects him: thief, bank robber, "and worser"—a murderer. As Rose takes care of her child, Livingstone forces her to give him her money and jewels, including the wedding ring from Ralph. Picking Livingstone's pocket as he goes by, Bunco recoups the treasures. In Livingstone's absence, Silas and Lindy come to visit, having been to the "Opery House." During the friendly conversation that follows, Ralph breaks in, wearing convict's garb and followed closely by the police. Rose and Bunco hide Ralph where the searching police cannot find him. When the police have gone, Silas and Lindy, asserting this is no place for them, quickly depart.

155

Ralph changes into civilian clothes provided by Rose. Livingstone returns. At gun point, Ralph forces him to put on the convict clothes, gags him and ties him to a bed; then Ralph and Rose depart, Ralph promising Livingstone further punishment. Livingstone frees himself and is pursued by policemen.

ACT IV: Old Hut in the Hills

Silas and Lindy have walked many miles from the city—Silas walking barefoot to spare his $1.20 shoes. After they go by, Ralph and Rose appear, having heard that Livingstone is being followed by bloodhounds. Ralph sees hope in the future as he takes his wife into a hut. In a nearby tent, Mother Tagger still has Bess under restraint. Bess pleads to die. Having had so much trouble already because she had no mother to guide her, she hopes for a mother in heaven, where she desires to go at once.

Jake Jordan, having served his term in prison, has come back to comfort Bess. Because Jake told the full story of sundry crimes, Ralph has a good chance to be freed (he had always insisted upon his innocence). He gives himself up to Officer Keough, who thinks Ralph will be declared innocent but for now must handcuff him. After examining Mother Tagger, who implicates herself by telling on Livingstone, the officer is convinced that Mother Tagger is a worse criminal than Ralph. Begging Ralph's pardon, he takes the handcuffs off Ralph and places them upon the wrists of vicious Mother Tagger.

Running from dogs and shooting at random, Livingstone bursts in, covered with blood. Silas, as constable of the neighborhood, demands that he surrender. Livingstone turns the gun upon Silas and fires several times: the revolver snaps because it is out of shells. Livingstone now encounters, by fists, first Jake and then Ralph. He seems to be winning when Jake shoots him and Silas catches him. Livingstone, being led away, tells Jake he'll meet him in hell. Jake replies: "No, guv'ner—I ain't goin' that way." Ralph and Rose fall blissfully into each other's arms.

38

WILLIAM VAUGHN MOODY (1869–1910)

The Great Divide (1906)

Drama of American contrasts in three acts

MAIN CHARACTER AND THEME: Drama of the true conflict in ideals and behavior between the genuine products of the American West and those of Puritan New England, as concentrated in the experiences of *Ruth Jordan*, nineteen, who is caught in "a Massachusetts-Arizona mix-up."

OTHER CHARACTERS:

Philip Jordan, thirty-four, Ruth's brother

Polly Jordan, Philip's wife

Mrs. Jordan, Ruth's mother

Winthrop Newbury, recent graduate of an Eastern medical college

Dr. Newbury, Winthrop's father

Stephen Ghent

Lon Anderson

Burt Williams

Dutch

Shorty, a Mexican half-breed

A Contractor

An Architect

A Boy

TIME: End of the nineteenth century.

PLACE: Southern Arizona; the Cordilleras of Arizona; Milford Corners, Massachusetts.

MUSICAL HIGHLIGHTS: Song with original words by Moody.

HISTORICAL NOTE: First produced in Chicago, April 1906, under the title of *The Sabine Woman*, with Margaret Anglin as Ruth. Later performed memorably at the Princess Theatre, New York, with Margaret Anglin and Henry Miller as Ruth and Ghent. Repeated in New York and London, 1907 and 1909. Besides being a professor at the University of

Chicago, Moody wrote other plays showing awareness of the dramatic upheaval caused by modern scientific thinking—*The Faith Healer* (1909) and a poetic trilogy on the Promethean theme of God-man relationships.

ACT I

As Philip prepares to put Polly on a train to San Francisco, because she can stand the desert no longer, Ruth shows her adoration for the whole surroundings of their Arizona cabin (adorned with blankets, pottery, weapons, and sacred images of local Indian tribes), especially for a gorgeous desert moon. She has recently joined her brother to develop a cactus-fiber plant, with money supplied by their mother, still in Massachusetts. Winthrop is called to treat a broken leg; before he goes, as he has done for years, he vainly entreats Ruth to love him. She professes to be looking for "a sublime abstraction—of the glorious unfulfilled—of the West—the Desert."

Because the workmen, gone to a Mexican blowout, have taken all the ponies, Ruth cannot go to see Polly off. Left alone, happy and singing, Ruth prepares for bed, not seeing sinister faces at the window. Finally, the door is broken through: Dutch, Shorty, and Ghent crowd in, as Ruth's gun misfires. Brutally, the three maneuver to possess her. She turns to Ghent for salvation. After buying off Shorty with a chain of gold nuggets, Ghent returns, wounded but victorious, from a square stand-up shoot with Dutch. Ruth then tries to beg off. Ghent promises she will not regret marrying him. Because he needs her for his return to manhood and as his inspiration to go to work on his rich mining claim, he cannot release her. Although he places his pistol where she can reach it, she does not shoot him. Instead, she tends his wound. After writing a note for Philip, and kissing her mother's picture (but not taking it), she leaves with Ghent.

ACT II

At the Ghent home in the Cordilleras, Ruth has won the admiration and loyalty of the miners who work for her husband. They cannot, however, understand why she weaves rugs and makes baskets (like some half-starved Navajo woman) in view of her husband's phenomenal success with the Rio Verde mine. Because Ruth is absent, Ghent delays settling with his architect and contractor on the fabulous new home. Returning, Ruth is cool as usual to Ghent. He gives her handsome jewelry and the plans for the $25,000 home. She says only, "My price has risen! My price has risen!" referring to the gold nuggets Ghent gave Shorty. Winthrop has followed her home: he is now physician at the End-of-the-Rainbow mines. He tells her that the Rio Verde is in litigation—it is news to her.

Eventually, Polly and Philip appear, the latter demanding explanations which Ruth superciliously withholds. She reproves her brother for insulting her husband, and even calls Ghent by his first name before her three old cronies. She is greatly distressed, however, to hear that her leaving ruined the cactus venture. When the others have gone, she tells Ghent that she has tried without success to love him. She requests release, offering the nugget chain, repurchased from Shorty with her own funds. Ghent refuses, especially when he learns they are soon to be parents. But when Philip, suspicious all along, returns to reassure himself, he takes his sister home to Massachusetts, at her request.

ACT III

In the Massachusetts home, the walls are hung with Revolutionary, eighteenth-century clerical, and Puritan family portraits. News is that the home has been redeemed by a benevolent relative and that Arizona Cactus Fiber, which Philip was forced to sell cheaply, is booming. Ruth mopes around, listless and mechanical, even where her child is concerned. According to Polly, she is a battleground of Puritan anxieties and natural love of the primitive in Ghent. Ghent arrives. His conversation with Mrs. Jordan discloses his role as savior of the home. He also hands her papers restoring to Philip the now valuable cactus mine. When Ruth learns all this, she prepares to leave a house Ghent has contaminated; when Philip learns it, he wants to fight his brother-in-law. Even Mrs. Jordan tells Ruth she should have died rather than allowed Ghent to "save" her as he did.

Intervening between Philip and Ghent, Ruth declares that this is her business and hers alone. Ghent restores to her the gold nuggets and invites her to explain them to their son. Preparing to depart forever, he tells Ruth that she has allowed the old gentlemen on the wall to delude her—that love and joy and supreme selfishness are more important than useless, self-destroying sacrifice. He admits that he came east just after she did, that his mine is almost stolen, that he could have it back by fighting if there were anything to fight for. She finally sees his point. Confessing that she has always loved him, she says she knew no other way to cleanse herself and him of sin. He is happy beyond words to have the chance to make a good life for their "little rooster." "And for us!" says Ruth. "For us!"

39

LANGDON MITCHELL (1862–1935)

The New York Idea (1906)

Manners comedy emphasizing divorce in four acts

MAIN CHARACTER AND THEME: The preparations of *Cynthia Karslake*—society girl and sportswoman, in her twenties, divorced wife of a young sportsman—to marry into a very staid New York family, already afflicted by a sensational divorce, and the resulting complications.

OTHER CHARACTERS:

Philip Phillimore, judge of the State Supreme Court

Mrs. Phillimore, his mother, a semiprofessional invalid, refined but unintelligent

The Reverend Matthew Phillimore, his brother, a high-church clergyman with a fashionable congregation

Grace Phillimore, his sister, about twenty, pretty and fashionably dressed

Miss Heneage, his aunt, in her sixties, relying on the influence of a large and steady income

William Sudley, his cousin, thoroughly insignificant in appearance but relying on his travels

Mrs. Vida Phillimore, his divorced wife

Brooks, Mrs. Phillimore's footman

Benson, her maid

John Karslake, a sportsman, specializing in horses

Nogam, his valet

Sir Wilfrid Cates-Darby, an English sportsman and connoisseur of choice femininity

Tim Fiddler, an English horse trainer

Thomas, the Phillimores' family servant

Choirboys

TIME: About 1906.

PLACE: New York City.

MUSICAL HIGHLIGHT: "Epithalamis."

HISTORICAL NOTE: A notable dramatic development of the theme of divorce at a time when divorce was just emerging as a serious threat to American social life. Outstanding in literary and dramatic quality, and as penetrating, perceptive satire. First performed at the Lyric Theatre, New York, November 19, 1906, with Marion Lea (the author's wife) as Vida, Mrs. Fiske as Cynthia, and George Arliss as Sir Wilfrid. The son of S. Weir Mitchell, American novelist, Langdon Mitchell also dramatized Thackeray's *Vanity Fair* in a play called *Becky Sharp* (1899), successfully acted by Mrs. Fiske.

ACT I

In the living room of Philip's house at 19-A Washington Square, the table is set for tea and the *Evening Post*, symbolic of the household's conservatism, is on the table. The topic for Miss Heneage and Miss Phillimore is how best to announce Philip's wedding on the next day, since both parties to be married have suffered divorce. Grace Phillimore's cousin, Sudley, drops by to expatiate on his recent trip to Cairo and to condemn the impending wedding as quite improper. When he hears that Cynthia's fortune is in the neighborhood of fifteen million dollars he is somewhat soothed. Philip, having decided in favor of his divorced wife a lawsuit brought by a dressmaker, comes in after a rugged day, grateful for Cynthia's calming nature. In the afternoon papers is the story of John Karslake's bankruptcy, making necessary the sale of his horses, his ex-wife's (Cynthia's) jewels, and her portrait by Sargent. Matthew arrives, demonstrating the social urbanity which accounts for his success with a fashionable religious congregation. Previously and caustically introduced by William, who noted her party in Cairo exclusively for divorcees, Vida comes in to discuss with her former husband (Philip) some B. and O. stocks they hold in common. She is quite gracious to John, who has come to see Philip on business, but who positively refuses to sell either to Philip or Cynthia his favorite racehorse, Cynthia K. Shocking Matthew, Cynthia tries to persuade Philip to lend John money to bet on a big race. Sir Wilfrid calls and is much flustered by the interrelationship of names and individuals, those divorced, those about to be married, and those unattached. He concludes that Americans are divorce-crazy, and that New York is bounded

162

on the north, south, east, and west by the state of Divorce. Flirting with Cynthia, he tries to get her not to marry her sober second choice, whom she obviously does not love, and to substitute him. Before the session breaks up, Cynthia has promised to meet John next morning (she is to be married at three in the afternoon) to see Cynthia K., the racehorse, and Vida has dated John for eleven and Sir Wilfrid for twelve at her apartment. John, en route to a dinner for his creditors, invites the company along, but only Vida and Sir Wilfrid accept. When John leaves, Philip wonders if the Creator can give any good reason for having made John. On her side, Cynthia, having listened to the horribly catty talk of the Phillimore household, lets go with a burst of hysterical laughter.

ACT II

Next morning, at Vida's apartment (furnished to please an empty-headed, pleasure-loving, fashionable woman), Vida briefs her servants on her two engagements. She gets John discussing his views on marriage—"three parts love and seven parts forgiveness of sins." John admits that he has been checking the validity of his divorce from Cynthia. On the other hand, Vida forces him into declaring a mad affection for her and a hatred for his former wife. Just as they are "near Eden" alone and losing, in Vida's phrase, the key under a rose bush, the footman Brooks announces Sir Wilfrid, but Benson, the maid, corrects with "your dressmaker, ma'am." John agrees to hide in Vida's clubroom on condition that he is let out by twelve for the sheriff's sale and later for the races. Vida uses her regular tactics on Sir Wilfrid, but the best she gets from him is that Cynthia is first in his heart and she a good second. Even so, Sir Wilfrid is in the act of proposing when Cynthia sweeps in. She has seen Fiddler and the horse nearby and wants to talk with John. When they do talk, her speech declares her disgust for him, but her nervous manner suggests she is still in love. She finally bets him the wedding gown against Cynthia K. that he does not have the nerve to come to the wedding at three and give her away. As a sportsman, he accepts. Philip comes by and is sent away empty-handed by Sir Wilfrid, who later begs Cynthia again to go the races with him that afternoon. Because John tells her this invitation is out of the question, Cynthia goes with Sir Wilfrid, ordering John to send Philip a telegram postponing the wedding until half-past seven.

ACT III

It is now 9:40 P.M. at the Phillimore's home, and no Cynthia. The choirboys have been given supper; the whole family feels completely disgraced. Cynthia has sent a second telegram saying she will arrive by ten. Arriving as promised, in the company of Sir Wilfrid, and even defending her racing escapade, she demands that Philip marry her. John is there also. Philip will marry her, but is outraged at the effrontery of John and Sir Wilfrid. Vida also arrives and tells John that since he obviously still cares for Cynthia, his best point is to court Vida openly. John agrees. After Cynthia comes back in, Vida flirts outrageously with John, even fainting in his arms; but when Cynthia is about to sprinkle her best Paris gown, Vida revives. Very shortly, however, Sir Wilfrid takes Vida away for champagne and lobster. John leaves with them after being explicitly told by Cynthia that Vida is not the woman for him. John says: "How dare you look me in the face with the eyes I once kissed and pretend the least regard for me?" He follows this statement with a bitter condemnation. Result is that Cynthia, after a few moments, once again kicks over the traces. Telling Philip she cannot marry him as she must go to prevent John's marrying Vida, she leaves the bridal party, causing Matthew to throw up his hands. This was the signal for the choirboys to begin singing: they burst lustily into "Enduring love; sweet end of strife!/Oh, bless this happy man and wife!"

ACT IV

At John's study and smoking room, kept exactly as Cynthia left it when she broke up her marriage with John, Matthew has come by and performed the marriage rites for Vida and Sir Wilfrid. Fiddler tells John that Cynthia K. has a touch of malaria, and further that John is to call his lawyer. When Cynthia arrives, Fiddler says the marriage is over—Cynthia taking this to mean the marriage of Vida and John. Seeing Vida and Sir Wilfrid, however, she learns the truth. Vida, in kindliness, hopes she has not married Philip, whom she describes as a tomb. Sir Wilfrid invites her to his English estate at Traynham, where, he says, there will soon be a covey of jolly little Cates-Darbys. Philip is outside with a hansom to take her back, but she firmly declines. Left with John, Cynthia reviews again the reason for their misalliance. They drink claret together and rediscover old memories. Only the fear of scandal at her remaining so late in John's house overshadows Cynthia's pleasure. But John finally tells her (news from his lawyer) that they are still married. Handing her a glass of benedictine he asks her to toast with it. In the glass is her wedding ring, which he slides out and places on her finger.

40

AUGUSTUS THOMAS (1857–1934)

The Witching Hour (1907)

Realistic drama of mental telepathy in four acts

MAIN CHARACTER AND THEME: How *Jack Brookfield*, a professional gambler, becomes involved in a murder case, politics, and his own strong efforts to overcome a gambler's way of life through his use of extrasensory perception.

OTHER CHARACTERS:

Jo, a Negro servant

Tom Denning, a fat indolent type

Harvey, an old Negro servant

Mrs. Alice Campbell, Jack's sister

Mrs. Helen Whipple, Clay's mother

Viola, Alice's daughter, an athletic Kentucky girl of nineteen

Clay Whipple, twenty

Frank Hardmuth, thirty-five, assistant district attorney

Lew Ellinger

Justice Prentice and *Justice Henderson* of the United States Supreme Court

Colonel Bayley

Mr. Emmett, a reporter

TIME: 1907.

PLACE: Louisville, Kentucky; Washington, D.C.

HISTORICAL NOTE: First performed at Hackett's Theatre, New York, November 18, 1907, for 212 performances. Followed the great excitement in America about parapsychological investigation that was one of the results of the founding by Sir William Barrett of the Society for Psychical Research in England in 1882. Thomas gained private information on the subject through being the press agent for Washington

Irving Bishop, a "thought-reader," in 1889. As a playwright, Thomas was prodigiously productive, writing or adapting seventy plays. Many of these dealt with the geographical and social regionalism of distinctive American states, such as Alabama, Arizona, Colorado, Indiana and Missouri.

ACT I

In Jack Brookfield's luxurious library, with such cultural appendages as a Corot, a Poe-esque bust of Minerva surmounted by a bronze raven, the Antommarchi death mask of Napoleon, and bronzes of Beethoven and Dante, Tom Denning comes looking for a game. Jack tells him no game until his lady guests go. When Jack offers cigarettes to the ladies, Alice says he is confusing Kentucky ladies with his Eastern friends. Harvey has "brewed" terrapin for the group. Two things about Jack are resurrected from the past: his great (vain) effort to win Helen and his mesmeric endowment.

When his sister Alice takes the others for a tour of Jack's gorgeous place, Clay Whipple wants to know what Frank, the assistant district attorney, was saying to Viola in the box at the theatre. Loving her madly, Clay has already asked Jack (her guardian) for her hand. In Clay's arms, Viola says "I will." Clay now insists they are engaged, but her mother Alice wants them to wait until Clay is definitely established in his architectural firm. Helen tells Alice that gambling broke up her romance with Jack. Helen and Alice discuss the proposed betrothal, including the fact that Clay is gambling with Jack's friends. Frank pushes Jack for his support in getting Viola to marry him. Jack tells him that besides the difference in their ages, Frank lacks the required character and morals; for example, he cheats the law he is sworn to support by permitting Jack's gambling emporium. Also Jack warns him that some day the truth will come out about who murdered the governor-elect: he does not want Viola mixed up in it.

Helen comes in to report that Tom is annoying Clay. Jack tells her he still hopes to win her back, even after twenty years; Helen says her views are unchanged. Justice Prentice comes to buy Jack's Corot; as they bargain about the price, each reveals a capacity for telepathy. Upon leaving, Justice Prentice tells Jack he has a strong psychic, i.e., hypnotic ability. Tom, now almost drunk, continues to tease Clay, using a scarf pin with a cat's eye, to which Clay has a compulsive aversion. In a frenzy, Clay swings a large ivory paper knife blindly and strikes Tom, who falls dead. Jack holds everything *in statu quo* until the doctor reports; after that, Clay will have the credit himself of notifying the police.

ACT II

In the library-living room of Justice Prentice in Washington, D.C., over a rubber game of chess, Prentice and Henderson discuss the Clay Whipple case, which has reached the highest court because the trial judge, needing to limit attendance, had the sheriff issue tickets of admission. Prentice leans toward rejecting a new trial; Henderson toward ordering one. Shortly after Henderson's departure, Jack brings in Helen and Viola to see Prentice. Prentice agrees that clairvoyance is definitely not a "bughouse" theory. Experimentally, Prentice cures Jack's headache. Helen introduces herself as the daughter of the Margaret Price whom Prentice knew years ago, and about whom that evening he had had intensive memories. She shows the justice a letter he wrote to Margaret, enclosing a spray of mignonette. Helen revives in Prentice's mind the story of a duel he fought with Henry Boland because the latter had frightened Margaret with a cat's-eye jewel. Helen begins to plead for Clay, who is under sentence of death. Prentice begs her not to, since the case is before the court. But Helen persuades him by discussing only the cat's-eye aversion, which in Margaret amounted almost to insanity, and which was handed down to her grandson, Clay.

Prentice is now convinced the case must be remanded and says the letter they have brought will be new evidence at the new trial. Asking for Margaret's handkerchief and receiving it, he muses, after the others have gone, over the presence of Margaret, there in the room, directing a decision of the United States Supreme Court. He recites Bret Harte's lines: "The delicate odor of mignonette. . . ."

ACT III

Jack confesses to Alice that he is working telepathically on *one* man on the jury he thinks is a friend; she calls his work spiritualism and lunacy. Frank promises to kill Jack if the newspapers print the story that Frank engineered the assassination of Scovill (the governor-elect). Not at all frightened, Jack accuses Frank of hounding Clay through two murder trials to even the score of his rejection by Viola, and to help his campaign for governor. Frank gone, Jack explains to Alice that he had to release the story now because if Clay is

168

reconvicted, Frank might be governor when the case comes up for clemency. Viola reports that the jury has asked for new instructions, expects to deliver a verdict within an hour, and will be happy to return to their homes. Prentice is impressed by their using the phrase "to their homes" on the ground that this is a kindly thought, not the thought of people about to convict. Viola gives Jack a note from Clay's lawyer, saying that Frank will shoot Jack on sight. Lew reports that Jack's charges have upset Frank's smooth control of the gubernatorial convention. Prentice and Jack think the telepathic commotion will filter through the mental screen and kill Frank's chances with the jury: 500,000 minds on twelve. Clay shows up, acquitted. Frank rushes in and thrusts a derringer against Jack's body; Jack tells him he cannot shoot the gun. The derringer drops from his hands. He wants to know how Jack did this to him.

ACT IV

The reporter Emmett wants Clay to report Frank's trial for his paper, if Frank is captured under the warrant out for him. Clay sorrowfully refuses, in spite of the kindness of the paper to him. In an experiment to help Clay, Jack tells him he holds the cat's-eye in his hand and wants Clay to put his hand over it, too. Through terrible vibrations, Clay does so. Jack then tells Clay that he was holding only his night key. He then orders Clay to go to the table drawer and take out the pin, which Clay does.

Lew has treed Frank: he wants to capture and turn him in for the big reward money. Jack sends Clay and Viola with a note to pick up Frank: he explains to Helen that, though a bit dangerous, this is the way to overcome fears.

By naming cards from the deck telepathically, Jack illustrates to Lew how he had won at gambling all along without knowing it. Now that he knows, he no longer cares to do it. He believes many people unconsciously have the ability. Viola and Clay bring Frank back. Jack is going to get Frank out of the state because just as he identified Lew's cards because he could read the thoughts of them in Lew's mind, so he had thought of Scovill's assassination the exact way it was done; and thus, Frank and he were unconscious conspirators, he the more guilty because he had always held great influence over Frank. Jack once more proposes to Helen ("Will you stand by *me* while I make my fight?"). This time she gives her hand: "You've made your fight, Jack, and you've won."

41

EUGENE WALTER (1874–1941)

The Easiest Way (1909)

Naturalistic drama in four acts

MAIN CHARACTER AND THEME: The attempt of *Laura Murdock*, an actress experiencing her first true love, to escape the demimonde existence into which she has fallen through having little ability and much girlish beauty.

OTHER CHARACTERS:

Elfie St. Clair, former chorus girl, mistress of a rich man

Annie, Laura's colored maid

Willard Brockton, forty-six, New York speculator, Laura's sponsor

John Madison, twenty-seven, for-mer newspaperman, determined to get rich quick in business

Jim Weston, forty-five, theatrical agent

Mrs. Williams, Laura's hostess on her Colorado vacation

Mrs. Farley, Laura's landlady

Offstage voices

TIME: About 1907.

PLACE: Ranch house near Colorado Springs, Colorado; New York City.

MUSICAL HIGHLIGHT: "Bon-Bon Buddie, My Chocolate Drop."

HISTORICAL NOTE: Brilliant and comprehensive analysis of New York City life just after the turn of the twentieth century, especially of that phase of the tenderloin district which includes the demimondaine and their sponsors in the business world. Play ranks with novels of Dreiser and takes cues from the plays of Ibsen and his English followers.

ACT I

Will Brockton shows his devotion for Laura by going from New York to Colorado to bring her home from vacation. He hears her say, nevertheless, that she will no longer be his mistress because she has fallen in love. When, however, he offers to back her in a new play, with the understanding that their old arrangement continue, she is tempted. Her true love, John Madison, knowing her past, proposes marriage, but he wants to wait until he has earned enough money to support her in style. Laura joyfully accepts, agreeing to get a job and, especially, to be faithful. Consequently, she rejects Will's offer and tells him good-by for good.

Later John confronts Will and expresses his contempt for men who make their money gambling and who prey on women. Amused by John's contempt, Will assures him he cannot support a girl like Laura—he will never earn money fast enough. In parting, though, both agree that if Laura should return to Will, she must tell John when and why.

ACT II

For six months Laura searches desperately for a job; everywhere she is thwarted. She has moved into Mrs. Farley's cheap theatrical rooming house, patches her clothes, has little to eat, and is far behind in her rent. Every day she gets a loving letter from John, but no money and no promise of his business success. Besides John's letters and his photographs about the room, the only other boost to her flagging morale is the theatrical agent Jim Weston, who lives in the rooming house and is equally destitute.

A visit from Elfie, showily dressed and well fed, shakes Laura's resolution. She finally breaks down completely when Mrs. Farley deliberately embarrasses her by demanding the back rent while Elfie is present, expecting Laura to get the money from Elfie. It turns out that Elfie is Will's messenger and that Will's influence had shut the door on her acting opportunities. When Will arrives, Laura surrenders. He gives her a roll of five $100 bills. But he also makes her write a letter to John in which she says she does not love him and is returning to Will. Later, she secretly burns this letter.

ACT III

Back in a rich apartment, Laura is unhappy and resentful of Will, in spite of good acting roles and general affluence. Will reads in the newspaper that John has reached Chicago as representative of a mining syndicate operating in the Nevada gold fields. Almost simultaneously, Laura receives a telegram which she tries to hide. Forcing the telegram from her, Will reads that John is en route to New York to marry Laura. She confesses that she burned the letter of renunciation and has continued her correspondence with John. On her solemn promise to tell John the whole story, Will agrees to leave her alone with him. But following the advice of Elfie, who insists that Laura owes Will nothing and owes herself a decent chance, Laura joins John in making plans to marry immediately and to occupy their new home in the West. John promises to come back for her in two hours. When Will returns, she is packing. Will knows she is lying when she says she has told John the full truth. Hearing Will declare he will warn John against her treachery, Laura grows hysterical. She repeatedly shouts that she is going to be married and is entitled to happiness.

ACT IV

Returning for her, John asks only her assurance that the rumor he has just heard of her and Will being back on the old basis is untrue. She promptly gives that assurance. Using his own key, Will enters and greets John casually. In an angry attack John is about to shoot Will when Laura prevents him. Laura now tries desperately to get John to understand that she stumbled only because of extreme destitution. He understands that, but he cannot forgive her lying to him. When Will tells him of the burned letter, John views Laura with pity. He tells her she is unmoral and incapable of decent sentiments. As Laura seizes her gun to kill herself, John merely calls Annie to observe that he is blameless; Laura throws the gun away. Ignoring her pleadings, John abandons her. In pitiful bravado, Laura unpacks her things and plans a gay, reckless evening. As the hurdy-gurdy in the street plays the grotesquely suggestive song, "Bon-Bon Buddie, My Chocolate Drop," Laura, resigned and hopeless, cries out: "O God—O my God."

42

VICTOR HERBERT (1859–1924)
with lyrics and book by
RIDA JOHNSON YOUNG

Naughty Marietta (1910)

Operetta in two acts

MAIN CHARACTER AND THEME: The adventures of *Marietta d'Altena*, an Italian contessa, who comes to French New Orleans as a casket girl to avoid marriage with an ancient, undesirable suitor. (Casket girls were sent to Louisiana by the French government to marry the French settlers.)

OTHER CHARACTERS:

Captain Richard Warrington (Captain Dick), leader of a band of adventure-seeking Americans

Simon O'Hara, his Jewish servant, who masquerades as an Irish-American

Sir Harry Blake, Irish adventurer, friend of Captain Dick

Etienne Grandet, son of the Lieutenant Governor (Acting Governor), also in disguise the famous buccaneer, Bras Prique

Lieutenant Governor Grandet, known as "Monsieur By-and-By"

Rudolfo, an Italian street musician, keeper of the Marionette Theatre

Florenze, secretary to the Lieutenant Governor

Manuelo, Bras Prique's right hand man, a pirate

A Handsome Indian

Adah, a quadroon, slave and sweetheart of Etienne

Lizette, a casket girl

Marie le Valleau, a quadroon, known as the Voodoo Queen

Nanette, *Felice*, and *Fanchon*, flower girls

Graziella and *Franchesca*, daughters of Rudolfo

Sambo, the back-scratcher
An East Indian, Night watchman,
Lamplighter, Sacristan, Knife
grinder, Flower girls, Street

sweepers, Quadroons, Dancers,
Captain Dick's Adventurers,
Pirates, Mexicans, Spaniards,
Indians, Others

TIME: 1750.

PLACE: New Orleans (under the French).

MUSICAL HIGHLIGHTS: "Italian Street Song"; "Voodoo Song"; "Captain Dick with Followers" (better known as "Tramp, Tramp, Tramp"); "Entrance of Governor"; "Casket Girls and Men"; "Dream Song" (really "Ah, Sweet Mystery of Life"); "It Never Can Be Love"; "If I Were Anybody Else but Me"; "Neath the Southern Moon"; "I'm Falling in Love with Someone"; "You Marry a Marionette"; "New Orleans Jeunesse"; "The Loves of New Orleans"; "Opening of the Ball"; "In the Sweet By-and-By"; "Live for Today"; "It's Pretty Soft for Simon"; "Naughty Marietta."

HISTORICAL NOTE: One of the thirty operettas of Victor Herbert, Irish-born but thoroughly American composer, who supplied a unique chapter in American theatrical history with such musical stories (besides the present most successful one) as *Mlle. Modiste* (1905), *The Red Mill* (1906), and *Princess Pat* (1915). Many of his libretti, including that of *Naughty Marietta*, were written by Rida Johnson Young, who also wrote the lyrics for Ernest R. Ball's "Mother Machree" and book and lyrics for Sigmund Romberg's *Maytime*. The story of *Naughty Marietta* is basically historical, combining the importation of casket girls as wives for colonists, carried out by Bienville from 1728 to 1750, with the exploits of such brilliant figures as Lafitte, who combined piracy with respectable business operations, and who, like Bras Prique, operated both in New Orleans and in Barataria Bay, about eighty miles to the south. They also commanded the very best political connections.

With due credit to Miss Johnson, much of the drama of *Naughty Marietta* is in the tension, lilt, and substance of the songs by Herbert, which have remained famous even to those who do not know their words because they tell a story all their own. *Naughty Marietta* was played in Syracuse and Buffalo before opening at the New York Theatre, New York, November 7, 1910, with Emma Trentini as Marietta and Orville Harrold as Captain Dick. It was enthusiastically received both in New York and on a national tour, in which Herbert joined.

174

ACT I

The Place d'Armes is picturesque with tall moss-covered trees, a levee with a glimpse of the Mississippi, arcaded booths for sellers of flowers and confections, and passing people of various nationalities—Mexican, Indian, Spanish, Negroes, among others. There is a gateway entrance to St. Louis Cathedral. Beside the large fountain, which is dry, beggars sleep.

As Etienne arrives, the lively girls tell him that New Orleans lost its thrill as Little Paris while he was away. The news is that Bras Prique has been raging and a mysterious voice has been heard, beginning a melody but never finishing it. When Adah whispers to Etienne that the Voodoo Queen knows him to be Bras Prique and is working on his image with sharp daggers and burning candles, Etienne says he likes the added danger. Manuelo passes a message to Etienne; he pretends not to know the pirate but gives him a secret reply.

As pirates get their knives ground, the "Tramp, Tramp, Tramp" of Captain Dick's men is heard approaching. These Canadian woodsmen, Tennessee mountaineers, Kentucky farmers, and Indians are colorfully dressed and rugged in appearance. Captain Dick lets it be known that they are on a double mission: to capture Bras Prique and to get wives from among the casket girls.

In pomp and state, the lieutenant governor marches in. He announces that every would-be groom must deposit one hundred pounds of tobacco. Ceremoniously, Captain Dick asks the governor to sign the king's warrant allowing his men to bring in Bras Prique. When things crowd him, the governor resorts to sleep (from which he can be awakened only by bottle-popping) and to his favorite phrase, "by-and-by."

The others gone, Etienne hears a snatch from a dream song, but sees no singer. The snatch has just two phrases, "Ah, sweet mystery of life" and "secret of it all," and then it trails off. When Etienne leaves, Marietta comes out of the fountain urn and introduces herself by singing "Naughty Marietta." Captain Dick intercepts her as she tries to get back to her hiding place. In conversation, both agree that love and marriage are for fools. Marietta confesses to having run thousands of miles to get away from marriage, but as a casket girl she has a problem of survival. Yielding to her begging that he provide her with a disguise, Captain Dick calls Rudolfo, who owes him a favor, and arranges for Marietta to wear the disguise of

Rudolfo's son. Before she leaves, Marietta says that the man who claims her heart will be able to finish her dream melody; Captain Dick assures her he will never try.

Meanwhile, the secretary has given the governor a message from the king demanding the return of the Contessa d'Altena, who ran away to New Orleans by bribing a casket girl to be substituted in her place. Afraid that he will merit the king's displeasure by not finding the contessa, the governor provides himself with a whipping boy, namely Simon. In a short while, Rudolfo and his band—among them Marietta dressed like a boy—return to sing a street song of old Napoli, "Zing, Zing." The Governor announces ten thousand francs reward for the contessa, who can be identified by her attempts to finish an unfinished melody. Captain Dick rebukes Marietta for inveigling him into a dangerous position. As people fight to capture Marietta, the cathedral bell saves her. Carted away by Rudolfo, Marietta throws a kiss to Captain Dick.

ACT II (*two scenes*)

Marietta has switched from Rudolfo's lost son to his daughter. Dressed as a girl, she flirts with Captain Dick and Etienne alternately. She tries to get Rudolfo to finish the song, promising, if he does, to love him like fire. Etienne insists that she come that night to the Quadroon Ball; Captain Dick forbids her; when Etienne tells her that Captain Dick is taking Adah, she decides to go. Adah, warned by the Voodoo Queen that Etienne will desert her for Marietta, glares at Marietta; whereupon Etienne says he will sell Adah, for her jealousy. Adah is now set on revenge. Marietta, on the other hand, teases Captain Dick into trying to kiss her, but runs away before he can. Rudolfo promises Captain Dick to prevent her going to the ball by locking her up; Rudolfo cannot find her.

In the ballroom, gaiety reigns—"Gambling, gambling, racing, dicing," according to the song. Etienne swears that no man will be allowed to go home sober. Quadroons sing: "We Are the Loves of New Orleans." Lizette sings: "I Wait for Mister Right."

Dressed in a Pierrette costume, Marietta comes in through the window, masked. According to the tradition of the ball, men crowd around to unmask her, and she is frightened. When Captain Dick comes forward to take her home, she dances off with Etienne. Later, Etienne reveals himself as Bras Prique, reveals his father as his co-conspirator and protector for half

176

the spoils, and suggests to his father that they strike up an alliance with Italy by having him marry Marietta and declare Louisiana a republic, with the governor as dictator. Bras Prique's men are ready to move in.

Captain Dick sings of a monumental change going on inside him: "I'm Falling in Love with Someone." At the auction, occasioned by Etienne's promise to sell Adah so that Marietta will marry him, Captain Dick outbids everyone for Adah. Angered and jealous, Marietta announces herself as the Contessa d'Altena and as the affianced of Etienne, who demands that the wedding proceed at once.

In exchange for Captain Dick's setting her free, Adah tells of Etienne's true name, Bras Prique, tattooed on his arm. As Simon sings, "It's pretty soft for Simon," Etienne sends for the priest, to get married. Captain Dick rips open Etienne's sleeve and unfolds his true identity; he then demands that the governor arrest the pirate. But the governor requires Simon, as whipping boy, to accept his son's punishment—as a kindness, he can be shot rather than hanged. Etienne promises to fight Captain Dick *after* the wedding. Now that all is revealed, especially Captain Dick's freeing of Adah, Marietta no longer wants to marry Etienne; the governor says she must.

Outside, Captain Dick completes the dream melody; Marietta joins him in singing and goes into his arms. When Sir Harry, having captured Etienne, brings him forward, Captain Dick says: "Let him go. I have won all I want in the world." Captain Dick and Marietta gloriously sing their "sweet mystery of life." Afterwards, Rudolfo leads the company in a finishing "Zing, Zing" song.

43

PERCY MACKAYE (1875–1956)

The Scarecrow (1910)

*Symbolical drama—called a tragedy of
the ludicrous in four acts*

MAIN CHARACTER AND THEME: Efforts of *Lord Ravensbane*, born of the machinations of a New England witch and the Devil, to rise from scarecrow to man.

OTHER CHARACTERS:

Justice Gilead Merton

Goody Rickby, known also as "Blacksmith Bess," who is in converse with the Power of Darkness

Dickon (the Devil)

Rachel Merton, niece of the justice

Ebenezer, Goody's dumb servant and Dickon's contact man

Mistress Cynthia Merton

Richard Talbot, Esquire, betrothed to Rachel

Sir Charles Reddington, the lieutenant governor

Mistress Reddington and *Amelia Reddington*, his daughters

Captain Bugby, the governor's secretary

Minister Dodge

Mistress Dodge, his wife

Rev. Master Rand and *Rev. Master Todd*, both of Harvard College

Micah, a servant

TIME: Late seventeenth century.

PLACE: A town in Massachusetts, with the colonial designs in architecture and furniture and the high elms that characterize the New England landscape.

HISTORICAL NOTE: Son of Steele MacKaye, popular American playwright of the 1880's, Percy MacKaye became a highly respected personality in the theatre. Besides writing straight dramas, including an historical play, *Jeanne d'Arc* (1906), he also wrote masques, pageants, operas, folk plays (especially of the Kentucky mountains), fantasies (especially in a New England setting), and a significant biography of his father (*Epoch*, 1927). He fought hard for a deeper appreciation of the educational values in playwriting and dramatic production. *The Scarecrow* is based on *Feathertop*, a story by Hawthorne.

ACT I

In a blacksmith shop, hammer rings on steel as Goody with the help of Dickon makes a sturdy scarecrow. Although fearful of the witch-hunters of nearby Salem, Rachel comes to pick up her purchase—a large mirror framed in old gold, embroidered with peaked caps and crescent moons. Goody assures her the glass will reveal all truth, although Rachel pretends to want the mirror for amusement only. Receiving her money, Goody guarantees delivery by dumb Ebenezer, her servant. Richard, who has followed Rachel, begs her not to deal with such people, and threatens Goody. Once Rachel has taken Richard away, Justice Merton comes. Goody reminds him of their amour years ago (when though she was pregnant, he banished her) and shows him the coat he left. He threatens her with hanging, but wavers momentarily before Dickon's threat to expose his immoral past. His departure calls Goody to grieve over the death of her bastard son, who would now be twenty-one. Dickon tries his hand at activating the scarecrow they have built out of broomstick-gourd-carrot-turnip-beet (the anatomy), bellows (the lungs), feather duster (the peruke), and corncob (the pipe); he succeeds. Dubbing the new creature Lord Ravensbane, he has him address Goody as mother, and leads him forth to sue for Rachel's hand. The nearby crows give loud acclamation.

ACT II

In Justice Merton's parlor, Richard stands before the Glass of Truth and comes off very well. Justice orders the servant Micah to remove this symbol of witchcraft; before he can do so, he must announce the visit of a nobleman,

Ravensbane, and his tutor (Dickon). Dickon bears a letter from Ravensbane's mother requesting Rachel's hand for her son who is heir presumptive to a fortune of £20,000. Ravensbane describes his home plot truthfully, but Dickon's explanations turn it into an ancient English castle with heirlooms. *Sub rosa*, Dickon informs the justice that here is his illegitimate son. The justice then tries to persuade Ravensbane to accept money and depart, just after Richard chides Rachel about taking too quickly to European fashions of smoking and flirtation. It is noticeable that Ravensbane has smoked perpetually on his morning call and has lost vitality when his pipe was removed. When Richard challenges Ravensbane to a duel, Ravensbane picks up and pockets the challenge glove, bows low to Rachel, and blows smoke in Richard's face.

ACT III

Under Dickon's instruction, Ravensbane offers flails as the weapon of the duel; the governor's secretary, Captain Bugby, Richard's second, considers the idea a stroke of genius. When Richard has later contemptuously refused to fight, Ravensbane woos Rachel ardently. She drives Richard out, receives Ravensbane's silk tassel, and says she will wear it at the reception if she decides to become his wife. Justice offers Dickon £10,000 to get Ravensbane off the premises, but before a deal can be arranged, the distinguished guests arrive, including the lieutenant governor, his daughters, and the masters from Harvard. Bugby has amused some of the guests with the story of the flails. At Dickon's instance, the justice presents Ravensbane as a soloist; the resultant crowlike song with crow chorus causes the audience to feel more and more the poisonous suspicion of witchcraft. Nevertheless, Rachel permits Ravensbane to fasten the tassel on her breast. At this moment, Richard pulls the curtain before the Glass of Truth and reveals Ravensbane to the company, but especially to himself, as a scarecrow. This realization is tragically important for Ravensbane, since for love of Rachel, Ravensbane had been defying Dickon and striving desperately to rise (above Richard's contempt) to manhood.

ACT IV

In his Hamletlike soliloquy, Ravenbane discourses not only upon the pangs of a scarecrow's realizing his true lowness, but also universally upon man's realizing his. The Image in the Glass will not let him forget the truth. He

180

turns to the moon, whose face, beautiful like Rachel's, beguiles him. He and the Image argue about his being a man:

> And prithee [says the Image] what's a man?
> Man's but a mirror,
> Wherein the imps and angels play charades,
> Make faces, mope, and pull each other's hair—
> Till crack! the sly urchin Death shivers the glass,
> And the bare coffin boards show underneath.

Ravensbane tries to kill the Image with an iron crosspiece from the fireplace. Assuring him that all mortals are ridiculous and despicable, Dickon tries to quiet him; he is nevertheless realizing himself more human by the moment. Noticing this point, Dickon informs him that although Rachel's mirror has given him soul, the breaking of the pipe will end everything about him. Goody comes by to tell Dickon that the hanging party is on the way to condemn the Glass and all who go with it. Dickon begs her not to worry.

Upon Ravensbane's insistence that he was born for Rachel, Dickon promises that he shall have Rachel for lover and wife if he behaves himself; to avoid pain to Rachel, he agrees to be silent. When the group arrives, Dickon tells them Goody has bewitched the mirror to get even with the justice; he sends them after her. When he turns to order the union between Rachel and Ravensbane, the latter commands silence and orders Dickon not to speak to his beloved. To Rachel he declares his love. Richard tells him that Rachel has again agreed to marry him, but Ravensbane says that he nevertheless owes all to her. With a noble speech, he breaks the pipe and chooses chaos and darkness. His dying words are, "Oh Rachel, could I have been a man—!" The Glass promptly shows him now to be a man. He asks whose is the image, and Rachel tells him it is his. With exalted joy he stands, announces "A man!" and topples over in death.

44

EDWARD SHELDON (1886–1946)

The Boss (1911)

Impressionistic drama in four acts

MAIN CHARACTER AND THEME: Impassioned desire of *Michael Regan* ("Shindy Mike"), who has risen from the social depths, to bargain his new-found wealth and power for the social status of an established but financially declining family through marriage.

OTHER CHARACTERS:

James D. Griswold, fifty, established contractor and social leader

Donald Griswold, his son, thirty

Emily Griswold, his daughter, twenty-eight, brilliant, beautiful, assured

Mitchell, the Griswold butler

Lawrence Duncan, Emily's society suitor

Davis, Regan's private secretary

Mrs. Cuyler, fashionable young woman

Gates, Mrs. Regan's butler

"Porky" McCoy, Regan's representative in the Fourth Ward

Scanlan, a Union representative

Archbishop Sullivan

A Cook, A French Maid, Lieutenant of Police, A Police Officer, Another Police Officer.

TIME: 1910.

PLACE: An Eastern lakeport (probably Detroit).

HISTORICAL NOTE: Educated as playwright under George Pierce Baker at Harvard, Sheldon developed a sure touch in the treatment of social and personal problems of representative Americans. *The Nigger* (1909) and *Lulu Belle* (with Charles MacArthur, 1926) treat of racial complications;

Salvation Nell (1908) and *Romance* (1913), of strong moral struggles. Sheldon was able to combine the idealistic and the practical in a keenly theatrical manner. According to Professor Quinn, Holbrook Blinn's Regan was masterly.

ACT I

Realizing that Regan, ex-barkeep and Irish tough, is on his way (through blackjacking and swindling) to control of the grain contracts in their city, which transports half of the wheat of Western fields to the world, the Griswolds, father and son, invite him to their home to try to make a deal to save their own contracting business. Emily comes in as they wait for Regan. She has been doing charitable work in Regan's district—the Fourth Ward. She is most distressed that the men there spend their money on drink and the women lack funds for food and for their children's clothes. Donald tells her why: if an employee does not leave half his pay in a Regan-owned saloon on Saturday night, he gets his quit-notice on Monday morning. Emily swears not to stop until she has a club house for the men and a cooking school for the women. If, says Donald, they can keep Regan away from the big contracts for a month, Donald can get his eight thousand men unionized, and on strike, and Regan will be ruined. On the other hand, Emily has been riding with Regan that very morning, and thinks him nice.

Duncan is shown in. He proposes to Emily, and is rejected because he shows no social responsibility. In the conversation, he disclaims responsibility for having sent her four dozen American beauty roses (at twenty-five dollars per dozen). Emily tells Duncan "her man" is out there in the wings somewhere.

Regan arrives; he tries to tip the butler. As he and the Griswolds talk, he shows full knowledge of the Griswolds' status and of the jam they are in. He is even aware that some of Griswold's bank dealings might win him a jail term—what with the outcry raised by the muckraker press. Griswold protests his honesty; Regan reminds him that it's what people think you do that counts. Brushing aside all their suggestions for delay, he boldly offers a merger, and agrees that the Griswold methods should predominate. There is one proviso: Emily must marry him. The men are about to throw him out, when he gets the opportunity to put his proposition flatly to Emily. She also is about to reject him disdainfully when she learns that if the deal fails the banks in the Fourth Ward will go under, carrying all the savings of the Fourth Warders. Then she accepts Regan, but on condition that it be a marriage in name only: "Everything stops at the church door." Regan considers this deal sharp, but accepts. Later, she asks to be let off; he refuses. They will be married at three the next day.

ACT II

Six months later, in his library, Regan shows his bravado by lighting his cigar with the copy of the *Record-Times* in which Donald tells how he unionized Regan's men and got them to strike. Emily is having a party. During the evening she rejects her husband's fabulous gift of a diamond frog with ruby eyes to celebrate their six months' anniversary. Porky reports that, according to orders, Hurley's Bar has been smashed; Porky is not spying on the union meeting because his wife just gave birth to a boy, who shall be named "Michael Regan Ignatius McCoy." Donald, whom Emily has not seen in five months, comes over to ask his sister to spy on her husband —he wants to know if and when Regan is importing Negroes from Georgia and Alabama to work the docks at one-fourth the white man's wage. Emily refuses—ashamed that Donald has broken his promise not to interfere, a part of her original agreement.

Scanlan, the union representative, tells Regan the union's demands, including a ten-hour day, their own saloon and no firings for not using Regan's, and a 10 per cent raise. Regan's answer is to knock Scanlan down. Emily vigorously protests. As the archbishop approaches, Regan hides the injured Scanlan. Regan rehashes old boyhood times with the archbishop. He promises to settle the strike by Sunday; he swears he knew nothing of the injury to Hurley when his bar was wrecked. When he has the archbishop almost convinced, Emily steps in to tell the latter of Regan's plan to import strikebreakers and of the injured Scanlan in the next room. Regan still tries to stop the archbishop from going to the strikers' mass meeting "to bury him," but the archbishop overwhelms him with the power of the Church. Later, Porky calls to tell him the archbishop is blasting him, to the cheers of the crowd. After accusing Emily of betrayal, he shouts, "I'll beat 'em yet!"

ACT III

Next morning at nine, Regan tells Emily he has been working industriously on a plan to turn the ocean grain traffic to Montreal, and he is succeeding.

184

He does not expect to make a profit, only to ruin the home city. Emily says she married him to save poor people and will not stand to see her sacrifice lost. Hysterically she says she's his wife and he must not do these things he has planned. "You lie!" says Regan. "Yer not my wife an' ye know it!" He tells her that had he received from her what his lowliest trucker receives— a woman to love him—things would have been different. She offers him a new bargain, but when he tries to kiss her, she stops him, with a cry of horror. Porky comes in to tell him that Donald, making a speech in Fourth Ward, was hit by a brick which Porky fired, and carried to the hospital in an undetermined condition. When this news gets out, a mob comes to get Regan, but the police interfere. Duncan takes Emily away, and Emily believes Regan guilty of ordering the attack on Donald in spite of his promise to give up all his schemes if she would stand by him. When she has gone, he pitifully proclaims his innocence. Finally, three plain-clothes policemen arrest him for assaulting Donald.

ACT IV

Three days later, in Regan's rooms at the police station, Regan dictates letters ending the Montreal prospect. His secretary Davis asks him not to give up so easily. Regan says he will be indicted for first-degree murder if Donald dies; he knows they will try to hang him. Porky comes in, most remorseful. He says he has confessed to his wife, and has come down to confess to the police that he is Donald's assailant. Regan roaringly forbids him. When Emily comes, Porky leaves quietly after shaking hands. She accepts Regan's offer to deed all the Fourth Ward mortgages to her: she is now boss of the Fourth Ward. In exchange, she tells him Donald is doing well. She begs him to forgive her for not believing in him: she will make up for everything; they will look ahead; she will be a real wife and helpmate for him. The inspector comes in to say that Porky has confessed, and Regan is free to go. Regan offers to free Emily so that both can start alone. Emily says she has just learned that she loves him. She sends for her chauffeur that she may drive her husband home. She has Regan straighten his hat, and then take it off. "Why?" says Regan. Half-laughing, half-crying, she replies: "Do you think I'm going to let you kiss me with it on?" He throws the hat across the room and catches her in his arms.

45

J. HARTLEY MANNERS (1870–1928)

Peg o' My Heart (1912)

Irish-American comedy in three acts

MAIN CHARACTER AND THEME: What happened when *Peg O'Connell*, a little Irish-American poor relation, a beautiful girl of eighteen with gleaming red hair, pits her simple ideals and spirited ways against the sophistication and moralistic crust of her cultured English relatives.

OTHER CHARACTERS:

Mrs. Monica Chichester, fifty, Peg's aunt

Ethel, Mrs. Chichester's daughter

Alaric, Mrs. Chichester's son

Christian Brent, twenty-five, married, pleasure-loving

Montgomery Hawkes, forty, a solicitor

Jerry, a gentleman who learns to like Peg

Jarvis, the footman

Bennett, the maid

Michael, an Irish terrier

TIME: Early 1900's, beginning on a June first.

PLACE: Regal Villa, Mrs. Chichester's old Tudor house in Scarborough, England.

MUSICAL HIGHLIGHTS: "Man, Dear"; "Valse Mauve."

HISTORICAL NOTE: Besides representing the unpredictability, vivacity, and humor of the Irish quality in American life, this drama is also suffused with a haunting poetic atmosphere. The play was dedicated to the author's sweetheart, who later became his wife, Miss Laurette Taylor. She acted in it 1,099 times: it became her most memorable vehicle and one of the most remarkable acting triumphs in American dramatic history. It opened in Los Angeles on May 26, 1912, for 101 performances; and in New York, at the Cort Theatre, December 20, 1912, for 604 performances. It later played a year in London. This was followed by tours by eight companies all over the United States for a total of 5,987 performances in three years. The author called the play "a comedy of youth" and of "Love's young dream."

ACT I: "The Coming of Peg"

The Chichesters learn that Gifford's Bank has failed: they are financially ruined. The daughter Ethel says she will teach; Alaric, the son, declares that he will put his hand to the plough. With disgust, Alaric remembers that Jerry comes that day—he and his family have taken a hill house nearby. Brent comes calling, presumably on the family but actually on Ethel. Telling her privately that he intends to separate from his wife, he offers her the chance to go away with him, promising to marry her later when he is legally free. She is tempted, but says that the longing for adventure has not yet risen within her. As they embrace, they do not see a strange beautiful girl of eighteen enter. She has some parcels and an unkempt disgraceful-looking Irish terrier. The girl refuses to tell who she is, saying only that she was told to wait; Ethel has her wait in the kitchen.

In the front of the house, the solicitor Hawkes is telling Mrs. Chichester about her brother's strange will. Under its terms, if Mrs. Chichester will undertake the upbringing of Margaret O'Connell, the daughter of her deceased sister and an impossible Irishman who lives in New York, she will be paid £1000 a year. If, after a year, Margaret is found to be unworthy, she will be returned to her father with a stipend of £250 annually for life. But if she proves worthy, her training will continue until she is twenty-one, at which time she will receive £5000 annually for life, and may do as she pleases.

At first, Mrs. Chichester refuses. At the family's request she reconsiders and accepts, since it will save them all from charity or the hatefulness of being poor relations. Hawkes warns her that the girl is not to know the conditions of the will except in a crisis. Margaret, who insists her name is Peg, is found in the kitchen and brought forth. She does not trust these relatives, especially when they separate her from her dog: she wants to return to her father, whom she does trust and adore. Her parcel breaks open—it contains a prayer book, a small Bible, a rosary, and a framed photograph of her mother. She is angry when her father is slurred. Immediately she earns Ethel's enmity by referring to the embrace in which Ethel was first seen. The family decide to isolate her from all company, especially from Jerry who is calling soon, until she is ready to be seen.

By a strange quirk, she and Jerry meet alone. Hearing her talk, he decides she is quite charming and tells her so. She talks of New York and old Ireland, of the lightning in the sky which kills according to the state of grace you are in, and of her father who can do anything but make money. Asked who he is, Jerry says he has been a doctor and a civil engineer in South America, but now he's a farmer. A moment later, she tells him she is going back to her father because "Sure it's easier to suffer the want of food than the want of love." Jerry persuades her to give them all a month's trial. When the others return, Jerry tells Alaric his cousin is adorable. Mrs. Chichester's anxious remark is, "She must be taught, and at once."

ACT II: "The Rebellion of Peg"

A month later, Peg, charmingly gowned, is the object of Brent's flirtations. When he tries to kiss her, she boxes his ears: Ethel sees a part of the scene and is disgusted with Brent. Brent nevertheless tries to get Ethel to agree to leave with him at once on a vacation trip to Norway, Moscow, and Siberia: he will await her answer at the hotel until one in the morning. At a family meeting to discuss what they shall tell Hawkes next day about Peg, the decision is hard to make: Peg tells them she disobeys so persistently because of the original sin in her. Later, watching Ethel, Peg becomes worried about the obvious anxiety displayed by "her model." Peg and Ethel have an argument, Ethel calling love sentimental rot, Peg describing it like this: "One day the world's all beautiful flowers and sweet music and sunshine. . . ." When Peg complains to Ethel about her interest in Brent, Ethel tells her never to speak to her again.

Jerry arrives in evening dress to take Ethel and Peg to a dance. Ethel immediately declines, pretending a headache. Peg asks Jerry not to ask permission of her aunt on her behalf because her aunt will say no, and she will have to disobey. Jerry does ask permission; Mrs. Chichester does refuse; and Peg, as she laughingly informs her aunt, does go anyway.

"Peg o' My Heart" (1912)

Returning from the dance, Peg sees Ethel, suitcase in hand, leaving to run away with Brent. Peg begs her not to do the most shameful thing a woman can do. With real sisterliness, she calls Ethel "Acushla." Before very long, Ethel is sobbing that she hates herself. Taking Ethel's bag, Peg assumes full responsibility when Mrs. Chichester discovers her—she does not want her aunt to know of Ethel's near-slip. But Jerry, who turns out to be Sir Gerald Adair, comes back and accepts his share of responsibility for Peg's misbehavior. Mrs. Chichester tells Peg she has disgraced them all. Ethel tries to confess, but faints. And Peg says next day she will go back to her father who "knows more about motherhood than any man in the world."

ACT III: "Peg o' My Heart"

Peg's leaving, of course, means the end of the Chichesters' regular income. At Mrs. Chichester's suggestion, Alaric proposes to Peg (he can suffer for £5000 a year): Peg laughs at his proposal and refuses him. Hawkes begs Peg to marry in England and uphold the dignity of her family (the Kingnorths). Even he proposes to her; but he at last agrees to get her steamer ticket.

As chief executor of the will, Jerry tells her the conditions and lets her decide. At first Peg asks her aunt, "You got paid for abusing me?" At last, she decides to stay. Jerry then announces that Gifford's Bank will reopen soon, and the Chichester fortune will be restored. Then Peg again decides to go. It begins to rain in torrents, with lightning and thunder. Fearful of the lightning, Peg returns from going toward the train station, deathly white, trembling. She asks Jerry to shut the storm out. He says he loves her, and will she be his wife. She asks if he has really proposed. He says yes. She says he, with his title, will be ashamed of her. His answer is simply, "I love you." She answers, "I love you, too, I do." The lightning continues. Jerry asks her what her father will say. Peg answers that he has always said: "Sure, there's nothing half so sweet in life as love's young dream!" As the thunder crashes, Peg hides her head on Jerry's shoulder.

BRONSON HOWARD (1842–1908)

The Henrietta (1887; 1913)

Business and society drama in four acts

MAIN CHARACTER AND THEME: Crisis in the business and romantic affairs of *Nicholas Van Alstyne, Senior*, called Old Nick in the Street, who for years has dominated Wall Street, his family, and much of high New York society.

OTHER CHARACTERS:

Dr. Parke Wainwright

Nicholas Van Alstyne, Jr.

Bertie Van Alstyne, his brother

Lord Arthur Trelawney

The Reverend Doctor Murray Hilton, a Shepherd

Watson Flint, a young broker

Musgrave, an old clerk

Mrs. Cornelia Opdyke, a handsome widow

Mrs. Rose Van Alstyne, wife of Nicholas, Jr.

Agnes, her sister, in love with Bertie

Lady Mary Trelawney, daughter of Nicholas, Sr.

TIME: About 1900.

PLACE: The Van Alstyne residence (with private office), and the office of Watson Flint and Company on the New York Stock Exchange; both in New York City.

HISTORICAL NOTE: Bronson Howard is sometimes called the first professional playwright in America. His appeal to audiences was great; his dramatic skill somewhat less than great. In farce-comedy, with *Saratoga; or Pistols for Seven* (1870); in social and international drama, with *The Banker's Daughter* (1878); and in Civil War drama, with *Shenandoah*

(1888), he was equally at home. The play was a triumph at its original production in 1887, running sixty-eight weeks and earning nearly half a million dollars. Somewhat revised in 1913 by Winchell Smith and Victor Mapes, and called *The New Henrietta*, it won a more modest success. In this version, Bertie was played by Douglas Fairbanks, Agnes by Patricia Collinge.

ACT I

An indication of the economic dictatorship of the Van Alstynes, Senior and Junior, is given by the clerk Musgrave, who testifies that he had saved six thousand dollars in thirty years, but that they had made half a million by one turn of the market the preceding Friday. Even so, Musgrave wonders about their new venture, the Henrietta Mining and Land Company. Nicholas, Junior, reads with great concern a letter from Gertrude, mother of his child, who tells him she has just learned he has a wife. Van Alstyne, Senior, warns his son not to gamble: he insists that although he may lie about minor matters, all his main ventures and big hauls are made by telling the honest truth. He has noticed that some big fish is swimming in the market and knows it is not Van Brunt, his ancient enemy. He brags of having won the Henrietta Company through a bluff in poker; and of buying and selling governors, legislators, and congressmen.

Among family and friends, Van Alstyne is also quite energetic. He is gentle with Bill James, his old schoolmate who just lost his fortune, partly because he expects to get the new fortune that James is sure to make, too. He hears from his daughter Mary that she is about to marry Lord Arthur Fitzroy Waldegrave Rawdon Trelawney. He is going to let the widow Cornelia invest her $300,000 estate well because he expects to marry her; but he promises to lead his rival for her hand, Rev. Hilton, down the primrose path, although he is Hilton's richest vestryman. With Agnes, who is in love with his son Bertie, he is all sweetness, encouraging her to continue her charities. In her presence, he even gives orders to save Van Brunt from bankruptcy.

But the other members of the Van Alstyne family have activities and troubles of their own. Dr. Wainwright comes in to warn Nicholas not to overtax his weak heart and to beware of Gertrude, whom he has been treating and who is very bitter. Bertie confesses his love to Agnes; she persuades him to burn his "girlie" pictures, especially those of the dancer Henrietta. She

191

also makes him promise to stop being lackadaisical, and to enter business. But his father rejects Bertie as hopeless, and says he will leave his whole fortune to Nicholas. He does give Bertie a quit-check for his share, raised to $500,000 when he hears of the proposed marriage with Agnes. Dr. Wainwright assures Nicholas' wife Rose that her husband is safe for the moment, and reveals to the audience that he himself loves Rose.

ACT II

The young broker Flint informs Nicholas that he knows the "bear" who has been trying to wreck Van Alstyne—namely, Nicholas. Flint refuses the latter's bribe and says he wants only his one-eighth of 1 per cent on any transaction of either side. As Wainwright arrives with news of Gertrude's death, Musgrave, the clerk, delivers to Rose a packet, brought by messenger, from a dying woman. Nicholas is able to convince his wife that the covering letter in the packet, asking the care of a fatherless child, concerns Bertie. Dr. Wainwright takes the remainder of the packet—a set of letters in the handwriting of Nicholas—and says he will deliver it upon demand. Van Alstyne and the Rev. Hilton engage in a battle of wits over Cornelia, during which Henrietta is variously identified as a chestnut racing filly, a ballet dancer, and the witch of Wall Street. Meanwhile Rose confronts Bertie with his crimes, saying he must break off with Agnes. When Wainwright sees how Nicholas has diverted suspicion from himself, he delivers the packet to Rose. Without looking at the handwriting on the letters in the packet, Rose hands them to Bertie, who does look at the handwriting and at his dismayed brother. Bertie cries out to Agnes, who faints. He then tosses the letters into the fire.

ACT III

In Flint's office, it is apparent from the condition of the market that today will bring the showdown between Van Alstyne and his mysterious bear. Henrietta Company, center of the attack, is going down—87, 85¼, 84. Van Alstyne is away on his yacht; all his stocks are falling. Henrietta is 79. Flint remarks that, whoever loses, brokers win. Bertie, wishing to top off his mad dissipation of the past ten days (since the letter crisis), gives Flint $50,000 to begin a fling on the market, ordering him not to buy Henrietta stock; meanwhile the Van Alstyne series has steadied: Henrietta is 83.

192

"*The Henrietta*" (1887; 1913)

Nicholas tells Flint he is trying to beat Henrietta down to 65, to ruin his father and leave himself a multimillionaire. It is after two—the market has less than an hour to run. Van Alstyne arrives unexpectedly just as his son is about to use his stocks in the bear raid. Henrietta again starts down. Telling Cornelia he must have her, Van Alstyne proposes, but noticing unusual activity on the ticker, he rushes to it and allows her to slip from his arms. Her "yes" turns to "no—no—no—no!"

It is two-thirty; Henrietta is down to 68; Van Alstyne tells Flint that if his son does not return with the necessary stocks in ten minutes, he will be wiped out. He throws Cornelia's $300,000 of assets into the battle. Flint reads on the tape that the Security Bank has failed. Nicholas returns, announcing that he has no securities. Henrietta has reached 65. Van Alstyne concedes his ruin, but tells his son that since he is only 55 years old, they can start over. A moment later, his son confesses that he has been working with Van Brunt to ruin his father; he gloats at being the master of Wall Street, but Wainwright, noticing danger signs in his physical condition, drags him away. Bertie returns, describing the uncouthness of Wall Street. At ten minutes to three, Bertie gives up $400,000 to buy 40,000 Henrietta shares at a time the enemy thinks his victory assured. Watching the final ticker, Nicholas sees Henrietta rising from 65 to 79 to 83 to 85 to 88 to 90, closing a point higher than the day before. He sinks into a chair, hearing the message that his father forgave him before he left the market. Dr. Wainwright turns him over to Hilton, but Nicholas says that no man like Hilton can teach him how to die when he has never shown him how to live. With that word he dies. Wainwright turns to the ticker to say: "Tick on! Tick on! Bring fortune and despair—to the living; the ear of a dead man cannot hear you."

ACT IV

Eighteen months later, Agnes thinks only of Bertie in spite of Rose's plans for her to accept Flint. Bertie has deliberately missed his European steamer and returned to her. Wainwright tells Bertie he is ready to clear him, but Bertie will not permit clearance at the expense of his dead brother. Informing Rose that Van Alstyne, has destroyed her inheritance, Cornelia, who had pulled a piece of the packet out of the fire, now delivers the truth about Nicholas, which Dr. Wainwright, although rejected through her love for a dead husband, was unable to do.

Spreading the rumor that Cornelia has $30,000 a year, Van Alstyne eggs Hilton on to propose to her; when she says she is glad he cares for her in spite of her loss of fortune, Hilton backs out—rushing to write his sermon. Van Alstyne then proposes; after one refusal, and his assuring her that her fortune is safe, he hears her say: "Keep the bonds and take me." Cornelia gives Bertie the bonds for a wedding present. Rose finally accepts Dr. Wainwright. Bertie's father compliments him on his skill in the market. Bertie does not tell him that it is based on flipping coins in the air.

47

EUGENE O'NEILL (1888–1953)

Anna Christie (1921)

Drama in four acts

MAIN CHARACTER AND THEME: Story of *Anna Christopherson*, twenty, tarnished daughter of a Swedish coal-barge captain, and her search for fulfillment through love in spite of the heartless machinations of "dat ole davil, sea."

OTHER CHARACTERS:
"Johnny-the-Priest"
Two longshoremen
A postman
Larry, the bartender
Christopher Christopherson, about

fifty, called Chris, captain of
the barge *Simeon Winthrop*
Marthy Owen
Three men of a steamer's crew
Mat Burke, a stoker
Johnson, deck hand on the barge

TIME: About 1920, fall.

PLACE: New York City; Provincetown; Boston.

MUSICAL HIGHLIGHT: Chris's song: "My Yosephine, come board de ship. Long time Ay vait for you."

HISTORICAL NOTE: First performed at the Vanderbilt Theatre, New York, November 2, 1921, with Pauline Lord as Anna. Winner of the Pulitzer Prize for the 1921–1922 season. Reappeared as musical play, entitled *New Girl in Town*, with Gwen Verdon as Anna, at the 46th Street Theatre, May 15, 1957. This drama is an excellent sample of O'Neill's power of characterization through living models and of his impressive development of atmosphere from actual places he frequented. Chris Christopherson was based on a roommate O'Neill had in New York—so thorough was his absorption of the character that even his Swedish background is intensively depicted. As to place, *Anna Christie* is one of several O'Neill plays set in Johnny-the-Priest's, really Jimmy the Priest's: O'Neill has reflected this waterfront dive with precision and insight.

ACT I

At "Johnny-the-Priest's," a saloon near South Street, New York City, Chris, almost drunk, is given a letter from his daughter Anna. It says that she will visit him soon. In alcoholic anxiety, Chris breaks the news to Marthy, who has lived on the barge with him, and Marthy agrees to move out, and no hard feelings. She also persuades him to get something to eat and to try to sober up for Anna.

Anna arrives while he is gone. No innocent, as her father had announced, she quickly displays herself as a woman of the world, hard and cynical. She orders a whisky, downs it in a gulp, and takes another. In conversation with Marthy, she tells of spending time in a prison hospital. She is here to meet her father, a janitor. Since he is a man, she does not expect much from him, but she hopes he will underwrite a rest cure for her.

Marthy informs her that her father is captain of a coal barge. Declaring that she will never live on a dirty barge, Anna goes on to say that her father "brought her up" by turning her over to her mother's cousins out West, who ruined her when she was sixteen. Later, after a period of good living, she was lured into prostitution, and there remained.

Chris, returning, greets her as "Anna lilla!" She refuses his effort at tenderness, his family memories, and the Swedish touch. First, she declines to go with him; then, hearing that the barge has excellent moonlight and vacation properties, she decides to take a chance.

ACT II

Ten days later, as the *Simeon Winthrop* lies at anchor off Provincetown, Anna says she loves fog and sea because they are making her over. She learns that her father's people were seamen, but she hears from Chris repeated warnings of the sea's treachery. "Any gel marry sailor," he asserts, "she's crazy fool!"

Suddenly, the sea casts up Mat Burke, a powerful, handsome, rough, bold, broad-chested six-foot stoker, one of four sailors rescued from an open boat.

196

When he tries to kiss Anna, she bangs his head against a bulwark and knocks him out. Coming to quickly, he curses her, then begs her pardon, then compliments her for being unique among women. He fascinates her with his story of the storm which scuttled his ship, and of other rough conflicts between man and Nature. He admits the sea is a monster—though clean— but swears he would have no other life. Before she realizes it, he is proposing marriage to her. When Chris returns, Anna leads Burke inside to rest. Chris hears him say: "You're the girl of the world and we'll be marrying soon and I don't care who knows it!" Chris shakes his fist at the sea and vows that he will die before she puts this dirty trick over on him.

ACT III

In dock at Boston, Chris continues to complain to Anna about Burke. Anna brusquely defends him, calling him the best man she has ever met, hinting that she loves him, but declaring that she will never marry him although she might have had she met him four years earlier. Burke tells Chris he will marry Anna before the day is out. Chris uses many arguments to dissuade him, but Burke is equal to them all. From calling him "no-good, sailor fellar" and "Irish svine," Chris condemns him for his girl in every port and for being impossible husband material. Burke admits his past but says his meeting Anna has transformed him. Chris finally attacks Burke with a knife, but Burke laughingly repulses him. At Burke's request, Anna declares her love, but her father tells Burke he has not won: Anna has not yet promised to marry him. Again queried, Anna says she can never marry him. Anna finally stops them both by parading before them the full sordid story of her past. Neither of them can take it: Chris moans; Burke raises the chair to kill her, but checks himself. Her protestations of love and deter- mination to be a pure wife accomplish nothing with him. He leaves her, cursing her and passionately blaming her for destroying him. Chris still blames "dat ole davil, sea." Anna is stoical.

ACT IV

Two nights later, Chris, drunk and overthoughtful, returns to Anna. She tells him she is tired of waiting for Burke, and will return next day to New York, and her old life. Chris says he will sail next day as bo'sun on a steamer, sacrificing himself to the sea in hopes it will leave Anna alone. Once more he calls her "Anna lilla," and this time she accepts the Swedish tenderness and lets him kiss her.

Burke returns. Peering blinkingly around the cabin, he begins: "Let you not be hiding from me, whoever's here—though 'tis well you know I'd have a right to come back and murder you." He describes his two days of desperation, fighting, and cursing—tormented with shame. Anna begs him to forgive her past and to take her freely for the future. He says he can never forgive. He tells her he has signed on board the *Londonderry* for Capetown. With wild, ironical laughter, she refrains from informing him that so has her father. Once she has sworn that she hates with deadly hate all the men of her past, he begins to soften. She swears and reswears that he is the only man she has ever loved. He promises they will be wedded in the morning and will be happy in spite of the devil.

Chris comes in and proposes a drink. When Burke demurs, Anna says he may as well drink with his new shipmate. Anna is to get a little house, to wait for her two men, but Burke vows that Chris's grandchild will soon be there to prevent any loneliness. When Burke learns that he, "a devout Catholic," is marrying among Lutherans, he is still not daunted: "'Tis the will of God, anyway." Raising her glass for a beer toast, Anna tries to enliven them, but Burke agrees with Chris that the sea, now dressed in fog, is full, as always, of dreadful tricks.

48

ANNE NICHOLS

Abie's Irish Rose (1922)

*Vaudeville-type sentimental-and-comic
drama in three acts*

MAIN CHARACTERS AND THEME: Repercussions in the marriage of *Abraham*
(Abie) *Levy*, member of an intensely Jewish family that hates the Irish,
to *Rosemary Murphy*, daughter of an intensely Irish father who hates
all but Catholics—especially Jews.

OTHER CHARACTERS:

Mrs. Isaac Cohen, a talkative
neighbor of the Levys

Isaac Cohen, her husband

Dr. Jacob Samuels, a rabbi, with
war experience

Solomon Levy, a prosperous Jewish store keeper, Abie's father

Patrick Murphy, a California
contractor, Rose Mary's father

Father Whalen, an Irish priest,
from California

Flower Girl

Six Bridesmaids

TIME: About 1920.

PLACE: New York City.

MUSICAL HIGHLIGHTS: "Maseltof"; "Oh, Promise Me"; "Wedding March";
"Too-ro-la-too."

HISTORICAL NOTE: Play presents interesting and accurate picture of Jewish-
American culture and a sketch of the Irish-American position, revealing
much of the custom and tradition that guide and restrict the assimilation
of transplanted cultures in America. Though without distinction as a
literary or an artistically dramatic vehicle, its theatricality was attested
by the fact that after Miss Nichols had been refused production by the

entire Broadway community, she borrowed money to put on her play, and it broke all records for consecutive performances up to that time. Opening at the Fulton Theatre, New York, on May 23, 1922, it played 2,532 consecutive performances and developed seven road companies. It has often been revived since, even on radio and television, and has been the parent of innumerable imitations. In 1927, it became a novel. Since the drama specialized in the improvement of relations among diverse peoples, its great popularity in the 1920's was probably a sign of reaction to the wave of bigotry of the early post-War period.

ACT I

As Solomon waits to hear from his son, Abie, who has unaccountably been away all day, he must listen again and again to Mrs. Cohen's revelations about her appendicitis operation and to the rabbi's urgings that most problems can be solved if people "concentrate." Abie calls his father on the telephone to say that he wants to bring a lady home to dinner. When Solomon asks if the girl is Jewish (Abie has usually brought home Gentile girls), Abie says wait and see. Solomon is anxious to get Abie married: "I want his grandchildren," says Solomon. As soon as Abie is married, Solomon will take him into the firm.

Very shortly Abie brings Rosemary in. Talking alone, they reveal that they have just been married by a Methodist minister. Since their first job is to win acceptance from Abie's family, Rosemary is introduced as Rosie Murpheski, an entertainer Abie met when he was with the American Expeditionary Forces in France during World War I. Solomon is distressed at Rosie's very short dress and her very bad habit of saying "shure!" and "blarney." He is shocked when Rosie says that her father's business is contracting; Abie quickly corrects this confession to "contracting for clothes." But Rosie proves to be so very sweet, and Solomon is so happy that his son has at last fallen in love with "a Jewish gel," that plans for the wedding move swimmingly. The date is set for the following week.

ACT II

Rosemary learns that her father's train is an hour late, and she is glad because she really wants to have the wedding ceremony completed (her second one with Abie) before her father gets there. To make Rosie feel at home, Solomon

200

has decorated his place with real orange trees of different sizes, overlaid with bunches and festoons of orange ribbons. When Patrick Murphy and his priest, Father Whalen, arrive, the Jewish ceremony is nearly over; Patrick is fearful that the orange decorations mean that his daughter is marrying a despicable Protestant; he has been told that his son-in-law-to-be is named Michael Magee. When the truth comes out, Patrick and Solomon begin what is almost a pitched battle. Father Whalen and Rabbi Samuels, on the other hand, find common ground in having both been war chaplains, and in having ministered to men outside their own communions when a proper chaplain was unavailable. Patrick, meanwhile, has found a loophole in the marriage: his daughter signed the register as Rosie Murpheski, and there is no such person. Solomon is entirely willing to have the marriage canceled. But when Solomon's lawyers assure him the present marriage is legal, let alone the one in Jersey City by the Methodist minister, both fighting fathers feel frustrated. At Rabbi Samuels' suggestion, Father Whalen gets permission to perform a Catholic marriage. When Patrick returns after making arrangements to take his daughter to California, he hears Father Whalen declare: "I now pronounce you man and wife. 'Those whom God hath joined together, let no man put asunder.' " Patrick cannot believe his ears. "My God!" he shouts. "They've done it again!"

ACT III

For over a year, Rosemary and Abie have lived in their modest apartment, disowned by both their fathers. Looking after her baby, Rosemary also prepares for a Christmas celebration, with a Christmas tree. The Cohens drop by, and Rosemary, innocently, sends Mrs. Cohen to look after her baked ham. There is also kosher food on the Christmas menu. Half in shame, the two fathers sneak in, bringing gifts for their grandchild and placing them on the Christmas tree. Their bitter debate continues, revolving at times around the recent freedom of the State of Ireland and of the Jews in Jerusalem. Solomon boasts that the Jews do not really need Jerusalem: "Ve own all the other peoples!" When the "grandchild" is brought out, it develops that Rosemary has had twins—Patrick Joseph Murphy Levy, who is given to Patrick, who incidentally wanted only a girl grandchild, and Rebecca Levy, given to Solomon, who wanted only a boy grandchild. In the swap of babies, the two grandfathers are reconciled. "Merry Christmas, Sol!" says Patrick. "Goot Yonteff, Patrick," replies Solomon.

49

EUGENE O'NEILL (1888–1953)

The Hairy Ape (1922)

Expressionistic tragic drama in eight scenes

MAIN CHARACTER AND THEME: The religion of brute force as expressed in the character and personality of *Yank* (born with the common name of Robert Smith), stoker on a transatlantic liner, whose goal is to win back the social importance which he suddenly learns he has lost.

OTHER CHARACTERS:

Paddy, a poetic Irish stoker

Long, a class-conscious stoker

Mildred Douglas, twenty, passenger on the liner, daughter of the chairman of the board of the company that owns the steamship line

Aunt, Mildred's aunt

Second Engineer

Fourth Engineer

A Guard, A Secretary of an Organization, Stokers, Ladies, Gentlemen, Members of the Crowd

TIME: About 1920—but perhaps timeless.

PLACE: On an ocean liner, an hour out of New York and two days later; Fifth Avenue, New York City; an island near the city; other places in New York City.

MUSICAL HIGHLIGHT: "Oh, Whisky Is the Life of Man!"; "Far Away in Canada"; "Miller of Dee."

HISTORICAL NOTE: In this drama, O'Neill uses the expressionistic scene-structure drama (as he did in *The Emperor Jones*, 1920) to accentuate the process by which his powerful evolution of character, situation, and internal meaning are revealed. Though showing the effects of O'Neill's learning his craft—it was written in 1921, during his third year as a professional writer—it has many deep probing devices and original touches. One of these is his adaptation of Rodin's *Thinker* as a pose for Yank and Yank's constant use of the word *think* in the stokehole to symbolize the power of awareness and Yank's instinctive urge to rise above brutality. It was first performed on March 9, 1922, at the Provincetown Theatre, New York, with Louis Wolheim as Yank, and later at the Plymouth Theatre, New York. Its initial run was 127 performances. It has become, however, a great favorite of college and amateur groups.

Scene 1

Deep in the fireman's forecastle of a transatlantic liner, an hour after the beginning of a voyage, the hairy-chested stokers raise a great tumult. They buzz about their adventures on land, tussle, and bawl for beer. Coming forward, Yank takes charge. He asks for, and gets, something stronger than beer. By request, Paddy sings. But his songs are too sentimental for Yank, who demands rough ways. Long's oration on the culpability of the capitalists is equally ruled out by Yank. In a wave of poetry, Paddy talks of the old days of ships and Yank listens, especially when Paddy asks if Yank wants to be a flesh-and-blood wheel of the engines. Yank says yes, he does. Only the engines have power, he insists. "And I'm steel—steel—steel! I'm de muscles in steel, de punch behind it!" Not the rich guys, but those in the stokehole, really belong, says Yank.

Scene 2

Two days out, on the promenade deck, Mildred and her Aunt quarrel, as usual. Aunt is tired of her exhausting low places, such as Mildred's tour of duty as social worker on New York's East Side, looking for morbid thrills. Calling her aunt a cold pork pudding, Mildred says her heart is in the smoke generated by her grandfather, who was a puddler, not in her father's gold. She therefore has arranged for the second engineer to take her on a visit through the stokehole.

Scene 3

In the stokehole, the men are taking a breathing spell. Yank calls them back to work; orders them to open the furnace up. Mildred, in a white dress, is right behind Yank, where the other stokers see her before he does. Yank is cursing the man who a moment ago blew a whistle to speed things up. Seeing the men in front of him stare, he whirls and faces Mildred. He glares into her eyes and is turned to stone. As she looks at his gorilla face, framed by the savage surroundings, she cries out and shrinks away. Saying "Take me away! Oh, the filthy beast!" Mildred faints. The engineers carry her out as Yank curses her.

Scene 4

Although the others have eaten and washed up, Yank, grimy and unwashed, sits in the forecastle like Rodin's *The Thinker*. The men jeer at him, saying he has fallen in love; he says he has fallen, but in hate. Paddy says that Mildred all but called Yank "hairy ape," and Yank is sorry he did not "bang" her. If she comes down again, Yank says, he'll fling her in the furnace. In any case, he is bound to get even with her.

Scene 5

On a fine Sunday morning three weeks later, Yank and Long are swaggering along Fifth Avenue in the Fifties, looking for people like Mildred. Long is in his shore clothes, topped off by a Windsor tie; Yank is in dirty dungarees. Yank talks of his parents and of how their throwing him out caused him to begin living by his muscle. As well-dressed people pass nearby, one or two bump into him, and Yank's ire against them rises. Finally, he lets drive a terrific swing against one man who brushes against him to reach the bus. The gentleman seems undisturbed by Yank's power and vehemence; he is only angry because he has missed his bus. Calling a policeman, he has Yank jailed.

Scene 6

In a cell on Blackwell's Island, Yank shakes the bars and recognizes that they are steel. As his fellow-prisoners try to quiet him, he talks still of "a skoit . . . dolled up all in white—in de stokehole." They tell him that he should join the I.W.W.'s if he wants to get back at the girl who insulted him. In a new fit of anger, he bends the steel bars with his hands because he knows that steel doesn't belong as fire (symbol of his greatness in the stokehole) does. The prison guards turn the hose on him and run to get a straitjacket for him.

204

"The Hairy Ape" (1922)

Scene 7

A month later, Yank tries the I.W.W. (Industrial Workers of the World) at their office. He pays his fifty cent initiation fee and is inducted. Then he talks of blowing up the plants of the Steel Trust. Believing him sent by the detectives to spy on them and report their explosive talk, the I.W.W. people throw Yank out. Even they do not think he belongs. A policeman comes by and hears Yank asking the Man in the Moon to clear up his confusion. Although Yank begs to be arrested, the policeman does not consider him worth bothering with.

Scene 8

Next day, at the monkey house of the Zoo, Yank is still in a quandary about who belongs and who does not, and about where he fits in the scheme of things. In this mood he challenges the gorilla whose kinship he claims since he has been called "hairy ape." He pounds on the rail of the gorilla's cage; the gorilla rattles his bars in reply. He tells the gorilla how lucky he is that he cannot think. Roaring back at him, the gorilla tries harder to get out. Still talking, Yank takes a jimmy, releases the gorilla, and offers to shake hands. Reacting to being mocked, the gorilla seizes Yank, cracks his ribs, throws him into the cage and shuffles off. Calling attention to himself in the cage, like a circus barker, Yank slips in a heap on the floor and dies. The monkeys set up a chattering, whimpering wail, perhaps at last conferring on Yank the honor of belonging.

50

MARIAN SPENCER SMITH

An American Grandfather
(printed 1924)

Immigrant-Americanization drama in one act

MAIN CHARACTERS AND THEME: Drama of the choice of *Fydor*, an expert carver, and his wife *Marta*, a young Rumanian couple, who on the threshold of becoming Americans envisage a challenge to their ideals.

OTHER CHARACTERS:

Jan, an old man   *Chita*

Stanislaus, a violinist   *Other immigrants*

Immigration Officer

TIME: 1924.

PLACE: Entrance point for immigrants (probably Ellis Island).

HISTORICAL NOTE: Printed in *Poet Lore*, Vol. XXXV (1924), 443–455. Typical of hundreds of immigrant and Americanization dramas which appear constantly in school magazines, play pamphlets, and short-play anthologies, and are acted in great quantity and faith throughout the land.

ACTION

The immigrants in gay costumes wait in the bare room, surrounded by miscellaneous piles of luggage. They are apathetical, bewildered, animated. Some dance to Stanislaus' violin. Briskly, the immigration officer calls their numbers—193, 194, 195—ushering them into the great country. Marta tells Fydor that they are only nine numbers away.

Marta wonders if American women wear shawls like Chita's or hats like the one she has especially bought. Once in America, she vows to have nothing but things American—shiny furniture, stoves under windows, rugs with flowers. Fydor is proud that Americans work only a few hours each day. In the evenings, adds Marta, Fydor can carve toys and sell them. "So much money we will make, it almost frightens me."

Behind them, says Fydor, are long hours in the field, cold winters with snow coming through the chinks, and numb fingers. They are happy to have come to America in their youth. The old—like Jan over there—cannot really appreciate America, where heat boxes along the walls create summer all the year.

The immigration officer has called 200. In America, says Fydor, everything is done by machinery, even the caring of children. For Fydor and Marta the entrance is crucial since they saved for three years to make the trip and have no life to go back to, not even a goat.

Jan boastfully says he will take out citizenship papers at once. His son and his four grandchildren want only Americans in the home. Thus, he will soon be an American grandfather. In his American house are machines that talk through the air and machines that make music comprehending violins, harps, and voices. They all quickly assure Stanislaus that no machine can equal his violin. Stanislaus envisions his first concert, which will banish the darknesses of his past. He shall play until people forget their fine clothes and fat purses and remember only their souls. Fydor can remember only work. In Matchin, his home town, he did with his hands the work of three men; in America, he will do the work of five men, and be correspondingly paid.

The immigration officer is puzzled: four immigrants left, and only three can be admitted. He refuses to argue about mistakes officials make; he will return in a few minutes and receive their decision as to who will go in.

They all agree to send Stanislaus ahead, with his music. Jan plays his trump card: the American grandchildren must have a grandfather. But Fydor and Marta have the prior numbers. When he returns to the Danube, they tell him, the black hawthorns on its banks will be turning pink.

They rise to go. Jan hands them the toys they must give his grandchildren. Then they decide to stay behind and let Jan go through, even against the opinion of the immigration officer. Marta cannot see America through the window: it is too dark.

51

GEORGE S. KAUFMAN (1889–1961)
MARC CONNELLY (1890–1964)

Beggar on Horseback (1924)

Part-realistic, part-expressionistic, psychoanalytic fantasy in two parts, based on Paul Apel's Hans Sonnenstössers Höllenfahrt

MAIN CHARACTER AND THEME: Using the international proverb, "Set a beggar on horseback, and he'll outride the devil," as a basis, the authors develop *Neil McRae*, a promising musician, alternately pulled by the demands of the time to make money and by his deepest artistic urges.

OTHER CHARACTERS:

Dr. Albert Rice, Neil's friend
Cynthia Mason, Neil's neighbor
Mr. Cady, a businessman from Neil's hometown
Mrs. Cady, his wife
Gladys Cady, his daughter
Homer Cady, his son
A Butler
Jerry, another friend of Neil's
A Businessman
Miss Hey and *Miss You*, secretaries to Mr. Cady

A Waiter, A Reporter, Jurors, A Guide, A Sightseer, A Novelist, A Song Writer, An Artist, A Poet.

In the Pantomime, Part II:
H.R.H., The Crown Prince of Xanadu
The Crown Princess of Xanadu
First Lady in Waiting
First Lord of the Bedchamber
A Lamplighter
A Policeman

TIME: The early 1920's: spring of the year.

PLACE: New York City; dreamlands.

MUSICAL HIGHLIGHTS: Low songs—"Sweet Mamma"; "The Frog's Party";

jazzy version of the Bridal Chorus from *Lohengrin*; Neil's symphony; Pantomime music.

HISTORICAL NOTE: Although separately active in many phases of theatre life, Kaufman and Connelly distinguished themselves together in the 1920's for their satiric comedies which laid bare the ridiculous pretensions and wrongheadedness of various individual areas of American life. Though biting deeply, they did not become overtly critical, and they did show proper respect for the high aspirations of the people they satirized. They wrote *Dulcy* (1921) and *To the Ladies* (1922) about wives helping husbands in business and *Merton of the Movies* (1922) about would-be movie stars.

PART I

In Neil's apartment, characterized by a huge grand piano, Cynthia and Neil's friend Albert discuss Neil—his artistic bent, his teaching music to get money, his general but likable improvidence. Neil arrives. As the three talk and drink tea Cynthia prepared, Neil confesses that he delays writing his symphony to do cheap, potboiling orchestrations like the "Sweet Mamma" he hears through the window. Conscience-stricken, he sits down and plays the second movement of his symphony (there is no first).

The Cadys come in. Mr. Cady thinks only of money; Mrs. Cady concentrates upon community and society; the daughter Gladys is called "the sunshine"—she brings candy for Neil's tea; Homer, the son, is always feeling bad. Mr. Cady offers Neil a job. From the window, "The Frog's Party," a Charleston-dance tune, makes Gladys want to dance; since Neil cannot dance, she dances with Albert. The Cadys gone, Albert advises an alliance with Gladys to give Neil comfort, money, time. He also gives Neil a pill and puts him to bed. Cynthia refuses Neil's marriage proposal and plans to move. By telephone Neil proposes to Gladys, who accepts.

The doctor's pill begins to work. Neil falls asleep and the scene changes crazily, although Neil remains in bathrobe with easy chair and piano in position. Neil and Gladys are married in a jazzy ceremony; the bride's bouquet is made of banknotes. The babel around him prevents Neil from composing. When the Cadys order him to play, his music is reminiscent of Cynthia, and Cynthia comes through the window. When Neil's music involuntarily turns jazzy, Cynthia fades. Neil ends his playing with a disconsolate crash.

Neil goes into Mr. Cady's widget business. He meets bewildering complications in just requisitioning a pencil. Catching the spirit of business, he amasses a subscription list of one million dollars. Gladys informs him that his life will be daytime success in Daddy's office and nighttime in swank night clubs. The jazz tunes evolve into Cynthian music, and Cynthia appears. Neil and Cynthia are proud of the symphony—the orchestra has programmed it—and are $177.77 rich from the products of their little red hen and little dun cow. Hearing Gladys' voice, Neil goes to it. After Gladys tears up the manuscript of his symphony, Neil is driven to a quadruple killing—each of the Cadys, blow after blow.

PART II

The courtroom where Neil is tried carries symbolic touches: Jurors are dancing teachers (reminiscent of Gladys forcing Neil to dance); Judge is a bewigged Mr. Cady; Prosecutor is Homer; Witness is Mrs. Cady. Arriving gaily, Gladys tries to kidnap the jury for a night club opening. Neil goes to a higher court: it is Mr. Cady on a higher stand. For his defense Neil introduces a Pantomime, entitled, "A Kiss in Xanadu," by Cynthia Mason and Neil McRae. It is the story of a Prince and Princess, separately seeking adventure outside the castle and becoming involved with each other, not knowing their respective disguises. Keeping their naughty dream a secret, they dutifully return to their humdrum existences.

Jury shouts "Rotten! Highbrow!" and declares Neil guilty. He is sentenced to be a song writer who does not use his imagination. From eight every morning he must work in a cell with great novelists, poets, magazine artists, scientists, and religionists, who have packaged stuff for public consumption. Eventually Neil rebels and agrees to die rather than continue. Albert gives him a pill to ease the pain of the knife. Cynthia promises to stay with him always.

A *real* knock on the door dispels the fantasy. A real Cynthia walks in. They agree they must never be parted. Gladys breaks the engagement. Cynthia glowingly remains, as Neil plays the Pantomime music.

52

HATCHER HUGHES (1881–1945)

Hell Bent fer Heaven (1924)

Folk drama in three acts

MAIN CHARACTER AND THEME: The remarkable influences of *Rufe Pryor*, thirty, a homeless religious fanatic, over the members of two established mountaineer families, the Hunts and the Lowrys, who had formerly engaged in a feud.

OTHER CHARACTERS:

David Hunt, eighty, snow-thatched but well-preserved

Meg Hunt, his daughter-in-law, a woman of forty-odd, strong, active

Sid Hunt, her son, young war hero

Matt Hunt, Sid's father, forty-five, vigorous mountaineer

Andy Lowry, young mailman

Jude Lowry, his sister, a longtime sweetheart of Sid's but much desired by Rufe

TIME: About 1920.

PLACE: Matt's house in the western Carolina mountains, not far from Asheville, near a river dam.

MUSICAL HIGHLIGHTS: "Turkey in the Straw," played on the banjo; Gospel hymns as follows—"None but Christ"; "I've heard of a beautiful city"; "Are you ready, are you ready fer the comin' o' the Lord?"; "I am bound fer the Promised Land!"; "Wonderful love! Oh, wonderful love!"

HISTORICAL NOTE: Representative of the regional drama of the mid-Appalachian area (Kentucky-Tennessee-Carolina mountains), concentrating

211

on the following explosive elements: deep sense of local isolation; Southern, even Confederate, sympathies; family feuds; religious fanaticism and religious fears; treacherous river and dam breaks; heavy rains; hard drinking; personal abnormalities.

ACT I

Sid, returning as hero from World War I, meets the taunts of his grandfather, who fought in the Civil War, the warnings of his mother against being over-sinful, and the suspicious behavior of Rufe, who has become interested in his girl, Jude. Sid tells how he captured many Germans by knowing when to look back after he had started running in battle, and then chasing the runners on the opposite side. Now that Sid is back, Matt dismisses Rufe for being a spiteful weakling, notwithstanding Rufe's having no place to go; at Sid's request, though, Matt retains him for one more month. Andy drops in with the mail; the shooting match he and Sid had planned is broken up when Sid's mother Meg says she is tired of shooting and killing. It is Rufe who introduces tenseness at this point by recalling the feud between the Hunts and Lowrys of years ago. The conversation drifts toward religion and the old-time Baptist preachers who could "lay out" the strongest parishioner with their fists and go right on preaching God's word. When liquor is mentioned, Rufe remembers a ten-gallon keg of powerful liquid which he uncovered one day when dynamiting for fish. While Sid is picking up his courtship with Jude from the point of their last lovers' quarrel, Rufe is plying Andy with liquor and subtly suggesting that the feuding, though many years gone, ended unequally since three more Lowrys were killed than Hunts. Andy, now drunk, swears to equalize things by killing six Hunts.

ACT II

A few minutes later, Andy does attempt a beginning at equalization. Forcing Sid to dance to banjo music as prelude to becoming the first Hunt to die, he is stopped only when Jude distracts him, and Sid is able to wrest his gun away. Rufe, meanwhile, warns Jude against marrying a sinner like Sid; he tells her also that his love for her is pure since, as desire, it originated in prayer meeting. Later, Sid receives Jude's promise that if a feud starts, she will be on the side of the man she loves, not of her blood kin. Sid and Jude are now officially engaged. Andy, somewhat sobered up, apologizes, and Sid returns his gun; but David and Matt think it wise to go over and have a talk with Andy's father to prevent a feud. Getting Andy alone, Rufe makes him believe that Sid plans to kill him on the road home. Because of deeply threatening weather, only Andy and Sid decide to go, the latter to beg Jude's hand of her father. Very soon after they leave together, a shot is heard and Sid's horse is seen returning without a rider. Even Jude declares that if Andy has killed Sid, she will destroy her brother with her own hands, and Meg upholds her but doubts that she has the strength. David and Matt have gone to settle things with Andy. Returning, Sid tells Rufe that Andy shot at him but missed. As he quizzes Rufe, he is forced to believe that Andy shot at Rufe's instigation. He rushes out to get to the dam to telephone ahead and prevent his people from renewing the feud on his account. When he has gone, Rufe talks to God and gets the order to blow up the dam and eliminate the blasphemer Sid.

ACT III

Fifteen minutes later, Matt and David return, driving Andy before them. Rufe swears that Sid has not been there; Andy swears that he did not kill Sid. In spite of knowing that he may be shot any minute, Andy makes no effort to soothe the tempers of his captors. Little by little the river rises from the bursting dam and begins to flood the Hunt home. Matt and David tie Andy up, but Andy tells Rufe that if Rufe does not tell the truth about who promoted his attack upon Sid, he will tell, and he and Rufe will go to destruction together. When the evidence seems to point certainly to Rufe as the general instigator of trouble, Rufe resorts to evangelical preaching, causing Meg and Jude to shout and sway. Rufe is about to kill Andy to eradicate him as a witness when Sid enters, torn, bruised, and muddy. Calling himself "the ghost o' Sid Hunt!" Sid corners Rufe and makes him, shrieking in terror, confess to all his crimes. When Sid goes to release Andy, Rufe tells Meg and Jude that Sid's ghost has been there. Sid brings Andy up and before the whole group accuses Rufe of dynamiting the dam to commit murder. Meg protects Rufe until he admits his acts, calling them the will of God; then she wants him killed. Rufe runs into the cellar for protection. But the water is still rising; other sections of the dam are expected to burst momentarily; the only way out is on a boat. Sid packs his family and

Jude and Andy in a boat and prepares to leave. Then Rufe begins to scream that he cannot swim, and they must not leave him to die. They do leave him, instructing him to call for salvation on the God who has directed him. Alone, Rufe prays, but as the water gets closer, he curses God, committing the unpardonable sin. The end of the play is his hysterical screams for help.

53

NANCY BANCROFT BROSIUS

Sue 'Em (1924)

Radio farce in one act

MAIN CHARACTER AND THEME: *The Dorn family*, its acquisitiveness and defensiveness.

TIME: An evening in 1924.

PLACE: A typical middle-class American apartment, but rather shabby and run-down.

HISTORICAL NOTE: First performed by Provincetown Players on radio station WGBS, New York, December 29, 1924: first radio play printed in America (New York: Brentano's, 1925). Therefore one of the earliest of the genre of plays written to the peculiar specifications of radio, sometimes called radio drama. Specifications include the following: dramatic action developed for hearing and not seeing; plot situations sufficiently simple to appeal to a universal audience; specific suggestion of lessons learned directly from life; rapid shifts in action to avoid monotony; O. Henry-like surprise endings; broad humor, suspense, and emotional reactions.

ACTION

Mrs. Dorn is getting the family ready to go to the movies and grumpily awaiting Mr. Dorn. Upon Mr. Dorn's return, he casually lets it be known that he was touched on the leg by a truck and accused by the truck driver and a policeman of jaywalking. Mrs. Dorn joins the accusers in berating her husband until Aunt Grace on the telephone asks if they are going to sue.

215

Seizing this cue, Mrs. Dorn convinces her husband that he is a very sick man. She plans to have him sue for two thousand dollars to compensate for his injuries. With the money she will visit her sister in Idaho and get a kitchen cabinet and some Haviland china.

Bill teases his sister about what she will wear at the trial. He then quickly goes out. Mrs. Dorn and Effie—the movie date called off—talk of internal bleeding and of sending Mr. Dorn to the hospital. Bill returns, telling of the mess he is in. He has just run over a man who is in the hospital about to die. Since the man is a friend of the mayor and will leave a wife and four children, Bill estimates that he will be sued for at least $100,000. Effie wonders if she will have to dress for two trials. Mrs. Dorn reaches a pitch of high indignation about the law supporting careless jaywalkers against honest drivers; she says she will fight Bill's suit to the death. Bill then tells her his story is a joke concocted to test her sincerity about the suit in behalf of Mr. Dorn.

54

LAURENCE STALLINGS (1894–   )
MAXWELL ANDERSON (1888–1959)

What Price Glory? (1924)

Realistic war drama in three acts

MAIN CHARACTERS AND THEME: Military and romantic exploits, under actual battle conditions, of two American marines—*Captain Flagg* and *Sergeant Quirt.*

OTHER CHARACTERS:

(Marines unless otherwise identified):
Corporal Gowdy
Corporal Kiper
Corporal Lipinsky
Charmaine de la Cognac, an attractive French girl
Private Lewisohn
Lieutenant Aldrich
Lieutenant Moore
Lieutenant Schmidt
Gunnery Sergeant Sockkel
Private Mulcahy
Sergeant Ferguson
A Brigade Runner

M. Pete de la Cognac, Charmaine's father
Another Brigade Runner
Brigadier General Cokeley
A Colonel
A Captain
A Lieutenant
Another Lieutenant
A Chaplain
Town Mayor
Spike
A Pharmacist's Mate
Lieutenant Cunningham
Lieutenant Lundstrom

TIME: World War I.
PLACE: France.
MUSICAL HIGHLIGHT: "Mademoiselle from Armentières."

HISTORICAL NOTE: Stallings and Anderson wrote this play while fellow members of the staff of the New York *World*. Only Stallings, however, had had war experience: he had lost a right leg as the result of being in the battle at Belleau Wood, and he had spent months in army hospitals. This drama belongs to the tradition of literature which debunks war as glory and inquires into war's true effects, a literature begun in America by Stephen Crane's *The Red Badge of Courage* (1895). *What Price Glory?* opened at the Plymouth Theatre, New York, on September 3, 1924, and had an initial run of 299 performances. During the 1948–1949 season, it received an interesting revival by the Hollywood Masquers Club with the following famous motion-picture stars in the cast: Gregory Peck, John Wayne, Maureen O'Hara, Pat O'Brien, Ward Bond.

ACT I (*two scenes*)

At a room in a French farmhouse, converted into headquarters for a company of United States Marines, Gowdy, Kiper, and Lipinsky discuss the latest methods for conquering women and handling alimony payments, with side references to the company commander, Captain Flagg. Quirt arrives to take over as First Sergeant and to allow Flagg to take ten days off. While Quirt is out looking for the captain, the latter comes in with Charmaine, his current sweetheart. She wants him to take her to Paris because she is afraid that, like her sergeant who went away, he will not return. Flagg swears to return but warns Charmaine to be true to him. When Quirt gets back, he and Flagg remind each other of their soldiering around the world and of their breaking each other from time to time. Flagg calls a meeting of platoon leaders, ordering them to give Quirt his head but to lock him up if he gets unruly. Flagg having gone, Quirt tries unsuccessfully to capture Charmaine. But when Quirt quiets the trouble-making Mulcahy with a single blow of his fist, Charmaine rushes into his arms and they hold a long kiss.

Eight days later, Flagg is reported on his way back, but not from full vacation. He was detained because of a quarrel with an M.P. over his swagger stick. Rumor is that Charmaine's father is going to complain that someone has taken advantage of his daughter. Flagg enters this picture, quite intoxicated. His temper is not helped by the news about Cognac Pete's complaint; or by Quirt standing over him yelling, "Think fast, Captain. Think fast." Using Lieutenant Moore as his interpreter, Flagg bargains with

218

Pete and finally orders Quirt to marry Charmaine. General Cokeley backs the order, but Quirt escapes by swearing he will go to jail before he will marry, and then Flagg will have no sergeant to lead the men to battle in twenty minutes. Cokeley promises Flagg a vacation if he will hang morale posters and bring back an Alsatian officer in good condition. The company marches away, and Charmaine has no luck beguiling Sergeant Ferguson, who has been left behind.

ACT II

In a wine cellar of a disputed battle area, soldiers are dirty and wearing eight days' beards. Kiper and Lipinsky unveil the brutishness and selfishness of war. Aldrich, who has lost an arm, is brought in, bloody but not groaning, squired by an unkempt Flagg. Moore rises to damn the army for throwing away the lives of its men. He says:

> And since six o'clock there's been a wounded sniper in the tree by that orchard angle crying "Kamerad! Kamerad!" just like a big crippled whippoorwill. What price glory now? Why in God's name can't we all go home? Who gives a damn for this lousy, stinking little town but the poor French . . . who live here?

Flagg begs him to sleep it off. Quirt gives him a little chocolate and reviews his own experience of getting shot. He then reports the losses to Flagg. With eloquent sardonicism, Flagg greets the new lieutenants; he says he cannot spare good corporals to train them. One of the lieutenants promptly volunteers for dangerous duty. Quirt comes back with a bloody wound on his right calf, trying to open his first-aid pack. Then when his leg has been patched, he and Flagg bark at each other about many things, including Charmaine. Flagg is about to go out on a risky detail, and Quirt begs him to get himself killed, for Quirt's sake. To their surprise, Lieutenant Cunningham proves tough and brave. Flagg captures his Alsatian lieutenant and comforts a dying Lewisohn as the curtain falls.

ACT III

Two days later, in Cognac Pete's tavern, Ferguson talks to Charmaine (almost to himself) about the returning troops—possibly cut in half. Men who say they like to fight, he calls liars. Charmaine wants to know when

Flagg will return. Quirt enters, shaven, crafty-faced, wearing a major's overcoat, but beneath it, the flannel pajamas of a wounded soldier. In the hospital, he says, he was given ether so they could lift his gold watch and eight hundred dollars. He hit a captain at the hospital, got locked up, and came out with aphasia, he says. Charmaine worries over his wound: he still calls her "Pittsburgh."

Flagg follows Kiper, Gowdy, and Lipinsky in—he is cold sober. He wants his men fed, billeted, and let out to drink and fight as they choose. When Charmaine returns, he tells her that war is no good with so many green little boys in it. Charmaine postpones their date; she also makes excuses to Quirt until he is beautiful again.

Later Flagg comes back, drunk and staggering. He and Quirt agree that the cure for drunkenness is a drink. Quirt and Flagg wrestle, threaten, and try to outbrag each other. Quirt declares: "Top sergeants is eternal. They don't never die." After getting chummy, Quirt and Flagg fall out again— over Charmaine. They play blackjack for Charmaine. Flagg wins, but before he can enjoy his victory under the three days' rest promised him, word comes that the battalion must go back to the fighting front. Flagg refuses to go—he has earned his leave. Charmaine agrees to stay with him. Then Flagg realizes that he has the religion of the profession of arms, and must go. Quirt comes down from the roof, kisses Charmaine, and screams, "Hey, Flagg, wait for baby!"

55

EUGENE O'NEILL (1888–1953)

Desire Under the Elms (1924)

Freudian realistic tragedy in three parts

MAIN CHARACTER AND THEME: The determination of *Abbie Putnam*, thirty-five and sexually vigorous, to gain security for herself first through ownership of land and finally through love, and the tragic consequences of that determination.

OTHER CHARACTERS:

Ephraim Cabot, seventy-five, owner of a New England farm and active beyond his years

Simeon, thirty-nine, his eldest son

Peter, thirty-seven, his middle son

Eben, twenty-five, his youngest son, but by another wife to whom Eben is devoted even though she has been dead for ten years

Young Girl

Two Farmers

The Fiddler

The Sheriff

Other folk from neighboring farms

TIME: 1850.

PLACE: New England.

MUSICAL HIGHLIGHTS: "Oh, Susannah"; "Lady of the Lake"; "Pop Goes the Weasel"; "Turkey in the Straw."

HISTORICAL NOTE: Probably the best example of O'Neill's adoption of Freudian psychology, which he used extensively in such later plays as *Strange Interlude* (1928) and *Mourning Becomes Electra* (1931). Even the elms on each side of the farmhouse reflect and project the Freudian atmosphere. Although the strong emphasis on sex caused the play to come under the eye of police authority in New York—especially since it followed by only six months the drama of miscegenation, *All God's Chillun Got Wings*—the play escaped serious injury through censorship. It was produced at the Greenwich Village Theatre, New York, on November 11, 1924, and added greatly to O'Neill's reputation as a dramatist, although it still showed the facile effects of the well-made play. Also an acting success, it offered Walter Huston as Ephraim, Eloise Pendleton as Abbie, and Charles Ellis as Eben.

PART I (*four scenes*)

As Simeon and Peter debate the question of leaving the farm and all their investment of hard work and potential inheritance to follow the Gold Rush to California, Eben, from the dining-room window, listens intently.

The three brothers have their supper. Eben informs the other two that it is useless for them to wait for their inheritance since the farm actually belongs to his dead mother, and she cannot sleep in her grave until Eben has rescued it for her. After supper, the elder sons tease Eben about going to visit the neighborhood prostitute who has served old and young men for many years.

Next morning, Eben wakes up the brothers with news that their father, at seventy-five, has remarried. Since this fact makes their waiting for an inheritance more dubious than before, Eben offers to give them three hundred dollars apiece if they will sign away their shares to him; then they can ride to California. Asked where he will get the money, he says he knows where it is hidden, and they will never find it if they do not deal with him.

Simeon and Peter finally sign. Pulling out a strip of flooring under the stove, Eben takes up a canvas bag and gives them their money, in twenty dollar gold pieces. When Ephraim and his bride, Abbie Putnam, arrive, Simeon and Peter stop only long enough to make sarcastic greetings—off then they go, singing their ho-for-California song. Eben's greeting to Abbie is spiteful—he accuses her of having been bought, like a harlot.

PART II (*four scenes*)

Eben and Abbie continue their strong competition for full possession of the farm as though Ephraim did not exist. As a strategy in the battle, Abbie tries

222

to stimulate Eben's interest in her sexually. Eben refuses her with contempt and returns to Minnie, the prostitute. When Abbie "reports" him to Ephraim, saying that he has tried to make love to her, the old man is ready to drive him away or even to harm him bodily at her bidding. Suddenly Abbie conceives in her mind the notion of luring Eben into a plot whereby she can have a son, which she will tell Ephraim is his. When she suggests to Ephraim that the Lord may give them a son, he vows that, if that should happen, he will withhold nothing from her.

Boldly, Abbie makes her attack upon Eben through his most vulnerable point, his mother's memory. First, she reassures Ephraim that he will have a son, by her, which he considers the crown of his rugged, frustrating life. Then when the old man leaves to sleep in the barn, she stares through the wall at Eben. From both directions, desire seems to move in electrical waves. Abbie seizes the opportunity to go into Eben's room and embrace him. Although he struggles periodically, remembering his vow to his mother, he cannot help submitting. Finally, Abbie leaves and says she will wait for Eben in the downstairs parlor, dedicated to his mother and locked up since she died. Terribly tempted, Eben cries out, "Maw! Whar air yew?"

In his mother's parlor, using both Jocastan and direct sexual advances, Abbie overwhelms Eben and seduces him. In the process, however, both fall genuinely in love with each other.

Next day, Abbie takes over the parlor completely, with Eben's blessing. Saying that he had a fine rest in the barn, Ephraim comments also upon Eben: he tells Abbie there is no hope in his youngest son—he is soft-headed, "like his Maw."

PART III (*four scenes*)

On a night in late spring of the following year, a big party celebrates the birth of an heir to Abbie and Ephraim. The neighbors, however, are not fooled, although they participate in the festivities. In secret, Abbie restrains Eben from announcing the truth, telling him that by waiting they will get their hearts' desires.

Half an hour later, Ephraim reveals to Eben that the farm now belongs wholly to Abbie: at her request, Eben has been cut off. Seeing in Abbie's behavior with him a scheme to get a father for her child and then to dispose of him, Eben swears he will kill her. Ephraim is grappling with him when Abbie comes up. Accusing Abbie of trickery, Eben promises to tell the old man the truth and then to pack up and leave for California. Repeatedly Abbie swears her love for him and her fidelity, and Eben does not believe her. Her last word on the subject is a promise to prove to him that she loves him . . . "Better'n everythin' else in the world!"

Just before dawn, Abbie runs up to Eben in the kitchen and tells him that she has smothered the baby. Eben is overwhelmed—the baby was the greatest living remnant of his mother's world. Despite Abbie's mournful declarations of love and requests for the renewal of his love, Eben goes out to report her to the sheriff.

Before the sheriff returns with Eben, Abbie has confessed to Ephraim that the baby was not his, and that she has killed it. Ephraim's condemnation is a summation of tragic loss hovering over the whole house. A few minutes later, Eben "confesses" that he helped Abbie kill the baby. Ephraim tells the sheriff to take them both—and goes out to round up the stock that he had turned loose in expectation of going to California, a trip he cannot make now that he has discovered Eben's appropriation of his gold coins. The sheriff, looking around, says that it's a jim-dandy farm and he wishes he owned it.

56

JOHN HOWARD LAWSON (1895–   )

Processional (1925)

Musical drama in four acts

MAIN CHARACTERS AND THEME: The story revolves around the lives of a number of persons symbolically engaged in the stresses of class conflict, but the most important are *Dynamite Jim Flimmins*, a young miner who had been jailed for strike activity, and *Sadie Cohen*, the daughter of the storekeeper. These two are torn between fear of social penalties and the inner urge to live freely, whatever the expense.

OTHER CHARACTERS:

Boob Elkins, newsboy

Isaac Cohen, Jewish storekeeper

MacCarthy and *Bill*, soldiers

Phillpots, a city reporter

The Sheriff

A Man in a Silk Hat, representing Big Business

Mrs. Euphemia Stewart Flimmins, Jim's mother

Old Maggie, Mrs. Flimmins's mother

The Jazz Miners:

Slop, the leader, who comes through the audience playing the jazz march, "Yankee Doodle Blues," which forms a background throughout the play

Jake Psinski, a Polish miner with fiery wild eyes and a starved face, who blows a long trumpet

Rastus Jolly, a Negro miner, who plays a banjo and sings

A Big Soiled Man, with a great beard, who manipulates a slide trombone

Felix, a middle-aged anemic man, who makes a ghostly effort to manage a badly dented French horn

Alexander Gore, a man of the hayseed type, who blows on the big bassoon

Dago Joe, a sleek, greasy Italian, who has an accordion

Wayne Whifflehagen, a man with a curious face, who plays a harmonica

Smith, young and serious, who brings up the rear banging on a big drum

TIME: About 1920.

PLACE: Outskirts of a large town in the West Virginia coal fields during a strike.

MUSICAL HIGHLIGHTS: Besides "Yankee Doodle Blues" are the following: "There's no land so grand as my land from California to Manhattan Isle" (reflecting land hunger), "Bow-wow Blues," "Runnin' Wild" (a theme song of the flapper era), "When them lovin' arms is waitin'/When them lovin' lips is hot."

HISTORICAL NOTE: A rather successful effort, though the play lacked the influence its author intended, to infuse American drama with emotional vitality through the use of vaudeville stereotypes and musical extravaganza. Lawson insisted that these song-and-dance characters, available on every street corner, were truer to life than the realistic characters one usually meets on the stage. *Processional* was produced by the Theatre Guild at the Garrick Theatre, New York, January 12, 1925, with George Abbott as Jim and June Walker as Sadie, and ran for 96 performances.

ACT I: On the Fourth of July

On Independence Day, the striking miners march by Cohen's store as the news spreads that soldiers have been sent to the coal fields to mingle coal dust and blood. Boob, to whom Sadie has given one garter, tries to get from her the other garter, and a kiss. He is driven from the store by Sadie's father. As part of the uproar and confusion, Psinski (of the Jazz Miners) returns with a flesh wound made by "some guy" who didn't like music. Phillpots, who has come to town looking for a good news story, meets Sadie, dances with her, and (like Boob) is driven off by her father. Yet Phillpots is the only one who does not run and hide when the Sheriff and the Man in the Silk Hat bear down upon the streets. A shot knocks the silk hat off the Man's head;

226

the Man is so unnerved that he cannot finish his patriotic speech. When the Sheriff sees Phillpots laughing, he threatens to jail him, but his threat dissolves when Phillpots gives him a drink of Johnny Walker whiskey and Phillpots promises to give him nationwide coverage. Psinski, arrested for the shooting, is further condemned when a copy of Omar Khayyám's *Rubáiyát* is found on his person. Phillpots and Psinski go off to visit the pigsties and barns the miners call homes, and Old Maggie predicts "a black time" for all.

ACT II: *Scene 1*—Dynamite Jim

Coming to the jail to visit Jim are his mother and grandmother: they tell him of the bitter times with "soldiers here thick as flies." Rastus, with the blues, is trying to break into jail; but Jim is trying to saw his way out. Jim succeeds. To avoid the two soldiers, Bill and MacCarthy, he hides in a nearby coffin. Sheriff raises the alarm for Jim. He orders the soldiers to break up the music-makers who keep the people upset. When the Sheriff has gone, Jim climbs out of the coffin and thanks Psinski for the file with which he sawed to freedom. Climbing back into the coffin, he gets Psinski and Rastus to take him to the Labor Temple.

ACT II: *Scene 2*—The Labor Temple

As young soldiers, MacCarthy and Bill are deeply frightened by their duties in the midst of an angry populace. The Sheriff tells them to use their whistles if they need help. Walking in the moonlight, Phillpots and Sadie exchange nicknames which indicate their ambitions: Phillpots is Mr. Zip, a man-of-the-world character; Sadie is Desdemona, a heroine of the theatre. Just after the couple moves on, Rastus and Bill arrive at the Temple with their coffin. Bill and MacCarthy behave gingerly in the vicinity of the Temple, but MacCarthy goes inside for a drink. Jim comes out of his coffin. Through fear, Bill has pulled his rifle into shooting position and fixed his bayonet. In a struggle, Jim wrenches the rifle from Bill's hand and jabs the bayonet down on the fallen body; the soldier quivers and lies still. Sadie, watching the scene intently, tells Jim he is a beast, and that she hates him—wants to kill him. In the vaudeville motif, Jim bends over Bill saying, "He's gettin' cold . . . his soul's gone up in the sky, his soul's a-sittin' in the moon; he had a mother too. I want my mammy's arms 'cause I done a black thing . . ."

ACT III: *Scene 1*—Mother and Son

Hidden by his mother and grandmother in their cellar, Jim is the object of a very comprehensive search. In one mood, Sadie warns Jim's mother of his being pursued; in another, she and Boob demonstrate the dances they expect to do when they get to Broadway. Sadie's father spanks her. The Man in the Silk Hat thinks Boob and Sadie should be placed in detention homes. Reading off a long list of charges against Jim, the Sheriff tells Mrs. Flimmins that they'll hang him on Lonesome Mountain, with birds pecking at him. Mrs. Flimmins strikes out against the tyranny of soldiers and the Man in the Silk Hat. When Mrs. Flimmins leads the Sheriff to the rear of the house, Sadie goes to the trap door and taps three times; thinking it is his mother, Jim opens the door, carrying his gun. Sadie gives him a paper from the miners, who tell him they will act soon. Unable to keep the Sheriff occupied, Mrs. Flimmins comes back to protect the trap door. Sheriff opens it and finds only Psinski; he and MacCarthy carry Psinski away. Knowing the Sheriff will not immediately return, Jim comes out and swears that he is going to fight again—he hasn't killed enough.

ACT III: *Scene 2*—What Happened to Sadie

Sadie tries, unsuccessfully, to get Phillpots to take her to New York. When Phillpots is gone, Sadie is met by Jim, who is avoiding the soldiers and the Ku Klux Klan, which has recently entered the policing operation. After a brief erratic love scene in which he promises to raise her high to the moon, steal a barrel full of diamonds, and reach up and pick a bunch of stars for her, he carries her into the mine.

ACT III: *Scene 3*—The Man Hunt

Caught by his pants on the fence, and hanging like a flag, Jim is captured. His capture is exultingly reported by the Man in the Silk Hat.

ACT IV: The Jazz Wedding

Sadie, six months pregnant, is living with Mrs. Flimmins. Both women are captured by the Ku Klux Klan, in spite of Phillpots' efforts at rescue. When

228

unmasked, one Klansman turns out to be Psinski, another to be Rastus. Jim enters, feeling his way with a cane: he is blind. After he was hanged, a farmer cut him down before he died and watched over him. In Charleston, he was tried and found innocent. His blindness resulted from his being hanged.

Sadie carries a gravestone inside her, she says, but wants her kid. To her, the unborn child is a prophecy of marching freemen—all the soldiers who have died from Bunker Hill to the Marne. This is in line with a telegram from Calvin Coolidge which states that all men are brothers.

Phillpots suggests that Sadie and Jim get married. In the same atmosphere, Psinski makes a speech about the meaning of the strike and is amazed when the Man in the Silk Hat tells him that the miners will get what they want. The Sheriff marries Jim and Sadie in a jazz ceremony, with a revised dog license that is sealed with Jim's blood. The whole town forms a wedding procession.

57

SIDNEY HOWARD (1891–1939)

The Silver Cord (1926)

Psychological drama in four acts

MAIN CHARACTER AND THEME: *Mrs. Phelps*, archetype of the Cannibal
Mother, self-revealed in all her magnetic charm, terrible power, and
Freudian implications, through three large dynamic phases: as a
woman-animal, starved of normal affection; as mother, draining
affection from her sons, regardless of their other obligations; as mother-
in-law and prospective mother-in-law, fighting hard not to be shut out
by invaders.

OTHER CHARACTERS:

David, her older son   *Hester*, Robert's fiancée
Robert, her younger son   *Maid* (mute)
Christina, David's wife

TIME: The mid-1920's.

PLACE: Mrs. Phelps' house in mature residential area of an Eastern city.

HISTORICAL NOTE: The most thoroughgoing analysis of the professional
mother yet produced by the American drama. Also a sample of the
penetrating and highly literary works of Sidney Howard, who for insight
and dramatic skill rivaled O'Neill in the 1920's and 1930's. This drama,
with Laura Hope Crews as Mrs. Phelps, had comparatively brief runs
in New York and London, but was, justly, well received by the critics.

ACT I

Bringing his wife to visit his mother, David finds himself fussed over because
of his two years' absence, and Christina, his wife, finds herself all but ignored.

"The Silver Cord" (1926)

Christina immediately realizes that her mother-in-law, though well past fifty, is aggressively feminine and vital. In the ensuing conversation, Christina and Hester disagree with Mrs. Phelps' idea that parents should pick their children's careers. Hester's view—"Have 'em. Love 'em. And then leave 'em be"—is so shocking to Mrs. Phelps that she dismisses her boys in order to investigate these women who are trying to filch her sons from her.

Her first tête-à-tête is with Christina. The going is quite hard for her: she is offended when she hears Christina say that she refused to marry David for six or seven months; she is chagrined by Christina's cold businesslike manner and by her insistence that New York is the only place for people to work. When she is unable to wangle a promise from Christina to give up her job at the Rockefeller Institute, Mrs. Phelps tries desperately to get Christina to agree to join her in persuading David to give up his prospects in New York and to settle down at home and build houses for a development she intends to call Phelps Manor. Now and then in the conversation, she begs Christina not to crowd her out, set her aside, or rob her. She is thoroughly resistant when Christina says that she and David have only a week to visit. At length, she tells Christina: "Be honest with yourself. You are sacrificing David!"

Following her apparently unsuccessful bout with Christina, she returns to Robert with the declaration: "Oh, Robin! I'm so lonely! So lonely!" Robert comforts her and tells her what an ideal mother she has been. She tells him: "... you are my son. David takes after his father." Going to work on Robert in earnest, she "convinces" him that he is not in love with Hester and has him promise, on his own initiative of course, to break his engagement. When David enters, at her command he kisses her fervently on the lips. Finally, Mrs. Phelps and the two couples sit down for cocktails. Chris's announcement that in four months she is to become a mother causes Mrs. Phelps to spill her cocktail on her lovely evening gown.

ACT II *(two scenes)*

In the living room that same evening, Mrs. Phelps is insulted when the girls joke sharply about her sons' baby pictures and withdraws the pictures from further consideration. She pours out her bitterness by saying openly that she knows several girls who might look well in the dress Christina is wearing. Later, Christina and David go outdoors to watch the children coasting in the snow. When Robert, at the window, describes their kissing, Mrs. Phelps orders him to call David in for fear of his catching pneumonia. Hester protests that David should be proud of Christina and her motherhood; Mrs. Phelps counters that babies are not a fit subject for Hester to discuss. Somewhat later, Robert picks a quarrel with Hester about where they are to spend their honeymoon; the quarrel leads to a break of their engagement. Hester returns his ring and goes into hysterics. When she gets Mrs. Phelps alone, Hester asks her why she instigated the break in Robert's engagement: Mrs. Phelps tells her Robert never really wanted to marry her. Hester then asks for the car so she can leave; Mrs. Phelps refuses. Hester is about to walk away from the house, but Christina persuades her not to.

That night, Mrs. Phelps comes down to David's bedroom, which has been preserved—morbidly so—as it was when David was a child, and which is separate from Christina's room. Lovingly she tries to recall their past. Hearing a knock, she leaves and David hopes his visitor is Christina. It is, instead, Robert, who complains that David is trying to turn his mother against him. Mrs. Phelps returns and the three argue about the engagement. Mrs. Phelps says she has a bad heart and "may go at any moment." Dismissing Robert, Mrs. Phelps turns her full pressure upon David and gets him tentatively to accept her plan for him to stay and build Phelps Manor and to promise to exert his influence on Christina. In a few minutes Christina arrives, and with a glance she and Mrs. Phelps pledge each other undying enmity; nevertheless, Mrs. Phelps kisses her son as she leaves, but only after telling him he should put on his dressing gown. With scientific thoroughness, Christina cuts through the façade and tells David frankly that his love for her is impaired by a sexual understanding between him and his mother. She insists that he take her to New York the next day. When Mrs. Phelps slips back in, in the midst of their heated argument, Christina says: "I'm going to have a baby by a man who belongs to another woman!" Mrs. Phelps stands in the door, white but steady. Christina refuses to apologize and leaves. The new conversation between mother and son is interrupted by cries from Robert and Christina: Hester has left by way of the dining-room window wearing no coat. She is found drowning in the pond. Calling to David who is rushing to save Hester, Mrs. Phelps tells him to get his coat. "Are you crazy? Do you want to catch pneumonia?"

232

ACT III

Because there was a loss of beauty in the house the previous night, Mrs. Phelps next morning fills the house with flowers. The doctor who visited Hester left word that Mrs. Phelps has nothing wrong with her heart, and that it would take a stick of dynamite to kill her. On her side, Mrs. Phelps has decided to announce that Hester went insane. She has already made boat reservations for herself and Robert to travel abroad. In addition, although Robert knows little about them, the plans for him to become an interior decorator are far advanced—Robert is enthusiastic in spite of his ignorance.

Coming down the stairs, Christina tells David she is leaving with Hester whether David comes or not. Standing on his principle of the "noble" mother, David wavers and hesitates and accuses his bride of jealousy and inconsiderateness. Christina and Hester finally depart, Hester swearing she will marry only an orphan, and Christina leaving David to his "self-centered, self-pitying, son-devouring tigress" who has "unmentionable proclivities suppressed on the side."

A moment later, breaking loose from his mother, David follows his wife. In the final scene, Robert kneels beside his mother as she recites over him a parody of St. Paul's dictum on love—"mother love suffereth long and is kind . . . hopeth all things; endureth all things . . . . At least, I think my love does?" Robert, engulfed, parrots: "Yes, Mother."

58

BEN HECHT (1894–1964)
CHARLES MACARTHUR (1895–1956)

The Front Page (1928)

Photographic drama and satire in three acts

MAIN CHARACTER AND THEME: The hectic career of *Hildy Johnson*, star reporter for the Chicago *Herald-Examiner*, and of other members of that individualistic breed known as crime reporters on the special occasion of a member of the breed deciding to break from the ranks and elevate himself.

OTHER CHARACTERS:

Crime reporters:
Wilson, American
Endicott, Post
Murphy, Journal
McCue, City Press
Schwartz, Daily News
Kruger, Journal of Commerce
Bensinger, Tribune
Mrs. Schlosser, wife of Herman Schlosser, another reporter for the *Herald-Examiner*
Woodenshoes Eichorn, a policeman
Diamond Louis always called Louie by the reporters, "ham" gunman, formerly a fruit vendor
Jennie, scrubwoman in the Criminal Courts Building

Molly Malloy, a girl friend of the condemned man
Sheriff Hartman
Peggy Grant, an attractive girl of twenty who plans to marry Hildy
Mrs. Grant, her mother
The Mayor
Pincus, who comes with a paper from the governor
Earl Williams, condemned to be hanged for murdering a policeman
Walter Burns, the managing editor of the *Herald-Examiner*
Carl and *Frank*, deputies
Two Policemen

234

"The Front Page" (1928)

TIME: A Friday night in 1927.

PLACE: The press room in the Criminal Courts Building, Chicago.

MUSICAL HIGHLIGHTS: "By the Light of the Silvery Moon" (on the banjo); "Three O'Clock in the Morning"; "Waltz Me Around Again, Jennie"; *"Ach du lieber Augustin."*

HISTORICAL NOTE: First significant portrayal of the modern American newspaperman in American drama; imitated widely on the legitimate stage, in the movies, and on television. Its satiric scope is far-ranging, including among other topics politics and politicians and their links to crime, persecution of radicals for their opinions rather than their deeds, the handling and mishandling of crime, the nature of prostitution as practiced in the big city, and the cynicism of public officials concerning racial elements. The journalistic dialogue and characterization, concocted by two master journalists, are never without sparks; many of the incidents are based on actual happenings and are presented in accordance with journalistic methods. Running for 276 performances after its opening at the Times Square Theatre, New York, on August 14, 1928, the play was a personal triumph for Lee Tracy as Hildy, and he was supported by an outstanding cast.

ACT I

In the busy press room, Murphy, Endicott, Schwartz, and Wilson are engaged in their usual poker game, and McCue on one of the telephones which are free to reporters is calling a woman who was the victim of a Peeping Tom. The reporters are on all-night vigil, awaiting the hanging of Williams, but some are monitoring other news sources. On Burns' repeated calling for Hildy, who is not present, Schwartz tells the others that Hildy has quit the *Examiner*: the news is, of course, unbelievable. The sheriff has refused to move up the hanging from 7 A.M. to 5 A.M. so that the reporters can make an early edition; of the sheriff's attitude, Murphy says: "That guy wouldn't do anything for his mother."

Bensinger, a precise, hygienic reporter, is giving his city desk all the details of the preparation for the hanging, including the fact that Williams will be examined by a new alienist, Dr. Max J. Eglehofer, of Vienna. Since Williams is a radical, the consensus among reporters is that the sheriff is eager to capitalize on his hanging to show his anti-Bolshevik sympathies; but, on

235

the other hand, Williams killed a colored policeman at a time when the colored vote is important, and this fact helps to seal his fate.

Hildy finally arrives. He tells his reporter pals that he, his fiancée, and her mother are leaving for New York on the 11:18 train that night; that he is getting married at once and has a job in New York with an advertising firm making $150 a week (compared to the $70 a week the *Examiner* pays him); and further, that his fiancée's uncle owns the company and has already advanced him $500 in cash.

In spite of Hildy, business for the reporters goes on. Molly, a North Clark Street prostitute, complains to the reporters about their making her innocent conversation with Williams appear as a rendezvous. The sheriff is accused of getting the Williams execution postponed twice so that Williams can be hanged three days before election to help the sheriff's "law and order" ticket. For his part, the Sheriff invites the reporters to cooperate to stamp out the Red menace; he pledges "to reform the Reds with a rope." He and the reporters haggle over the number of tickets each gets for the hanging. As Hildy is saying good-by to his friends, Earl Williams breaks out of jail. Hesitating only slightly, Hildy drops his suitcase and calls Burns to report the shocking event: he tells Burns he is "on the job!"

ACT II

The Crime Commission has offered a reward of ten thousand dollars for the capture of Williams. While the other reporters telephone to their offices routine details and human interest stories, Hildy secretly calls Burns and tells him he has paid the assistant warden $260 of his wedding money for the real story. It is that during the examination by the alienist Eglehofer, the sheriff gave his gun to Eglehofer; Eglehofer, reconstructing things, gave the gun to Williams; and Williams shot Eglehofer and escaped. Hildy must work hard to get Peggy and her mother to understand why he cannot leave his big story at once. Meanwhile, Pincus has brought from the governor a reprieve for Williams, but the mayor does not want to accept it. He offers Pincus a good job for saying that the reprieve was not delivered, and Pincus temporizes. Getting $150 from Diamond Louie, Hildy is again on his way to the station when Earl Williams falls through the window into the press room where Hildy is alone. Hildy pushes Williams into the toilet and telephones the story to Burns. Returning, the other reporters find Hildy talking to Molly and suspect that the conversation concerns news of Earl; rather than give them any news, Molly jumps out of the window. Mrs. Grant, who has come to hurry Hildy, sees the whole thing. Because she refuses to keep quiet, she is carried off and locked up by Burns' men. Burns then turns to Hildy and, by showing him what a momentous story he has in his hands—one which can wreck the city administration—gets him to postpone his wedding trip one more time. After Burns has ordered ten men to come for the desk in which Hildy has locked Williams, so that the *Examiner* can claim full credit for capturing and returning Williams, Hildy, rejecting Peggy's pleas to leave, sits down to write his story.

ACT III

Protecting his investment in Williams, Burns promises Bensinger a high-paying job with the *Examiner* to remove Bensinger's interference. Somehow, Mrs. Grant has been lost and Hildy goes out to find her; he is stopped by the sheriff and the reporters and accused of having a special tip on Williams. When the sheriff discovers that Hildy has the gun which played a part in the prisoner's escape, he places both Burns and Hildy under arrest. Mrs. Grant wanders into the press room and accuses Burns of having her kidnapped because she knew he was hiding a murderer. Burns and Williams had decided previously that three taps on the desk were a signal: when Burns accidentally gives the signal, Williams inside responds, and the sheriff has the desk surrounded. Williams offers no resistance. As the sheriff is taking Burns and Hildy to be locked up, Pincus returns and insists upon serving the reprieve. Hildy then accuses the sheriff and the mayor of wanting to hang an innocent man just to win the election. The reprieve must therefore be accepted by the discomfited officers.

This time, Hildy is really through. He makes things up with Peggy, and Burns gives his blessing, kissing the bride. For a present, he gives Hildy his valuable watch. But once Hildy is gone, Burns sends a wire to the chief of police of a town Hildy's train will soon reach to have Hildy arrested for stealing his watch.

59

THOMAS JOB (1900–   )

Giants in the Earth (1928)

*Tragedy of the northwest frontier in a prologue and three acts,
based on the epic novel (1927) by Ole Rølvaag*

MAIN CHARACTER AND THEME: Drama of the gargantuan efforts of Norwegian families of the late 1870's and the 1880's to master the Dakota frontier, and of one family in particular, that of *Per Hansa*, a short, stocky, brown-bearded Norwegian immigrant.

OTHER CHARACTERS:

Beret, Per's wife

Ola (also called Olamund), Per's older son, age eight when the drama begins

Peter Victorious, Per's younger son

Hans Olsa, Per's oldest friend from Norwegian days

Sorina, Hans's wife

Syvert Tönseten, would-be deacon and justice of the peace, a

pompous friend of Per's with whom he came to Dakota

Kjersti, a plump, red-faced woman, Syvert's wife

Aslak Tjome, an elderly man

Mrs. Tjome, his crippled wife

Crazy Bridget, an Irish conjure woman

Henry Solum, a young farmer

Men and Women of the Congregation

TIME: 1873–1880.

PLACE: Dakota prairie.

MUSICAL HIGHLIGHTS: Ballad: "A cosy little cot in a nook on the plain"; "Oh Jesus see/My misery"; "No tongue can tell/How low it fell/In sin's dire degradation."

"Giants in the Earth" (1928)

HISTORICAL NOTE: A notable reduction of a great novel of American history, accomplished with the blessings of the novelist. The original settlement is depicted, the growth from sod to frame houses, the hugeness and depth of the country, the spreading prairie, the big silent skies, the plagues of grasshoppers, the cattle and the crops, and the terrible storms of snow and wind. Legends and religions of Norway and America are skillfully intermixed, even Indian lore. First performed by Carleton Players, Carleton College, Northfield, Minnesota, December 17, 1928.

PROLOGUE

It is 1873, with a covered wagon in the background; one sees the camp and campfire of Per and his family, the scene characterized mainly by sky, grass, and aloneness. Per promises Beret a real home and real pleasures. But Beret can remember only their sin—Ola is the child of that sin—and she is superstitious about its evil consequences. Begging her to forget the past, Per concentrates upon his present jobs: land to plough, house to build, food to get for winter. After saying good night to her husband, Beret prays: "Do not hunt us out in these lonely places."

ACT I

On a Sunday afternoon in June, six years later, the congregation has gathered in a large clumsy sod building with a wreath of wild flowers over the door. The religious service is interrupted by Beret's wild behavior. The minister has Per take the sick Beret out. During the service, Per's new son is christened Peter Victorious. Maddened by the grasshopper plague, Beret has wanted to kill the child—to give him back to Satan. Grieving over her behavior, Per says: ". . . happiness and I have been cold friends for many a long day." But Ola is proud of his father for catching 156 wild ducks in one night. Per has also caught badgers.

The minister calms Beret by telling her that Peter Victorious is a fine, brave name. After he leaves, however, Beret talks to her mother, who has been dead for years. Per fears that Beret is a fine craft that cannot sail rough seas. Beret listens tensely as Hans Olsa tries to get Per to let him keep Peter, for the child's protection. Per definitely refuses, praising his wife. He compares his bleak grimy house with the beautiful palace, white fence, and grand white

239

gate he had promised her in America. Hearing Per defend her, Beret gets new spirit: she dresses up, and she chides her husband and son for boxing on the Lord's Day.

ACT II

It is the following February, in the bedroom in Hans Olsa's house. From spending the night in the shed to protect his cattle, Hans Olsa has caught cold. Beret sings for his recovery, and Crazy Bridget puts a steaming poultice and a charm over Hans Olsa's chest. Later, Beret begins to prepare Hans Olsa for what she believes is his impending death. She says he must think of higher things—he needs the minister, not the doctor. After Per sends Beret on an errand, Hans Olsa talks of the ugly winter: he says the Snow King would freeze in it. He also says that it is a man's job to tame the prairie. Per replies: "You can't lose if you've got the guts to stick at it long enough." Reacting to Beret's meditations, Hans Olsa gives Per orders for his death—he loses all hope. He says he must have a minister to avert the dark doors of hell. "It is a terrible thing," he continues, "to fall into the hands of the Living God."

ACT III

In the kitchen of Per's frame house, Beret tells Per he must go to get the minister for Hans Olsa. Per shows her that it is quite impossible—it is thirty miles to the James River, and a new storm is brewing. To the young Peter, Per, grimly joking, says that his mother, always so tender, is trying to drive his father into the arms of death. Sorina, Hans's wife, urgently wants someone to go for a doctor, not a minister: she believes Hans Olsa is sinking rapidly. When she leaves, Beret again gets after Per to save Hans Olsa's soul. Uselessly, he points to the sky, discusses the snowy miles, the ease with which a man can get lost, the power of the cold, the winter with claws in it. Eventually, Per gives in. Borrowing skis, not waiting for coffee, he swings off. Ola again is proud of his father, who has assured him that their farm will be the best on the prairie, who handles the big skis with great skill, and who has told Ola that taming the prairie has been hard, but fun. Per has also told Ola to look after Peter: he has left without saying good-by to Beret.

When Per's friend Tönseten comes, he cannot believe that Beret would send her husband into such a storm. Beret tries to believe that Per will turn

240

back if things get too difficult, but Tönseten says she knows Per is not the kind to turn back ever. Beret begs Tönseten to go after Per and make him come back; Tönseten says it is far too late. Frightened, Beret says no wind can beat Per Hansa. Tönseten answers: "You can't beat the prairie." As her fears mount, Beret at the window calls Per repeatedly, moaningly, brokenly.

60

PHILIP BARRY (1896–1949)

Holiday (1928)

High-society drama in three acts

MAIN CHARACTER AND THEME: Difficulties faced by *Johnny Case*, thirty, promising broker from the lower ranks, with ideas, as he pursues romance and business success in the highest New York society.

OTHER CHARACTERS:

Linda Seaton, twenty-seven, looks twenty-two

Julia Seaton, twenty-eight, Linda's sister, beautiful

Ned Seaton, twenty-six, Linda's brother

Edward Seaton, fifty-eight, father of Linda, Julia, and Ned, veteran Wall Street and society leader

Susan Potter, thirty

Nick Potter, thirty-four

Laura Cram, thirty-two

Seton Cram, thirty-six

Henry, fifty, butler

Charles, younger servant

Delia, about thirty-five, house-maid

TIME: Christmas season, 1928.

PLACE: An extremely large and well-furnished Stanford White home in the richest residential section of New York City.

MUSICAL HIGHLIGHTS: Intermittent music from an old-fashioned music box, an electric gramophone, and a male singing group called the Scotch Songbirds.

HISTORICAL NOTE: First produced November 26, 1928, Plymouth Theatre, New York, with Hope Williams (to whom the author dedicated the printed play) as Linda. Directed by Arthur Hopkins. Sets by Robert

242

Edmond Jones. One of a number of plays in which Barry, without pursuing the conventions of manners comedy, dissected and portrayed the upper middle classes with sympathy, but with insight and sharpness. Other examples include *In A Garden* (1925) and *Tomorrow and Tomorrow* (1931), about the search for the security of true love within the complicated walls of society; *Paris Bound* (1927) and *The Animal Kingdom* (1932), about the intricacies and realities of marriage and divorce; *Hotel Universe* (1930), a one-act full-length play about a group of young American lost sheep probing for truth in a European vacation setting. The nearest Barry came to authentic manners comedy was *The Philadelphia Story* (1939), which mirrored Philadelphia "main-line" society and which gave Katherine Hepburn a profitable opportunity as Tracy Lord, on both stage and screen.

ACT I

Johnny and Julia, having met at Lake Placid, are determined to be married within a month. Johnny is amazed at the richness of Julia's surroundings, but Julia is more concerned with how she is going to get her father (she has no mother) to agree to so quick a marriage. Her brother Ned, though sympathetic, seems unable to fight his father even for his own life, and generally resorts to drink. Linda, more courageous, is impressed by Johnny, and helps the two lovers with their campaign. Upon her questioning, Johnny tells her of his secret plan—not yet broached to Julia—calling for a temporary retirement as soon as he makes a few thousand, so that he can relax and discover himself before settling down to work the rest of his life. Linda is fearful that this plan will not pass muster with either Julia or her father, but she is not hopeless. The first encounter between Johnny and Edward, the father, is indecisive, but each feels the other's peculiar strength and quality. Johnny readily confesses his struggles as a poor boy in Baltimore; Edward is politely touched. but less than encouraging.

ACT II

Edward agrees to the early wedding, but plans a huge New Year's Eve party— three hundred guests—to announce the engagement. Disgusted, Linda says: "A hundred million dollars knocking together never made many sparks that I could see." Linda tries to satisfy her sense of the occasion with her own small party up in the playroom that all her life has been a place of reality and dedication. With her up there are the Potters, and much of the time, Johnny. In between the two parties, word leaks out that Johnny has just made a killing of $40,000 and established himself on Wall Street as a promising brokerage organizer. This means that by applying himself to "the reverence for riches," he can be a millionaire soon. Near the end of Linda's party, Nick Potter leads the group, including Johnny, in a satirical delineation of the rise of a self-made tycoon. The real excitement, however, comes when having received congratulations from Edward and Julia on his financial coup, Johnny springs upon them his plan "to retire young and work late," and enthusiastically urges Julia to help him put it in force at once. Julia indignantly refuses and assures her father that she will bring Johnny around. On the stroke of midnight, a bewildered Edward is heard announcing the engagement (with misgiving in his heart) and wishing the engaged pair and the guests "a most happy and prosperous New Year."

ACT III

Twelve days later, Johnny is missing and Julia is still uncompromising. Linda learns from the Potters that Johnny has reserved a single cabin on the French Line to sail with them that night. Linda finds it impossible to believe that people in love can be so casual and stubborn about their mutual happiness. Meanwhile, Ned hints to Linda that he knows she is in love with Johnny and urges her to grab him; Linda pointedly ignores the hint. When Johnny arrives from Lake Placid, he sees Linda first. She is not downhearted when he tells her he is going to surrender to Edward and Julia because she thinks that love should rank even above one's dreams. Trying to surrender decently, Johnny finds Edward planning his honeymoon and his whole life with Julia. Withdrawing his surrender, he implores Julia to leave with him at once. This she indignantly refuses to do. Once Johnny is gone, Linda is amazed that Julia seems undisturbed. Compelling Julia to confess that she does not love Johnny, Linda flies to join the man she has always loved. At Julia's declaration that Linda has no chance, Ned, raising his glass, savagely challenges her: "Any bets?... Any bets, Julia?"

61

ELMER L. RICE (1892–   )

Street Scene (1929)

Drama in three acts styled to show the interlocking fates of people in the melting pot of the American city

MAIN CHARACTER AND THEME: Although the play lacks a full-fledged main character, *Rose Maurrant*, twenty, a pretty Irish office worker, is the principal character. Like a modern morality play, the drama revolves around Rose's family life and its tragedy, her efforts at romance, and her desire for freedom from the evil concentration of too many heterogeneous people in one place.

OTHER CHARACTERS:

Residents of the apartment house:

The Kaplans—

Abraham, sixty, Russian Jew of leftist philosophy

Shirley, his daughter, a teacher, thirty-three

Samuel, his son, twenty-one, honor student in college and aspiring lawyer, who cuts across racial lines to fall in love with Rose

The Fiorentinos—

Filippo, Italian musician and music teacher

Greta, his fat German wife

The Olsens—

Carl, the janitor

Olga, his wife

The Maurrants (besides Rose)—

Frank, forty-five, often away from home

Anna, his attractive wife of forty

Willie, his disorderly son of twelve

The Hildebrands—

Laura, a woman deserted by her husband and about to be dispossessed

Charlie and *Mary*, her two children

The Joneses—

George

Mary, his wife

Vincent, his son, a New York cab driver

Mae, his daughter, a vulgar shop-girl of twenty-one

Daniel Buchanan, typical white-collar slave and expectant father

Agnes Cushing, an old maid

Non-residents:

Steve Sankey, in his early thirties, collector for the milk company

Alice Simpson, spinster, who works for the Charities

Harry Easter, thirty-five, good-looking, Rose's office manager

Dick McGann, vacuous youth of twenty-one, who takes Mae out

Dr. John Wilson, an obstetrician

Officer Harry Murphy

Two other Policemen; *A Milkman*; *A Letter Carrier*; *An Italian Iceman*; *A Special Officer*; *Several Workmen* from the excavation next door; *Two College Girls*, nineteen; *Two Music Students*, eighteen and seventeen

Marshal James Henry

Fred Cullen, his assistant

A Grocery Boy; An Old-Clothes Man; A Huckster; A Janitor from a neighboring house; *A Mulatto Girl; Six or Eight Neighborhood Women; An Interne; An Ambulance Driver; Two Furniture Movers; Two Young Nurse Maids; An Undersized Man and a Tall Athletic Woman*, dressed to play tennis; *A Shabby, Middle-aged Couple; A Sailor with Two Girls; Passers-by*

TIME: 1920's—a hot June evening and the next day.

PLACE: Walk-up apartment house in a mean quarter of New York City.

HISTORICAL NOTE: One of the earliest successful dramas to do what John Dos Passos did in *Manhattan Transfer* and *U.S.A.*—to plait in a single strand the multifarious impulses of modern city life. The revolt of youth and the radical agitations in the twenties are also given due dramatic recognition. First produced January 1, 1929, at the Playhouse Theatre, New York; ran for 601 performances. Winner Pulitzer Prize for 1929. Musical version in collaboration with Kurt Weill and Langston Hughes, produced at Adelphi Theatre, New York, January 9, 1947. Rice made a reputation also with analytical dramas of various significant American characters, such as Mr. Zero, a clerk displaced by automation in *The Adding Machine* (1923), and the self-describing title characters in *Counsellor-at-law* (1931) and *Dream Girl* (1945).

246

ACT I

Aside from the variety expressed through colorful racial and national origins, different degrees of assimilation into American culture, different occupations, and intensive prejudices, the people of the apartment house are busy every minute reflecting their individual reactions to their close living, their family conflicts, their struggle for daily bread, and the oppressive heat. Mrs. Maurrant is a matter of unusual concern because, being neglected by her husband, she receives visits from Steve Sankey, a married man with two children. When at home, Maurrant openly expresses his anti-Semitism and his contempt for Mr. Kaplan, who talks constantly of the need for socialism. Mr. Maurrant is also determined that his daughter shall live a decent life, and he scolds her for allowing her office manager, Harry Easter, a married man, to take her dancing and keep her out late. When Rose begs him to take his family out of this area where his daughter sees so much cruelty and immorality, his son is subjected to brutality and gossip about his mother, and his wife is starving for wholesome living, he is little concerned. Rose rejects Easter's offer to get her a job as a showgirl and an apartment; she is kind to Sam Kaplan in spite of his weakness before the bully, Vincent Jones. She enjoys his reciting Whitman to her. Before she goes to sleep, however, she is called back to the reality of painful living that surrounds her—she must call the doctor for Mrs. Buchanan, whose wild screams of approaching childbirth pierce the early morning sky.

ACT II

All around her, Rose continues to see indifference, immorality, and unexpected intermittent beauty. She wonders how it can continue, and wishes she and her family could be free of it all. Hearing hints of the gossip concerning his wife, Maurrant announces that he will be out of town for a while, on his job. After he leaves, Shirley Kaplan asks Rose not to intervene between her brother and his aspirations to be a lawyer; Shirley tells Rose her romance with Sam is unsuitable for racial and cultural reasons. Mrs. Maurrant, meanwhile, gets word to Sankey, the collector for the milk company, that Maurrant will be away and that he may visit her. When Sankey arrives for the visit, Mrs. Maurrant pulls down the shades. Into the areaway below, the marshal and his assistant are dumping the belongings of the Hildebrands, who are being dispossessed. Maurrant suddenly returns. Before Sam, who sees him, can shout a warning upstairs, Maurrant has rushed up to his apartment and shot his wife and her lover, the latter dying instantly, the former just after she reaches the hospital. Momentarily, Maurrant escapes. Rose accompanies her mother to the hospital and watches her die.

ACT III

Easter returns to beg Rose to let him help her in her bereavement; she declines—she cannot accept his version of happiness. The police capture Maurrant, but allow him to say good-by to his daughter before they take him away. He tells her how deeply he regrets having lost his head: he remembers how his wife looked at him just before he killed her. Rose also separates herself from Sam, who is willing to give up his future to be with her. Perhaps, she says, they can be together in the future. For now, she must make a home for her brother Willie and build a new life for herself. Most of all, she must move out of New York City, maybe to Jersey where there is more room. At the end, a shabby couple come to occupy the apartment from which the Hildebrands have been dispossessed, and to start a new cycle of crushing tragedy.

62

MARC CONNELLY (1890–1964)

The Green Pastures (1930)

A religious fable in two parts suggested by Roark Bradford's southern sketches, Ol' Man Adam an' His Chillun (*1928*)

MAIN CHARACTER AND THEME: Adventures of *The Lord* in creation: his faithful believers and his faithless creatures, as seen through the eyes of simple folk who believe in God's manlike and godlike qualities.

OTHER CHARACTERS:

Mr. Deshee, the Sunday School teacher

Myrtle, Carlisle, Randolph, Three Boys, and Other Children, members of Mr. Deshee's Sunday School class

A Heavenly Cook

A Custard Maker

First Mammy Angel

A Stout Angel

A Slender Angel

Archangel Gabriel

Choir Leader

Adam

Eve

Cain

Cain's Girl

Zeba, Cain the Sixth's Girl

Cain the Sixth

Boy Gambler

First Gambler

Second Gambler

Voice in Shanty

Noah

Noah's Wife

Shem

Three Women

Flatfoot

Ham

Japheth

Two Cleaners

Abraham

Isaac

Jacob

Moses	*King of Babylon*
Zipporah, Moses' wife	*Prophet*
Aaron	*High Priest*
A Candidate Magician	*Five Girls*, the King's Favorites
Pharoah	*Two Officers*
The General	*Hezdrel*
First Wizard	*Angels*
Head Magician	*Townspeople*
Joshua	*Babylonian Band*
First Scout	*The Choir*
Master of Ceremonies	

TIME: Sunday School time.

PLACE: A lower Louisiana town; Earth; Heaven.

MUSICAL HIGHLIGHTS: "Rise, shine, give God the glory"; "When the saints come marchin' in"; "Certainly, Lawd"; "So high!" (a jump-up); "Bright mansions above"; "Turn you round"; "Run, sinner, run"; "My soul is a witness for the Lord"; "A city called Heaven"; "My Lord's a-writin' all de time"; "Go down, Moses"; "Mary, don't you weep"; "I'm noways weary and noways tired"; "Joshua fit de battle of Jericho"; "A blind man stood in de middle of de road"; "March on"; "Hallelujah, King Jesus." Also "blues" by Zeba.

HISTORICAL NOTE: According to Mr. Connelly, this play was written not to describe a racial community but to demonstrate the power of faith and the kind of faith needed by a world in danger of losing its faith. It was a phenomenal success. After opening at the Mansfield Theatre, New York, on February 26, 1930, it played in New York for two years and toured the country for many more years. In the difficult role of God, Richard B. Harrison achieved an outstanding success. The play was made into a motion picture, and was acted several times on television in the 1950's.

PART I (*ten scenes*)

Reading and interpreting the Bible to his Sunday School class of ten youngsters, Mr. Deshee makes clear that Heaven was a real place, with fish fries, "b'iled custard," and "ten cent seegars." God, he tells his children, probably looked like Reverend Dubois. As he goes back to the creation story, the lights go down. When they come up, Heaven is just as he said it was. The Angels are people the little children can understand. When God approaches, Gabriel cries out, "Gangway for de Lawd God Jehovah!" and the Angels sing to Him that they have all been baptized and redeemed. God takes a "seegar" with the others; he makes new firmament to improve the richness of the custard. When he finds he has created so much firmament as to endanger the health of the children, he drains the firmament off into mountains and valleys, oceans and lakes. Then he finds he must go to Earth on an inspection tour. He leaves Gabriel in charge of Heaven.

On Earth, God installs Adam and Eve in Eden. In the darkness, Mr. Deshee has the children tell him the story of the loss of Eden and the meanness of Cain. After this, the lights go back up again, and God observes the wickedness of Cain and Cain's Girl: he shakes His head. Later, back in his office, after preventing Gabriel from blowing his horn and ending time, God is told by Gabriel of the burden of the prayers from Earth. He had almost forgotten about the little place which so much displeased him three or four hundred years ago. Returning, he sees more and even greater wickedness in Cain the Sixth and Zeba; he sees gamblers with loaded dice and all kinds of sinning. He is utterly disgusted. Only a visit with a country preacher named Noah calms him somewhat. Still believing in mankind because of Noah and because of an inner faith in his experiment, he makes an arrangement with Noah whereby the people now living will be washed away—except Noah and his family. He orders Noah to build the Ark, and gives him precise specifications. Two animals of each kind are to be placed in the Ark. Building by God's instructions, Noah is ridiculed by the sinful people. But according to Noah's predictions, the rains actually come, for forty days and forty nights, and all the people except Noah and his family are drowned. When it is all over, God says to Noah: "Well, now we'll see what happens."

PART II (*eight scenes*)

In God's office, Two Heavenly Cleaners take notice that the Earth, though very small in the scheme of things, is using up progressively more of God's time. Speaking to that point, God mentions to Gabriel that he is employing an inordinate number of thunderbolts and not getting the best results. But he is pleased with a few specimens—men like Abraham, Isaac, Jacob, and their families. He still believes he can make something of this man-creation.

251

In Heaven, Isaac tells God that Moses, coming along now, is also to be trusted. God says he has been noticing Moses; in fact, he is going to turn over the whole Land of Canaan to Isaac's descendants—Moses' people.

Going down to talk to Moses, God shows him and his brother Aaron, both field hands, a few tricks. Then, he prepares them to face Pharaoh, who has many magicians and loves magic. When Moses and Pharaoh finish "tricking each other," Moses has struck down the oldest boy in every house of Pharaoh's people, and Pharaoh has at last agreed to let Moses' people go free. God does not let Moses take his people into Canaan, but he does let Moses watch as Joshua takes them in.

In the dark, Mr. Deshee is telling the children once more that even this Canaan scheme of God's did not work. ". . . dey went to de dogs again. And dey went into bondage again. Only dis time it was the City of Babylon." Following his announcement, the next scene resembles action in a New Orleans night club. In this setting, idol-worshipping kings and venal high priests drive God to his limit. He announces to all that he repents of man and will deliver him no more.

Every day, for hundreds of years, God has received Abraham, Isaac, Jacob and Moses; every day, they have asked him to go back to their people; every day, he has refused. A recent admittee to Heaven, Hosea, a prophet, does not worry God by coming into the office; he merely walks back and forth in front of the office. God feels his shadow on the wall. Suddenly, God tells Gabriel that the commotion is all because of Hezdrel. Jerusalem is under siege, and Hezdrel is one of the defenders. So poignant is Hezdrel's petition, which is not exactly a prayer, that God worries. He tells Gabriel: "Even bein' Gawd ain't a bed of roses." Going to the window, he tells Hezdrel: "I know yo' fightin' bravely, but I ain't comin' down." Later God goes down, without promising anything. He learns from Hezdrel that they fight in the faith of the Lawd God of Hosea—not of the old God of wrath and vengeance. By such faith God is indeed impressed.

He tells Gabriel his problem is quite serious. Now, he realizes that maybe even God must suffer. A voice is heard describing a man carrying a cross up a high hill and being nailed to it. God rises and murmurs "Yes!" as if in recognition. As he smiles after so long a time, the Angels sing, "Hallelujah, King Jesus."

63

GEORGE S. KAUFMAN (1889-1961)
MORRIE RYSKIND (1895–   )
with lyrics and music by
IRA and GEORGE GERSHWIN

Of Thee I Sing (1931)

Musical comedy and drama of political satire in two acts

MAIN CHARACTER AND THEME: The presidential campaign of *John P. Wintergreen*, whose platform is one word—love; the methods of conducting the campaign and the repercussions.

OTHER CHARACTERS:

National Campaign Committeemen:

Louis Lippman, Jewish, later Secretary of Agriculture

Francis X. Gilhooley, Irish, later Secretary of the Navy

Hotel Chambermaid

Matthew Arnold Fulton, who owns a string of newspapers, later Secretary of State

Senator Robert E. Lyons, from the South

Senator Carver Jones, from the West

Alexander Throttlebottom, the Vice Presidential candidate, later the Vice President

Sam Jenkins, Fulton's assistant, later secretary to the President

Diana Devereaux, a bathing beauty, first very Southern, then very French

Mary Turner, secretary, who makes wonderful corn muffins

Miss Benson, Mrs. Wintergreen's secretary

Wrestlers—*Vladimir Vidovitch*, the Harlem Heaver, and *Yussef Yussevitch*, the Terrible Turk

The Chief Justice and eight *Associate Justices*

Scrubwoman,   The   French Ambassador,   Senate   Clerk,

Guide, Photographers, Police-   *Newspaperman, Senators, Flun-*
men, Secretaries, Sight-seers,   *keys, Guests*

TIME: The early 1930's.

PLACE: All over the country; New York City; Washington, D.C.

MUSICAL HIGHLIGHTS: "Who is the lucky girl to be?"; "My Mary makes corn muffins"; "Of thee I sing, baby"; Inaugural address: "I have definite ideas about the Philippines"; "We're the one-two-three-four-five-six-seven-eight-nine Supreme Court judges"; "Oh, it's great to be a secret'ry"; "Everybody wants to know: what about Miss Devereaux?" "Who cares . . ."; "She's the illegitimate daughter"; "Because, because, because, because—"; "The country thinks it's got depression"; *"Garçon, s'il vous plait"*; "Jilted, jilted"; "I'm about to be a mother"; "Posterity is just around the corner"; "Oh trumpeter, trumpeter, blow your golden horn"; "I was a beautiful blossom."

HISTORICAL NOTE: Brilliant and comprehensive satire of American national politics and of political perspectives among the people, up through the 1920's. The Gershwin songs, patterned at times after Gilbert and Sullivan, are a lasting contribution to musical comedy literature. Drama ran for 441 performances, beginning on December 26, 1931, at the Music Box Theatre, New York, and received the Pulitzer Prize in 1932.

ACT I (six scenes)

The first scene, set in any city in America, is a political parade in progress. The name of the presidential candidate is boldly displayed; that of the vice-presidential candidate is lost in shadow. Slogans proclaim Wintergreen's worth because his "flavor lasts" and because he represents "the full dinner jacket," among many other things. Also, "He's the man the people choose—/ Loves the Irish and the Jews."

In a shabby hotel room, the president-makers decide to steer their campaign away from such issues as war debts, wheat, and immigration, and to stick to trusted political clichés, such as what Lincoln said, Southern chivalry and hospitality, and opposition to Russian Bolshevism. What they need most, however, is a keynote slogan. They find it in one word—love. It is decided that the candidate Wintergreen shall hold a great beauty contest and fall in love with and marry the winner; he will then make love continuously until election day. Throttlebottom, the vice-presidential candidate, must be hidden away.

254

"*Of Thee I Sing*" (1931)

At Atlantic City, the beauty contest is in full swing. Diana Devereaux seems far ahead because of her capacity to throw her arms right around everyone's neck and because of other marked and studiously charming Southernisms. In casual conversation with Mary Turner, however, Wintergreen is deeply impressed by her sincerity; when he eats her corn muffins, he falls in love with her and gets her promise to marry him. Diana wins the contest but loses the man. She demands justice.

In Madison Square Garden, the campaigners compete for attention with wrestling matches. Eventually, Wintergreen and Mary get the stage, and as he has done all over the country, he once more wins her love and gets her promise to marry him. Turning to the audience, he challenges them: "Citizens, it is up to you! Can you let this glorious romance end unhappily!" The meeting ends with the campaign song, which has this chorus:

> Of thee I sing, baby,
> You have got that certain thing, baby,
> Shining star and inspiration,
> Worthy of a mighty nation,
> Of thee I sing!

Naturally, Wintergreen sweeps the country, taking every electoral vote. In Atlanta, Georgia, he got 12,736 votes to 1,653 for Jefferson Davis; in Hollywood he ran ahead of Mickey Mouse and Gloria Swanson's First Husband. On the motion picture screen that flashes the returns, Wintergreen is shown leading King George and Queen Mary in Manchester, England, and losing only to Mussolini in Rome, Italy (828,638 to 0). Throttlebottom is shown getting his shoes shined before entering the election booth, but one sees only the feet.

The Chief Justice, on Inauguration Day, combines the inaugural oath with the marriage ceremony. At the end his pronouncement is, "I hereby pronounce you President of the United States, man and wife." Cutting through the jubilation is Diana's threat to sue for being jilted.

ACT II (*five scenes*)

The duties devolving upon the President begin to come clear: serving the cause of disarmament by scrapping two battleships and building four; having the Secretary of War collect his gambling debts; and solving the problems of farmers and sailors by having them exchange places. The President's wife also has duties, such as buying 148 lamb chops, a carload of asparagus, and 75 loaves of bread for a single state dinner, By being a member of a guided tour inspecting the White House, the Vice President learns that he has a duty to preside over the Senate: he hurries thereto. The Diana Devereaux matter begins to flare up dangerously: New Jersey, Nebraska, and Louisiana, among other states, have passed resolutions in Diana's favor. When the French Ambassador discovers Diana's Gallic origins, he threatens war to protect France's honor. At last the politicians decide that Wintergreen must resign, but he and Mary determine to hold their ground.

As presiding officer of the Senate and heir apparent to the presidency, Throttlebottom tries to hurry the proceedings impeaching Wintergreen. After much maneuvering—which includes voting five thousand dollars for flowers to be sent to a Senator's wife on her birthday and a report of the Committee on Unemployment showing that it has succeeded in bringing more unemployment to the nation—impeachment is defeated when Mary steps forward and announces that she is going to have a baby. This momentous fact makes the impeachment of the President unthinkable. It also causes the French Ambassador to feel more aggrieved since France's birth rate is declining, and if Diana had become the President's wife, this new event would have worked in France's favor. The Ambassador calls Mary's announcement "American trickery of the most reprehensible sort!" Eventually, France agrees to let the baby proceed if Wintergreen will promise to turn him over to France immediately after he is born. The President refuses.

As the time for the baby's arrival grows nearer, the Supreme Court goes into session to decide its sex. In spite of the great justices, twins are born— a boy and a girl. The French Government is pacified when Wintergreen, remembering Article Twelve of the Constitution which puts the President's obligations upon the Vice President when the former is unable to fulfill his duties, turns Throttlebottom over to Diana. With a great burst of music, a canopied bed from the White House, hung with gold, and silver, and bald-headed eagles, is pushed forth. In it is Mary Turner Wintergreen, a twin on each arm. The crowd bursts into song, which is naturally "Of Thee I Sing, Baby."

64

S. N. BEHRMAN (1893–   )

Biography (1932)

Manners comedy in three acts

MAIN CHARACTER AND THEME: Concerning the publicity value of a very free
and cosmopolitan soul, *Marion Froude,* and how the story of her life
stirs excitement in many quarters of high society.

OTHER CHARACTERS:

Richard Kurt, twenty-five　　　　*Leander Nolan*

Minnie, a German maid, fifty　　　*Warwick Wilson*

Melchior Feydak, a Viennese　　　*Orrin Kinnicott*
composer　　　　　　　　　　*Slade Kinnicott,* his daughter

TIME: About 1930.

PLACE: New York City.

HISTORICAL NOTE: First produced by the Theatre Guild, Guild Theatre,
New York, December 12, 1932, with Ina Claire as Marion. Although
accepted as one of the leading American exponents of manners comedy
because of the present play, *The Second Man* (1927), *Rain from Heaven*
(1934), and other examples, Behrman has written other types, ranging
from drama of controversial social problems to that of warm human
relations.

ACT I

Kurt, waiting for Marion in her apartment, is impatient with Minnie and
Feydak until he learns that Feydak is a composer (like most Americans, he
mistakes Feydak for his late brother, Victor, who wrote the popular operetta

Danubia). Kurt is about to leave when Marion comes in, as usual indomitably alive. She has been walking on Fifth Avenue. Dismissing Kurt for thirty minutes, she gives vent to her happiness at talking with Feydak, whom she has not seen since she buried Victor (whom she had joyously lived with and almost married) six years ago. Feydak learns she has been short on commissions—she who had painted the great of the world, communist as well as capitalist. In independence, Marion refuses Feydak's offer to accompany him to Hollywood. Answering the doorbell, she greets Leander Nolan, a middle-aged man resembling the late President Warren G. Harding. When Feydak is gone (she promises to meet him soon at a speakeasy), she recognizes Nolan as her childhood friend and a candidate for United States Senator from Tennessee. He offers to let her paint him in oils, and she thinks she might. Upon Kurt's return, Marion diplomatically dismisses Nolan. Kurt wants her to do a serial autobiography for *Every Week*, a magazine with three million circulation, which he edits. He hands her a two thousand dollar advance. She hesitates; and then she begins to see the fun of it. He wants her to concentrate on how she was not very good, only clever. Waving her check after Kurt is gone, she says she must fill in the spaces between "I was born" and "I meet Richard Kurt."

ACT II

An afternoon three weeks later, Marion is happy touching up Nolan's portrait and making notes for her book. Feydak comes by, as does another old friend, Warwick Wilson, the movie star, who devastates Minnie with his good looks. Late for his posing, Nolan enters, full of anxiety over the announced autobiography. He warns Marion to keep him entirely out. If she will give up the whole idea, he promises her many commissions, including one from his rich prospective father-in-law, Orrin Kinnicott. He simply cannot have his career ruined. Marion bids him good-by and agrees to part friends, but he will not go. Nolan offers Kurt a big job in Washington in exchange for killing the autobiography. Kurt is wounded only by realizing that Nolan is still another of Marion's early lovers. Refused on both sides, Nolan lashes out with threats; Kurt is merely intrigued at this prospective boost to the Tennessee circulation. After Nolan has gone, Kurt receives a call from his boss, obviously under pressure. He tells Marion that if he is fired, he will publish the book on his own. Marion tries hard to learn why

Kurt is so passionately critical and vindictive. After a while, Kurt confesses the influence of the tragic deaths of his parents, his resulting loneliness, and his love for Marion.

ACT III

Two weeks later, Kurt, Nolan, Kinnicott, and Slade (Nolan's fiancée) are gathered at Marion's, talking things over. After miscellaneous pyrotechnics, including incriminations and insults, Marion clears away everybody except Kinnicott, who suggests that he could correct her troubles by metabolism. Before very long, he has made a date with Marion for dinner the next evening at his widower's penthouse. Later, Kurt and Marion quarrel; Kurt bounds out; and Marion burns her manuscript in the Franklin stove. Nolan comes back, having broken with both Kinnicotts, and proposes marriage to Marion. Marion declines, telling him she loves Kurt. Finally, she tells Kurt she must part from him because she cannot join his crusade, and he can never understand the essential her. A telegram, which has come earlier, is from Feydak, inviting her to accept the commission he has got her to paint the prizewinners of the Motion Picture Academy and to go on with him to Honolulu and China. Marion and Minnie joyfully pack.

65

EUGENE O'NEILL (1888–1953)

Ah, Wilderness! (1933)

Comedy in three acts

MAIN CHARACTER AND THEME: Nominally dealing with the social development of *Richard Miller*, sixteen, the play by its dramatic terms stresses the strength and vagaries of the American fireside.

OTHER CHARACTERS:

Nat Miller, fifty-seven, owner of the *Evening Globe*, Richard's father

Essie, fifty, his mother

Arthur, nineteen, his elder brother

Mildred, fifteen, his sister

Tommy, eleven, his younger brother

Sid Davis, forty-five, Essie's Puckish brother

Lily Miller, Nat's sister, forty-two, an old-maid schoolteacher

David McComber, store owner in the town, father of Muriel

Muriel McComber, fifteen, Richard's girl

Wint Selby, a classmate of Arthur's at Yale

Belle, twenty, a fast college girl

Norah, Irish servant in the Miller house

Bartender

Salesman

TIME: July 4 and 5, 1906.

PLACE: A small town in Connecticut, probably New London.

MUSICAL HIGHLIGHTS: "Waltz Me Around Again, Willie"; "Waiting at the Church"; "Poor John!"; "In the Sweet Bye and Bye"; "Bedelia"; "Then You'll Remember Me"; "Dearie."

"*Ah, Wilderness!*" (1933)

HISTORICAL NOTE: The drama points up the moorings and excitements of the Miller household, and moral and intellectual challenges, both contemporary and perennial. Evidences of middle-class standards of value are seen in the Millers' Buick and their dressing for driving in linen dusters, veils, goggles, and caps; in Arthur's padded shoulders and peg-top trousers; in the Ivy League atmosphere, predominantly Yaleish; and in jokes about Theodore Roosevelt, the radical Emma Goldman, Nick Carter, and the Sandow Exerciser. The entire play is O'Neill at his best, his material fully digested and absorbed, delivered with beguiling realism and haunting poetic and nostalgic effects. First performed by the Theatre Guild at the Guild Theatre, New York, October 2, 1933, with George M. Cohan as Nat Miller, Gene Lockhart as Sid, and Elisha Cook, Jr., as Richard. Initial run: 289 performances. Transformed in 1959 into a successful musical entitled *Take Me Along*, starring Jackie Gleason.

ACT I

Although it is just 7:30 on the morning of the Fourth of July, breakfast is over and the Miller family looks forward to its holiday preparations. Young Tommy has been warned to keep his firecrackers away from the house. Arthur announces that he and Bert Turner are taking Elsie and Ethel Rand canoeing; Mildred is on her way to the beach, with Anne Culver. When Elsie says she and Lily are going to sit around and rest and talk all day, Nat says that he has a better suggestion: a drive around town in the Buick, and out to the lighthouse and back. Essie and Lily agree. Although apparently detached, Lily has been particularly interested in Sid's talk—about his new job on the paper in Waterbury and his determination to refrain from his accustomed heavy drinking when he and Nat drop by the Sachem Club picnic. Lily and Sid would have been married years ago if he could have stopped drinking or she could have been the wife of a man who drank heavily, even though she has always loved him.

Only Richard is unaccounted for. These days, according to his father, Richard has been preoccupied with the "red meat" of love, poetry, and socialistic reading. When called to account by his father, he readily confesses his belief that the Fourth of July is a stupid farce—there is no liberty anywhere. In his hand, as he comes forward, is Carlyle's *French Revolution*. Surprised that his father has read the book, he must also defend himself against his mother's charge of hiding "vile" books. Essie can identify them only vaguely, but Richard proudly identifies them as the works of Oscar Wilde, Bernard Shaw ("the greatest playwright alive today"), Algernon Swinburne, and Omar Khayyám.

Seeing Mr. McComber—the father of Muriel, Richard's present love—coming up the walk, Arthur and Mildred flee to catch the 8:20 trolley, and the others clear out so that Nat can be alone with the guest. McComber immediately charges Richard with "being dissolute and blasphemous" and shows Nat letters and poems, in Richard's handwriting, which (after McComber leaves) even Nat describes as "warm." But in the presence of McComber, and in spite of the letter's threat to take his advertising out of Nat's paper, Nat defends his son vigorously.

The "warm" literature turns out to be Swinburne's "Anactoria," which talks of the complete merger of lovers, body and soul. Called on the carpet, Richard denies any faint intention of seducing Muriel: he says, sincerely, that he loves her and hopes to marry her. Even so, his father gives him the letter McComber had brought, dictated by McComber, in which Muriel tells him she is through with him, completely. Richard, to himself, calls her a little coward, but he obviously does not mean it: he is only expressing his deep hurt. Like a little boy, he says he feels sick. When his mother turns to stay with him, he bids her go: he wants to be alone!

ACT II

At six that evening, Essie is dictating the dinner preparations to her second-girl, Norah. Lily, helping her, talks of Sid, still insisting that she cannot marry a man who drinks. Richard appears, completely disillusioned, sure that life is just a joke. He is ready to go "out, then, into the night," with Shaw's Marchbanks; but his mother warns him not to go far—dinner will be ready very soon. When Wint Selby comes by, looking for Arthur, he talks Richard into coming along with him. Wint has engaged "a couple of swift babies" from New Haven, but lacks funds to treat them both. Richard volunteers to go—throwing himself away like this suits his present mood—and he has eleven dollars saved up. Sid arrives, delightfully tipsy, and Lily is dismayed. At dinner, Nat tells for the thousandth time the story of his swimming prowess and once again insists that he cannot eat bluefish because of its poisonous oil. This time disgusted, Essie tells him that he has been eating bluefish for years under the name of weakfish: he is sure now that he is poisoned. After flirting with Norah, Sid becomes the life of the party, and even Lily laughs, though she is sick at heart. Richard sums up the situation by saying that, like all women, Aunt Lily is ruining a man's life—this time, Uncle Sid's, by keeping him dangling—and that he for one will follow Omar's advice and drink without caring to know whence nor why.

ACT III *(two scenes)*

At ten that night, Richard is with Belle in the back room of a bar in a small hotel—Wint has gone off with Belle's friend, Edith. Belle has little luck in getting Richard to "warm up" and have some fun. Nursing one glass of beer for a long time, Richard speaks poetically about life. He even tries to reform Belle. When she accuses him of wasting her time, he gives her five dollars just for kissing him. Richard is quoting Oscar Wilde when a salesman comes up and takes Belle away. By now Richard has had another drink or two and is well intoxicated and unruly; the bartender and the salesman throw him out. When the salesman warns the bartender that there may be trouble because it was Nat Miller's son who was just thrown out, the bartender eases his conscience by chasing Belle away.

At eleven, the family is gathering again. Tommy and Mildred tell of the good times they had, each in a different way. Looking quite pleased, Arthur comes in whistling. At his mother's request, he sings "Then you'll remember me." As Sid blatantly begs forgiveness of Lily, under the romantic spell of Arthur's singing, Arthur sings "Dearie" and "Waiting at the Church," very popular tunes of the time. Eventually Richard arrives, fully inebriated, his trousers dirty and torn, shouting lines from Omar and Ibsen. After a minute or two, like a sick little boy, he falls into Essie's arms with "Ma! I feel—rotten!" Sid, who has full experience in this line, puts him to bed. Nat quiets Essie's fears about Richard.

ACT IV *(two scenes)*

Nat is trying to wait for Richard to awaken, but Richard takes too long—his father must go to work. During the waiting, Nat and Essie discuss what must be done with Richard; at first Essie advocates stern measures, and then when Nat agrees, she says she does not want Richard hurt. Nat receives an unsigned letter (it is a part of Belle's vengeance on the bartender) telling him that Richard was at the Pleasant Beach House and that the bartender served him knowing him underage. This arouses new fear, but all decide to tread gingerly with Richard. When Richard comes down, he tells his mother he is not worried about the immorality, just about the fact that drinking did not make him feel good, as it does Uncle Sid. Later, his Uncle Sid teaches him about the ill effects of drinking and unrequited love. But Richard's life is enlivened by a letter Mildred brings him from Muriel, who has been imprisoned by her father but who threw the letter, folded many times into a tiny square, out of her window. The letter says she still loves him and wants the two of them to sneak out that night and meet along the beach.

Richard is at the meeting place before nine and has time to soliloquize on his strange fate. Muriel arrives, and under the new moon a tender love scene develops between these daring young sweethearts, sixteen and fifteen years of age. They talk of their love as though it were utterly reckless and timeless. But Muriel, about to let Richard kiss her, is shocked and over-whelmed when she hears of Belle. She fights to leave; she hates him. But soon she forgives him, and lets him kiss her. They swear undying love and faithfulness. They even plan their honeymoon, distant though it is. Richard (quoting) tells her she is "my love, mine own soul's heart, more dear than mine own soul, more beautiful than God!"

Simultaneously, Essie and Nat are delving through the books confiscated from Richard's room. Parental duty again looms high, but the problem of how to handle a delicate Richard delicately remains extremely difficult. Nat and Mr. McComber have made up; Richard will still go to Yale; he can still be friendly with Muriel. When Richard arrives, he is floating on many clouds. Warned again by Essie to talk to Richard when the time comes, Nat gives Richard his unique lecture on the facts of life. The talk is not a great success, but Richard demonstrates that his spirit has been uplifted and continues to rise.

When Richard has gone upstairs, his parents look at the moon, quote Omar, and kiss like young lovers. Nat says autumn has beauty—and winter, too, if you are together.

66

JACK KIRKLAND (1901–   )

Tobacco Road (1933)

*Tragedy of the soil in three acts from
the novel (1932) by Erskine Caldwell (1903–   )*

MAIN CHARACTER AND THEME: Story of *Jeeter Lester*, fifty years a dirt farmer, as the final basic representative of Georgians attached to the soil for life, and refusing to separate from it in spite of suffering depression and degeneracy through steady poverty and moral starvation.

OTHER CHARACTERS:

Dude Lester, sixteen, Jeeter's last son of a brood of seventeen children, sadistic and careless of all feelings but his own

Ada Lester, about fifty-three, Jeeter's wife of forty years, thin, gaunt, pellagra-ridden

Ellie May, eighteen, Jeeter's daughter, attractive in figure, but spoiled by a harelip

Grandma Lester, Jeeter's mother, an old bent hag in ragged black clothes

Lov Bensey, thirty, who works at the chute and is married to Pearl

Henry Peabody, a neighboring farmer, who resembles Jeeter

Sister Bessie Rice, forty, portly, formerly a woman of loose morals, now an evangelist, who likes young men

Pearl, fourteen, Ada's pretty, yellow-haired daughter, who refuses to consummate her marriage

Captain Tim Harmon, son of Captain John, who promised Jeeter lifetime occupancy of the land

George Payne, officer of the bank in Augusta

TIME: About 1930.

265

PLACE: Jeeter Lester's farm situated on a tobacco road in the back country of Georgia.

MUSICAL HIGHLIGHTS: "Shall We Gather at the River."

HISTORICAL NOTE: Play belongs to the world-wide list of dramas in which preoccupation with the soil and struggle for everyday shelter and food through the soil are basic considerations. Its use of picturesque symbols —such as broom sedge, ready for burning, the coal-grimed overalls of Bensey, the mask of the cynical banker—of colorful and authentic language, and of theatrical effect, drab but disturbing, elevate it to a place of historical significance in the American drama. In spite of widespread critical disapproval, the drama is an American original and deservedly popular as such. First performed at Masque Theatre, New York, December 5, 1933, it accumulated 3,182 consecutive performances, and has been many times revived. Henry Hull was first in a long line of Jeeter Lesters.

ACT I

In the hope of getting a load of wood off to Augusta so that he will have a few dollars for food, Jeeter patches the tire of his old automobile. He tries to get Dude to stop throwing his ball against the house because the vibration is causing the shingles to fall off. Dude bitterly refuses. Although without seed-cotton or guano, Jeeter still hopes to plant a crop this year—he has not planted one for seven years. Dude sadistically teases his father about the prospect of his being buried in the corn crib and having his face eaten away by rats, the fate of Jeeter's father. Ada thinks only of being buried in a stylish dress, but she cannot expect this favor from any of her seventeen children.

Lov Bensey comes by with a load of winter turnips, and the whole Lester family is excited, not having eaten for some time. Since Lov paid seven dollars to Jeeter for Pearl, he wants Jeeter to compel Pearl to consummate their marriage, but he will not willingly share his turnips. Using Ellie May as a decoy, Jeeter steals the turnips and runs away into the woods with them. Returning, he shares a few with his son, his wife, and his mother.

Sister Bessie comes by to pray for the sinful Lesters. While conducting her religious service, she falls in love with Dude. When Peabody, a neighboring farmer, tells Jeeter that Captain Tim, Captain John's boy, is coming back, Jeeter is hopeful that he can get credit to start a crop. He and Dude prepare to burn off broom sedge, to that end.

266

ACT II

Very early next morning, Bessie returns to get Dude: she says the Lord has approved of their marriage. Dude is not interested until she tells him that she is prepared to invest the eight hundred dollars received from her husband's insurance in a new automobile, expressly for him to drive. Without anger, Lov comes back to say that Pearl has run away and that he *must* have her back. When Lov goes, Pearl appears and rushes to her mother—she will talk with no one else. Ada assures Jeeter that Pearl is not his child and that therefore he has nothing to say about her future. She says Pearl is not going back to Lov; she is going to Augusta to live a city life. Meanwhile, Ada and Jeeter practice a maneuver that results in their stealing a sack of corn meal from Morgan Prior nearby, to avoid starvation. While they are gone, Lov tries once more to talk to Pearl, but she will not even listen to him, let alone answer him. Ada, returning, beats Lov with a stick, and Jeeter says he has no right to interfere. He tries to get Lov interested in Ellie May, who because of her harelip has been much neglected, but Lov cannot abide her ugliness: besides, he must have Pearl.

Bessie and Dude return from the city, Dude blowing the horn of the new car almost continuously—to blow an automobile horn is Dude's greatest joy. Bessie marries Dude in a ceremony which she herself conducts; married, she drags him indoors. But Captain Tim and the bank officer Payne tell Jeeter that he will get no credit; Captain Tim has lost the land to the bank, and Payne, as the bank's representative, wants to try modern methods on the land. His suggestion that Jeeter move to Augusta and work in the mills is contemptuously rejected by Jeeter who says he's a farmer and nothing else. The only thing that will satisfy Payne is a land rent of one hundred dollars a year, and he wants the first one hundred dollars before he goes back to town next morning. Thus, Dude is rescued from his husbandly duties because he and Bessie must go over into Burke County to get the one hundred dollars from Jeeter's reliable son, Tom.

ACT III

Jeeter is up at dawn next morning, wondering why Dude and Bessie have not returned. Lov is back again, offering a large slice of salt pork if Jeeter will help him get Pearl back. Ada is adamant, and Lov again leaves without

Pearl. But Bessie and Dude report that Tom has sent no money, and Jeeter is very much distressed. Since Dude has wrecked the new car several times, Jeeter tries to get Bessie to agree to let him use it to haul his wood into the city, to get a small payment for the banker, but Bessie flatly refuses. Driven to drastic measures, Jeeter captures Pearl and sends Dude in the car to get Lov: he is going to accept Lov's offer to pay two dollars a week if Jeeter will turn Pearl over for good. Trying to prevent this indignity to her daughter, Ada gets in the way of Bessie's car and is run over by her son. Dying, she bites Jeeter on the hand and makes him free Pearl, who flies off just as Lov appears. Jeeter sends Ellie May to console Lov, and Ellie May is quite happy.

To his dead wife, Jeeter says: "You shouldn't have done that, Ada. One way and another it didn't do anybody much good except maybe Pearl." Since Jeeter has entirely ruled out any possibility of leaving his land, whatever the bank does, his final act of pinching the earth between his fingers and rubbing it, with atavistic love, into dust, is a savage declaration of faith.

ROBERT E. SHERWOOD (1896–1955)

The Petrified Forest (1934)

*Realistic drama of the romantic
American West in two acts*

MAIN CHARACTER AND THEME: The story of *Gabby Maple*, a desert heroine, torn between her American and French backgrounds, and the adventure which came to her through a strange, foreign love and an unexpected visit from a group of escaping killers.

OTHER CHARACTERS:

Gramp Maple, Gabby's grandfather, who has lived on the desert for fifty-six years and who adores desperadoes

Boze Hertzlinger, football hero, who works in the gas station and who wants Gabby to love him

Jason Maple, forty, Gabby's father, who married a French girl after World War I

Paula, the Mexican cook

Two Telegraph Linemen

Alan Squier, thirty-five, ex-writer, a poetic hitchhiker

Herb, a cowboy

Mr. and Mrs. Chisholm, high society folk from Dayton, Ohio

Joseph, their Negro chauffeur

Jackie, Duke's machine-gun man

Duke Mantee, a hunted killer

Ruby, another gunman

Pyles, who drives Duke's car

Legion Commander, Another Legionnaire, Sheriff, A Deputy, Another Deputy, Radio Voice

TIME: Autumn 1934—afternoon and evening of one day.

PLACE: Black Mesa Bar-B-Q, gas station and lunchroom at a lonely crossroads in the eastern Arizona desert, on the edge of the Petrified Forest.

ROBERT E. SHERWOOD (1896–1955)

HISTORICAL NOTE: Play exemplifies the attention of Sherwood to problems of American life in the 1930's, to the impact of America's natural resources upon life, and to the emergence of the twentieth-century "bad man"—of the type of Capone, Karpis, and the Barkers—as contrasted with the nineteenth-century "bad man"—of the type of Jesse James and Billy the Kid. It represents also the the rise of Humphrey Bogart, as Duke Mantee, to full acting stature. In the poetic role of Alan Squier, Leslie Howard won honors in both stage and screen versions of the play.

ACT I

Jason, a devout Legionnaire, speaks sharply to a telegraph lineman eating in his restaurant because the latter has been praising revolutions, American and Russian, as the best means of improving the lot of working classes. Jason promises himself to track down the lineman and get him fired. His real anxiety, however, is rooted in the fact that Gramp refuses to take the nine thousand dollars he can get for the restaurant and set Jason up in the auto-camp business in Los Angeles; on the desert Jason feels defeated.

Gramp is hardly concerned. He has heard that Duke Mantee is coming their way. Since he was shot at by Billy the Kid many years ago, he has considered gunmen very important individuals. When Gramp leaves to get the mail, Boze pursues Gabby onto the scene: they are at loggerheads because Gabby likes to read François Villon's poetry but Boze likes to talk about his football exploits and his determination to have Gabby make love to him. As Boze kisses Gabby, Alan Squier drifts in for a meal. Although seedy and dusty, he is ultrapolite and soft spoken. As Alan's meal is being prepared, Gramp comes in with a copy of the Denver *Post* which says that Duke Mantee and his gang killed six and wounded four in Oklahoma City and are the object of an intensive search. Jason, now dressed in his horizon-blue Legion suit and armed with a revolver, leaves for his Legion meeting, expecting to help the sheriff catch Mantee.

Alan and Gabby find that they have much in common: Gabby still hears from France, where her mother (who divorced her father after she returned home) has a new husband and family—for a long time her mother has begged her to come over for a visit; Alan has recently returned from France after being married for eight years to a rich woman who provided him with the opportunity to become an artistic writer. Besides these contacts, both are in

270

love with the poetry of François Villon. Gabby even shows Alan her bad paintings, which she is ashamed to show others. So deeply does Gabby learn to trust him that she offers to underwrite a trip to France, with money she will receive in Gramp's will, if Alan will stay until Gramp dies and take her with him. Alan declines. Asking and receiving a good-by kiss, he is caught by Boze. Calling him a panhandler (when he cannot pay his bill for the food), Boze is ushering him out roughly when the Chisholms arrive, requiring fifteen gallons of gas for their Deusenberg, and other services. Gabby arranges for Alan to ride with them and gives him a silver dollar from the cash register. When the Chisholms and Alan are gone, Boze succeeds in getting Gabby to agree to go out in the moonlight with him.

But once again Boze is interrupted, this time by Duke Mantee and his gang, all formidably armed. Gramp is delighted. Paula, thoroughly frightened, is hardly able to cook the meal demanded by the killers. After Duke gets his captives quiet and settles down to wait for his girl friend and the rest of his gang, Alan strolls in on foot, reporting that the Chisholms' big car was commandeered by Duke.

ACT II

Half an hour later, the radio reports that Duke's pursuers have organized "the greatest man-hunt in human history," a monster dragnet from St. Louis to the Pacific Coast. Since Duke insists they all stay together, the whole group hear Boze confess true love to Gabby and Gabby, in return, say that it is only Alan she loves. All drink freely except Gramp, whom Gabby restricts. Boze, watching his chance, gets possession of a shotgun and covers Duke, but when he turns to cover the Chisholms, who re-enter after also walking back, Duke shoots him in the hand with a revolver, and recovers the shotgun. Duke allows Gabby to go out with Boze to attend to his wound. But Duke has also been obliged to reprove Alan for asking Gramp why he doesn't die and give Gabby a chance to live. If Alan had not apologized, Duke says he might have had "to put the lug" on Alan for talking disrespectfully to an old man.

When Mr. Chisholm tries to buy freedom for himself and his wife, Duke takes all his money but does not let him go. Following Boze's spectacular action, Alan decides to make an even more heroic stand. He takes out his five thousand dollar insurance policy, signs it over to Gabby, gets the

271

signature witnessed by the Chisholms, and then gets Duke to promise to shoot him as the last act before Duke's departure. Duke says, "I'll be glad to." Alan then asks the others not to tell Gabby what will happen. To the Chisholms, Alan reintroduces Duke as a romanticist like himself—he could have been across the Mexican border had he not been waiting for his girl.

In the meantime, Mrs. Chisholm is inspired by the proceedings to express semipublicly her disgust for her husband and the high-society life, when all along she wanted to be, and could have been, a great actress, as attested by a letter she received from Max Reinhardt. She offers herself romantically to Duke, whom she admires as the real man her husband is not.

As the time gets short, Alan tells Gabby (all the others listening) that he loves her and wants her never to give up her artistic dreams. Jason and the other Legionnaires return; Jackie, Duke's chief gunner, disarms them. They tell Duke that his girl friend, Doris, and her associates have been captured and that Doris is telling the police all she knows. As Duke prepares to leave, Alan begs him not to waste his life on avenging Doris, but to run for freedom since he is going to die anyway.

Duke asks the group not to spoil their pleasant evening by forcing him to kill someone as he makes his escape. The sheriff and his men begin firing on Duke, and Duke and his men answer abundantly. Eventually, Duke's Jackie is killed. Duke has maneuvered the sheriff's men to one side, and he prepares to escape on another. He takes the Chisholms, their chauffeur, and two Legionnaires as shields; he rejects Gramp, who wants to be taken.

Now assured of Gabby's love, Alan wants to live. But when Duke asks him, "Do you still want it?" Alan says yes. Duke obliges just before he escapes. Gabby is inconsolable as Alan dies in her arms; she says she will bury him in the petrified forest nearby. When Gramp tells her of Alan's insurance gift, she shows that she understands what Alan intended. She repeats the words from Villon:

> Thus in your field my seed of harvestry
> Will thrive—for the fruit is like me that I set—
> God bids me tend it with good husbandry:
> This is the end for which we twain have met.

68

SIDNEY KINGSLEY (1906–   )

Dead End (1935)

Naturalistic drama in three acts

MAIN CHARACTER AND THEME: The main character is a gang of six boys, as follows: *Tommy McGrath*, leader of the gang; *Dippy*, a gawky, cretinous, adenoidal Polish boy; *Angel* (originally Angelo), an Italian boy, a sometime shoeshine boy; *Spit*, so-called because of an abnormal reliance upon solving things by spitting on people; *T.B.*, a 16-year-old tubercular; *Milty* (Milton Schwartz), a Jewish boy, who is new in the tenement.

OTHER CHARACTERS:

Gimpty Pete, a young architect, who won his name by having a leg twisted by rickets

Doorman, giant in powder-blue uniform with gilt buttons and braid

Old Gentleman and *Old Lady*, residents in the East River Terrace Apartments

A Colored Chauffeur

Governess

Philip Griswald, little rich boy who lives in the Apartments, nephew of Judge Griswald

Mr. Griswald, Philip's father

Mr. Jones, Mr. Griswald's business associate

Drina, Tommy's sister

"Baby Face" Martin, twenty-eight, Public Enemy Number One

Hunk, short and squat, one of "Baby Face's" boys

Kay, Gimpty's high-class girl friend, who lives in the Apartments

Jack Hilton, early forties, Kay's sponsor

Fat Lady, with tiny black dog
Three Small Boys
Second Chauffeur
Two Second Avenue Boys
Mrs. Martin, "Baby Face's"
   mother
Patrolman Mulligan

Francey, the girl "Baby Face"
   returned to see
Three G-Men, Policeman, Plain-
   clothesman, Interne, Medical
   Examiner, Sailor, A Crowd

TIME: The early 1930's.

PLACE: Lower Manhattan, New York.

MUSICAL HIGHLIGHT: Chugs and shrieks of tugboats on the East River.

HISTORICAL NOTE: Drama vividly portraying the spawning, nurturing, and education of the slum adolescent, often called the juvenile delinquent. The dead-end district Kingsley chooses is directly adjacent to a set of exclusive terrace apartments. On this point Kingsley quotes Thomas Paine as follows: "The contrast of affluence and wretchedness is like dead and living bodies chained together."

Obviously, much effective observation and scholarly research went into the making of this play, as has been true of most of Kingsley's dramas, such as *Men in White* (1933), about hospital doctors, and *Detective Story* (1949), about precinct policemen.

ACT I

On first acquaintance with the Dead End boys, the audience is impressed by their bad language, reflecting a raw attitude toward life, their restless activity, their respect for money even in small amounts, their ability to swim and dive (in the filth-covered river), and their brutal pitiful efforts to maintain self-respect. The other boys, for example, constantly try to perform T.B.'s feat of coughing up saliva filled with blood, but it is beyond their reach. In great glee they deride Philip, the little rich boy beyond the high terrace and the white iron gate. Their initiation ceremony over Milty is primitive, but ritualistic. Tough as they are, they respond to sincere love from without, as when Tommy upholds his sister, Drina, when she gets Milty his three cents, unjustly taken from him. And the comedy in their behavior is genuine because beneath the distortion visited upon them by the slum atmosphere which is not of their making, they are real people.

The power of the slum to generate delinquency is revealed when Gimpty recognizes the man in the expensive suit as the notorious outlaw, "Baby Face" Martin, in spite of his expensive remade face. Readily admitting that he is a graduate of the entire Dead End educational system, Martin belies the strength to which he has aspired through outlawry by returning on two sentimental missions—one to see his mother, the other to see his first love. That he is risking his life to pursue these missions is a tribute to his weakness, not to his strength.

In Dead End, strangely, there is also intellectual appeal. Tommy deigns to compete with Philip in a contest naming the Presidents of the United States. All the boys listen to Gimpty talk about evolution and its powerful effects.

When Kay comes into the picture, the boys truly recognize loveliness, though with crude outward phraseology. Kay herself is torn between the easy, immoral life of the Apartments and her love for Gimpty, who sets up a drawing board to sketch on the riverside. For her, love is all right, but so far it does not inspire her to return to the crushing ways of poverty. Even so, she joyfully follows the lame Gimpty to his room, where they can be alone.

ACT II

Enjoying a game of poker, the boys face a problem: how to lure Philip away from his chain of protection and debase him with one of their ceremonies. Meanwhile, they accept a challenge from the Second Avenue boys for a gang fight on Saturday—just sticks and bare knucks, no bottles or rocks. Martin comes up to advise them—he who is an expert on fighting and who has a loyalty to his sector. He warns them to disregard the rules, saying: " . . . when yuh fight, dee idee is tuh win. It don' cut no ice how." As Gimpty and Kay continue their bizarre love talk, the gang catches up with Philip, Tommy taking his watch as an extra bonus. Kay tells Gimpty she has been invited to go on a yachting trip with Jack: if she goes, it will be for months, and she will doubtless be saying good-by to all that is represented by their love. Gimpty begs her not to go, but can offer her little as alternative.

Meanwhile, Martin has his conferences with his mother and his sweetheart. Both are great failures. In the first, his mother refuses his blood money and tells him to stay away from her; in the second, the young girl who introduced him to love is now a hardened prostitute with a terrible, visible disease, and even the hard-crusted Martin is deeply disillusioned. The

275

$4200 reward for Martin's capture becomes more and more inviting to Gimpty as these events develop.

Philip's father has called the police, and the search is on for the boys. Catching Tommy, Mr. Griswald is unable to hold him because Tommy cuts a deep gash in his hand with a knife. Excitement rises when Gimpty, trying to get enough money to hold Kay, calls in the G-Men on Martin. In the fight, a G-Man is shot, but Martin is riddled with bullets. After Martin has been cleared away, Spit is seen telling the police about Tommy, to save his own freedom.

ACT III

Tommy is sought, but not yet caught: he is himself the seeker—Spit must pay for "snitching." Despite his $4200, Gimpty does not succeed in charming Kay: she says they would have a year of comfort, and then, money gone, they would despise each other. Gimpty waves good-by to her as the yacht whistles past. Tommy finds Spit; only Tommy's sister prevents him from carving Spit up with his knife. When his sister tries to get him to flee the police, Tommy shows character by remaining. But Mr. Griswald will not listen to Drina's pleadings, or to Gimpty's well-documented declarations that reform school does nothing but create new "Baby Face" Martins. As they take Tommy away, T.B. tells him of a good friend in "rifawm school" he knows Tommy will like. The only hope is in Gimpty's assurance to Drina that, with his new money, he will get Tommy the best lawyer available.

The other boys carry on in the best Dead End tradition.

69

GEORGE GERSHWIN (1898–1937)
IRA GERSHWIN (1896–   )

Porgy and Bess (1935)

Folk opera in three acts based on the novel (1925) by DuBose Heyward, who also collaborated on the opera

MAIN CHARACTER AND THEME: The adventures in love and fighting of *Porgy*, a crippled Negro beggar who drives a goat cart, and his fellow denizens of Catfish Row, formerly a mansion of the aristocracy, but now a tenement on the waterfront of Charleston, South Carolina.

OTHER CHARACTERS:

Bess, age somewhere between twenty and thirty, originally Crown's woman

Crown, a big, bullying stevedore

Serena, a religious woman, wife of Robbins

Clara, wife of Jake

Maria, a shopkeeper, sometime friend of Bess

Jake, the head fisherman

Sportin' Life, a dope peddler and general good-timer

Mingo and *Robbins*, dice players in the Row

Peter, who sells divorces

Annie, a girl in the Court

Lily, Peter's girl

Strawberry Woman

Jim, a former cotton worker, who takes up fishing

Undertaker

Nelson, a man in the Court

Frazier, a lawyer

Crab Man

Mr. Archdale, a white man

Detective

Policeman

Coroner

277

Scipio, a mouth-organ player
A Chorus of Catfish folk
The Charleston Orphans' Band

Other Residents of Catfish Row,
Fisherman, Children, Stevedores,
Others

TIME: The 1920's.

PLACE: Catfish Row, Charleston, S.C.

MUSICAL HIGHLIGHTS: "Summer-time"; "Gone, Gone, Gone"; "It Take a Long Pull to Get There"; "Oh, I Got Plenty o' Nuttin'"; "Buzzard Song"; "Bess, You Is My Woman Now"; "Oh, I Can't Sit Down"; "It Ain't Necessarily So"; "What You Want Wid Bess?"; "Oh Dey's So Fresh and Fine" (Strawberry woman); "Here Come de Honey Man"; "I'm Talkin' About Devil Crabs" (Crab man); "I Wants to Stay Here"; "Oh, Doctor Jesus"; "There's a Boat Dat's Leavin' Soon for New York"; "Bess, Oh Where's My Bess?"; "Oh Lawd, I'm on My Way."

HISTORICAL NOTE: Often considered the outstanding native American opera. The outstanding dramatic accomplishment of the Gershwin brothers who for fifteen years dominated the American musical-comedy stage. *Porgy and Bess* opened at the Alvin Theatre, New York, on October 10, 1935, with Todd Duncan and Anne Wiggins Brown in the title roles. Although it played only 124 performances on its initial performance, it remained in circulation for a number of years, and like *Oklahoma!* became a national drama. Its second New York appearance, opening at the Majestic Theatre on January 22, 1942, lasted for 286 performances. In the 1950's, it recruited a new cast, once again played a national circuit, and under the encouragement of the State Department represented America on the cultural scene in many foreign countries for several years.

ACT I (*two scenes*)

After Clara sings the "Summer-time" lullaby to her baby, the spotlight falls upon a spirited dice game. Crown, Robbins, Jake, Mingo, and Sportin' Life are the central characters in the game before Porgy arrives. More and more under the influence of alcohol and cocaine, Crown grows reckless and dangerous. When Robbins wins at dice, Crown threatens him; they fight; Crown delivers a killing blow, and Robbins is dead. Shaking Crown to his senses, Bess gives him money and sends him into hiding. One by one, the people of the Row refuse shelter to Bess, now homeless with Crown gone.

As a result, Bess turns to Porgy's room, shuddering away from Robbins' body and the weeping Serena over it.

In a penetrating, comprehensive chant, the Row mourns for Robbins—"Gone, gone, gone, gone, gone, gone, gone." At first, Serena refuses Bess's contribution for the saucer in which money is being collected to pay for Robbins' funeral; but, learning it is Porgy's money, Serena accepts. The Chorus tells Serena that the Lord will care for her and Robbins' fatherless children; even Porgy prays for her. Breaking into the ceremonies, a detective accuses Peter, the divorce seller, and orders him held until Crown is caught. The detective also informs Serena that if Robbins is not buried by tomorrow, his body will be turned over to the medical students. Serena sings her plaint, "Ole man sorrow sittin' by de fireplace." Saying it will cost him twenty-five dollars to bury Robbins, the undertaker nevertheless accepts the fifteen dollars in the saucer and agrees to perform the burial. Bess sings of the train leaving for the promised land, telling all to get on board.

ACT II (*four scenes*)

Following the playing of the chimes of St. Michael's, Jake, the head fisherman, and his men sing the fishermen's song, "It take a long pull to get there." Although Clara begs Jake not to take his ship *Seagull* out into the September storms, Jake says he must—he needs money to give his boy a college education. Annie, the girl from the court, reminds the fishermen of the picnic that day. As Porgy is heard singing, "Oh, I got plenty o' nuttin'," the other residents of the Row comment on how Porgy has changed since Bess came into his life. Just after Maria drives Sportin' Life from her shop, brutally assuring him that she will tolerate no dope peddlers, Lawyer Frazier enters the Row wanting to seal Bess a divorce from Crown for $1. When Frazier learns that Bess was never really married to Crown, he charges Porgy $1.50 for Bess's divorce. Archdale, another lawyer, follows Frazier. He warns Frazier to stop selling phony divorces and promises Porgy he will post bond and see to Peter's release. But all of this activity becomes a minor consideration when the buzzards fly low and worry the Row people. Porgy sings, "Buzzard, keep on flyin'."

When Sportin' Life tempts Bess with a snifter of "happy dust" (cocaine), he is discouraged by Porgy's powerful grip. This act of protection causes Porgy to sing "Bess, you is my woman now," and Bess to sing agreement.

Although Bess is willing to stay at home with Porgy, Porgy urges her to go on to the picnic without him. Alone but happy, Porgy again sings, "I got plenty o' nuttin'."

At the picnic on Kittiwah Island, there are African drums and dancing. Sportin' Life sings, "It ain't necessarily so." A steamboat whistles in the distance. Coming upon the church members dancing, Serena calls shame upon them. She also orders them to the boat. As Bess moves to obey Serena, Crown whistles to her from the thicket. He tells her he has plenty to eat, but is lonely. He tells her also he will come for her in two weeks. Her reply is to say that she is now with Porgy who needs her, and that he needs a younger girl. Pleadingly, Bess sings, "What you want wid Bess?" As the boat gives a final whistle, Crown seizes Bess and hurls her into the palmetto thicket.

Having come the eighteen miles from Kittiwah in a state of collapse, Bess lies in Porgy's room, feverish and raving. Serena lifts a prayer for her: "Oh, Doctor Jesus." She tells Porgy that by five o' clock, Bess will be well. Through the court echoes the colorful selling songs of the strawberry woman, the honey man, and the crab man. Fulfilling Serena's prediction, Bess is well, after a week's illness. She swears that she wants to stay with Porgy and asks Porgy to protect her when Crown comes. Porgy promises. Then all the Row people sink in terror as they hear the hurricane bell and feel the wind rise.

The terrible storm rages. In Serena's room, the people sing. Bess thinks of Crown in the storm and knows that he must be dead. But Crown has escaped the storm: he pushes in Serena's door. Scorning the praying folk, he calls for Bess and throws Porgy on the floor. To Serena's warning of blasphemy, Crown says that if God had wanted to kill him he has had plenty of chances. The thunder, he tells them all, is God laughing at them. In defiance, he sings, "A red-headed woman makes a choo-choo jump its track."

Looking out of the window, Bess sees Jake's boat upside down in the river. She moans and notifies Clara, Jake's wife. Clara gives Bess her baby and goes into the storm looking for her man. Only Crown is brave enough to follow Clara. The storm blots out the lamp. All the others rock in terror, moan, and pray.

ACT III (*three scenes*)

The chorus begs Clara not to be downhearted at Jake's loss. In a news-giving manner, Sportin' Life suggests that Bess now has two men, discounting

280

the common belief that Crown was also killed by the storm. After the crowd leaves, Crown enters stealthily and moves toward Porgy's door. Above him, a shutter opens slowly—an arm extends with a long knife. The arm plunges the knife into Crown's back. The knife is withdrawn and hurled to the center of the stage. As Crown staggers to an upright position, Porgy leans from the window and closes both hands around Crown's throat. Porgy kills Crown and hurls him to center. Laughing victoriously, Porgy says Bess has a *man* now.

The detective and the coroner come to accuse the sick Serena of killing Crown in revenge for his killing Robbins. When they face a hard alibi for Serena, they turn to Porgy. They want him only to identify Crown, but Porgy resists in spite of Bess's urging him to go with them. Sportin' Life tells Porgy that if Crown's killer identifies him, Crown's wound will bleed, and the police will then know the killer. The detective takes the resisting Porgy away with him.

Struggling to fight off Sportin' Life and his "happy dust," Bess at first succeeds, then fails. So nervous is she that she must have one sniff of the happy dust and then she yields to Sportin' Life's full temptation. Singing "There's a boat dat's leavin' soon for New York" and promising Bess mansions, silks, and satins, Sportin' Life lures Bess away.

It is a lovely morning. Porgy, jailed for contempt when he refused to look upon Crown to identify him, has returned with presents for most of the Row people. For Bess he has many bundles, but he cannot find her. Serena and Maria tell him that he is lucky: Bess has gone back to happy dust and red eye (whiskey), and forward to Sportin' Life and hell. Bess gave Serena Porgy's child to raise. Mingo says she has gone to New York.

Porgy calls for his goat. Waving aside all warnings, he is off for New York, singing, "Oh—Lawd, I'm on my way . . . .."

70

LAURENCE STALLINGS (1894–   )
MAXWELL ANDERSON (1888–1959)
EDWIN JUSTIN MAYER (1897–1960)

So Red the Rose (1935)

*Motion-picture play from the novel of
the same title (1934) by Stark Young (1881–1963)*

MAIN CHARACTER AND THEME: How war and romance challenged the deepest
fibres of the aristocratic *Bedfords* of Tennessee in the trying times of the
1860's, as a family, as individual members, and as representatives of a
colorful passing civilization.

OTHER CHARACTERS:

Malcolm Bedford, master of the plantation, later a Confederate major

Sally Bedford, wife of Malcolm

Vallette Bedford, brilliant daughter of Malcolm and Sally

Edward Bedford, Vallette's elder brother

George Pendleton, Edward's friend

George McGehee, member of a related aristocratic Southern family

Yankee Boy

William Veal, loyal Negro slave

Duncan Bradford, cousin of Vallette, an older man

Mary Cherry, the spinster sister of Malcolm

Middleton Bedford, the spoiled younger son of Malcolm and Sally

Cato, a slave leader

Major Rushton

Confederate Sergeant

Six thousand extras

TIME: 1860–1865.

PLACE: Tennessee, near Shiloh.

282

"So Red the Rose" (1935)

HISTORICAL NOTE: This play represents the motion-picture drama and the drama of the Southern aristocracy which was swept away by the Civil War. Although following the general outlines of Young's best seller, it is quite different in many respects—e.g., the whole action has been transferred from the Natchez, Mississippi, area, so intensively developed by Young, to a setting close by that of the famous Battle of Shiloh. In transmission to the screen, the story has also been simplified, to broaden its appeal. Its stars were two Virginia-born actors—Margaret Sullavan as Vallette and Randolph Scott as Duncan.

ACTION

At Portobello, in Tennessee, the Bedford family lives in the greatest glory of the Old South. Malcolm Bedford is surrounded by a large family and many slaves. Vallette is her father's favorite and the sentimental boss of the plantation. She rules with pleasant tyranny every one except her cousin Duncan, who, in his independency, seems to consider Vallette a flirt, unworthy of serious consideration. He is, however, secretly in love with her and is able to touch her deeply by his talk and behavior.

When Lincoln is elected President and Tennesseans, generally, talk of secession and fighting, Duncan does not hesitate to say that for the South to go to war would be stupid and senseless. Meanwhile, Edward, his mother's favorite, has returned home from military school, bringing along his friend, George Pendleton. Edward's return is the occasion for a great round of parties, balls, dinners, and horseback riding. In all these, Vallette is the star. She does not hesitate to try to make Duncan jealous by a heavy flirtation with George.

The news of the firing on Fort Sumter causes great joy at Portobello, as it did everywhere in the South, which envisioned a quick, easy victory. George is one of the first Southern gentlemen to enlist, and one of the first to die. Abiding by his principles, Duncan refuses to go to war. Edward wants to enlist but restrains himself until the effect of George's death unsettles complacency throughout his world. Edward, avoiding a farewell with his mother, slips quietly away to join the Confederate Army.

Malcolm is the next member of the family to be thoroughly aroused. He is angered and his pride is irreparably damaged when a Northern raiding party rides through Southern lines and reaches Portobello. Malcolm himself is roused out of his bed and forced at sword point to show the raiders a safe road back to their lines. Despite his age, Malcolm joins the army.

Portobello is soon swept by rumors that a great battle has been fought at nearby Shiloh. Waking her household in the dead of night, Sally, Malcolm's wife, leads Duncan, William, the slave, and others to the battlefield. Among the dead and wounded of this terrible battle, Sally finds the body of Edward. In deep despair, she brings the body home. Now overcome by grief and a sense of being needed, Duncan, crushing back his principles, goes off to war.

With only women left among the family at Portobello, the slaves, hearing that the Yankees are winning, revolt. In the midst of the revolt, Malcolm returns, critically wounded. Valette hides from him the story of the rebellion of his slaves: she and William are able to calm the slaves for a while. But Malcolm dies. The slaves break out and leave the plantation.

As the war grows worse for the South, Confederate soldiers flee in disorder past Portobello. None of them has any news of Duncan. One day, a Confederate group drives a Yankee detachment before it, and a young Union soldier stumbles into Portobello. Placing him in Edward's room, Valette nurses him. Before very long, the Confederates demand the Yankee boy—they say he must hang as reprisal for Confederates indiscriminately hanged by Yankees. Even though Duncan is in command of the Confederate detachment, Vallette refuses to deliver the boy. After a stormy scene, in which Vallette and Duncan display their old spirit in new lights, Duncan yields. The Yankee boy is saved.

Shortly after this episode, another group of Union soldiers takes over Portobello. The historic old mansion is burned to the ground; the proud Bedfords are compelled to move into slaves' quarters. Sally and Vallette pull the plow to till the fields and sow the crops. They seem barely able to get the everyday necessities.

The war over and lost, the exhausted South works bravely to rebuild. Vallette shows herself deeply matured by her wartime experiences. One day— after quite a long time, it seemed to Vallette—Duncan staggers home. In their deep and sensible love, Vallette and Duncan find the strength and vision to make together the struggle to rebuild and to reacquire the old glories.

71

CLIFFORD ODETS (1906–1963)

Waiting for Lefty (1935)

Agitprop, expressionistic drama in seven scenes

MAIN CHARACTER AND THEME: The pivotal character, *Lefty Costello*, a respected union leader, never appears. The theme of the play is whether or not a union of taxicab drivers, in meeting assembled, will vote to go on strike.

OTHER CHARACTERS:

Harry Fatt, union head, executive secretary, but in the pay of the cab owners

Fatt's Henchman, a gunman

Joe Mitchell, a cab driver

Edna, his wife

Miller, former lab assistant but now a cab driver

Fayette, an industrialist

Sid, another cab driver

Florrie, his sweetheart

Irv, Florrie's brother and head of their household

Tim Clayton, a union speaker

Dr. Barnes, attached to the Hospital

Dr. Benjamin, formerly an interne in the Hospital, now a cab driver

Agate, a union member

Voice (*Clancy*)

Man

The Audience

TIME: 1935.

PLACE: New York City.

MUSICAL HIGHLIGHT: "Sweet Rosie O'Grady" for soft-shoe dance.

HISTORICAL NOTE: Sample of the agitprop drama of the 1930's which reacted to the Great Depression by depicting particular events of class conflict and their socio-dramatic solution. Play won a contest of New Theatre

League, had two Broadway runs within a year (during 1935), and because of its unique production elements is often revived by amateur, especially college, groups. Representative also of Odets' thoroughgoing analysis of the middle-class crisis are a number of plays between 1935 and 1950, including *Awake and Sing* (1935), *Paradise Lost* (1935), and *Golden Boy* (1937), plus two others dealing sharply with the screen and stage industries: *The Big Knife* (1949) and *The Country Girl* (1950).

Scene 1

Curtain rises on a bare stage where six or seven men sit in a semicircle. Fatt talks directly to the Audience, who are presumably taxicab drivers; the men seated behind him are a workers' committee. Telling the Audience that this is no time for a strike, and that more promising strikes than theirs could ever be have failed, Fatt in return hears grumbles and yells of "Where's Lefty?" Backed by his gunman, leaning against the proscenium down left, Fatt allows the opposing speakers to be heard. As they emerge, one by one, the center of the stage goes dark and a spotlight picks up the action of each contributory episode. The first episode concerns the speaker Joe. Smoke from Fatt's cigar sometimes invades the spotlighted scene. Each scene closes with a blackout.

Scene 2 (Episode I. Joe and Edna)

Edna suddenly tells Joe, just come home from driving his cab, that he is less than a man to allow his furniture to be taken for nonpayment of notes and his children to have nothing to eat. She has put "the kids" to bed so they would not know they had missed a meal. The second month's rent is due tomorrow. Pitifully, Joe offers her $1.04 which he says is his net for the day. She tells him that the cab owners "make suckers" of the drivers, and the drivers are too spineless to hit back. When she suggests that they strike, he says that "strikes don't work." Even so, says Edna, he must do something about his two children who continue to have colds because they get no orange juice. When he gives weak answers, she takes off her apron and swears she will leave him and rejoin her old boy friend, his ex-rival, Bud Haas. Finally, in response to her energetic pounding, he says he will go down to 174th Street and look up Lefty Costello. He concludes with a statement to the Audience: "We gotta walk out!"

Scene 3 (Episode II. Lab Assistant Episode)

Miller, a lab assistant, is discovered talking with Fayette, an industrialist. Much impressed by Miller, Fayette is offering him a raise of twenty dollars a month—on one condition: Miller is to devote his chemical ability to work on a new poison gas. Orders have come from above, says Fayette; perhaps Miller did not know a new war was so close. Miller refuses, remembering the twelve million killed and twenty million wounded in the last war. Fayette raises his offer to thirty dollars a month added to Miller's present salary; then to forty dollars. On Miller's final refusal, Fayette fires him. "No hard feelings?" says Fayette. "Plenty of hard feelings!" replies Miller, who hits his former boss in the mouth and gets a job driving a cab.

Scene 4 (Episode III. The Young Hack and His Girl)

Irv tells Florrie that whether she loves Sid, the cab driver, or not, she must get rid of him—he is a financial liability. Irv is responsible for the family and cannot afford to take care of Sid and Florrie in addition to everything else. Florrie promises to talk straight to Sid. When he arrives, they discuss their dreams and plans and try to be cheerful, but the realities cancel out their efforts. In spite of Irv, Florrie is willing to go with Sid, but Sid says she would only curse him eventually. He declares his love; almost simultaneously, he hears her say her family needs the nine dollars she makes every week. They dance, holding each other tightly; he does his imitations and his soft-shoe act. The scene ends suddenly as he falls on his knees and buries his face in her lap.

Scene 5 (Episode IV. Labor Spy Episode)

Fatt has imported "a man from Philadelphia" to tell at firsthand how badly the cab drivers' strike in Philadelphia went. In the midst of his story, the speaker is identified as a labor spy, who has helped to break strikes up and down the East Coast—in coal, shipping, textiles, and steel. He is a member of an outfit which specializes in labor spying. When Fatt wants proof from the identifying speaker, the Voice gives proof: the labor spy is the Voice's brother. Voice chases the labor spy from the room.

Scene 6 (Episode V. Interne Episode)

Dr. Barnes draws the assignment of transferring important patients from Benjamin, the most competent interne in the Hospital, to Leeds, an incompetent, but the nephew of a senator. By slow degrees, Benjamin learns that his ward is being discontinued next month; and so is he. His discontinuance is based largely on his being a Jew and in spite of his brother Jews on the Hospital Board. Learning through a telephone call that Leeds has lost one of Benjamin's patients, Dr. Barnes so informs Benjamin and further states that he wishes he had the courage to resign. Benjamin says he will get a job—perhaps driving a cab—and will study and work and learn his place.

Scene 7

Agate rises to criticize the do-nothing policies and tactics of Fatt and the other union officers. Fatt and his gunman try to quiet him, but he breaks away and continues talking. He tells the Audience they are dying by inches. Now, they can choose slow death or fight. He praises Edna; he asks Sid, Florrie, and Dr. Barnes to fight. Man breaks in to say that Lefty has been found behind the car barn with a bullet in his head. Agate cries for union to "put fruit trees where our ashes are." He asks the Audience: "Well, what's the answer?" All cry: "Strike!" Agate says: "Louder!" All cry again and again: "STRIKE, STRIKE, STRIKE!!!"

72

MAXWELL ANDERSON (1888–1959)

Winterset (1935)

*Blank-verse tragedy, with social implications,
in three acts*

MAIN CHARACTER AND THEME: Crusade of *Mio* (*Bartolomeo Romagna*), son of a man executed ostensibly for murder but actually for his radical ideas, to clear his father's name. Drama is one of many literary works based on the celebrated Sacco-Vanzetti case (1921–1927): Mio's father is the equivalent of Vanzetti.

OTHER CHARACTERS:

Trock, a gangster just released from the penitentiary

Shadow, his lieutenant

Garth, former member of Trock's gang

Miriamne, his sister

Esdras, an old rabbi, father of Garth and Miriamne

The Hobo

First Girl

Second Girl

Judge Gaunt, who tried the Romagna case years ago

Carr, friend of Mio

Herman, gawky shoe salesman

Lucia, organ-grinder

Piny, his friend

A Sailor, Street Urchin, Policeman, Radical, Sergeant

Nonspeaking:

Urchins, Two Young Men in Blue Serge

TIME: Probably the early 1930's.

PLACE: An apartment building under a bridgehead on the bank of a river in New York City.

MUSICAL HIGHLIGHT: Beethoven's "Archduke Trio" on the violin.

289

HISTORICAL NOTE: One of America's most productive dramatists, Anderson nearly always aimed high and showed considerable range in theme and method, but he did not maintain the highest possible standard of performance. Like *Winterset*, his play *Gods of the Lightning* (1928— with Harold Hickerson), deals with the Sacco-Vanzetti case mainly because he felt that the persecution of men for their ideas was an undermining of the true spirit of democracy. He wrote dedicatedly on phases of economic and political life in such plays as *Saturday's Children* (1927) and *Both Your Houses* (1933). He also tried valiantly to revive the poetic drama in America not only with *Winterset* but also with *Elizabeth the Queen* (1930), *Mary of Scotland* (1933), and *The Masque of Kings* (1937). In *High Tor* (1937) he attempted poetic expression also, and further, a revivification of American legend. In *Valley Forge* (1934), he enlarged a brief but important incident of American history, especially interpreting the great American hero, George Washington. In the last quarter century of his life (1935 on), his dramatic scope was even greater than that just outlined. In the first production of *Winterset*, Burgess Meredith as Mio was a notable aid to Anderson's sociopoetic purposes.

ACT I (*three scenes*)

In the early dark of a December morning, Two Young Men in Blue Serge, obviously hired killers, lean against the masonry, matching bills. Trock, just out of jail, rails at Shadow about the meanness of a society that wants to keep him in jail for life. The penitentiary doctor gave him only six months to live. In the cellar apartment of the building, Miriamne asks her brother Garth about a threatening letter he has received. Esdras, their father, comes in to say he must speak alone to somebody. But it is with Garth that Trock, the somebody, wants to talk; he dismisses Miriamne and Esdras. Garth tells him that some professor has been looking up a certain old case; he assures Trock that *he* cannot talk, being as deep in the case as Trock. Trock orders him to stay at home. When Trock has gone, Garth admits to his sister that he once saw a gang rob a payroll and that one member, Trock Estrella, did a murder for which Romagna paid the death penalty, and that he sits guilty and fearfully fiddling. Garth says he is tired of living in fear. Miriamne says it is better to tell the truth and die; Esdras, that Miriamne is young.

Under the bridge that evening, two girls discuss their love life. Also, Judge Gaunt goes everywhere proclaiming that he decided on the evidence and that he has an errand to do. Carr and Mio appear, Mio discussing his nonidentity on the Pacific Coast, where he has been wandering. When Mio looks interestedly at Miriamne, Carr warns him to be careful. The warning sets Mio off on a bitter refrain of being the son of an executed father, whom he knows to have been innocent, and of a mother who died of grief. He speaks eloquently of his impassioned need to vindicate his father. He talks of his new interest—this Professor Hobhouse—who has found new evidence. Around Mio, Lucia plays on his organ and the street dance starts. Miriamne refuses the Radical, but dances with Mio. Policeman stops the dancing, in spite of heavy protests, especially from Radical, and even from Judge Gaunt, who despite pronouncements on his dignity and knowledge of the law, does not impress Policeman because of his bedraggled appearance. Having defended Policeman tongue in cheek, Mio eventually demands apology of him, and is threatened by him. A sleet storm begins. Trock hovers nearby. Miriamne admits to Mio that she is a Jew and believes in nothing; Mio correspondingly doubts the existence of chivalry, honor, freedom, and enduring love, except on paper. In spite of their infidelism, they quickly declare their enduring love for each other; she says she will follow him anywhere. Miriamne says she knows for whom he looks but urges him to avoid death, although she grieves to send him away. To show him what she means, she pulls him back into the shadows as Trock and Shadow go by, Shadow warning Trock that he cannot kill everybody, including this Judge, and get away. Trock tells him they are through; he extracts Trock's gun. As he leaves, Trock signals the Blue Serge Men; two or three shots are heard. Carr comes in to say that Shadow's body has fallen in the river near riptide, where it will never be found. Miriamne goes in. Carr urges Mio to forget any business in these parts.

ACT II

From Garth's violin is heard the sad movement of Beethoven's "Archduke Trio." Miriamne tries to get Garth to go away; he says he is safer here. Awaking from deep sleep, Judge Gaunt identifies Garth and complains about the shadow cast by Professor Hobhouse. Mio comes and reviews the evidence with Gaunt and the others; Gaunt tells him that Garth's evidence was the only possible missing link, and now that Garth has declared his ignorance of the case, Romagna's guilt is definite. Mio threatens Gaunt, who says Mio displays the same murderous spirit his father had. Coming in from the other room, Miriamne tries to comfort Mio, who feels at his worst now as he faces even the possibility that his father was guilty. Garth tries to drive a wedge between Miriamne and Mio, but unsuccessfully: the lovers again declare their love, but Mio is doubtful of its future. Trock returns and threatens each person, to make sure he is safe; if necessary, he will take the Judge for a ride with a couple of chauffeurs, for good. Covered with blood, Shadow returns from death's door, but when he tries to fire the pistol he points at Trock, he cannot: the gun falls from his hand, and he is taken into the next room. With a lead left by Shadow, Mio wades into Trock, who accuses Shadow of the murder. Assuming courtroom procedure before Gaunt, Mio places Trock, Shadow, and Garth in their respective places, and accuses Gaunt of having known. Gaunt pleads the execution of one man against disgrace of the law. In spite of Trock's threatening him, Mio is jubilant that his father's innocence is at last definitely established. Policeman and Sergeant come, looking for Gaunt. Mio screams to them that Trock is guilty of two murders, but when he directs them to the other room, Shadow's body is gone, and even Miriamne lies to protect her brother. Policeman and Sergeant take Gaunt away. Trock and Gaunt are no longer fearful of Mio. Telling Miriamne that she might have picked some other stranger to dance with, Mio expresses sublime sorrow that her face has come between him and his mission. Miriamne begs him not to leave because Trock will be waiting. "Let the four winds blow," he says, "the four winds of the world, and take us to the four winds." He goes.

ACT III

Trock comes out into the rain and says words to his gunmen, too low to be heard. Mio comes out, trying the rain. When Miriamne begs him to come back into the house, he declines because they do not speak the same language. She asks forgiveness for betraying him; he only asks if there is a path along the bank; she says yes, the one Shadow took. Mio says a funeral oration for Shadow as Garth and Hobo take his body to dump it. Because he cannot bargain principle, Mio cannot accept help from Esdras on condition he avoid involving Garth. He tells Miriamne that the hour he is living now is forever, and "how does one spend a forever!" He also refuses Miriamne when she swears her love and asks only that he let her brother go. When Carr offers to hide him at a Grand Street place, once again he refuses, though tentatively. He asks God to teach him how to forget hate; Miriamne reminds him that his father would have forgiven. So impressive is her suggestion that he kisses her.

Esdras comes in, bloody from a beating by Trock. He tells Mio that Trock wants all the six months the doctor promised him, and therefore will come for Mio. But now Mio *wants* to live, for love's sake. Esdras goes to seek an escape route for him. When Mio tries to follow, he meets the quick rat-tat of machine guns and comes back slowly, his hand pressed under his heart. With his last breath he rebestows his love upon Miriamne. Miriamne calls the guns upon herself by proclaiming into the night that she is not silenced, and she knows all Mio knew. The machine gun speaks again, and she sinks. She scorns Garth's hands and begs Mio to notice why she is dying, but she ends with "Oh, now he'll never know." Over them Esdras says words, praising their honor, their taking defeat implacable and defiant, their dying unsubmitting. He calls Mio his son, and prepares a proper burial for them both.

73

GEORGE S. KAUFMAN (1889–1961)
MOSS HART (1904–1961)

You Can't Take It with You (1936)

Comedy drama in three acts

MAIN CHARACTER AND THEME: The joyful, though often overwhelming, adventures of *Martin Vanderhof*, known as Grandpa, a wiry little man of seventy-five, who leads his family through the complexities of American business civilization, carrying the banner of doing-what-one-likes rather than what-one-must.

OTHER CHARACTERS:

Penelope Sycamore, usually called Penny, Martin's daughter, a round little woman in her early fifties, who paints and who writes plays that are never produced

Essie Carmichael, Penny's elder daughter, who at twenty-nine devotes most of her time and energy to an effort to be a ballet dancer (she wears her dancing shoes throughout)

Rheba, in her early thirties, the colored maid

Paul Sycamore, in his mid-fifties, Penelope's mild-mannered husband

Mr. De Pinna, a bald little man with a serious manner

Ed Carmichael, in his mid-thirties, Essie's husband, a printer and a xylophone player

Donald, very dark, pleasant, Rheba's boy friend

Alice Sycamore, a lovely fresh girl of 22, Penny's younger daughter

Wilbur C. Henderson, an Internal Revenue agent

Tony Kirby, Alice's ardent suitor, who happens to be her boss's son

Boris Kolenkhov, enormous, hairy, and loud, a relic of the defunct Russian monarchical society

"You Can't Take It with You" (1936)

Gay Wellington, a loose, generally intoxicated actress, picked up by Penny to read for the plays

Mr. Anthony Kirby, Tony's father, Alice's boss, deeply aware of his wealth and business responsibilities

Mrs. Miriam Kirby, his wife, Tony's mother

Leader, Mac and Jim, three men from the Department of Justice

Olga Katrina, a former Russian Grand Duchess, cousin of the late Czar, now a waitress at Childs' Restaurant in Columbus Circle

TIME: About 1935.

PLACE: New York City, near Columbia University.

HISTORICAL NOTE: This play is one of several created by two American masters of the type of comedy which leans toward farce but which simultaneously depicts the foibles of its contemporary society, upper, middle, and lower class. As Brooks Atkinson has said, these comedies are characterized by fantastic wit and humor, are compact in form, and swift in tempo. The first product of the collaboration was *Once in a Lifetime* (1930); other notable samples were *The Man Who Came to Dinner* (1939) and *George Washington Slept Here* (1940). Besides being skillful playwrights, in this collaboration and singly, both Kaufman and Hart are adept at production and direction. *You Can't Take It with You* took only five weeks to write and was first produced by an all-star cast on December 14, 1936, at the Sam H. Harris Theatre in New York. It had an initial New York run of 837 performances (two years). Since then, it has had a long, uniformly successful career in both the professional and amateur theatres.

ACT I (*two scenes*)

As usual, everyone in the Vanderhof household is working in his favorite medium: Penny is typing on her eleventh play; Essie is furiously dancing and making candy, called "Love Dreams"; Paul and Mr. De Pinna are manufacturing skyrockets, for selling, and other sensational fireworks; Rheba is preparing dinner, consisting of cornflakes, watermelon, candy, and some kind of meat (the kind she cannot remember); Donald is feeding flies in large quantities to the snakes that have turned the goldfish aquarium into a solarium. In addition, Ed is printing all kinds of cards, some of which carry ominous warnings about the nature of American government, though Ed intends no harm. Grandpa arrives late—he has been engaged in one of his most inspiring hobbies: attending a commencement exercise at Columbia University. Meanwhile, Essie dances to a selection Ed plays on the xylophone, one in which Ed and Beethoven collaborated. Following all this, Alice warns the family that they must be on their good behavior for the dinner visit the next night by Tony and his elegant parents. Also, Grandpa, who simply walked out of his job thirty-five years ago but who all along has received a handsome income from property, has a visitor. The visitor is Mr. Henderson, who first tries to reason with Grandpa and then must threaten him with dire punishment if Grandpa does not begin paying the income tax he has deliberately neglected for twenty-two years (since the Income Tax Amendment was placed in the Constitution). Grandpa cannot be persuaded that the Government will use his payments intelligently. Mr. Henderson rages and threatens but leaves in a hurry when Paul and Mr. De Pinna test their firecracker bomber. Tony arrives to take Alice to the Monte Carlo Ballet—the mere idea disgusts Kolenkhov, who knew Bakst and Diaghilev of the great era of Russian ballet.

Returning home from the ballet, Tony follows Alice in. Very pointedly, he declares his love. Alice admits loving him too, but tells him she believes her free-wheeling family would never be acceptable to his strait-laced family. As though to prove her right, as they talk, different members of the family make embarrassing appearances. Essie, for instance, reports to Ed in passing that Grandpa has approved the idea of their having a baby. Tony assures Alice that his parents are not free from peculiar ideas—his mother believes in spiritualism—and Alice eventually agrees to become engaged to him. But she warns Tony that she loves her family, strange though they always seem. As though to celebrate their engagement, Paul sets off for them some "new red fire," which blazes and sheds a soft glow over the room. Despite her fears of coming calamity in the clash of families, Alice tells her father: "Everything is beautiful. It's the most beautiful red fire in the world."

ACT II

It is a week later. The family has finished dinner. Trying to get Gay Wellington to concentrate on reading a play, Penny fights a losing battle with the gin bottle and glass Gay is concentrating upon. Only when Gay sees the

296

snakes in the solarium does she pour the gin back into the bottle; but then, instead of reading the play, she "passes out" cold. Ed announces that a man has been following him for several days as he has delivered candy with his original printed messages inside. No one believes him. Carefully and somewhat anxiously, Alice supervises preparations for the visit of Tony and his parents the next night. Alice is anxious that everyone shall behave himself. Despite his years and grown children, Paul, Penelope's husband, plays with an Erector set, building the *Queen Mary* this week to supplant last week's Empire State Building. Having found an old portrait Penny had started of a discus thrower in a Roman costume, Mr. De Pinna persuades Penny to return to her painting, after eight years. Penny is reminded of Charlie, the milkman, who, like Mr. De Pinna, came into the house almost accidentally and stayed for five years. Charlie had died in the house and was buried as Martin Vanderhof (Grandpa's name) since the family never learned his last name. Kolenkhov comes in to drill Essie on her dancing. Donald, Rheba's boy friend, complains of having to go a considerable distance to pick up his relief check every week—it breaks up his week. As Grandpa once more expresses his delight in having walked out on the compulsive life of business thirty-five years ago, Penny comes downstairs wearing her artist's smock, a flowing black tie, a black velvet tam-o'-shanter (at a rakish angle), and carrying palette, paints, and brushes. Joining her is Mr. De Pinna in his stripped-down Roman costume. Grandpa is now playing with darts and Kolenkhov is putting Essie through the dizzy paces of pirouette and entrechat when Rheba ushers in the Kirbys—in full evening dress. Only Grandpa manages to meet the occasion. Before long, Tony has apologized for mixing up the dates, Mrs. Kirby is frightened by snakes, Alice is staggered with embarrassment, Donald is sent to the store to buy frankfurters, canned corn, and half a dozen bottles of beer, Gay stumbles intoxicatedly across the room, and Kolenkhov gives Mr. Kirby a wrestling lesson, which leaves the fine gentleman flat on his back. Penny rescues the situation by playing a game of free association with the Kirbys. But the rescue backfires because through the game Mr. and Mrs. Kirby learn that their secret thoughts are not complimentary each to the other (Mrs. Kirby, for example, reveals that years ago she had found her honeymoon quite dull). Into this maze of growing misunderstanding three Justice Department figures come to arrest Ed; it seems that the printed messages he has been placing in the candy have been carrying such injunctions as "Dynamite the Capitol!" and "Dynamite the Supreme

Court!" Not only are the Kirbys prevented from leaving; everyone else in the house must be rounded up. Mr. De Pinna protests that he had better be allowed to get his pipe from downstairs. He is told to shut up. While one of the officers is reporting to his chief on the large supply of gunpowder belowstairs, enough to blow up the city, Mr. De Pinna's fuming pipe reaches the fireworks. A year's supply of bombs, big crackers, little crackers, sky-rockets, and pin wheels goes up at once. Only Grandpa is reasonably calm. He says, "Well, well, well!" and sits down.

ACT III

On the next day, Donald is reading to Rheba the account in the paper of the arrest of thirteen defendants who, after spending the night in jail, were given suspended sentences for manufacturing fireworks without a permit. Among the defendants was Anthony W. Kirby, of Wall Street, holder of many high social connections. Most of the family, at home, are subdued. Penny and others grieve because Alice has broken with Tony and is determined to go, all by herself, on an Adirondacks vacation. Tony comes and bravely tries to talk sense into Alice's head, for the time being without success. Meanwhile, Kolenkhov brings Grand Duchess Olga to dinner: there is so much food about to be wasted and the Grand Duchess needs a change from the fare at Childs' Restaurant where she is a waitress. As the Grand Duchess prepares blintzes for the whole company, Grandpa and Mr. Kirby argue the question of living freely or in accordance with one's social and business obligations. Interspersed in the conversation, Tony begs an adamant Alice to marry him. Tony finally brings his father to a disadvantage by revealing the contents of old letters in which his father had told of wanting to be a trapeze artist and a saxophone player. Tony also confesses that he had deliberately brought his parents to the Vanderhof mansion on the wrong night so that the Kirbys could see in action a loving, understanding family. Alice's taxicab arrives; she is ready to depart. Grandpa has her wait a moment: he once again tries to convert Mr. Kirby to a life in accordance with his true stars. At this moment, the Grand Duchess comes in from the kitchen to ask how many blintzes will be required. Mr. Kirby is deeply impressed: he asks Tony if they should not stay for dinner. Alice and Tony are reconciled. Grandpa discloses that he has settled the income tax matter by letting the Government know that Martin Vanderhof (remember the milkman?) has long since died

298

and been buried. Mr. Kirby sidles up to him to study his shrewd methods of income tax adjustment. As the whole crew sit down to feast on the Grand Duchess' incomparable blintzes, Grandpa thanks God for the fine way things are going.

74

JOHN STEINBECK (1902–   )

Of Mice and Men (1937)

Naturalistic tragedy in three acts

MAIN CHARACTERS AND THEME: Of bright plans for the future ardently held by two migrant agricultural laborers, *George Milton* and his inseparable idiot pal *Lennie Small*, working under conditions that make bright futures nonrealizable.

OTHER CHARACTERS:

Candy, stoop-shouldered old worker with right hand missing

The Boss, superintendent for a big land company

Curley, the Boss's son, an ex-boxer

Curley's Wife

Slim, a skinner, boss of a team of barley-thrashers to whom George and Lennie are assigned

Carlson and *Whit*, other barley-thrashers

Crooks, a Negro stable buck

TIME: About 1937.

PLACE: Grain fields in Salinas River valley, California.

HISTORICAL NOTE: The only significant excursion into the dramatic field by the distinguished novelist of America in general and California in particular. His fictional treatment of California includes both legendary and realistic phases, and Steinbeck is strong in both. The material of the current play was developed in novel form a few months before the play was produced. In the same manner, Steinbeck published *The Moon Is Down*, a novel, and it was produced as a play on the day of its novel publication (April 7, 1942). It had the noble purpose of laying bare the real brutality and tyranny of the Nazi spirit and the resultant natural, insuppressible resistance of free men, but it was only partially successful. Supporting Steinbeck's writing in *Mice and Men*, Broderick Crawford won an enduring reputation as Lennie.

ACT I (*two scenes*)

Having received work cards and bus tickets from Murray and Ready's agency, George and Lennie spread out on the river bank at night before reporting to work next day. George separates Lennie from a dead mouse he has been using as a pet. They mention the "bad thing" Lennie did, which resulted in their having to leave Weed posthaste. Supper is a can of beans. To make Lennie behave, George talks of the easy life he would lead if he did not have to care for Lennie. On the other hand, Lennie makes him repeat again and again the story of their plans for the future (having a dream, they are better off than other ranch workers)—their little house, a couple of acres, a cow, a pig, and rabbits which Lennie will be allowed to tend. Red and blue and green rabbits, like those Lennie saw at the Sacramento fair.

Next morning, in their new bunkhouse, Boss complains of their arriving too late to go out with the morning team. Boss is suspicious of George's domination over Lennie, not allowing Lennie to answer questions. Later, Curley comes in, flexing his muscles (as always), and gives indication that he will set George and Lennie in their places; he is particularly determined to tackle Lennie, who is big and powerful, and whose conquest would be a feather in the cap of the small-sized, small-minded Curley. George warns Lennie that if there is trouble, he is to hide in the brush by the river, where they had slept the previous night. Curley's Wife, most suggestive in dress and behavior and heralded by loud carnation perfume, comes in, presumably looking for Curley but actually because she is lonely. Most specifically George warns Lennie against having anything to do or discuss with her. As Slim gives away pups from the litter of nine his dog had, Lennie begs for a brown and white one, to pet.

ACT II (*two scenes*)

George is telling Slim about Lennie—how completely obedient he is, even to jumping into the river, at George's behest, without being able to swim.

He also tells of the trouble at Weed, when George would not let go of a girl wearing a red dress and very nearly got both of them lynched. Because Candy's old dog smells unconscionably bad, Carlson finally persuades Candy to let him be shot: Slim is giving Candy a pup from the new litter. As Candy waits to hear the shot, he and the others are deeply touched. Whit tries to get George to go into town for fun with the girls, but George hesitates because of the expense and the need of saving for the future home. Lennie makes George tell the whole story of the home again, with embellishments. When Candy overhears it, he wants to be part of the plan. He has $250 he received for losing his right hand bucking barley, and another $50 he saved up. At first George resents the intrusion; but then, he figures that with the $50 each of the three of them will make the next month, the total of $450 might buy a piece of property he knows about, from some old owners that are "flat bust." So Candy is admitted, and now the plan is threefold. Because Curley's Wife still hangs around, she and George have another quarrel. The big quarrel, however, comes when Curley finally "chooses" Lennie, to bolster his morale. Seizing his hand, Lennie (once again) will not let go, and Curley's hand is broken in many places. In an effort to save the jobs of George and Lennie, Slim tells Curley he had better say his hand was caught in a machine if he does not want to become a laughingstock.

Because the other fellows, even George, have gone into town, Lennie comes by to visit Crooks, who is isolated because of racial prejudice and full of resentment. Hearing of the plan—Lennie cannot help talking about it—Crooks also wants to be a part. Eventually George comes to get Lennie. Curley's Wife appears again, demanding to know the real truth of her husband's injury. So deeply does she irritate George that he is about to strike her when he sees Boss standing in the door.

ACT III (*two scenes*)

Lennie pets his little dog to death and is in the barn trying to revive him and then covering him with hay when Curley's Wife appears, suitcase in hand, ready to leave the place she has found so dismal. She and Lennie speak of their respective golden futures, in alternate monologues rather than in dialogue. Proving to Lennie that she is beautiful, she takes Lennie's hand and has him rub her hair. Lennie's fingers close on her hair and hang on. When she struggles and tries to scream, Lennie's other hand closes over her

302

mouth. Eventually, he wrenches her neck around and breaks it. Realizing that he has "done a real bad thing," he heads for the secret meeting place George had ordered him to, taking his dead little dog along for tender burial.

Candy finds the girl's body and calls George, who immediately figures out the truth. Appropriating Carlson's Luger pistol, he has Candy call the others. Curley leads the lynching party and commands each of them to shoot Lennie on sight, "in the guts." In consultation with Slim, George is forced to rule out the possibility of Lennie's being saved from Curley's mob and put away in an asylum. He finds Lennie in the meeting place and has him hide among the tules while he diverts the rest of the party. Then, as Lennie looks across the river and he and George repaint again the picture of their "little place . . . with   cow . . . pig . . . chickens . . . alfalfa . . . rabbits . . ."   George   places Carlson's Luger back of Lennie's head and fires. Lennie crumples and falls behind the brush.

75

ROBERT E. SHERWOOD (1896–1955)

Abe Lincoln in Illinois (1938)

Biographical drama in three acts

MAIN CHARACTER AND THEME: The crucial and revelatory thirty years in the life of *Abraham Lincoln*, from the time of the educational struggles of his early twenties to that of his leaving Springfield to assume the Presidency the day before his fifty-second birthday.

OTHER CHARACTERS:

Mentor Graham, a middle-aged patient schoolteacher

Ann Rutledge, daughter of the owner of Rutledge Tavern in New Salem

Ben Mattling, Revolutionary veteran of New Salem

Bowling Green, an elderly fat judge, staunch friend of Abe's

Mary Todd of Springfield, twenty-two (on first appearance), short, pretty, sharp

The Edwards' Maid

Jimmy Gale, Seth Gale's eight-year-old son

Aggie Gale, Seth's wife

Gobey, a Negro freed by Seth's father

Stephen A. Douglas, Abe's rival candidate for United States Senator from Illinois in 1858

Ninian Edwards, young, prosperous, handsome Whig leader

Joshua Speed, Abe's quiet, very dear friend

Trum Cogdal, New Salem citizen, who subscribes to the Cincinnati *Journal*

Clary's Grove Boys—*Jack Armstrong, Bab, Feargus, Jasp*

Seth Gale, frontiersman going to Oregon

Nancy Green, wife of Bowling Green

William Herndon, law clerk for Stuart and Lincoln, attorneys-at-law in Springfield

Elizabeth Edwards, Ninian's wife

Willie, nine, *Tad*, seven, and *Robert*, seventeen, Abe's three sons in 1860

The Lincolns' Maid

Crimmin, a shrewd, humorous fixer

Barrick, a soft Episcopalian dignitary

Sturveson, elderly, wealthy, and blank

Jed, telegraph operator

Phil, who takes bulletins at the Lincoln headquarters in Springfield

Kavanagh, a captain in the Secret Service

Cavalry Captain, Soldiers, Railroad Men, Townspeople

TIME: 1830's to 1861.

PLACE: New Salem, Illinois; Springfield, Illinois, and environs.

MUSICAL HIGHLIGHTS: "Tippecanoe and Tyler, Too—"; "Old Abe Lincoln Came out of the Wilderness"; "John Brown's Body"; "Glory, Glory, Hallelujah."

HISTORICAL NOTE: Literarily, dramatically, and historically outstanding, this drama won respect and popularity from the time of its opening, appropriately in Washington, D.C., on October 3, 1938, and ten days later at the Plymouth Theatre, New York. Its New York run was 472 performances, and during that run it won the Pulitzer Prize for 1938–1939. Without undue glorification or debunking, it depicts in an absorbing manner the peaks and valleys, the humor and sadness, and the fierce self-analysis of America's greatest statesman. Raymond Massey was widely acclaimed for his interpretation of the Lincoln role.

ACT I *(three scenes)*

In Mentor Graham's cabin in New Salem, late at night, Mentor teaches Abe, a ragged backwoodsman, the moods of grammar. For the imperative mood, Mentor introduces his pupil to Webster's famous speech on "Liberty and Union," a reply to Calhoun's right-of-secession speech. Studying the potential mood, Abe lingers on his economic failures, on his father's fruitless moving, on his own fear of cities and death. He is reminded of his mother's death from "milk sick," of the deer running over her grave, and of his inability to kill deer thereafter. Receiving from Mentor Keats' poem on death, and reading it aloud, Abe is much impressed.

In the Rutledge Tavern on the Fourth of July, Judge Green, Trum, and

305

Ninian Edwards, the young Whig, drink casually while waiting to talk to Abe. Some Andy Jackson worshippers from Clary's Grove—Jack, Bab, Feargus, Jasp—capture the tavern and are about to "tan" Ninian when Abe, now the postmaster, arrives. He votes himself into Ninian's spot but manages to avoid a fight by telling Jack that his wife awaits him for the picnic. Nevertheless, Jack cannot leave without warning Abe to stop reading so much if he wants to remain champion wrestler. Ninian and the other Whigs broach to Abe the prospect of his running for the legislature: it would mean three dollars a day toward helping him pay off his one thousand five hundred dollar debt, some scrap of importance, proximity to a good library and to fine lawyers. Abe cannot make up his mind. He does listen sympathetically to Seth who is being forced to give up his plans to go to Nebraska in order to return East to a sick father and a measly thirty-six acres that will tie him down for good. Most awkwardly, Abe sympathizes with Ann over the apparently fading interest of her absent fiancé. At last he declares his love, offers himself, and receives some encouragement, but no definite answer. He then goes to tell Judge Green a joke—he will run for the legislature.

At Judge Green's house, Abe is devastated by Ann's death—Ann who showed him purity and beauty in the world, and whom he loved more than everything else. He wants to die to be with her again. As had Mentor, the Judge marvels at the combination of things good, bad, and mysterious in Abe.

ACT II (*five scenes*)

It is five years later in the law office of Stuart and Lincoln in Springfield. Billy Herndon, their clerk, twits Abe about being so much opposed to slavery—Abe had told of being outraged by seeing twelve Negroes chained on the Quincy boat—and not supporting the Abolitionists. When Judge Green and Josh tell Abe how much they worry about him, Abe says he's improving: he has settled his debts at seven cents on the dollar, has shaken hands with President Van Buren, and is as well off as a man internally at war with himself can be. He fears being a congressman and having to vote for or against any kind of war, remembering his experiences in the Black Hawk War, where he did not fire a shot. Ninian comes to take Abe to a reception where Ninian's sister-in-law, Mary Todd, who speaks French, will inspect the male eligibles.

Six months later, Elizabeth Edwards, Ninian's wife, is much disturbed because her sister Mary, daughter of the president of the Bank of Kentucky, is contemplating marriage with the boorish Abe. At the end of the scene, the lights fade on Mary's eyes melting upon Abe.

A few weeks later, on the afternoon of New Year's Day, Josh, Abe's close friend, is greatly disgusted because he has been unable to get Abe to withdraw a letter he has written Mary, canceling their engagement and telling her his ardor has cooled. Abe has already received a wedding cane from Ninian, who simultaneously gave warning of Mary's inordinate ambition and drive. Josh puts Abe's letter in the fire and compels him to deliver his sentiments in person. On his way out, Abe is forced to defend himself against Billy's claim that he does not believe in the Constitution if he will not fight more vigorously against slavery.

Abe is out on the prairie, two years later, with the Galeses, who are at last headed for Oregon. As he helps Seth minister to his son, who has swamp fever, Abe and Seth discuss the great opportunities in the West. But Seth realizes the disadvantages also: he is taking Gobey, a freed Negro, with him, and has already had to rearrange his route to avoid trouble. Seth swears to be ready always to fight to keep the Western lands free. On Seth's persuasion, Abe raises a prayer for the sick boy. He asks God not to condemn the boy to the imprisonment of death, and to allow him his birthright of "great plains and high mountains, of green valleys and wide rivers," as befits an American. After praying, he quietly dedicates himself to the cause of men like Seth.

Abe is again in the Edwards' home, confronting Mary. He begs her forgiveness and asks her to marry him. In accepting, she makes him promise to pursue his real destiny. He assures her that, having deliberately turned down the chance to go West, he knows that his true direction is with her. Mary says: "Whatever becomes of the two of us, I'll die loving you."

ACT III (*four scenes*)

On a summer evening in 1858, in an Illinois town, Ninian announces that the two speakers on the platform, both candidates for United States Senator, having completed their main speeches, are ready for rebuttal. Ninian introduces Mr. Stephen Douglas first. Warning his audience to beware of Abe's homely innocence, Stephen insists that Abe has muddled the issue by harping on the condition of Negro slave workers and ignoring the low condition of Northern white workers who labor fourteen hours a day and who

307

engage in strikes in Massachusetts and Illinois. Abe replies that the white slaves would not change places with black slaves because the former have in their hands the remedy for their slavery. He says that the doctrine of inequality, supported even in one case, can rend its supporters. To remain a free nation, we cannot leave slave states alone. We must not let other nations taunt us as hypocrites. More specifically, he says: "A house divided against itself cannot stand. This government cannot endure permanently, half slave and half free."

In the Lincoln home in Springfield, Mary is complaining of many things but most of Abe's not telling her that three men are coming by that evening to interview him as a possible presidential candidate. In Abe's absence, the three—Crimmin, Barrick, and Sturveson—decide that Abe is a great politician and can win.

On Election Day, November 6, 1860, everyone in the Illinois State House awaits the returns. Telegraph instruments clatter. Abe is far behind in New York, but gaining: the New York *Herald* and August Belmont are confident of defeating him. Because of edgy nerves awaiting the returns, Abe and Mary quarrel; Mary leaves, greatly disillusioned. Abe does not seem to want to win, and Billy calls attention to the danger of winning, what with secession in the offing. Finally, the big dispatch comes: the New York *Herald* has conceded that Abe has carried New York by twenty-five thousand votes and has won the election. Abe refuses to go out to the people. There is, however, shouting and singing everywhere, especially "Old Abe Lincoln Came Out of the Wilderness." When he leaves, Abe now has a Secret Service escort.

The date is February 11, 1861; the place, the railroad yards at Springfield. The Secret Service officers discuss the problem of defending a President whom the South has promised to kill before he can take office. From Billy comes the report that Abe wants his old office and shingle kept in place since he intends to come back to Springfield and practice law as if nothing had happened. But he emphasizes the words, "If I live. . . ." At length Abe responds to the crowd's demands for a speech. He begins by asking them if they like his new beard: the crowd roars approval. He then goes on to talk of the great danger to the dream of freedom on which our nation rests, and of the possibility that mankind may never again have the chance to nurture freedom. Begging the people for their support, he asks also their prayers. The train leaves as the crowd sings "John Brown's Body" and "Glory, Glory, Hallelujah."

76

ARTHUR ARENT (1905?–   )

"...one-third of a nation...":
A Living Newspaper (1938)

Agitprop drama in two acts and eleven scenes

CHARACTERS AND THEME: Lacking a single main character, unless it be the composite Poor American, called *Little Man*, looking for a decent place in which to live, this drama, produced under the auspices of the Federal Theatre Project of the United States Works Progress Administration, shows the evils of bad housing, how these have naturally developed over the years, and the best remedies. Since one of the purposes of the Federal Theatre Project was to employ actors who were out of work, more than one hundred acting roles were written into the script.

TIME: From 1705 to the 1930's.

PLACE: New York City, especially its slum tenements, but the author states that the same drama could be developed for Boston, St. Louis, Chicago, Philadelphia, or—in the words of President Franklin D. Roosevelt— "one-third of a nation!"

HISTORICAL NOTE: The use of the living newspaper style was an evolution from the agitprop drama of Europe and is related to the expressionism of O'Neill, Rice, and Odets. The living newspaper had no regular plot involving conflict affecting a single set of characters, but it was unified around an overpowering theme. Episodes evolving the theme in successive stages were presented, and then elaborated through devices intended to heighten and deepen their effect, as though one were reading

309

a newspaper with penetrative understanding. Chief devices were the loudspeaker, the free use of spotlights and of black and white screens, cubicles, striking songs, projection on screens, voices of inanimate things, and ballet movement. This play was produced and published under the general direction of Hallie T. Flanagan; it was first presented at the Adelphi Theatre, New York, on January 17, 1938, and ran for 237 performances. Since its time, playwriting and productive techniques have profited from its experiments.

ACT I (*six scenes*)

Scene 1. Fire: A big fire develops in a typical crowded slum section. A small boy shooting craps in the alley warns the tenants, who grab a few personal belongings and run. A man is trapped on the fire escape when the ladder gives way.

Scene 2. Investigation: Setting abstract, impressionistic, not realistic. Newspaper explains that fourteen persons died in the fire. Three inspectors testify that the building was unsafe, but it did not violate fire laws because it was an old building and new laws apply only to new buildings. Landlord, who legally was not compelled to testify, admits his building was a fire trap but says the blame is upon "whatever it was that made New York City real estate the soundest and most profitable speculation on the face of the earth."

Scene 3. Land: Again abstract setting. Story of how real estate values in the city grew, from 1705 to the present. Even Aaron Burr in 1794 dropped a rent investigation when he received some land in payment. With the growth of the city and the coming of overcrowding, rents go higher and higher. John Wendall testifies: "... we followed four cardinal rules: never to mortgage, never to sell, never to repair, and never to forget that Broadway moved uptown at the rate of ten blocks in ten years."

Scene 4. Looking Backward: The Little Man, searching for an apartment is told his chances are 3600 to 1. Scene 4a: Why They Came—Irish Family: Leaving a cottage, green grass, and the hot sun of Ireland, the family, expecting great improvement, is now in a one-room flat, where the roaches prevail and the toilet is usually stopped up. Scene 4b: What They Saw— Steve and Joe: Steve and Joe and Mary live a confused and complicated life because of their crowded housing and alley-dwelling. Mary tells them of the money her boss hides in his store; she and Joe go off to get it. Scene 4c: What They Got—Jewish Family. What they got from their housing was cholera, tuberculosis, spinal meningitis.

Scene 5. Appoint a Committee: Little Man sees committee reject the report for action.

Scene 6. Renting: Following charwomen's dusting rooms to "disinfect" them, the rooms are rented by landlords to Italians, Irish, and Jews of low economic status, three to five persons per room. One prospective tenant asks if these are the "cholera" rooms. The landlord lies—says emphatically they are not; tenants do not believe him and demand their money back. Landlord angrily shouts: "You've got to have a place to live."

ACT II (five scenes)

Scene 1. The Law: New laws continue to come forth, from 1869 on, regulating bad housing, but laws cannot change old houses. Investigation of violations shows that Trinity Church, one of the earliest landholders in 1705, now has the worst tenements.

Scene 2. Crosstown: Little Man, in 1933, asks for tour of present conditions. Scene 2a. Frank, thirteen, and Sammy, twelve, argue over a "busted" homemade skate scooter. Frank squelches Sammy by accusing him of having to sleep in the same bed with his sister. Scene 2b. Little Man and Guide watch couple move into apartment. Husband begs wife to have baby. Wife refuses because, she says, baby will become either a "Peg-Leg" Lonergan or a "Two-Gun" Crowley. Little Man's wife calls him to apply for an apartment. From Tenement House Commissioner he learns that on file are 19,000 applications for 1,622 apartments. Scene 2c. In Harlem, men argue over bed which three share in eight-hour shifts. Scene 2d. Rent strikes develop in Harlem, Bronx, East Side, and Brooklyn.

Scene 3. What Price Housing?: Philanthropist begins with plans to build rooms to rent for seven or eight dollars. Taxes, mortgages, labor, building mistakes, and insurance bring rent up to twenty-five dollars.

Scene 4. Government Housing: Montage, in 1937, shows various scenes of the debate on the Public Housing Bill, especially the two chief opponents—Senator Wagner, of New York, for, and Senator Byrd, of Virginia, against. The Wagner-Steagall Bill passes!

Scene 5. Looking Forward: Newspaper helps Little Man to figure out

311

that the $526,000,000 voted by the Bill for better housing will give New York $30,000,000 to do a $2,000,000,000 job. At same time, Newspaper quotes the budget figure for Army-Navy appropriations as $3,125,000,000—"more than enough to clear out every slum in New York." Little Man's wife says: "We're going to holler, and we're going to keep on hollering until they admit in Washington that it's just as important to keep a man alive as to kill him."

77

THORNTON WILDER (1897–   )

Our Town (1938)

Presentational drama in three acts

MAIN CHARACTER AND THEME: Biographical sketch of an American town, presented through direct and indirect dramatic methods by a *Stage Manager*, who is, at times, historian, actor, and interpreter.

OTHER CHARACTERS:

Dr. Gibbs, the town physician

Joe Crowell, eleven, newsboy

Howie Newsome, thirty, the milk-man

Mrs. Gibbs, the doctor's wife

Mrs. Webb, wife of Mr. Charles Webb and a neighbor of the Gibbs family

George, sixteen, and *Rebecca*, eleven, children of Dr. and Mrs. Gibbs

Emily, sixteen, and *Wally*, eleven, children of Mr. and Mrs. Webb

Professor Willard, of the State University

Mr. Webb, publisher and editor of the Grover's Corners *Sentinel*

Woman in the Balcony

Man in the Auditorium

Lady in the Box

Simon Stimson, organist of the Congregational Church

Mrs. Soames, member of Mr. Stimson's choir

Constable Warren

Si Crowell, eleven, another news-boy

Baseball Players

Sam Craig, thirty, a Grover's Corners boy who went out west (to Buffalo) and became a businessman

Joe Stoddard, in his sixties, the   *Two Assistant Stage Managers*
 undertaker   *People of the Town*

TIME: 1901–1913.

PLACE: Grover's Corners, New Hampshire.

MUSICAL HIGHLIGHTS: "Blessed Be the Tie That Binds"; "Art thou Weary, Art Thou Languid"; Handel's *Largo;* "Love Divine, All Love Excelling"; "Wedding March" from *Lohengrin.*

HISTORICAL NOTE: Borrowing and adapting the presentational drama—generally employed by Oriental drama, in which the main action is presented directly rather than suggested—Wilder gives an incisive, accurate, and exciting account of an American phenomenon, a mill town. He defines it as a cross between country (with its bobwhites, crickets, chickens, gardens) and city (with its gradually emerging suspicions of neighbors, and its toughness). Using simple language and no scenery, Wilder gets to the heart of the town without the depressive naturalism of the town literature of the late nineteenth century. First performed at McCarter Theatre, Princeton, New Jersey, on January 22, 1938, it later played 336 performances at the Henry Miller Theatre, New York, with Frank Craven as Stage Manager in an indelible role of American stage history. Martha Scott was distinguished as Emily Webb.

ACT I: The Daily Life

Stage Manager describes the general outlines of the town—its residential areas, its businesses, its churches, its landmarks. Introducing the Gibbs and Webb families, he has them act out their early morning routines. He has Professor Willard testify as to the town's rock value and its population; he has Mr. Webb report on the voting and educational habits and on the town's general culture. Interpolating from time to time, Stage Manager himself ties these individual contributions to the bigger culture of the nation and of the twentieth century. Later, he allows Emily Webb and George Gibbs to talk from their respective windows of their studies and of the moonlight. He lets the choir practice and allows the audience to hear gossip of the intoxicated condition of the choir director. Before Mrs. Gibbs returns from practice, Dr. Gibbs gently chastises his son for not helping his mother sufficiently, but raises his allowance and charges him to improve. At 9:30 P.M., the town is rapidly going to sleep.

ACT II: Love and Marriage

It is three years later (1904), and just after the high school commencement. George and Emily have decided it is time for them to be married, and the wedding is on the church docket. Not just the Webb and Gibbs families, but the whole town recognizes the sanctity, the necessity, the glory, and the excitement of marriages: preparations are rife. Customs must be observed; advice (which will hardly be followed) must be given. To get the full picture, Stage Manager carries time back to the earlier days of the courtship of the marriage candidates—when they first began to realize that they were made for each other. Stage Manager, himself, serves them the ice-cream sodas over which they fall more deeply in love. In his curious way, George proposes.

Soon, everyone is in church for the wedding. En route, the principals have misgivings, but these are merely part of the game. Stage Manager performs the ceremony—unique and uninteresting each time—and people cry, and people say, "Aren't they a lovely couple?" The wedding over, Stage Manager calls for a ten-minute intermission.

ACT III: Death and the Meaning of Life

This time, nine years have passed. Stage Manager resets the scene of Grover's Corners to catch up with growth and deterioration. He brings the audience to a graveyard, strategic for understanding the town. On this spot, he grows more philosophic even than usual; "We all know that *something* is eternal. And it ain't houses and it ain't names, and it ain't earth, and it ain't even the stars—... that something has to do with human beings." Actually, the town is gathered to say its last farewell to Emily Webb Gibbs.

The dead and living of the town are on the spot, only they converse dead with dead and living with living, and cannot converse across the line. Since Mrs. Gibbs had already died, Emily can talk with her: she is affected by the fact that her funeral is being held in the rain. She tells Mother Gibbs how they used the legacy she left them: to buy a "ce-ment" drinking fountain for the stock, one that never overflows.

Only the Stage Manager can rise above the dividing line between life and death: he tells Emily she can relive any day of her selection and watch herself reliving it at the same time. Emily chooses her twelfth birthday—February 11, 1899. At first, she is deeply touched and pleased; but as the day rolls on, she is poignantly aware of the lack of passion in the living operation as she observes it from this objective coign of vantage. She wants to be taken back to the realms of death, and is. She seems to have learned that in the long run, the townspeople are measured by death, where through the ignorance, blindness, selfishness, and slow learning of life, people seem even more blameworthy. When will they understand, thinks Emily.

But Stage Manager is not entirely hopeless. It is eleven o'clock in Grover's Corners; tomorrow's going to be another day.

78

HOWARD LINDSAY (1889–   )
RUSSEL CROUSE (1893–   )

Life with Father (1939)

Comedy in three acts
from the book (1935) by Clarence Day

MAIN CHARACTER AND THEME: How a businessman Father (*Clarence Day, Sr.*), in his forties, attempts to dominate his family in spite of the quiet power of his wife, a determined mother, and the stresses and magnetic forces of a rapidly growing city and American civilization.

OTHER CHARACTERS:

Annie, the new maid, a young Irish girl

Vinnie, Clarence's wife and mother of his four red-headed sons

The Sons:

Clarence, seventeen

John, fifteen

Whitney, thirteen

Harlan, six

Margaret, the cook, a small Irishwoman of about fifty

Cora, Vinnie's attractive country cousin of about thirty

Mary, Cora's friend, a pretty small-town girl of sixteen

The Reverend Dr. Lloyd, rector of the Episcopal Church

Delia, new maid

Nora, another new maid

Dr. Humphreys, the family physician

Dr. Somers, a consulting physician

Maggie, still another new maid

TIME: The late 1880's.

PLACE: The Day home at 48th Street and Madison Avenue, New York.

317

MUSICAL HIGHLIGHT: "The Happy Farmer"; "Sweet Marie."

HISTORICAL NOTE: The spirited though tender conflicts of the drama reveal much of the moral framework of upper-class life of the time—standards of material value and ethics, business methods, political prejudices, and aspirations of the young. The growing city is reflected—its geographical expansion, the rumored corruption of the Tammany administration, the enlarging taxes, the horsecars and private cabs (brougham and victoria), the show places in Chinatown and the Bowery, and echoes of an increasingly powerful Wall Street. Dialogue is both subtle and explosive, and often sparklingly humorous. Opening at the Empire Theatre on November 8, 1939, it ran for 3,216 performances, closing on July 12, 1947, and breaking all records for consecutive performances of a drama in New York.

ACT I (*two scenes*)

It seems that Vinnie is always inducting new maids. At the beginning of this scene, she is telling Annie about the individual napkin rings and the respective diets of each member of the family. Soon Father is heard from upstairs, loudly complaining that the necktie he wants to wear today has not been pressed. Downstairs, Vinnie is quite calm, reviewing the catechism with Whitney. Father comes down complaining again about the clothes made by his London tailors. But later at breakfast he both praises Margaret for the goodness of the bacon and condemns her for the coffee, which he calls slops. For Father, small annoyances are the unbusinesslike practices of Vinnie and the church, but a large annoyance is the management of the city. Father sums it up: "Why did God make so many damn fools and Democrats?" Talking to Mayor Hugh Grant as though the mayor were sitting before him, he warns that the people of the city of New York will not tolerate tax raises and the plundering of their pocketbooks. Meanwhile, Vinnie, entertaining Cora and Mary, fails to note that her son Clarence has been devastated by one of Mary's smiles.

With the help of Vinnie, Dr. Lloyd hopes to talk Father into making a large contribution to the building of the new church. Father pleads his own poverty and the poor business planning of the church in wanting a new edifice. Later, Father explodes because Vinnie arranges for him to take her, Cora, and Mary to dinner; but before very long, he is showing the beautiful Mary how to play tiddlywinks and hurrying Vinnie up for the date. In the course of

318

conversation, he reveals that he·has never been baptized: this sets up for Vinnie a new project to which she becomes utterly devoted. If Father has not been baptized, Vinnie wonders if they two are even married!

ACT II (*two scenes*)

The following Sunday, Father makes quite a disturbance when Dr. Lloyd preaches about the baptized: Father makes known to the minister his displeasure. Wearing his father's trousers, Clarence finds that he simply cannot kneel in church and later that the trousers make him dictatorial with Mary. Later, Father reads Clarence a hilarious lecture on women, of which the substance is, *be firm*. When Vinnie and Father get together over the bills, Father is firm but makes little headway against Vinnie's business attitudes; he finds himself once more being told that he *must* be baptized so that the two of them can be truly married. He postpones the issue. But Clarence has an issue he is not postponing: to get a new suit of clothes which his father will not buy him, Clarence tries to get John to give him the new job he has, selling on commission. He needs the new suit badly, because of Mary, even worse than he did when planning for Yale next year. But because he will not promise to write first, Mary will not say good-by to him when she leaves. As soon as Mary is out of the door, Clarence sits down and writes to her.

Vinnie is sick. John's new job is to sell "Bartlett's Beneficent Balm," a cure-all. To try out the medicine, Clarence puts a teaspoonful in the tea that is being taken up to his mother. Two doctors are required to restore Vinnie to health. Believing that his cooperation will hasten her recovery, Father promises, voluntarily, to be baptized; and then he is horrified that he has done so.

ACT III (*two scenes*)

Despite his panic at needing fifteen dollars for his new suit, Clarence does not succeed in wangling the money from Father. Father is equally dilatory with Vinnie about following through on his promise—of a month ago—to be baptized. Even so, Vinnie had made all the arrangements; he is to go to a church where he can be baptized secretly and without fuss. The scene ends with Father showing affection and gratitude for Vinnie's being married to him for twenty years by giving her a beautiful ring. Proud of the ring, Vinnie

319

nevertheless suggests that a diamond necklace would be an even greater token of affection. Although Father balks at showing that much affection, Vinnie is so happy with him that she sings. He is happy because she is.

Clarence, at last, has his new suit: he got it by exchanging the picture of the pug dog by which Father was so much horrified. Vinnie tries to show Father that since it was an exchange, the suit will cost him nothing, but Father knows there's something wrong with that kind of mathematics. Vinnie has also ordered a suit for Father to be baptized in, and she is dressed (for the occasion) like a bride. When the subject of religion comes up, Father reaches heights in his normal profanity; but when he learns that the cab to take him to be baptized is costing two dollars an hour, he is still profane but willing to speed things up.

79

LILLIAN HELLMAN (1905–   )

The Little Foxes (1939)

Drama in three acts

MAIN CHARACTER AND THEME: The brutal and devastating warfare conducted against members of her own family by *Regina Hubbard Giddens* in order to guarantee herself a more-than-fair share of the Hubbard family resources.

OTHER CHARACTERS:

Addie, fifty-five, and *Cal*, middle-aged, Negro retainers in the Hubbard household

Birdie Hubbard, about forty, the nervous, somewhat flighty and poetic wife of Oscar, and the only Southern aristocrat in the family

Oscar Hubbard, in his late forties, a hard-working businessman

Leo Hubbard, twenty, Oscar's son, possessing a weak kind of good looks

William Marshall, forty-five, a a self-possessed businessman from the North

Benjamin Hubbard, fifty-five, the senior member of the family, a bachelor, graceful but inclined to be tyrannical

Alexandra, seventeen, daughter of Regina and Horace

Horace Giddens, forty-five, Regina's sick husband

TIME: The spring of 1900.

PLACE: A small town in the South (probably Louisiana).

HISTORICAL NOTE: Revelatory picture of life in the South among the upper classes at the turn of the century, especially that part which reflected the beginnings of a Southern industrialist class sponsored by Northern capital. Both the traditions of the South and those of the super-power American capitalist are reflected. The passing of power from aristocrats to crude money-makers is indicated. While clearly demonstrating the analytic power of Miss Hellman, one of America's most skillful dramatic analysts, the play also is remembered for the significant contribution of Miss Tallulah Bankhead's acting in the role of Regina. The play is also a masterpiece in dramatic construction. It ran for 410 performances after opening at the National Theatre, New York, on May 15, 1939. Miss Hellman had won respect in 1934 with *The Children's Hour*, a penetrating drama about a girls' school. She won even greater respect in 1951 with *The Autumn Garden*, an incisive play about people in their forties.

ACT I

The Hubbards are entertaining Marshall, the businessman from Chicago, at dinner because he has brought them an interesting proposition. He proposes to build an effective cotton mill near the center of cotton production. For an interest of 49 per cent, he will invest $400,000; for a controlling interest of 51 per cent, the Hubbards are to put up $225,000 and make other necessary arrangements. Expecting great riches, the Hubbards discuss, each one, what they will do with their share of the profits. There is only one hitch: although Ben and Oscar Hubbard have two-thirds of the Hubbard share of the money ready to invest, Regina and Horace, her husband, have not yet produced the other third. Horace has for five months been in a hospital in Baltimore and will not discuss the matter in his correspondence. So far, the brothers have been willing to accept Regina's assurances, but now that contracts are about to be signed, money must be forthcoming. By shrewd bargaining, Regina gets Ben to agree that Horace will have 40 per cent of the Hubbard share for his one-third contribution, the extra percentage to come from Oscar's share. Oscar bitterly disagrees, but can do little to stop the bargain; he is somewhat pacified by Regina's promise that she will *consider* allowing her daughter Alexandra to marry his son Leo. Before their little meeting is over, she has also promised to send Alexandra, Horace's favorite of all people on earth, to Baltimore to bring her father back so that the transaction may proceed. Alexandra's complaint that her father may be too sick to travel is brushed aside. And Birdie's loud protest against Alexandra's marrying her son Leo

322

is joined by Alexandra (who says she will not marry at all, but certainly not Leo)—but both seem to be voices crying in the wilderness.

ACT II

Alexandra is behind schedule in bringing Horace from Baltimore. In a private conversation, Oscar tells Leo he must behave more responsibly if he is to help make the family fortune—must give up outside women and work harder at the bank. Casually Leo confesses that without permission he had looked into Horace's safe-deposit box at the bank and seen $88,000 worth of Union Pacific bonds, which have lain there untouched for fifteen years, just appreciating. Oscar toys with the dangerous idea of having Leo "borrow" the bonds, to use as collateral; they would gain Leo a secure place in the transaction, providing Horace is not going to use them. A few minutes later, Horace and Alexandra arrive. Horace is surrounded by medicines he must take to stay alive—he is an extremely sick man, and somewhat hopeless. After a few preliminaries, Horace ironically expresses his appreciation for being wanted home. He also makes clear that he will never sanction a marriage between Alexandra and Leo.

Although Horace is too fatigued to want to talk about the mill, Regina and Ben almost force the discussion upon him. Ben tells Horace how he "swung" the deal, promising the Marshall Company unlimited water power, no racial troubles, no strikes, and other desirable things. Horace is slow responding; he goes upstairs without giving a definite answer; Regina follows him to wrest an answer from him. In her absence, Ben and Oscar decide to "borrow" Horace's bonds and consummate the deal at once. When they are gone, Horace and Regina have another brief meeting. It concludes with Regina still unable to win him over and calmly telling him: "I hope you die. I hope you die soon. (*Smiles*) I'll be waiting for you to die." Alexandra shrieks for her father not to listen.

ACT III

Two weeks later, Horace, sitting near the window in his wheel chair, has received his safe-deposit box from Manders, a bank officer. Birdie talks voluminously around him, saying that her family looked down upon the Hubbards because they made their money cheating poor Negroes. Asked why she married into the family, she replied that Ben needed the superior cotton on her family's plantation and had Oscar to marry it for him. Enjoying the conversation with just Birdie, Alexandra, and the servant Addie, Horace announces that he is about to make a new will to prevent his money going places he would be ashamed of after his death. Cal returns from the bank where Horace had sent him and relates the incident of Leo's discovery that Horace had acquired his safe-deposit box.

A few minutes later, Horace is telling Regina about the theft of his bonds, and further that he is going to let her brothers get away with it. His new will, he says, will give the bonds to her and everything else to Alexandra. Regina's answer is to tell him how much she holds him in contempt. Then Horace has a sudden heart attack. Standing before him, Regina will do nothing to help him, particularly will not give him the medicine he needs, that is nearby. Waiting until he is completely helpless, Regina finally calls for Addie and Cal. She goes up to Horace, when they have removed him upstairs, and Leo, Ben, and Oscar meet downstairs.

Leo informs his father and his uncle that Horace knows about their theft of the bonds. They are panic-stricken, unable to determine what way to react. Regina comes down to say that Horace is unconscious. Without looking at them, she informs them that Horace told her about the bonds that afternoon. Believing that they can escape through the loophole that Horace gave permission for them to use the bonds, Ben, Oscar, and Leo prepare to leave. But Regina calls them back sharply. She tells them that if they do not do precisely what she orders, she will put them all in jail. They scoff at her threats until they learn that Horace is dead. Regina shows no sign of grief. Threatening them with a trial in court, she tells them she must have 75 per cent of the profits, or they will suffer the consequences. Their only counter-attack is in Alexandra's question of what her father was doing on the staircase, but they have no palpable case against Regina there.

When they are gone, Alexandra tells her mother she is leaving—she is not going to Chicago with Regina. Alexandra quotes Addie to the effect that some people eat the earth and others stand around while her mother does it. When Regina asks if Alexandra would like to sleep in her room that night, Alexandra turns to her and asks: "Are you afraid, Mama?"

80

WILLIAM SAROYAN (1908–)

The Time of Your Life (1939)

Drama of the poetry of living, in five acts

MAIN CHARACTER AND THEME: Drama of *Joe T.*, a well-to-do bohemian, and his friends, who attempt to battle those influences in life which prevent their thinking of themselves as always glorious.

OTHER CHARACTERS:

The Newsboy

The Drunkard

Willie, about twenty, a marble-game maniac

Nick, a young Italian-American who owns "the honky-tonk" in which most of the action takes place

Tom, thirty, big, handsome, innocent, who runs errands for Joe

Kitty Duval, a "burlesque queen" who when she does not believe in herself is a plain Polish girl from Ohio named Katerina Koranovsky

Dudley Bostwick, twenty-five, miseducated, who wants true love

Harry, who fancies himself a comedian but who is actually a good dancer

Wesley, a colored piano player, very good

Lorene, thirty-seven, overbearing and funny-looking, Dudley's wrong number

Blick, the head of the Vice Squad

Arab, who has been to Mecca and who plays a wonderful harmonica

Mary L., who secretly patronizes Nick's place

Krupp, a policeman, thirty-nine, who feels that his duties degrade him

McCarthy, a longshoreman-ideal-
ist, a boyhood friend of Krupp

Kit Carson, really Murphy, a
trapper who claims varying ages

Nick's Ma

A Sailor

Elsie Mandelspiegel, a nurse in
the Southern Pacific Hospital,
the object of Harry's affections

A Killer (elegant prostitute)

Her Side Kick

A Society Lady

A Society Gentleman, her husband

First Cop

Second Cop

Sam, man-of-all-work at Nick's

Anna, Nick's daughter

TIME: Afternoon and night of a day in October, 1939.

PLACE: Nick's Pacific Street Saloon, Restaurant, and Entertainment Palace
at the foot of the Embarcadero, San Francisco; also, a suggestion of
Room 21 at the New York Hotel, upstairs, around the corner.

MUSICAL HIGHLIGHTS: "The Missouri Waltz," Wesley's piano-playing;
Arab's harmonica-playing; Newsboy's "When Irish Eyes Are Smiling";
Salvation Army's "The Blood of the Lamb"; "My Country, 'Tis of
Thee" on the marble machine.

HISTORICAL NOTE: The second produced drama of William Saroyan, who
introduced into the American theatre a convincing faith in the magic
of believing in the inherent goodness of people and in their endless
capacity for delight and mystery, if they will only *live* their lives. The
play was brought to New York on October 25, 1939 (Booth Theatre),
and won both the Pulitzer and the Critics' Circle awards as the outstanding American play for that season. Other above-average Saroyan
plays in the same vein are *My Heart's in the Highlands* (1939), *The
Beautiful People* (1942), and *The Cave Dwellers* (1957).

ACT I

Although it is afternoon, Nick's Saloon is full of active people, who, long
frustrated, are trying to fulfill the deep secrets of their hearts. Nick, with
the *Racing Form*, is trying to bet a few winners and beyond that is trying to
give unhappy people a chance to be happy; Arab, the harmonica player,
sipping a glass of beer, is worried because everywhere there is "No foundation. All the way down the line. . . . " He wants to help supply this lack.
Willie is trying to win out over the marble machine, which represents Destiny
to him—he patiently inserts nickel after nickel and patiently "plays" the

326

levers; Dudley is in the telephone booth trying to reach his beloved Elsie, the nurse, and pouring out his heart to wrong numbers. As the afternoon goes on, Harry comes in, straining to convince Nick that he is a comedian and making no one laugh; and Wesley wants any kind of a job and faints from hunger before he can give a demonstration of his ability. But later, and somewhat by accident, Harry emerges as a wonderful dancer and Wesley as an excellent pianist: Nick adds both to his payroll because they bring joy to his customers.

The central story, however, seems to revolve around Joe, the well-to-do bohemian, who sits in the saloon day and night, drinking champagne, sending Tom on strange errands—such as to buy two dollars worth of toys at the Emporium—and trying through conversation to get people to see the best in themselves and to act upon it. In this manner he meets Kitty Duval, whom Fate has condemned to status as a cheap prostitute, but who thinks of herself as a burlesque queen. Even when Kitty's faith falters, Joe revives it within her. He is especially pleased when Tom falls in love with her: Joe believes in the redemptive power of love, no matter who the lovers are. Joe and Nick find an enemy in Blick, who seems to believe that everyone is a lawbreaker at heart.

ACT II

Because of his faith in people, Joe is always making discoveries in unexpected places. Mary L., whose last name he never learns, has been to Paris, as he has been, and thinks many of his kinds of thoughts. The Newsboy, who has been in and out, turns out to be a glorious soloist with "When Irish eyes are smiling," although he is Greek. McCarthy is involved in a longshoreman strike not because he is a patriotic union member but because he believes deeply in people. Joe, himself, believes in dreams sooner than in statistics. But Kit Carson, who comes in late, is more than a believer; he talks a dramatic autobiography, ranging from his experiences of love with a midget weighing thirty-nine pounds to his herding cows on a bicycle. Joe, he says, is the only man who has ever believed him all the way.

Joe gives Tom eighty dollars to put on a horse who is a 15-to-1 shot. The horse wins by a nose, but Tom arrived at the bookmaker's too late to place the bet. He is much distressed because with the money, he might be able to marry Kitty and stop her from crying. Joe is willing to rise from his seat—he reveals himself as a cripple—to help Tom stop Kitty from crying.

ACT III

In her cheap hotel room, Kitty tells Tom and Joe of her past dreams. Kitty is improving when a Sailor comes down the hall to talk business with her. Tom drives the Sailor away, but Joe decides that he will help Kitty's recovery by taking the three of them down to Half Moon Bay for supper, and to give Tom and Kitty a chance to dance together.

ACT IV

Back in the Saloon, Dudley has found his Elsie. As a nurse she has seen so much misery that she finds it hard to believe in Dudley's kind of love. But she is willing to try, although she knows the disillusion of the morning after, and she leaves with Dudley who embraces her shyly, as if he might hurt her. At their show of tenderness, a nearby streetwalker bursts out laughing. Nick asks the streetwalkers to leave his place because Blick and his men are becoming very strict. But Krupp, a policeman of many years, is finding the unkindnesses he must commit on his job so distasteful that he is thinking of resigning from the force. Arab, observing everything, still thinks that life is without foundation, but when he begins to play his harmonica, he seems to be giving a poetic commentary on life's most golden possibilities. As Wesley describes his playing: "That's deep, deep crying. . . . That's crying a thousand years ago. Some place five thousand miles away." Following this, the music and dancing in Nick's Saloon reach a very high peak of quality.

ACT V

When Joe has transferred Kitty from her room in the New York Hotel to the respectable and very elegant St. Francis Hotel, Tom wants to know where he gets his money. Joe is ashamed that, like most well-to-do people, he gets his money not from rich people who can spare it but from poor people who cannot. "Money," he says, "is the guiltiest thing in the world," and he does not want to hear any more about it.

His commentary seems to introduce a society couple who have come to Nick's, at the instigation of the wife, instead of going to the Mark Hopkins. So shocked is the husband by the weird behavior of Nick's people—such as a chewing gum contest between Tom and Joe and Joe's pointing a loaded revolver around—that he drags his wife out bodily, talking of divorce if she, a settled woman, insists upon staying. Blick returns and begins to question Kitty severely; angered, she tells him flatly that she is a prostitute. When Wesley protests Blick's treatment of Kitty, Blick beats Wesley. Tom is about to attack Blick, but Joe has called a friend and arranged to get Tom employed as a truck driver. He gives Tom and Kitty money, tells Kitty to ride with Tom to San Diego, and orders the two of them to get married. He tries to shoot Blick, but his gun will not fire. A few moments later, Kit Carson comes in and confesses that he has just killed Blick. But the killing is more symbolic of the elimination of ugly shadows from around people who are trying to live, than it is of murder.

81

JAMES THURBER (1894–1962)
ELLIOTT NUGENT (1899–)

The Male Animal (1940)

Comedy with social emphasis in three acts

MAIN CHARACTER AND THEME: The determination of *Tommy Turner*, thirty-three, a young, ambitious associate professor in Midwestern University, to live up to his liberal ideal and his sense of academic freedom in the face of serious threats to his immediate job, his academic standing generally, and his marriage.

OTHER CHARACTERS:

Ellen, Tommy's wife, a pretty young woman of twenty-nine or thirty

Patricia Stanley, a pretty, lively girl of nineteen or twenty, Ellen's sister

Wally Myers, six-feet-one, one hundred and ninety pounds, a football player who likes Patricia

Dean Frederick Damon, sixty-five, head of the English Department and Tommy's immediate superior

Michael Barnes, a senior student, editor of the college paper

Joe Ferguson, thirty-five, all-time All-American from Midwestern, now a popular, successful businessman

Mrs. Blanche Damon, Dean Damon's wife

Ed Keller, thirty-eight, a rich trustee, an arch-conservative real estate man, who contributed the Keller Building

Myrtle Keller, in her late thirties and a slightly faded blonde, Ed's wife

"The Male Animal" (1940)

"Nutsy" Miller, a bandleader who is circulating a student petition	*Newspaper Reporter*
Cleota, the Turners' colored maid	*Voice of Radio Announcer*

TIME: About 1939.

PLACE: Living room of Professor Turner's house in a Midwestern university town.

MUSICAL HIGHLIGHTS: "Happy Birthday to You"; "Who's Afraid of the Big Red Team?"; "I Can't Give You Anything but Love"; "Who?"; "Oh, We Don't Give a Damn for the Whole State of Michigan."

HISTORICAL NOTE: In the authorship marriage of James Thurber, one of America's outstanding humorists and incisive socio-literary critics, and Elliott Nugent, son of the popular actor, J. C. Nugent, and a distinguished actor in his own right, the American theatre was most fortunate. Dealing effectively with the general subject of academic freedom, Thurber and Nugent contribute also an accurate picture of an area which drama generally finds hard to portray with truth—college life. The fact that they were collegians together at Ohio State is helpful, but incidental. Their points are more effectively made than usual mainly because they command a range of humor from subtle to broad and an understanding of their complex characters rather than a preachment, an anti-educational stance, or a cold analysis.

ACT I

The occasion is the Homecoming Celebration, the big game with Michigan, and Ellen's birthday. It is complicated by the fact that Michael, editor of the school paper, has written an editorial in which he condemns the trustees as fascists, because they have ignorantly fired as Reds two liberal professors, and praises Tommy as the hope of education because he had read to his classes on the same day letters from Lincoln and Vanzetti, the famous anarchist. In the midst of plans for the Homecoming festivities, Dean Damon must come to see Tommy about the matter. Tommy says he has not yet read the Vanzetti letter—he had only planned to do so some day—but he will not, under pressure, promise never to read it. Tommy and Ellen and Damon get involved with Joe Ferguson, the all-time Midwestern hero, who used to love Ellen and is now being divorced, and with Ed Keller, the trustee who flatly tells Tommy that he must not read the letter. When Ellen asks

331

Tommy privately not to endanger his job by reading the letter, a quarrel ensues, and Tommy retires upstairs with a downcast feeling. Ellen dances with Joe, and the two seem to pick up their romance where they left it off. At Tommy's suggestion, Ellen and Joe lead the others off to the Dixie Club while Tommy stays at home.

ACT II (*two scenes*)

On the next day (Big Game Day), shortly after noon, Dean Damon comes looking for Tommy again because the trustees, especially Keller, are aroused at having been called fascists by Michael in the *Literary Magazine.* Keller and the other trustees are threatening to kill the "Endowment Fund." Patricia, Ellen's sister, who likes Michael, has tried to talk to him on the telephone, but he hung up. When, however, Michael comes to see Patricia, she refuses to talk to him, and he is distressed. Michael tells Tommy, who is just entering, that you can't do much with a woman who refuses to understand you and prefers half-witted football players.

His comment is appropriate, for immediately Tommy and Ellen get into an argument about Ellen's preference for a successful Joe and Tommy's stubbornness in reading radical letters to classes at the expense of his job. In a silly but understandable way, they agree to separate. When Joe arrives, Tommy, who is drinking, drags him into the decision and tries to make him promise to take care of Ellen properly. Ellen declares a plague upon both of them and goes upstairs, whereupon Tommy sends Joe to comfort her since he is Ellen's choice. Michael comes back to talk to Tommy about the incomprehensibility of women and the sensitive demands of the male animal. After Ellen has alarmed the house by throwing things, Tommy prepares a hot-water bottle for Joe to use to keep Ellen's feet warm and sends them both off to the game.

Two hours later, Tommy and Michael are still drinking. After a review of male animals up through the animal kingdom, Tommy concludes that they consistently fight for their females. When Joe brings Ellen home, Tommy alcoholically wades into him but does harm mainly to himself. Ellen has packed her bag to leave with Joe, but Tommy insists on having Joe fight things out in the back yard. Joe finally accepts and goes outside. A few minutes later, when Patricia and Wally have returned, Wally helps Joe bring Tommy in—unconscious from the fight.

332

"The Male Animal" (1940)

Two days later, Ellen has returned from her mild escapade and the reporters are hounding Cleota, the maid, trying to get Tommy's side of the rumor that Tommy is about to be fired as a radical. Michael appears and asks Tommy's forgiveness for creating troubles; once again, he is unable to win sympathy from Patricia. Joe returns and tells a now-sober Tommy that he passed out from hitting his head on a bench, not at Joe's hands. When Keller arrives and tells Tommy that the only way he can save himself from destruction is to issue a statement dissociating himself from Michael and the whole editorial problem, Tommy replies by persuading Keller to listen to the Vanzetti letter. Hearing the letter, Keller now knows that it is not inflammatory, but he wants Tommy to submit to the trustees and not read anything, out of respect for authority. When Ellen announces that she and Joe are going away together, Keller is even more deeply shocked. His remarks to Ellen cause Tommy to invite him out into the back yard. And even Dean Damon shows a spark of courage by opposing Keller's tyranny, as also do the students who are circulating a petition.

When Keller finds out that the star football players have signed the petition, he is somewhat shaken, but he is still determined to kick Tommy out of school. In return for his view, Tommy puts him out of the house. Patricia defends Michael, suspended from school, and is ready to go away with him if necessary. Because Tommy has changed from "nice" to "wonderful," Ellen is now a little bit afraid of him; she leaves off dancing with Joe to return to Tommy's arms for good.

book by
MOSS HART (1904–1961)
lyrics by
IRA GERSHWIN (1896–)
music by
KURT WEILL (1900–1950)

Lady in the Dark (1941)

Musical psychological drama in two acts

MAIN CHARACTER AND THEME: The psychoanalysis of *Liza Elliott*, in her late thirties, editor of *Allure*, a fashion magazine, but distinguished for her severity in dress and manner.

OTHER CHARACTERS:

Dr. Alexander Brooks, a good-looking psychoanalyst in his middle forties

Miss Bowers, Dr. Brooks' secretary

Miss Foster, twenty-five, Liza's secretary

Miss Stevens, receptionist in Liza's office

Maggie Grant, in her early forties, the acidulous, lusty, earthy fashion editor of *Allure*

Alison DuBois, another member of the *Allure* staff

Russell Paxton, staff photographer

Charley Johnson, advertising manager

Randy Curtis, handsome, rugged, powerful movie star

Joe and *Tom*, office boys

Kendall Nesbit, young fifty and rich, Liza's sweetheart

Helen, Ruthie, Carol, and *Marcia*, models

Ben Butler, the handsomest boy in Liza's high-school class

Barbara, a blonde, the prettiest girl

"Lady in the Dark" (1941)

Jack, another of Liza's early friends

Twelve Men in Faultless Evening Clothes

A Boy

A Tall Distinguished Man followed by A Zouave

Crowd at the Club Seventh Heaven

Liza's Father and Mother

Boy and girl graduates of Mapleton High

David, Liza's classmate when she was seven

Mrs. Bennett

Liza at three, seven, and ten

TIME: About 1940 to begin with, but going back to 1904.

PLACE: New York City and Mapleton, Liza's home town when she was a girl.

MUSICAL HIGHLIGHTS: "Oh, Fabulous One in Your Ivory Tower"; "Huxley Wants to Dedicate His Book to You"; "Just One Life to Live"; "Girl of the Moment"; "Of Beauty Untainted"; "We Sing the Praise of Mapleton High"; "This is New—"; "The Princess of Pure Delight"; "Oh, Promise Me"; "Ta ra ra, tazing, tazing, tazing—"; "Russian Composers"; "Jenny"; "My Ship."

HISTORICAL NOTE: An example of a drama which deals with the practice of psychoanalysis, and of the works of two notable contributors to the American stage, Moss Hart and Kurt Weill. It was produced at the Alvin Theatre, New York, on January 23, 1941, with an all-star cast, among whom were the following: Gertrude Lawrence as Liza, Danny Kaye as Russell, Macdonald Carey as Charley, Victor Mature as Randy, and Bert Lytell as Kendall. Initial run: 305 performances.

ACT I (four scenes)

Because she has mysteriously gone to pieces, Liza has come to see Dr. Brooks, the psychoanalyst. She tells him she has been an editor for ten years, likes her work, has a normal love life, and does not particularly believe in psychoanalysis. Somehow, she has gradually been experiencing vaporish states of terror for six months, and they are coming closer together. She can sleep now where formerly she was an insomniac. Recently, she threw a paperweight at her advertising manager, Charley. With Kendall, her lover, her relations have been fine—she has lived with him for some time because his wife refuses to divorce him; he has financially backed her magazine for twelve years.

335

When Dr. Brooks says she must begin trial analysis at once or he cannot take her case, Liza yields. Her first thought is of a song from her childhood, a few bars of which she can remember, but no words. Then she drifts into her recurring dream:

Lights dim. Liza is given the most elegant treatment—a chauffeur in a blue Duesenberg; a blue soap box for a speech she wants to deliver on Columbus Circle; adulation from the patrons of the Club Seventh Heaven. The people in her dream are the members of her staff in real life, but transformed; for example, her chauffeur Beckman is Russell, her staff photographer. Dr. Brooks notes the contrast between the Liza who in dreams is the object of such songs as "Oh, Fabulous One" and "Girl of the Moment" and in reality is the austere editor.

Liza's office has been thrown into an uproar by Randy Curtis, the movie star, whom one of the secretaries calls a "beautiful hunk of man." He has come to *Allure* to be photographed for a future issue. When Randy gets to Liza, she is quite casual with him, as she is also with Kendall who wants to take her home. Only Charley, the advertising manager, still irritates her. Cancelling her busy schedule, she lies down on the couch in her office and dreams once more. She dreams of her high-school graduation, but Randy, whom every woman wants, is in the dream. To her, the valedictorian, he sings, "This is new." Later, wedding bells ring: she and Kendall are about to marry. Charley appears to be murmuring the marriage ceremony, but he interrupts to say that this woman does not love this man. Liza contradicts; the chorus agrees with Charley; the dream ends in nightmare.

After receiving a worried Maggie, the fashion editor, who says Liza cried over her yesterday's dream, Dr. Brooks later receives Liza. He inquires into her partiality for plain clothes. Also, he wants to know why she intends to break her date with Randy when in the dream she was so proud to be seen with him. He wonders if she scorns and hates other women because she is afraid of them, especially so the more she makes them beautiful. When Dr. Brooks tells her she does not dare compete with pretty women, Liza breaks off her analysis and asks Dr. Brooks to submit her bill.

At 6:30 next evening, Liza's office is in an uproar. It is almost press time, and Liza has not been seen for hours. When Liza arrives, she tells Maggie she has been driving around Long Island since 7 A.M. Later, she tells Kendall she does not want to marry him, but he insists that she must, now that his wife has promised to divorce him. Charley comes in to say that he is leaving:

he is not angry, he is taking less money at *Town and Country* where he is going—he merely wants to be the boss. When she gets angry, he tells her: "Rage is a pretty good substitute for sex." She throws a cigarette box at him as he strolls out whistling. Liza begins to cry. Randy comes to take her out and he hopes she will not dress, for he is sick of glamour. She *will* dress! As she dresses, she cries. Seeing her dressed, Maggie tells her she is a fitting representative of *Allure,* magazine of beauty.

ACT II (*three scenes*)

Still unable to decide on a sound policy for her life, Liza, in her office, drifts again into dreaming. She finds herself on trial for indecision—specifically, she cannot decide whether the magazine will have a circus or an Easter cover, whether she will marry Kendall or no, what kind of woman she wants to be. Charley is the prosecutor; Randy, the defense lawyer. Liza defends herself by singing of Jenny, who could never make up her mind, and who got away with it. But the ensemble demands that she make up her mind.

As the lights come up, Liza is once more in Dr. Brooks' office. She has gone back to her early childhood when her mother was considered beautiful and she an ugly duckling; when little David Reed did not want to be a prince if she, and not Barbara, was to be the princess; when her mother died, and she felt no grief; when Ben, the handsomest boy, after dating her, the most popular girl, left her flat for Barbara, the most beautiful girl. Dr. Brooks sums it up: all along she has resented beautiful women because they have robbed her. She has stopped competing against them, but her longing remains.

In Liza's office, a week later, Charley tells Maggie that he admires Liza greatly but sees through her pose. Liza comes in from lunch with Randy, who is obviously fascinated with her. Later, Kendall calls—he realizes that love is over between them. When he leaves, Liza feels herself becoming freer all the time. She realizes that her life with Kendall was a flight from something she dared not face. Then Randy is back. He wants Liza to marry him. He confesses that he is frightened at being an actor and by all the publicity he gets: to him Liza suggests peace and courage, and he needs her eternally. He will call later for his answer.

Charley finally returns to try to apologize. He says he can't apologize, but he thinks Liza is fine. Liza now asks him to stay on as co-boss, and maybe later, as full boss. Between the two of them, they change the format of the magazine. Maggie, seeing them, is amazed; she remains as Charley goes to get the July layout. Liza tells Maggie she might have made a great new mistake and married Randy, who is another Kendall, full of insecurity. All Maggie can say is, "Well, for God's sake!" Liza likes Charley's layout. She begins to hum her secret song; Charley knows the words, has known them since he was a kid. Charley asks if she knows the words. She replies: "Yes—I know all the words—now."

Liza sings her precious "My ship," and Charley joins in.

83

EUGENE O'NEILL (1888–1953)

Long Day's Journey into Night (1941, 1956)

Psychological drama in four acts

MAIN CHARACTERS AND THEME: Although *Mary Cavan Tyrone*, fifty-four, married for thirty-five years to *James Tyrone*, sixty-five, is the pivotal character, the play is a family drama, revolving around all four Tyrones —*James, Mary, James, Jr.*, thirty-three, their elder son, and *Edmund*, twenty-three, their younger son.

OTHER CHARACTER:

> *Cathleen*, early twenties, a buxom Irish peasant, who is second-girl (servant) in the Tyrone household

TIME: August, 1912.

PLACE: The Tyrones' summer home, New London, Connecticut.

MUSICAL HIGHLIGHTS: Mary's playing of a Chopin waltz; the foghorn which is heard recurringly, with a great variety of theatrical effects.

HISTORICAL NOTE: Intensive autobiographical drama, observing the classical unities, and perhaps O'Neill's last masterpiece. Reminiscent of Strindberg and Freud, the story is a seething eddy of currents in which the family bond and the interrelationships of characters by twos and threes push against the vain but powerful efforts of each individual for self-expression. The colorful life of the town is incidentally developed— quack doctors, druggists, houses of prostitution, real estate slickers, among other elements. Though terribly analytical, the drama is poetic in the best and highest senses. Authorship completed in 1941, but play withheld from production for fifteen years. First performed, after O'Neill's death, in Stockholm, Sweden, by the Royal Dramatic Theatre, February 10, 1956. It had its American première in Boston on O'Neill's sixty-eighth birthday, October 17, 1956, and reached New York, Helen Hayes Theatre, on November 7, 1956, with Fredric March as Tyrone (James, Sr.), Florence Eldridge as Mary, Jason Robards, Jr. as James, Jr., and Bradford Dillman as Edmund (really O'Neill himself). Winner 1957 Pulitzer Prize.

ACT I

Recently returned from hospital treatment, Mary is complimented by the three other members of her family for looking so well. The spirit of good cheer remains until Tyrone is angered by what he calls Edmund's socialistic ideas and until notice is taken of Edmund's awful spells of coughing. It even returns when Tyrone in his best stage manner—he is a retired, successful actor—praises his wife for her beautiful eyes and kisses her. Out of Mary's hearing, James and Tyrone discuss Edmund's cough, which is serious: the doctor has promised to call that afternoon and let them know if Edmund has consumption. James takes occasion to upbraid his father, a big property owner, for relying upon such cheap physicians as this Dr. Hardy. Tyrone strikes back, accusing his elder son of being trifling, unable to make money, and a failure at acting jobs his father has thrown his way.

From Edmund, their conversation moves to Mary. Despite earlier compliments, they reveal their fears that Mary has returned to the dope addiction which they thought had been cured in the hospital. Coming back to them, Mary shows, through nervousness and detachment, definite signs of her old affliction. When her favorite son and personality, Edmund, returns, she hovers over him, complaining once more because her husband never has given her a real home. But even Edmund tentatively indicates to her that she must be careful not to yield again to the old temptation, and this suggestion causes her to condemn the air of suspicion in which she must always live. Edmund begs her not to worsen her condition by worrying about him. When trapped by his almost open accusations, she simply denies that there is anything wrong with her at all, practicing self-deception on a grand and rigid scale.

ACT II (*two scenes*)

That afternoon, the two sons compare notes and are compelled to conclude that their mother is again lost in narcotics. James accuses her outright; Edmund reproves him for so doing. When Tyrone comes in, he adds to Mary's uneasiness by indicating that he was a fool to believe that she could shake off her old ways. Once more, emphasizing her lack of home and true home environment, she says she doesn't know what he is talking about.

The tension builds as Tyrone gets a telephone call from the doctor. He passes a message to Edmund to be sure to see the doctor at four that afternoon. When, swept by nervousness, Mary retreats upstairs, James cynically observes that she is getting another narcotic boost. Tyrone says they must live through the experience, as they have through earlier ones, and have some faith. Edmund quotes Nietzsche: "God is dead: of His pity for man hath God died." To James alone Tyrone gives the news that the doctor called to report that Edmund actually has consumption; James is sure his father will find the cheapest way to get him treated.

When Mary returns, she is told by her husband that James is going into town with Edmund, and he is also going on a business errand. He asks if she has anything to do. She says she will drive into town (with the car and chauffeur Tyrone has provided) to get some necessities at the drugstore. More and more, her conversation drifts backward to the painful or glorious past—her life in the convent or the great pain she suffered bearing Edmund which, through a quack doctor who gave her overdoses of narcotics, set her on the road to addiction. She talks also of her dead son, Eugene, and her husband tries to get her to leave off such thoughts. Before going to his appointment with the doctor, Edmund begs her to exert her will power and try again to shake off her awful trouble—they will all help. At first reverting to her rigidity, she later admits she has become a great liar, especially to herself. Some day, she says with great poignancy, she will not have to feel guilty any more—"some day when the Blessed Virgin Mary forgives me and gives me back the faith in Her love and pity I used to have. . . . ." She says, then she will scream in agony, but will laugh through sureness of herself. In turn, she begs Edmund not to drink. When they are all gone, she says she is glad to be alone, she wanted to get rid of them—"their contempt and disgust aren't pleasant company." But at last, with a despairing laugh, she inquires: "Then Mother of God, why do I feel so lonely?"

341

ACT III

Mary and Cathleen have returned from the drugstore, and Mary gives Cathleen drinks from Tyrone's sacred bottle. Afterwards, they will restore the bottle level with water. When Cathleen asks why *she* never went on the stage, Mary replies that she was brought up in a respectable home. Later, Cathleen speaks of the shocking behavior of the druggist when she offered him the paper on which was the prescription for Mary's "rheumatism medicine." Once more, Mary's conversation reverts deeper and deeper into the distant and ecstatic past, this time into the period of her being courted by the handsome young Tyrone. When she hears someone returning, she is glad to give up her horrible loneliness. Tyrone and Edmund have returned, but James is still out, no doubt engaging in riotous living on his half-share of the ten dollars Tyrone provided his sons with earlier that afternoon. As they drink sociably, Mary still re-creates the past, going back, back—this time to her wedding and her wedding gown.

But Edmund wants to talk of himself and the awful news he has just received: that he must go to a sanatorium. His mother insists the doctor is lying. In the course of their conversation, Edmund blurts out that it's hard having a dope fiend for a mother. Later Mary, alone, says: "I must go upstairs. I haven't taken enough." But when, in a few minutes, she excuses herself from dinner and Tyrone accuses her of doing so to take more poison and become a mad ghost before the night is over, she calmly tells him she doesn't know what he is talking about. She wants to know why he says such mean, bitter things to her—he's as bad as their sons.

ACT IV

Around midnight, Edmund returns. His father, parsimoniously, warns him to douse the lights when he comes in, and Edmund calls him a cheap skate. As they become more and more intoxicated, Edmund recites passages from Dowson and from Symons' translations of Baudelaire; his father chides him for not sticking to Shakespeare and the other *good* poets. He says Edmund might have been a writer if he had had better taste. When Tyrone mentions that Dante Gabriel Rossetti was a dope fiend, the conversation once again reaches Mary. Again Edmund says his father's cheapness—in not getting a good doctor when she needed one—set his mother down her

342

awful road, and is going to do the same kind of thing to him. Tyrone eloquently defends himself, especially in saying that the Hilltown Sanatorium, though state-supported and therefore inexpensive, is the best place available for him. Further accused of miserliness, Tyrone reviews his early life and demonstrates how his money values rose out of a childhood fight against the most abject poverty. He also speaks of the restriction placed on his acting by being able to make forty thousand dollars a year from a single role. Edmund is glad to hear these things—he understands his father better now. From his own experience at sea, he relates similar feelings, ending on the note that he will always be a stranger who never feels at home, always a little in love with death.

James returns, heavily intoxicated, telling a drunken story of his trying to save a fat prostitute from being fired and not being appreciated. James tells his brother that all along he has envied him and warns him that he will try to pull him down at every opportunity. When James calls Mary "a hophead," Edmund punches him in the face. Their brotherly give-and-take is full of variations from deep antagonisms to maudlin demonstrations of respect, and many degrees in between. Finally, James drops into a drunken stupor; Tyrone appears, and condemns his son's wretched appearance.

Wearing a sky-blue dressing gown over her nightdress and carrying her wedding gown on her arm, Mary makes a triumphal entry. She is talking to Sister Theresa at the convent. The others try to talk to her, but she goes doggedly on with her ancient scene. At last, James breaks through to recite Swinburne's "A Leave-taking," which begins "Let us rise up and part; she will not know." Then all four are talking—James still reciting his Swinburne, Edmund speaking of his imminent trip to the sanatorium, Tyrone commenting on how deeply Mary is enmeshed, Mary going ahead with her story of thirty-five years ago. The story reaches its peak with the vibrant lines: "Yes, I remember. I fell in love with James Tyrone and was so happy for a time."

84

RICHARD WRIGHT (1908–1960)
PAUL GREEN (1894–)

Native Son (1941)

*Expressionistic sociological drama in ten scenes
based on Wright's best-selling novel (1940)*

MAIN CHARACTER AND THEME: Biography of a young American, *Bigger Thomas*, twenty-one, fighting to overcome the naturalistic handicaps of being black and of being forced to live in a Chicago slum.

OTHER CHARACTERS:

Hannah Thomas, fifty-five, Bigger's mother

Vera Thomas, sixteen, his sister

Buddy Thomas, twelve, his brother

Clara Mears, twenty, his sweetheart

Jack Henson, "G. H." *Rankin*, *Gus Mitchell*, cronies of Bigger, about his age

Ernie Jones, a café and night-club owner

Henry G. Dalton, about fifty-five, a capitalist

Ellen Dalton, about fifty, his wife

Mary Dalton, twenty-two or twenty-three, their daughter

Peggy MacAulife, forty, the Daltons' Irish cook and maid

Jan Erlone, twenty-eight, a labor leader

Jeff Britten, forty-five, private detective and local politician

David A. Buckley, forty, state's attorney

Edward Max, an elderly radical lawyer

Miss Emmet, a social worker

First Newspaperman

Other Newspapermen, Neighbors, Guards, Judge, Prisoners, Others

TIME: Late 1930's.

PLACE: The Black Belt of Chicago.

MUSICAL HIGHLIGHTS: "Every Time I Feel the Spirit/Moving in My Heart I Will Pray"; "Swing Low, Sweet Chariot"; carol singers; "Death Lament."

HISTORICAL NOTE: Dramatization of an epochal novel by the first fully accepted American Negro novelist. Probing with conviction the depths of the Negro problem in America, the novel was a best seller for a long time. When it was rewritten for the stage, Wright was joined in collaboration by Paul Green, who had already achieved a distinguished reputation as an analyst of social problems in his native North Carolina, especially those with racial emphasis, as a depicter of rebellious personalities (e.g., his war drama, *Johnny Johnson*, 1936), and as a successful writer of historical pageants (such as *The Lost Colony*, 1937, and *The Common Glory*, 1947). *Native Son*, acted originally without intermission, received an impressive production by the Mercury Theatre, under the direction of Orson Welles, with Canada Lee playing Bigger. Opening at the St. James Theatre, New York, on March 24, 1941, it ran for 114 performances.

Scene 1

In their poverty-stricken flat, where mother, daughter, and two sons sleep in a single room, the Thomases awake for the day. Hannah shows her religious background by opening the day with a spiritual; against "this racket" Bigger rebels. He sleeps because he has no job—Vera chides him for relying on leaving his name at agencies: she thinks he should go out and *find* a job. At the breakfast table, Hannah reads the Bible to her children, although Bigger is interested only in killing a big rat he has named "Old Man Dalton," for the owner of the row of dilapidated flats in one of which the Thomases live. Miss Emmet, from the welfare agency, arrives to minister to the Thomases, who are on relief. Though deploring Bigger's bitter, rebellious attitude, she has recommended him for a job driving the car for Mr. Dalton. In all honesty, she has reported his stint in the reform school, where he went for stealing automobile tires. When his mother gives him fifty cents to go to the corner store for washing supplies, Bigger takes the money and goes to his cronies instead.

Scene 2

His cronies discuss a robbery they have planned, which will enable them to divide $150. As they talk, they see an airplane above, and these deprived boys, Bigger leading, act out the frustrated power suggested to them by the plane and by what they could do if they had the chance. Later in the talk, Bigger resents remarks of his cronies, threatens them with gun and knife, withdraws from their robbery scheme, brags to them of his new job, and walks superciliously out, tossing the fifty cents his mother had given him on the ground before them—"buy you some hash," he orders.

Scene 3

Though aware that Bigger is a risk—the record shows that Bigger has a color complex, accentuated by the death of his father in a race riot when Bigger was ten—Dalton hires him. Mary somewhat wildly spouts radical talk before him and tells him that his job will be to do what she says. For his first task, he is to drive her to Ernie's, a place Bigger knows well, and to discuss the emancipation of the workers with her radical friends. She hopes Bigger will be unlike most colored people who have no desire to improve their condition by fighting. Later, Peggy shows Bigger how to operate the furnace in her house.

Scene 4

Returning home that night with a heavily intoxicated Mary, Bigger is ordered to take his charge to her bedroom. Before he can get away, she "passes out." The blind Mrs. Dalton, hearing her daughter come in, goes to her room to investigate. Fearing exposure, Bigger crouches in hiding. Mrs. Dalton satisfies herself that Mary is all right, though reeking with liquor, but before she can return to her own room, Mary begins to revive. Sure that if she revives he will be doomed, Bigger places a pillow over her head to prevent her making a noise. In the process Mary is smothered. Feeling himself blameless, but knowing no one will listen to his story, Bigger takes Mary's body and stuffs it in the furnace.

Scene 5

In the investigation which follows, Bigger implicates Jan Erlone, the labor leader, saying that Jan brought Mary home. Dalton tells Jan that, their

346

political and economic differences aside, all he wants is to find his daughter. Jan cannot understand why Bigger, whom he has befriended, will tell lies on him.

Scene 6

At Clara's one-room kitchenette apartment, Bigger displays terrible tensions. His words and actions, running from deep fear to shows of manic superiority, frighten Clara deeply. Lying on her floor, he writes a ransom note to Dalton, asking ten thousand dollars for the return of Mary. He says they may as well cash in on the incident. But Clara senses that he is more deeply involved than he is saying.

Scene 7

At the Dalton home, cold inside because the furnace is not working, the persistent First Newspaperman all but wrings a confession from Bigger. He cajoles Bigger into shaking down the furnace, from which falls an earring which the First Newspaperman picks up. Rushing out, Bigger yells, "I didn't do it! I didn't do it!"

Scene 8

Bigger hides out in an empty room on the top floor of an abandoned house. By soliloquy, he reveals an almost insane reaction to being pursued. Clara, whom he sent to get papers and food, returns; but the mob has followed her. In the course of gun-fighting, Clara is shot and killed by a bullet from outside. Bigger is captured by two policemen who, fearing the outcry from such folk as Max, the attorney, take him away to jail instead of letting the mob have him. From this point on in the play, recurrent murmurs of the mob suggest the angry reaction of a massed uncaring society.

Scene 9

Bigger is being tried. Buckley, the State's attorney, and the judge will not let Max bring in evidence blaming society for Bigger's deed. But Max manages to get across, eloquently, the point that a human being of natural impulses, brought up in a supposed land of freedom and forced to live as Bigger was, is bound to commit abominable crimes; and the people who compel or permit the criminal to live and think as he does are at least accessories. Gaining the floor, Buckley rules out all this kind of philosophy as irrelevant. He notes that Max has offered no evidence to deny the facts of Bigger's guilt, or even to mitigate the punishment. At the end, the judge commands, "Bigger Thomas, stand up." The murmur of the mob continues.

Scene 10

In the cell block, Bigger has ten minutes to live. His family and Max have come to tell him good-by. His little brother assures him he will have a nice funeral. In spite of a strong plea by the Daltons, the governor sends a telegram refusing to interfere. As Bigger begins edging toward the death house, the "Death Lament" of the other prisoners rises like a chant.

85

LILLIAN HELLMAN (1905–   )

Watch on the Rhine (1941)

Drama in three acts

MAIN CHARACTER AND THEME: *Kurt Müller*, forty-three, a good-looking former engineer, who, having left Germany in 1933, has become an outstanding fighter against Nazism in Germany and against the insidious spread of fascism throughout the world.

OTHER CHARACTERS:

Anise, sixty, the Farrelly housekeeper

Joseph, tall middle-aged butler

Fanny Farrelly, sixty-three, widow of Joshua Farrelly, who was a distinguished liberal and a famous globe-trotting American diplomat

David Farrelly, thirty-nine, Fanny's son, a lawyer

Marthe de Brancovis (née Randolph), an attractive woman of thirty-one or thirty-two, American society girl who married European royalty

Teck de Brancovis, forty-five, the Rumanian count Marthe married

Sara Müller, forty-one or forty-two, Fanny's daughter, Kurt's wife

Joshua, fourteen, *Babette*, twelve, and *Bodo*, nine, the children of Kurt and Sara

TIME: Early summer, 1940.

PLACE: The large Farrelly house, built in the nineteenth century, on an estate twenty miles from Washington, D.C.

MUSICAL HIGHLIGHTS: Kurt's piano-playing—segments of Mozart's "Rondo in D Major," Haydn's "Minuet in A Major," Mozart's "Minuet in B Flat Major"; German soldiers' song, "Wir zieh'n Heim, wir zieh'n" and its paraphrase, "And So We Have Met Again."

HISTORICAL NOTE: Perhaps the outstanding dramatic representation of the period centering in the early 1940's when the whole world was being forced to choose between active support of liberal ideas or default into the dynamic religions of Nazism and other forms of fascism. The drama brings the subject fiercely home to those Americans who imagined neutralism a possibility. The workings and weaknesses of the Nazi regime are spelled out in considerable detail. Possessing much natural wit and humor, keen character analysis, vivid dialogue, and consummate dramatic construction, the drama justly earned the Pulitzer and Critics' Circle awards and a wide public hearing. Opening at the Martin Beck Theatre, New York, on April 1, 1941, with Paul Lukas as Kurt, it ran initially for 378 performances.

ACT I

Fanny is waiting to greet her daughter Sara, who has not been home for twenty years, and her family, but the first spotlight of the play centers upon a triangle—David, Marthe, and Teck. Marthe and Teck, it seems, have come to the end of their marriage, although Teck denies it; visiting in the home of the Farrellys, they have but eighty-seven dollars left between them and must make fresh plans. Among Teck's "assets" is a set of friendships at the German embassy where he hopes to get money by playing poker and perhaps by making himself useful in other ways. Among Marthe's indefinite plans is pursuit of her great admiration for David. Teck, however, warns against any plans in that direction.

The Müller family—Kurt, Sara, and the three children—have come down on an earlier train, to save money; they thus are forced to guide themselves out to the Farrelly estate. As Fanny renews acquaintance with her daughter and her son-in-law, who was not a favorite with her when Sara married, many facts are disclosed—mainly, that the family has done a good deal of moving about in Europe, that the family is inured to hardship and danger, and that Kurt has not practiced engineering for a long time. Kurt openly declares himself an anti-Nazi. When Teck comes into the conversation, Teck

350

and Kurt immediately recognize their roles as deadly enemies. Teck has Joseph remove Kurt's baggage to a place where he may examine it surreptitiously.

ACT II

About ten days later, as the Müller children demonstrate great vitality and originality on the vast estate so different from their accustomed restricted lodgings, Fanny prepares to celebrate Babette's birthday. In conversation Teck reveals that David and Marthe have been seen shopping together in a rich jewelry store. On her side, Fanny reveals (from her gossip channels) that Teck has been a large winner at poker in the German embassy. Little by little, the secret warfare between Teck and Kurt breaks into the open. Both disclose that they have stores of hidden ammunition and resources with which to fight, but neither seems ready yet for a decisive engagement. Eventually, a side issue precipitates open engagement. Before David and Fanny, Marthe declares her love for David and tells Teck she is not going with him when he leaves shortly. When David enters the conversation, Fanny tries to restrain him. But David makes it clear that he is already involved, and that he has a definite interest in Marthe. Teck is now ready to make his offensive. He tells Kurt that, through the German Embassy and other sources, he knows that Kurt is a key member of an underground group fighting the Nazis in Germany, and that one of the other key members has been captured. He knows that Kurt will try to deliver his fighting companion and that he carries in his luggage $23,000 to be used in the anti-Nazi cause. For $10,000 of the $23,000, Teck will not reveal to the German Embassy where Kurt now is. With a head start, Kurt has a chance to deliver his friend; if the Germans can pin him down, his chances are gone. When Teck goes to pack, Kurt is amazed that Teck can imagine he will part with $10,000 of this precious fund when, to protect it, he allowed his own children to go hungry. Though his situation is desperate, he plans to leave for Germany at once.

ACT III

Having caught, as he thinks, Kurt in his net, Teck applies the pressure. David and Fanny learn that this is not merely a European contest but one involving all people, on one side or the other. Since Kurt will not part with any of his money, David offers Teck $2500 in cash and a check for $7500, postdated one month, to allow Kurt a month to get to Germany. While David and Fanny go to get all the cash they have in the house, Kurt, telling Teck that he should not gamble with his life, attacks him. In the struggle, Kurt overpowers Teck and takes him outside. When David and Fanny return, Kurt tells them frankly what he must do. He is going to borrow their car, with Teck's body secured in the back, dispose of the body, and drive to catch a plane to Brownsville, Texas, whence he expects to make his connections. They can report him immediately and kill his chances, or they can give him two days' respite before calling the police. Understanding the depth of his cause and of his dedication, they choose the latter course. Fanny also contributes the cash she has in hand. With deep farewells to his family, Kurt leaves. The whole estate seems to reflect an awareness that his uneven struggle is to try to restore shape to a twisted world. Kurt promises his children that they will live to see the day when the distortion will be eliminated.

86

RICHARD RODGERS (1902–   )
OSCAR HAMMERSTEIN, 2nd (1895–1960)

Oklahoma! (1943)

Musical drama in two acts based on the highly considered folk play,
Green Grow the Lilacs (1931), by Lynn Riggs (1899–1954)

MAIN CHARACTERS AND THEME: The main story concerns a love affair carried on by representatives of two antagonistic areas of Oklahoma life— *Laurey Williams*, who owns a farm, and *Curly McClain*, a handsome cowboy, who happens to be the best bronc-buster and bulldogger available.

OTHER CHARACTERS:

Aunt Eller Murphy, Laurey's aunt
Ike Skidmore, who owns a ranch where the Box Social is held
Fred and *Slim*, friends of Curly
Will Parker, a farmer who has been to Kansas City and who loves Ado Annie
Jud (called Jeeter in Riggs' play) *Fry*, a ranch hand on Laurey's place, of mysterious past, behavior, and appearance
Ado Annie Carnes, a girl with roving eyes

Ali Hakim, a Persian peddler, attracted to Ado Annie
Gertie Cummings, who likes Curly but is willing to settle for the peddler
Girls of the Community—*Ellen, Kate, Sylvie, Armina, Aggie*
Andrew Carnes, Ado's father, very skillful with a rifle
Cord Elam, the federal marshal
Boys of the Community—*Jess, Chalmers, Mike, Joe, Sam*
Singing and dancing choruses representing Oklahoma folk

TIME: About 1900.

PLACE: Indian Territory, later (in 1907) to be admitted as the state of Oklahoma.

MUSICAL HIGHLIGHTS: "Oh, What a Beautiful Mornin"; "The Surrey with the Fringe on Top"; "Kansas City"; "I Cain't say No"; "Many a New Day"; "It's a Scandal! It's an Outrage!"; "People Will Say We're in Love"; "Pore Jud"; "Lonely Room"; "Out of My Dreams"; "The Farmer and the Cowman"; "All er Nuthin' "; "Oklahoma!"

HISTORICAL NOTE: *Oklahoma!* is epoch-making in many ways: it is drama in the broadest and best sense, utilizing dialogue, decor, singing, ballet, costume, and lighting with blending and unified force; by making the story real and significant, instead of a peg for songs or production numbers, it created a new vogue in musical plays; it established a lasting record for continuous performances of a musical drama on the American stage, closing on May 29, 1948, after 2,248 performances on Broadway; its title song was actually adopted by the state of Oklahoma as a state anthem; since its first New York run, it has become a national drama and has represented the theatre in many parts of the world.

Group life of folk people of pre-Oklahoma territory is explored and territory customs, prejudices, and patriotism are blended in. Such a custom as the shivaree—a somewhat bawdy ceremony in which bride and groom are dragged from the nuptial couch on wedding night—is included, though much cut down from the massive and wonderful sketch of *Green Grow the Lilacs.* Likewise, Rodgers and Hammerstein have supplanted Riggs' use of folk songs, such as "Ta whoop ti aye ay, git along, you little dogies!" and "Green grow the lilacs," with their own songs which have become American folk songs. It is notable, however, that much of Riggs' dialogue and descriptive background is used with little or no change throughout *Oklahoma!*; and even the songs, particularly the "Surrey Song," most often stem directly from Riggs' phrases and folk poetry. This is not odd since Riggs was born in Indian Territory, where his father was a cowpuncher, and his upbringing was completely among the people he depicted. Rodgers and Hammerstein changed the basic Oklahoma idiom to a more sophisticated Broadway style, not always an improvement. Outside influences are well used, in the visit to Kansas City and in the character of the Persian peddler.

Oklahoma! was first called *Away We Go.* Under the production of the Theatre Guild, it opened at the St. James Theatre, New York, on April 1, 1943. Its success was the composite effort of many accomplished artists in the American theatre, most notably the following: Alfred Drake as Curly, Joan Roberts as Laurey, Howard da Silva as Jud, Celeste Holm as Ado Annie, Joseph Buloff as Ali Hakim; Rouben Mamoulian as director, Agnes de Mille as choreographer and dance director, and Lemuel Ayres as set designer.

ACT I (*three scenes*)

As Aunt Eller churns away in front of Laurey's farmhouse, Curly comes on, singing, "Oh, what a beautiful mornin'." In spite of help from Aunt Eller, Curly has very little luck trying to persuade Laurey to go to the Box Social with him. He manages to gain some attention from Laurey with an idea he develops in song, entitled, "The surrey with the fringe on top." When told there is no such rig, however, Laurey wants to drive Curly away, but he adds some touches to his surrey, in song, and pleads the right of using his imagination. Laurey is enchanted for a moment, but soon flounces indoors.

Will, the farmer, has just returned from Kansas City, having won fifty dollars roping steers at the Fair. He has brought a "Little Wonder" picture-machine for the father of his girl friend, Ado Annie. Answering the demands of the boys, he tells of his trip musically, assuring them, "Ev'rythin's up to date in Kansas City./They've gone about as fur as they c'n go!"

Meanwhile, Curly learns that Jud, the ranch hand, who with his work holds Laurey's farm together, has a great affection for Laurey. He confesses to Aunt Eller that the rig he was singing about is not imaginary after all—that he really "h'ard it over to Claremore." In panic, however, Laurey begs Aunt Eller not to go to the Social in Curly's surrey since she is afraid to ride alone with Jud, whom she has promised to accompany. She describes her abiding fear of Jud and her corresponding inability to dispense with him.

Annie comes by to say that although she still likes Will, she likes Ali also. The peddler has many strange and interesting things to sell, including "The Elixir of Egypt," which told Pharoah's daughter which prince she ought to marry. Laurey buys the elixir for "two bits" while Aunt Eller tells her she throws her money away. Annie's romantic problem grows complicated: though telling the peddler she must marry Will, she is talking intimately with the peddler when her father comes up. His shotgun leveled, Andrew wins a

355

proposal for Annie from Ali, who promptly sings of being "Trapped! . . . Tricked! . . . Hoodblinked! . . . Hambushed!" Annie leaves to spread the news of her betrothal. Laurey and Curly, together again briefly, express the precariousness of their romance by singing that they must not seem too friendly together or "people will say we're in love!"

In the smokehouse, where Jud lives, are shocking covers from the *Police Gazette*. Curly comes to visit him and tries to get him to hang himself: he paints an attractive picture of the glory Jud could thereby win, and he and Jud develop the picture through "Pore Jud is daid!" In the discussion which follows, Curly makes Jud aware that some of Jud's mysterious past is known. In their rivalry, both fire shots to demonstrate their skill and courage. After Curly leaves, Jud and Ali discuss switch-blade knives and women. Ali gone, Jud sings his promise to "git me a womern to call my own."

Before she goes to the party, Laurey has a dream—in ballet form—in which she sees Jud nearly killing Curly and herself surrendering to Jud to save Curly's life. She is waked by Jud, actually standing over her and saying, "Wake up, Laurey. It's time to start fer the party."

ACT II (*three scenes*)

At the Skidmore ranch, Andrew interrupts the dance to sing a song of peaceful coexistence: "The farmer and the cowman should be friends." According to custom, the girls' boxes are auctioned off to the men who will spend time with the respective girls. In the auction, Will, after making a deal with Ali, gets Annie. By selling his favorite saddle, gun, and horse, Curly manages to bid fifty-three dollars for Laurey's box against a persistent effort by Jud. Jud and Curly shake hands, but Curly is still suspicious. Although Will and Annie set the date for their wedding, Will is impelled to warn her that he expects complete fidelity—"All er nuthin'."

In a quarrel on Skidmore's kitchen porch, Laurey fires Jud and orders him not to return to her place again. She tells Curly she still fears Jud, and she promises to marry Curly. Leaving Annie to Will, Ali gives her a long kiss which he calls a Persian good-by, but Will matches this with a longer kiss which he calls "a Oklahoma hello."

Laurey and Curly, married, must have a shivaree—it is the will of the people. Meanwhile, Gertie has married Ali and receives from Will "a Oklahoma hello." In the midst of the shivaree, after Curly is pulled from the

356

house and hoisted on the shoulders of his friends, Jud reappears. He attacks Curly; they fight with fists; Jud pulls a knife; Curly grabs his arm and throws him; Jud falls on his knife, groans, and lies still. When Cord Elam, the marshal, comes to arrest Curly, he meets heavy protest from the crowd who say that Curly should not be locked up on his wedding night. The crowd declare Curly not guilty and end things by singing "Oh, what a beautiful day!"

87

TENNESSEE WILLIAMS (1914–   )

The Glass Menagerie (1944)

*Expressionistic-type drama, semifantasy,
in eight scenes*

MAIN CHARACTER AND THEME: The story of *Laura*, a shy crippled woman of twenty-three, on whose success her family's hopes depend, whose highest achievement and deepest frustration is symbolized in the collection of a menagerie of hundreds of tiny, finely-carved glass animals.

OTHER CHARACTERS:

The Mother—*Amanda*   The Gentleman Caller—
The Son—*Tom*, a merchant sea-   *Jim O'Connor*
man, the narrator

TIME: 1944, 1935, and the Past.

PLACE: An apartment in a St. Louis tenement, next door to the Paradise Dance Hall.

MUSICAL HIGHLIGHTS: Continuous "fiddle-music" in the wings to symbolize that the drama is webbed in memory; the old records Laura plays on her phonograph; "Dear One, The World Is Waiting for the Sunrise" and other old popular music of the 1915–1920 period, from the dance hall.

HISTORICAL NOTE: Perhaps the outstanding artistic accomplishment of Tennessee Williams to date. Play is a triumph of sound and delicate theatrical maneuver; in language, it is simultaneously tenderly poetic and brutally analytical and realistic. First major success of Tennessee (born Thomas Lanier) Williams in the full-length field and last great acting success of Laurette Taylor. First performed by Civic Theatre in Chicago, December 26, 1944; and then for a run of 561 performances at the Playhouse, New York, opening March 31, 1945. Decay and inadequacy of certain middle-class values of the early twentieth century are clearly portrayed. Williams continued to pursue this type of analysis in such notable plays as *A Streetcar Named Desire* (1947), *Summer and Smoke* (1948), *Cat on a Hot Tin Roof* (1955), and *Sweet Bird of Youth* (1959). The first and third of this group won both Pulitzer Prize and Critics' Circle Award for their respective seasons.

Scenes 1 to 6 are considered Act I, which is entitled "Preparation for a Gentleman Caller"; Scenes 7 and 8, Act II, entitled, "The Gentleman Calls."

Scene 1

The narrator, Tom, dressed as a merchant sailor, enters from the alley and sets the psychological stage. He also demonstrates that social backgrounds will play a very influential role. He introduces the four visible characters— and a fifth character, his father, who absconded many years before and who appears only in a large photograph hanging on the wall. Passing off-stage, he takes off his sailor outfit and awaits his normal cue. Behind the portieres, Amanda is heard telling Laura and Tom—the three are at breakfast—to eat properly. As usual, her conversation is on two levels: the present, representing her cramped physical and psychological quarters, and the past, when she was the belle of Blue Mountain, a high society in aristocratic Mississippi, and pursued by the scions of that society. She is especially emphatic about her adeptness in the art of conversation. In opposition to her mother's plethora of gentlemen callers (as many as seventeen at one time), Laura confesses she has none: she's afraid she will be an old maid.

Scene 2

A few days later, Amanda comes in overwhelmed. She tells her daughter that Rubicam's Business College has reported that Laura has not been attending school. Laura admits that after one period of extreme nervousness, during which she vomited publicly, she had been going out every day as though to school, but visiting instead the museums and flower galleries. Amanda is flabbergasted at Laura's thus depriving herself of a future. She tells Laura that there must be more to life than her glass menagerie. When asked if she ever had a beau, Laura replies that, in high school, she liked a boy named Jim who sang in the senior-class operetta: the boy had called her "Blue Roses" because she had once stayed out of school with pleurisy. Laura thinks her chances for a boy friend are greatly restricted by her being *crippled;* her mother will not permit her to associate herself with the word.

Scene 3

Amanda begins to move steadily toward the objective of getting her daughter at least one gentleman caller. Meanwhile, Tom and Amanda quarrel because Tom frequents the movies to fight off his deep frustration at working in the warehouse of Continental Shoemakers for $65 a month. Amanda vows not to speak to Tom again until he apologizes to her.

Scene 4

At five in the morning, Laura admits a mildly intoxicated Tom, who has been searching for his door key. Tom tells Laura of a big evening at the show when the magician changed water into whiskey and used him as proof of the reality of his product. Since Tom arises at six, he has less than an hour to sleep.

Scene 5

In too short a while, Tom hears his mother's "Rise and shine!" and he answers, "I'll rise—but I won't shine." Amanda sends Laura to the store, and Tom apologizes. Accepting his apology, Amanda says she would have spoken to him anyway since she must have his cooperation in finding a beau for Laura. She wants Tom to invite someone from his work place, an eligible young man who doesn't drink. Amanda tells Tom she has seen his correspondence with the merchant marine, but before he leaves, he should put a reliable person in his place. Tom says he will try to find a young man, though he has little hope.

Scene 6

Very casually, Tom reports that he has invited a young man to dinner for the next night. Quite shocked, Amanda begins the necessary preparations—the cleaning, the food, the clothes, and all. Tom leaves, warning her not to expect too much—Jim, the invited guest, does not know he is to be "a gentleman

360

caller" and Laura is a very strange candidate for romance. Nevertheless, when Tom has gone, Amanda calls Laura to look at the little silver slipper of a moon and make a wish. When asked what she shall wish for, Laura is told: "Happiness! Good fortune!"

Scene 7

As narrator, Tom tells of his very casual dealings with Jim since their days in high school. Down at the warehouse, Jim calls him Shakespeare since Tom has always tried to write. In the apartment, Amanda is dressing Laura, who objects to being a trap for young men. Her mother once again reviews the way young men were properly entrapped by eligible girls in the aristocracy of the Old South, where she was brought up. When Laura finds that the gentleman caller is Jim O'Connor, she says she cannot possibly appear because he was the boy she used to like. But at her mother's insistence, she answers the door and admits Jim and Tom; then she promptly becomes ill. Amanda keeps the conversation going at the dinner table.

Scene 8

After dinner, the lights in the apartment go out because Tom used the money earmarked for the light bill to pay his fees for the merchant marine. Taking Amanda's "lovely old candelabrum," Jim goes to talk to Laura who has lain down to recover herself. Very slowly he brings her to a warm conversation. Laura shows Jim the year book which contains his picture: he obligingly autographs the picture. Although she swears she cannot dance, never has danced, he picks her up and makes her dance. During the dance, however, he knocks off the table the prize of her menagerie—the glass unicorn. Laura forgives him; she awards him the unicorn as a souvenir. Jim also kisses Laura, but immediately begs forgiveness because he says he is engaged and must even then leave to get his girl at the station. To Laura's question, will he call again, he answers, "No, I can't."

When Amanda learns that they have entertained some other girl's gentleman caller, she is furious and angry. She refers to her daughter as a poor cripple; she chastises her son, and he threatens to leave. "Go, then!" says Amanda. "Then go to the moon—you selfish dreamer!"

As Amanda and Laura stand huddled behind the scrim, Tom confesses that his memories of trips about the world always return him to Laura.

88

HOWARD RICHARDSON (1918–   )
WILLIAM BERNEY (1920–   )

Dark of the Moon (1945)

Folk drama and fantasy in two acts

MAIN CHARACTER AND THEME: The hauntingly fearful adventures of *John,* the witch boy, who becomes human to gain his love.

OTHER CHARACTERS:

Barbara Allen, the human girl John loves
Floyd Allen, her brother
Mrs. Allen, her mother
Mr. Allen, her father
Marvin Hudgens, her human suitor
Preacher Haggler
Mr. Sumney, the storekeeper
Mrs. Sumney, his wife and the midwife
Edna Sumney, their daughter, one of Barbara's social competitors
Uncle Smelicue, the guitar player

Hank Gudger, Edna's lover
Miss Metcalf, who has trouble finding a man
Townspeople and church members representing at times a Greek chorus as follows—*Mr. Atkins, Mr. Bergen, Mrs. Bergen, Burt Dinwitty, Hattie Heffner, Greeny Gorman*
Witch folk as follows— *The Dark Witch, The Fair Witch, Conjur Man, Conjur Woman, Three Other Witches*

TIME: Indefinite.

PLACE: Buck Creek in the Great Smoky Mountains and the ridge peaks up above where the witches live.

362

MUSICAL HIGHLIGHTS: "Smoky Mountain Gal"; "Down in the Valley"; "Jes a Pitcher from Life's Other Side"; "John Williams"; "Up on Old Baldy All Covered with Snow"; "'Tis the Old Time Religion"; "As I Wander"; "You Got to Walk That Lonesome Valley"; "He's Washed in the Blood and Saved by Grace"; "No Never Alone"; "The Ballad of Barbara Allen."

HISTORICAL NOTE: Based on "The Ballad of Barbara Allen" and set in the American counterpart of the Scottish Highlands, this play reveals convincingly the superstition, religious fervor, and stimulating character of mountain folk, and the hate, fear, and envy that provide the sad ending of the ballad. Performed at the 46th Street Theatre in New York for 322 performances, opening on March 14, 1945; also performed in London in 1949. Music by Walter Hendl.

ACT I (*four scenes*)

Driven by his love, John, the witch boy, begs the Conjur Man to make him human; he is willing to work in the field with a mule and plow; he wants to enjoy dancing and guitars and singing in church. Conjur Man tells him to stay away from church since, if transformed, he cannot be *all* human. When Conjur Man refuses, he turns to Conjur Woman, who makes him confess that he loves the blue-eyed Barbara Allen with the copper hair. He is surprised, however, to learn from Conjur Woman that as a result of their love-making, Barbara will soon give birth to his child. Amidst increasing thunder and lightning, and threats from the Fair Witch, Conjur Woman promises to transform him if he will bring her spider webs, graveyard dirt, and the claws of twenty bats. The proviso is, however, that if Barbara is not faithful for a whole year, John will be a witch again.

In Buck Creek, the central square is roped off for the Saturday night dance. Edna hints that Barbara had better find a husband soon if she does not want to be disgraced. This hint leads to a hair pulling between Edna and Barbara. Unseen by the others, John comes in and asks Barbara for a dance. Marvin, Barbara's suitor, resents John and fights him, but he is eliminated by a stroke of lightning. John and Barbara dance, even through the rain that stops the others. Comforting Barbara, who is afraid of lightning, John tells her that the two of them have at least a year together.

At the Allen cabin on Chunky Gal Mountain, Mr. and Mrs. Allen discuss how difficult it has been to get a husband for Barbara—her behavior has been too untrustworthy. Preacher Haggler comes by, and, after a few rounds of "corn likker," suggests to the Allens that John would make a good husband. Preceded by his lonely eagle, John arrives and asks for Barbara's hand. Barbara accepts. The Dark Witch and the Fair Witch warn John not to remain human, but John brushes them aside. Even Marvin's efforts to renew his suit for Barbara do not change Barbara's mind about John: she tells him she is mighty proud to marry him.

In the general story of Buck Creek, everyone talks of the strange happenings recently. Most strange was the robbing of the ring with the green stone from the finger of Agnes Riddle's dead body. Again, John and Marvin have a contest—this time weight lifting, and again John wins by what approaches witchcraft. At John's insistence, Preacher Haggler performs the ceremony for John and Barbara, although Barbara must supply the $2.50 fee and John cannot write his name on the document. The wedding ring turns out to have a green stone that shines in the dark (Agnes' ring).

ACT II (*five scenes*)

John and Barbara live in their cabin, but through much interference. When John goes out to chop wood, the Fair Witch and the Dark Witch set him dancing, and he cannot explain to Barbara why he has chopped so small an amount. John also refuses to go to church to disprove the accusation around town that he is a witch.

Mrs. Sumney, the midwife, confirms John's witch nature because the baby born to Barbara was a witch and is now burning. When Preacher Haggler comes to pray for Barbara, John comes in and chases out those who pray. He confesses to Barbara that he was a witch when they made love before, but that now he is human, and from now on their children will be human. The Witches later warn John about the inability of humans to understand anything or to feel secure. Of Barbara, they tell him: "Kiss her, but you're alone, boy. Kiss her, but you're lost."

Up on the mountain range, Conjur Man bets the Witches that they will get John back. If they do get him back, they want "the life of Barbara Allen." If they do not, they will leave John alone. The church meeting will be the test.

The Church of God in Buck Creek is filled with worshippers and evangelical music on Sunday evening. The "good" people quickly get the spirit and bring pressure to bear upon the sinners. At first, Edna and Barbara refuse the mourners' bench because they have no "sorrer." Later, when confession time comes, many sinners unfold their hidden wickedness. The pressure turns full force on Barbara, who that night will complete her year of faithful living with John. To free her soul and to drive John back to being a witch, the religious group closes around Barbara and compels her to submit to Marvin. As the group shouts her salvation, John's voice is heard, calling Barbara.

Barbara is now on the ridge looking for John to swear that she was forced to be unfaithful. John is begging Conjur Woman for more time. She cannot grant his ardent request; she assures him that when the moon comes out, Barbara will die and he will be a witch boy again. When John meets Barbara, he is impelled to tell her of her impending death and of the song almost sung. Although he has told the Witches he will always love her, he tells Barbara that he cannot promise to find her—a witch has no soul; he has just three hundred years, and then he becomes fog on the mountain. She gives him the green stone that shines in the dark as a memento. The moon comes; Barbara dies in John's arms. Fascinated by the moon, he leaps away from her to join his eagle. A few minutes later, he gives the green ring to the Fair Witch, runs back to Barbara lying on the rocks, pushes her body with his foot, and runs at last toward his screaming eagle.

89

GIAN-CARLO MENOTTI (1911–   )

The Medium (1946)

Opera in two acts

MAIN CHARACTER AND THEME: The mysterious experiences of *Madame Flora*, known to her intimates as Baba, a spiritualistic charlatan who is caught in the web of her charlatanry.

OTHER CHARACTERS:

Monica, Baba's daughter

Toby, a mute, member of Baba's household

Mr. and Mrs. Gobineau, who come every week to Baba to communicate with their son,

Mickey, who died at age two

Mrs. Nolan, who comes for the first time, to get a message from her daughter, Doodly, who died a year ago at age sixteen

TIME: About 1945. Time of day: ambiguous.

PLACE: Madame Flora's squalid room in flat on outskirts of a great city.

MUSICAL HIGHLIGHTS: "Where, Oh, Where Is My New Golden Spindle and Thread?" (Monica); "Mother, Mother, Are You There?" (Monica); "The Sun Has Fallen and It Lies in Blood" (Monica); "Up in the Sky Someone Is Playing a Trombone and a Guitar" and "Monica, Monica, Can't You See—That My Heart Is Bleeding, Bleeding for You?" (imaginary duet between Monica and Toby); "Toby, What Are You Doing? Come Here, Toby. I Want to Talk to You" (Baba); "Afraid, Am I Afraid? Madame Flora Afraid!" (Baba).

HISTORICAL NOTE: Representative of modern American opera by an Italian-born American composer. In the past fifteen years Menotti's operas, highly dramatic in content, have developed American themes with great skill and success. Besides *The Medium*, his most significant contributions have been *The Telephone*, produced with *The Medium* at the Ethel Barrymore Theatre, New York, May 1, 1947; *Amahl and the Night Visitors*, a Christmas musical play about the Three Wise Men, produced annually on network television; and *The Saint of Bleecker Street* (1954). Marie Powers won universal praise as Mme. Flora in *The Medium*.

ACT I

As Toby, kneeling beside an open trunk, makes himself a costume with silk, bangles, and bead necklaces, Monica sings. Baba comes in and scolds Toby for dabbling in her things. She warns him that he will pay if anything in the séance goes wrong. When Monica asks where she has been, Baba throws her a roll of bills and says she spent the night on Mrs. Campi's steps and collected the money owed her. Monica says she should not have done it: Mrs. Campi is so poor.

The three complete preparations for the séance. Baba helps Monica into her white dress and white veil; Toby tests the manipulation of lamp, table, and properties of the puppet theatre, including levers and cables which levitate the table. When the doorbell rings, Toby hides in the puppet theatre and Monica runs off to the right. The Gobineaus and Mrs. Nolan come in and talk of the loved ones they hope to see. As the conversation continues, Mrs. Nolan, new to these activities, is almost hysterical.

Baba returns. At her signal, Monica sings, presumably in the voice of the dead Doodly Nolan, "Mother, mother, are you there?" After some hesitation, Mrs. Nolan converses with her. Doodly tells her mother not to cry for her; tells her also to burn her gloves and schoolbooks, to give away her dresses, to burn her shoes and bracelets, and to keep only the gold locket. Mrs. Nolan can remember no locket. When she rises to go closer, Doodly vanishes. Although Mrs. Nolan is distraught, the remainder of the séance is devoted to Monica simulating the voice of the Gobineaus' baby son.

Suddenly, Baba feels a mysterious touch on her throat. Hysterical and terror stricken, she runs wildly up the stairwell, asking who touched her. The others try to quiet her; she chases the visitors out. They leave asking, "Why be afraid of our dead?" Baba, shaking, tells Monica they must never do this again—must give back all the money. She accuses Toby of

367

having caused the disturbance. She tells Monica that Toby is not to be trusted.

In a beautiful lullaby, Monica rocks Baba gently:

> The sun has fallen and it lies in blood.
> The moon is weaving bandages of gold.
> O black swan, where, oh where—is my lover gone?
> Torn and tattered is my bridal gown,
> And my lamp is lost, and my lamp is lost.
> With silver needles and with silver thread,
> The stars stitch a shroud for the dying sun.

In spite of Monica's efforts, Baba still hears strange voices, calling for *mother*, and a little child's laughter. Brushing aside Monica's calming assurances, she sings, "Oh, God, what is happening to me? What is this darkness? Kneel down, kneel down—and pray God to save our souls."

ACT II

It is evening a few days later. Monica and Toby, alone, dance and play. Imagining that Toby is making love to her, Monica sings his song of love and, reversing her character, sings her reply.

Baba is heard dragging herself up the stairs. Dark and disheveled, bottle in hand, she calls Toby to her. Reminding him of her kindness since the days when she found him roaming the streets of Budapest, she promises never to be angry with him or to punish him again, but she must know if he was the one who clutched her throat. As she gets no answer, after repeated pleadings, her fury grows. She swears she will make him talk, and spit blood.

Without making advance arrangements, the Gobineaus and Mrs. Nolan have returned for a séance. Baba calls them fools and confesses that her séances were all trickery. They dispute her, offering evidence which convinces them. Besides, they say, this talking to their dead is their only joy. Baba gives them their money back and drives them out.

Then she turns to Toby and tells him, in spite of Monica's protests, to leave also. Monica tries to leave with Toby, but Baba will not let her. Alone, she hears again the mysterious voices. Repeated drinks do not restore peace to her. She admits her fear of the dead in spite of her bloody past. After laughing hysterically and asking God to forgive her, she falls asleep.

"The Medium" (1946)

Toby comes up the stairwell and scratches softly on Monica's door. Moving to the trunk, he causes the lid to fall sharply. Baba calls to the noise. Getting her revolver, she shouts, "Speak out or I'll shoot!" When the curtain moves, she fires at it several times. Pushing it back, she sees Toby clutching the curtain; a second later, he tumbles headlong downward. After a delay, Monica gains entrance and sees Baba kneeling by Toby, asking, "Was it you? Was it you?"

90

WILLIAM WISTER HAINES (1908–   )

Command Decision (1947)

Military drama in three acts

MAIN CHARACTER AND THEME: Tribulations of *Brigadier General K. C. Dennis*, forty, Commander of Fifth American Bombardment Division, Heavy, stationed in England, who, in trying to defeat the Germans in a vital phase of the war, must wrestle with nonmilitary problems, such as interservice rivalry, political interference, and yellow journalism.

OTHER CHARACTERS:

War Correspondent Elmer Brockhurst, who represents *Coverage*, a big popular magazine

Tech. Sergeant Harold Evans, graduate gunner, aide to Dennis

Colonel Ernest Haley, a Regular Army man, Dennis' executive officer

Captain Lucius Jenks, former hero but now being held for court martial

Major General Roland Goodlow Kane, fifty, Dennis' superior officer

Brigadier General Clifton C. Garnett, late thirties, secretary to the United Chiefs in Washington, on tour of inspection

Major Homer Prescott, Kane's aide

Colonel Edward Martin, Division Leader in Flight, Garnett's brother-in-law

Lt. Jake Goldberg, German escapee, bombardier

Major Desmond Lansing, Assistant Chief of Staff for Intelligence

Major Belding Davis, Division Weather Officer

Major Rufus Dayhuff, Division Medical Officer

370

> *Mr. Arthur Malcolm* and *Mr. Oliver Stone*, Congressmen on tour of inspection
>
> *Captain George Washington Culpepper Lee*, an officer
>
> returned from flight, a bit disorderly
>
> *Noncommissioned Officer Photographer, Enlisted Armed Guard*

TIME: World War II, probably 1944.

PLACE: England.

HISTORICAL NOTE: The best American drama dealing with battle operations of World War II. Written by a soldier who rose to lieutenant-colonel in the Army Air Corps, and one who was a combat air officer, this drama is well supported by statistics, visual exhibits, realistic dialogue, and other impressive detail, without losing its theatricality. It goes deeply into the questions of true loyalty and military ethics and into the war that is fought by and between military experts and civilian bosses. First performed at the Drury Theatre, Cleveland, December 12, 1946, it came to the Fulton Theatre, New York, October 1, 1947, where it remained for 408 performances.

ACT I

While burdened with preparations for important air attacks over Germany, Dennis must stop to prepare charges against Jenks, formerly an heroic flyer but now refusing to fly because he says Dennis' bombardment plans take unnecessary lives. At this point, Dennis receives an unexpected visit from his commander, Kane, who is accompanied by a troublemaking magazine reporter, Brockhurst, and by Garnett, from the highest headquarters in Washington. Although knowing that his audience is deeply prejudiced against his plans because of the great loss of life and planes entailed, Dennis frankly explains his Operation Stitch, abbreviation for "Stitch in Time." Through a Czechoslovakian engineer who defaulted to the Allies, Dennis has acquired a sample of a new German fighter plane, the Focke-Schmidt. He and his best flying officer, Martin, have tested it. In addition, the daily reports prove its worth. The sum total of its significance is that when it gets into full production—because of its altitude capacity, great speed, and maneuverability—it has the power to run the Allies out of Europe within sixty days. Operation Stitch is therefore for the purpose of destroying the plants which manufacture Focke-Schmidts at Posenleben, Schweinhafen,

371

and Fendelhorst. Since these plants were expressly placed deep inside the German borders, bombers must make a large part of the run without fighter cover: thus many bombers and crews must of necessity be lost. Posenleben has already been disposed of. But after Martin returned from the second step of Stitch, he reported that Schweinhafen was untouched, although a town just like Schweinhafen had been leveled. Forty-four bombers and four hundred expensively trained airmen had been lost, although a torpedo factory had been hit.

Dennis' problem now is to get his superiors all along the line not to interfere with his plan to return to Schweinhafen and then to destroy Fendelhorst. In addition to Kane, who sometimes has lacked strength to face up to his superiors and to the United Chiefs, who are half Navy men, Dennis must contend with Brockhurst, who pretends to represent the indignant public, the weather, always subject to change, and the policy meeting of Joint Chiefs in two days. He knows he can personally lose everything, but he is determined to move forward.

ACT II (*two scenes*)

By making a bargain to save Jenks for political reasons, Dennis gets permission to use his own discretion about going back to Schweinhafen. He immediately goes back, sending Martin as commander of the bombing force —Martin, who is Garnett's brother-in-law. In his conversations with Kane and Garnett, Dennis reviews the whole story of the unpreparedness of America in the air and of her woeful neglect of plane-building until the war emergency arose. Before leaving, Martin warns Dennis to be pleasant with the congressmen who are coming to inspect him next day. Martin says nothing to Kane of Garnett's offer to relieve Kane's sister, Helen, of further worries by making Martin a brigadier general over a B-29 unit in the Pacific theatre.

At noon the next day, the congressmen arrive. One of them, Malcolm, is from Jenks' home state: he is very bitter with Dennis and says he is butchering boys and planes to build up his personal record. Malcolm even persuades Kane to radio Martin that he may return if he wants to, without completing his mission. As the reception for the congressmen proceeds, news comes in from Martin that Schweinhafen has definitely been destroyed this time. But a moment later, Martin radios that he is on fire and going down. Malcolm is terribly indignant. When Dennis mentions that he must do Fendelhorst the next day before the weather defeats him for a month (during which the terrible fighters will be rolling off assembly lines), Kane relieves him of command and sets Garnett in his place. Kane is going to recommend Dennis for the Legion of Merit.

ACT III

Next day, Garnett awaits Kane's orders as to whether to give the airmen a light, relatively safe assignment or to send them on heavy duty. Garnett canvasses the whole situation—the morale of the men after the change in command, the weather, the new significance of Dennis' strategy. At last he hears from Kane, telling him to use his own discretion. He turns to Dennis for advice; Dennis can tell him only that commanders must make and abide by their own decisions. Under orders from Washington, Dennis is preparing to go home for rest before reassignment: he tells Garnett good-by. Garnett immediately orders the Fifth Division to attack Fendelhorst the next day. Before Dennis can leave, Garnett reads him a message that has just come from Washington, sending him to the Pacific and a B-29 command, with its inevitable second star: he will be Major-General Dennis.

91

SAMUEL and BELLA SPEWACK (1899–   )
COLE PORTER (1893–1964)

Kiss Me, Kate (1948)

Musical comedy in two acts

MAIN CHARACTER AND THEME: Tribulations and triumphs of *Frederick Graham* (Petruchio), thirty-two, writer, director, actor, and superman, who is trying to prepare a modernized version of Shakespeare's *Taming of the Shrew* for Broadway production.

OTHER CHARACTERS:

(In parentheses, the Shakespearean role portrayed by the characters):

Harry Trevor (Baptista), an actor playing a heavy role

Lois Lane (Bianca), second female lead, in love with Bill

Ralph, stage manager

Lilli Vanessi (Katherine or Kate), the female lead, a motion-picture star, once married to Fred

Hattie, Lilli's Negro maid

Paul, Fred's Negro dresser

Bill Calhoun (Lucentio), an actor, trying to be a gambler

First Gunman

Second Gunman

Stage Doorman

Harrison Howell, a Washington dignitary, Lilli's fiancé

Specialty Dancers, Conductor, Stage Boys, Electricians, Cab Driver, Singers, Paul's Two Pals, Haberdasher

TIME: 1940's.

PLACE: Ford's Theatre in Baltimore, opening night of a tryout show.

374

"*Kiss Me, Kate*" (1948)

MUSICAL HIGHLIGHTS: (words and music by Cole Porter) "Another Op'nin', Another Show"; "Why Can't You Behave?"; "Wunderbar"; "So in Love"; "We Open in Venice"; "Tom, Dick or Harry"; "I've Come to Wive It Wealthily in Padua"; "I Hate Men"; "Were Thine That Special Face"; "I Sing of Love"; "Kiss Me, Kate"; "Too Darn Hot"; "Where Is the Life That Late I Led?" "Always True to You in My Fashion"; "Bianca"; "Brush Up Your Shakespeare"; "I Am Ashamed That Women Are So Simple."

HISTORICAL NOTE: One of the notable musical comedies of the American theatre, developed by one of the most talented composer-lyricists, Cole Porter. Utilizing the full force of Shakespeare and carrying a modern musical plot, *Kiss Me, Kate* achieved deserved great popularity. Four million Americans saw it in various runs after its New York opening on December 30, 1948 (its initial run in New York was 1077 performances) and one million Englishmen cheered it in London. It lives on in amateur, semiprofessional, and professional revivals.

ACT I (*nine scenes*)

In last minute arrangements for their Baltimore tryout, Fred and Lilli, as stars of the production, curse each other *sotto voce* for personal reasons going back to their former marriage and divorce. Bill comes in to tell Lois that he has lost ten thousand dollars gambling and has signed Fred's name to his IOU's. Lois is anxious about this act: she hopes for Fred to make her a Broadway star. In their dressing rooms, Fred and Lilli continue their quarrels, Lilli calling attention to the fact that her new boy friend, Howell, has put up the money for the production. Through a mix-up, the flowers Fred sent Lois are received by Lilli—she thinks they celebrate the first anniversary of their divorce, and she is quite pleased. Meanwhile, two gunmen from the establishment where Bill lost the money descend upon Fred and warn him that he will pay immediately, or else.

The play gets started. Baptista lets the suitors know that Bianca cannot be given until the waspish Katherine is married. Petruchio arrives, singing, "I've come to wive it wealthily in Padua." With fervor, Katherine sings, "I hate men." Petruchio makes the deal for Katherine with Baptista, and Katherine rails at her new fiancé. Having now read the card on the flowers and knowing that they were a gift from Fred to Lois, Lilli, as Katherine, slaps Fred, as Petruchio, with considerable force. He paddles her hard, as Fred. After the scene, both pretend to be deeply and physically wounded.

Lilli announces she is quitting the show at once. She calls Howell and tells him to come for her: she is ready to marry and settle down without further delay. In spite of Fred's threats to have her barred from the theatre for life for contract violation, Lilli has Hattie pack her things. To save his show, Fred admits having signed the IOU's and tells the gunmen he will pay them off if they will keep Lilli from leaving. They quickly cooperate, and Lilli, as Katherine, does the next scene, the marriage scene, with guns pointed at her. At the end of the singing and dancing, in celebration of the wedding, Petruchio carries off Katherine, kicking and pummeling in wild, useless protest.

ACT II (*eight scenes*)

The intermission over, Fred announces that the mule scene has been cancelled because Miss Vanessi is unable to ride the mule tonight. Lilli does the scene at Petruchio's house, where Petruchio does the real taming of the shrew—starving his bride, refusing her pretty clothes and baubles. He comes downstage and tells the audience of his campaign. When he tries the bridal door, however, it is locked. Taking out his address book, he sings, "Where is the life that late I led?" At the end of this song, which discusses his previous and many amours, he backs into the bridal door, and it opens. Throwing away the address book, he exits through the door.

Howell arrives with an ambulance and two nurses to take Lilli away. Amazed to find Lilli performing when he expected her in a state of collapse, he is further surprised to have Lois identify him as the Harold Murgatroy with whom she went on an escapade to Atlantic City. Overhearing her, Bill accuses her of infidelity. She sings, "Always true to you in my fashion," to assure Bill that her extra-curricular love affairs will never bedim her love for her true sweetheart.

From Lilli's dressing room, Howell makes the most precise arrangements for the wedding. Lilli wants Howell to use his influence in Washington to call out the FBI and release her from these gunmen. With help from the gunmen, Fred depicts for Lilli the unbearable life she will have with Howell (on his 30,000 acres in Georgia, where Lilli will be alone with Howell and his tenant farmers). All this time, Howell, tuckered by the excitement of his rescue work and wedding plans, has been snoring happily away.

"*Kiss Me, Kate*" (1948)

Outfitted as members of the company, the gunmen move about. One of them calls Hogan, his boss, to report in. He is told that Hogan has been displaced (and dispatched) by Gumpy, who though lacking executive skill is in command of the gambling operation. Fred is thus released; he in turn releases Lilli, who plans to leave while Howell still sleeps. Alone, Fred reprises "So in love."

Despite her apparent departure, when called for the final scene, Lilli appears and sings the song by which Katherine chides women for not accepting the joy of obedient wifehood: "I am ashamed that women are so simple." Petruchio seizes and kisses her, as Fred to Lilli; she returns the compliment. In real reunion, they lead the company in "So kiss me, Kate."

92

ARTHUR MILLER (1915–   )

Death of a Salesman (1949)

Naturalistic drama in two acts, with flashbacks

MAIN CHARACTER AND THEME: The pathetic story of *Willy Loman*, sixty-three, who, after thirty-five years in the business of selling, is forced to confront his failure as salesman and human being and all the terrible implications of the realization of failure.

OTHER CHARACTERS:

Linda, fifty-three, Willy's wife of thirty-five years

Biff, thirty-four, his older son

Happy, thirty-two, his younger son

Bernard, Charley's son, one of Biff's early playmates

The Woman, Willy's girl friend in Boston years ago

Charley, next-door neighbor of the Lomans

Uncle Ben, in his sixties, Willy's older brother, who succeeded

Howard Wagner, Willy's boss, a young man

Jenny, Charley's secretary

Stanley, a waiter at Frank's Chop House

Miss Forsythe, a cover girl whom Biff and Happy pick up at Frank's Chop House

Letta, Miss Forsythe's friend

TIME: The present.

PLACE: New York City; Boston; unidentified places.

MUSICAL HIGHLIGHTS: "Roll Out the Barrel" (whistled on the recorder by Wagner's seven-year-old daughter); also appropriate music to guide and lead the flashbacks.

378

"Death of a Salesman" (1949)

HISTORICAL NOTE: The best-known play by one of the most promising play-wrights of the late 1940's and the 1950's. This play undoubtedly deals with an epic theme in American drama—the capacity of and opportunity for the little man in America to fulfill the American dream with all its paraphernalia of phony advertising, back-slapping, and Babbittry. In this sense, it is almost a morality play—the main character being named Loman, i.e., low man, and his sons, Biff (for the driving individualist) and Happy (for the pursuit of happiness.) But it does not qualify as a morality play because of its naturalistic revelation that the whole atmosphere is full of inescapable booby traps for the aspiring little man. Likewise, it does not qualify as tragedy since its leading character is not an important person from the start. It was, nevertheless, created with great dramatic and theatrical device, skilfully produced and acted, and extremely well received in New York and throughout the nation. Directed by Elia Kazan, the New York production offered Lee J. Cobb as Willy, Mildred Dunnock as Linda, Arthur Kennedy as Biff, and Cameron Mitchell as Happy. It opened at the Morosco Theatre on February 10, 1949, and ran for 742 performances on its initial presentation. Whatever Miller's weaknesses, he is still the most ambitious of the analytical playwrights of his period, as evidenced by the following dramas, which uniformly aim high and usually hit some-where near the center of their targets: *The Man Who Had All the Luck* (1944), *All My Sons* (1947), *The Crucible* (1953), *A View from the Bridge* (1955).

ACT I

Returning home from a road trip, Willy is upset. He even had trouble holding the car on the road. The road being hazardous, he is going to ask his boss to give him a local assignment. Still agitated, he asks about his son Biff, a rolling stone who has just come home. As Willy and Linda continue to talk, the lights come up on the bedroom of Biff and Happy. They are worried about their father who seems to be losing his grip. But Happy is also worried about Biff and his lack of stability. Biff confesses to twenty or thirty different kinds of jobs all over the Middle West and Southwest. As they talk, they make dreams of how wonderful their lives would be if they could carry things together. Their dreams, however, seem empty in view of the many opportunities each has had and the places they occupy now—Biff making bold

379

but rootless plans for what he would do if he had a ranch and Happy talking only in terms of his conquest of women.

The light goes back to their father, and from him to his vision. Talking in big, fancy terms to his sons (who in the vision are years younger), he tells them how great they can be in boxing and football, without half trying. Before very long, however, Willy's big talk is smothered under a list of realistic financial necessities introduced by Linda. In another vision, Willy sees himself in one of his philandering escapades in Boston. The Woman caters to his ego by calling him a great "kidder" and by thanking him for his gift of stockings. Linda, at home, must mend her stockings.

Back in the realm of reality, Charley, sensing Willy's difficulty, offers him a decent job, and Willy out of pride gets insulted. In a new vision, he sees his brother Ben fabulously successful—diamond mines in Africa. This vision accentuates the difference in "touch" between the two brothers. In reality again, Linda is giving her sons the unpleasant facts of Willy's decline, even the fact of his apparently trying to kill himself with the car and with a gas pipe. As a result, Biff promises to remain at home, and the sons both promise to take over a part of the burden from their father. When Willy returns, Biff tells him of a prospect he intends to pursue: long ago, Bill Oliver promised to stake him in business; he is going to see Bill tomorrow and get enough money to open a sporting-goods store. After some confusion, his father thinks Biff has "a one-million-dollar idea!" and knows now that the Lomans are on their way. Just this little prospect has caused Willy to fly again on his carpet of counterfeit dreams.

ACT II

Next day, everything seems bright for the family. While the boys go to search for their pots of gold, Linda wants Willy to visit his boss, demand a local position, and get a two hundred dollar loan—with a part of the money, they will make the last payment on the house and own it, after twenty-five years. The boys have invited Willy to dinner at Frank's Chop House downtown.

But out in the street, things go quite sourly. Instead of getting favorable answers from his boss, Willy is fired completely. Going by to see Charley, Willy borrows the two hundred dollars (Charley had been giving him fifty dollars a week all along, to make ends meet) but again superciliously refuses

380

a job under Charley, although he now has no job. At the restaurant, Biff and Happy pick up two girls and leave their father miserably alone, beating his fists on the floor of the men's wash room. Biff also has no good news from his venture: Bill Oliver does not even remember him.

In the course of the day, Willy experiences various visions, which are in juxtaposition to corresponding realistic events, as in Act I. In one of these, after a realistic quarrel with Biff about the Oliver fiasco, Willy experiences once more the awful time in Boston when Biff caught him in a hotel room in Boston with The Woman, called him a fake, and weepingly deserted him.

At home, Willy cannot even make sense of what remains of his life, let alone cope with it. Driving off in his car, he crashes in a frenzy of sound. In a requiem scene (epilogue), Linda mourns his death, calling him a good man and calling attention to the fact that they are now free, the house being paid for. Biff's summation is the most expressive: "He had the wrong dreams. All, all wrong." But whether self-destroyed or murdered by his civilization, Willy is forever dead.

93

JOHN MURRAY ANDERSON (1886–1954)
and various authors

New Faces of 1952 (1952)

Musical revue in two acts

MAIN CHARACTER AND THEME: Although creative and somewhat original, this revue follows regular revue style by setting performers and audience against the foibles, absurdities, and ridiculous behavior of prominent people and movements of its time. Its chief object for satire is the pompous, self-important person or group that does not know itself to be ridiculous. In contradistinction to most revues, which down the years have highlighted individual stars like Will Rogers, Bert Williams, W. C. Fields, Anna Held, and Jack Benny, *New Faces of 1952* specializes in performers whose fame is not fully developed. It has twenty-seven sketches: thirteen in the first act and thirteen in the second, and one running sketch which begins in the first act and develops in the second. Although most revues are international in range, this one introduced a special international flavor, especially in exploiting the personalities of Robert Clary, born in Paris, and Eartha Kitt, who, though born in South Carolina, acquired her unusual style in Greece, Egypt, Paris and Istanbul, where she was "discovered" by the producer, Leonard Sillman.

TIME: 1950's.

PLACE: Many parts of England and America, especially New England; New York and the South.

HISTORICAL NOTE: The revue is a form of drama which partakes of the qualities of both the vaudeville sketch and a vignette drama. Each sketch contains at its core a dramatic situation, even when it comprises a single song. Developed on the European continent, it reached a kind of perfection in England, as for example in the Charlot's Revue which in the 1920's introduced Gertrude Lawrence to the dramatic world. In the United States, the revue or the near-revue has been popular for most of the twentieth century. It is usually the product of a number of musical and literary (or pseudoliterary) artists. Among the more striking revues and revue-sequences of America have been Florenz Ziegfeld's *Follies* (first produced in 1907), George White's *Scandals* (first produced in 1919), and Earl Carroll's *Vanities* (first produced in 1922). Revues with strong political and social emphasis include *Pins and Needles* (1937—which introduced Harold Rome as lyricist and composer and which ran for 1108 performances), *Sing Out the News* (1938), *Call Me Mister* (1946—which had 734 performances), and *Lend an Ear* (1948). Often the revue has effectively introduced or established talented performers who in other mediums have found a hearing difficult.

ACT I

"Opening" strikes out against the reliance of contemporary literature upon conventional forms. Its main character is the Reader. Music and lyrics by Ronald Graham; dialogue by Peter de Vries. In "Crazy, Man," by Ronald Graham and Roger Price, an analogy is drawn between politicians and the "hepcat" or "jazzhound." "Lucky Pierre," also with music and lyrics by Ronald Graham, depicts the stir created by famous French visitors and introduces Robert Clary. In "Guess Who I Saw Today," the wife discovers her husband in a very romantic café deeply involved with a sweetheart. Its music is by Murray Grand, and its lyrics by Elisse Boyd; the piece is sung and acted by June Carroll. "Restoration Piece," with dialogue and lyrics by Alan Melville and music by Arthur Siegel, brings the manners of the period of the English Restoration (late seventeenth century) into close comparison and contrast with those of today.

"Love is a Simple Thing," with music by Arthur Siegel and lyrics by June Carroll, sung and danced by a large company, attempts to bring love back from all the psychological and literary complications through which it has been drawn, especially in more recent times, to something that just *is*. Satire on Boston as a setting for romance and as a suppressor of books is cleverly developed in "Boston Beguine," written and composed by Sheldon M. Harnick and sung by Alice Ghostley. "The Bard and the Beard," makes use of the Shakespeare-Shaw rivalry, which Shaw himself exploited, but from the particular standpoint of recent revivals in America of related Shakespeare-Shaw plays by Sir Laurence Olivier and his wife, Vivian Leigh. It was written and composed by Ronald Graham, June Carroll, Arthur Siegel, and Sheldon Harnick. Showing the assumption of womanhood by a Scottish girl on her seventeenth birthday is "Nanty Puts Her Hair Up," with lyrics by Herbert Farjeon and music by Arthur Siegel. Nanty's arrival at this critical stage generates ripples in her entire neighborhood. "Oedipus Goes South," written and acted by Ronald Graham, is a satire on Southern writers who deal with deep and weird psychological situations but who are in need of extensive psychological treatment themselves. Another satire on pompous social ways is "Time for Tea," with lyrics by June Carroll and music by Arthur Siegel. Contrasting international aspects of love, "Bal Petit Bal" (music and lyrics by Francis Lemarque) shows a young couple falling in love during a Bastille Day celebration in France, at a block dance where men dress like American cowboys: to the lovers, however, the noise and bustle are meaningless. This number was exquisitely done by Robert Clary, singing in English, and Eartha Kitt, singing in French. "Three for the Road," by Ronald Graham, satirizes memory songs, the practice of romantic waltzing, and that of taking off masks at a witching hour of masquerades; in the last situation, the ultraromantic young man, frantic to have his girl remove her mask, wants her to put it back on as soon as he views her face.

ACT II

The "Entr'acte" is a mélange of several skits already done. In "Don't Fall Asleep," by Ronald Graham, the romantic wife with the intoxicated husband renews her marriage declaration at a critical time. "After Canasta—What?" pokes fun at the canasta (card-playing) craze of the time. "Lizzie Borden," with music and lyrics by Michael Brown, revives, with uproarious effect, the story of the Fall River spinster who allegedly murdered her father and stepmother with an ax. Dealing with the schoolboy who falls in and out of love with his teacher, "I'm in Love with Miss Logan," written and composed by Ronald Graham, was very convincingly delivered by Robert Clary. "Penny

Candy" (music by Siegel, lyrics by June Carroll) describes the jaded socialite who wishes she could return to the simple desires of her childhood. "Trip of the Month," by Paul Lynde travesties all kinds of "of-the-month" operations. "Whither America? (Another Revival?)" burlesques America's future in a world of new discoveries. Ronald Graham's "Convention Bound" calls attention to the political nominating conventions of the year, and his "The Great American Opera" is a take-off on Menotti's *The Medium*, which had recently been professionally produced. In "Monotonous," with music by Siegel and lyrics by Carroll, Eartha Kitt sings very specifically—referring to famous people in the news—of how a too full life is self-defeating.

The running skit, "He Takes Me Off His Income Tax," with music by Arthur Siegel and lyrics by June Carroll, shows the businessman claiming huge exemptions for his philandering activities. In differing forms, it is used to introduce other skits.

94

WILLIAM INGE (1913–   )

Picnic (1953)

Midwestern domestic drama in three acts

MAIN CHARACTER AND THEME: Invasion of a small Kansas community by
Hal Carter, "a show-case husky, handsome young man," at the time of
the Labor Day picnic.

OTHER CHARACTERS:

Helen Potts, head of her family, keeper of an invalid mother

Millie Owens, Flo's younger daughter

Bomber, paper boy

Madge Owens, Flo's older daughter

Flo Owens, Mrs. Potts' neighbor, head of her family

Rosemary Sydney, who teaches school and boards with the Owenses

Alan Seymour, Madge's wealthy boy friend

Irma Kronkite and *Christine Schoenwalder*, Rosemary's friends and fellow teachers

Howard Bevans, Rosemary's boy friend

TIME: About 1953.

PLACE: Yard shared by Flo Owens and Helen Potts in small Kansas town.

HISTORICAL NOTE: With *Picnic* and *Come Back, Little Sheba* (1950), Inge
won a reputation as a most promising dramatist specializing in the
Midwestern region, especially his native Kansas. Although this promise
is not advanced in *Bus Stop* (1955) and *The Dark at the Top of the Stairs*

(1958), Inge is still warmly respected for his honest efforts to probe the depths of family and community life with some attention to poetic insights.

ACT I

Having exchanged a fine breakfast by Mrs. Potts for doing some cleaning up, Hal in T-shirt preens on the front yard. When Bomber comes along and seizes pretty Madge by the arm, Hal drives him away, but is in turn driven off by Flo who (showing signs of wear at being both mother and father to her daughters) tries to get Madge to concentrate on winning Alan. Flo queries Madge about Alan's lovemaking, but Madge talks most of her uneasiness when Alan and his friends talk of college and Europe. Flo warns that a pretty girl does not have long, while Millie, who has won a four-year scholarship to college, recalls that they had to burn the schoolhouse down to get Madge out of it. Coming casually into the conversation, Rosemary expresses a cavalier attitude towards men, including her "friend-boy" Howard, but she continues to look quizzically at handsome Hal. Alan comes by in his car to take Millie swimming. Rosemary complains of Millie's reading such books as Carson McCullers' *The Ballad of the Sad Café*, until Alan says it's all right. It turns out that Hal and Alan are former college chums and fraternity brothers: Hal still owes Alan the one hundred dollars he borrowed to get his Hollywood screen test. The others gone, Hal tells Alan of failing the test because he refused to have new teeth; like a bad boy, he gloatingly tells of his return trip, when he became intimately involved with two beautiful girls who took his money, and then went home where his drunken father died and where he gave to his mother the gas station he inherited. When Hal, now barechested, asks Alan for a job, Alan refers him to a Sinclair Oil work gang, where he can come up through the ranks. He makes Hal put on his shirt and lines him up for Millie's date at the picnic. Later, Alan shows deep interest in Madge, especially in her beauty (she was Queen Neewollah—Halloween spelled backwards—for the Chamber of Commerce). Alan assures Flo he can handle both Madge and Hal. When Alan and Madge are alone, he kisses her tenderly; she is sorry, and afraid, that he must at his father's behest return to college. He will return at five to take her to the picnic. Two symbolic revelations conclude the act: Hal tells Alan his misgivings about picnics; and Madge, alone, is intrigued—once more in her life—by the train whistle.

ACT II

Even Millie is pretty, dressed for the ball, that afternoon. Flo comes down complaining of Hal's dirty towels and commanding Madge to be sure there is no drinking. Alan and Hal drive up in Alan's two cars. When Hal begins to be expansive about his business opportunities, Alan deflates him by telling everyone he has got Hal a job on the pipeline. Howard locates a bottle; he and Hal drink; afterwards, Rosemary leaves off her coyness, dictated by her delicate position as a teacher, and drinks heartily. Then, all dance: when, at length, Hal and Madge dance together, "it's like" (in Mrs. Potts' words) "they were *made* to dance together." Millie has been sneaking drinks, and is soon intoxicated. When Rosemary, also slightly intoxicated, forces Hal to dance with her and later embarrasses him with her brashness, he breaks off the dance, and she accuses him of being "a low character." Flo demands that all this drinking stop. Subsequently, Rosemary and Howard go for a ride and at her mother's orders, Madge goes up to change her dress. Alan takes Flo, Mrs. Potts, and Millie, with some supplies, to the picnic. Madge tries to console Hal, who feels low, realizing the truth of Rosemary's condemnation (he confesses that he was in reform school at fourteen). Trying to cheer him up, she kisses him. He returns her kisses passionately. Picking her up, he carries her off, assuring her that they are not going to the picnic.

ACT III (*two scenes*)

It is after midnight; a great harvest moon shines in a murky, blue sky. Howard and Rosemary return from an evening of amorous adventure; Rosemary cajoles Howard into promising to return in the morning and to take her to be married. When they have gone, Hal and Madge return from an evening of similar adventure. Hal is again self-condemnatory because he cannot control his sexual passions and does not want to hurt someone he deeply cares for. But when he kisses Madge good night, once more they are both overcome. Madge finally breaks away, leaving Hal alone, despising the day he was born.

Next morning, Flo is genuinely worried: she is afraid of Alan's attitude, since Madge never got to the picnic; she thinks Hal belongs in the penitentiary. Bomber teases Millie about the gossip which says that Madge was seen making love under the bridge. Alan comes in, much broken up at being

"Picnic" (1953)

rejected. Howard returns as he promised, and a very humorous wedding
sendoff for Rosemary ensues. Hal has slipped in, and hides in the woodshed.
As the wedding party leaves, Hal comes out to Madge, just to say good-by.
Alan and his father had sent the police for him, saying he stole the car. He
knocked out one of the officers and swam the river to get away. Before Flo
he declares his love and his respect for Madge. Before long, with his fists he
defends himself against Alan, making sure not to hurt him. Not disguising
the difficult future ahead, he still begs Madge to come with him to Tulsa
where he expects to get a bellhop's job. The freight train he is going to "hop"
whistles in the distance; he kisses Madge and runs for it. Flo's outrage is
extended by Madge's loss of Alan: he is going to Michigan with his father,
and it is obvious that he is through with the Owenses. After Millie goes to
school, and while Mrs. Potts and Flo discuss love, Madge comes down,
suitcase in hand. She is ready to ride the bus to Tulsa. She knows the possible
bad outcome, but can no longer cope with her driving love for Hal. She
tells her mother to say good-by to Millie, whom she greatly respects. When
she has gone, Mrs. Potts consoles Flo.

389

95

JOHN PATRICK (1905-   )

The Teahouse of the
August Moon (1953)

*Satirical dramatic tale in three acts based on
the novel (1951) about Okinawa by Vern Sneider*

MAIN CHARACTER AND THEME: *Sakini*, whose age is between thirty and sixty, an Okinawan interpreter and fabulous Oriental, directly presents, after the fashion of the Chinese theatre, and projects the story of how the United States of America brought the fine fruits of democracy to Tobiki Village in Okinawa.

OTHER CHARACTERS:

From the United States Army of Occupation:

Colonel Wainright Purdy III, commanding officer

Sergeant Gregovich, assistant to Colonel Purdy

Captain Fisby, in his late twenties, recently transferred to Colonel Purdy from "Psychological Warfare"

Captain McLean, the psychiatrist from Awasi, a wild-eyed man in his middle forties.

From the Okinawan community:

Lotus Blossom, geisha girl

Old Woman, on way to visit grandson who is mayor of Tobiki

Old Woman's daughter, who must accompany Old Woman

The Daughter's Children and their Goat, who must accompany Old Woman's Daughter

Lady Astor, Miss Higa Jiga's goat

Ancient Man, who just wants to go on a trip

390

Mr. *Hokaido*, champion wrestler who thereby qualifies as Chief of Police

Mr. *Omura*, ancient Tobikian, the mayor

Mr. *Sumata*, nervous citizen in torn straw hat

Mr. *Samuta's Father*

Mr. *Seiko*, young artist who, because he draws lovely pictures of golden wheat stalk, qualifies as Chief of Agriculture

Miss *Higa Jiga*, aggressive unmarried lady with heavy glasses, president of the Ladies' League for Democratic Action

Mr. *Keora*, who gives pleasant gifts

Mr. *Oshira*, a very old citizen

Villagers

Members of the Ladies' League for Democratic Action

TIME: Just after the close of World War II (about 1946).

PLACE: Okinawa—American headquarters and Tobiki Village.

MUSICAL HIGHLIGHT: "Deep in the Heart of Texas."

HISTORICAL NOTE: A clever comparison of the ways of East and West, full of humor and folk wisdom; apparently authentic picture of the traditional life of natives; a richly amusing depiction of Army bungling and red tape; much penetrating satire on democracy—its weakness when not fully practiced and its suffering by comparison with the sincere ways of supposedly benighted peoples. American industrial acumen and the American capacity for organizing the trivial and the immoral are developed. On the Okinawan side are many insights, such as the natural and acquired gifts of people who are much-conquered. Drama won both Pulitzer and Critics' Circle prizes for the 1953–1954 season and ran for 1020 performances after opening at the Martin Beck Theatre, October 15, 1953, under the direction of Maurice Evans, with David Wayne as Sakini.

ACT I (*three scenes*)

Sakini presents the Okinawa community and its culture, a combination of deep natural characteristics and the contributions of such conquerors as Chinese pirates, English missionaries, Japanese war lords, and American marines. Before long, he prepares the stage by which Colonel Purdy delegates to Captain Fisby the absorbingly important job of bringing the glory of democracy to the Okinawan hinterland. Under Plan B, handed down direct

391

from Washington, Tobiki Village is to receive the full treatment—lectures on democracy, a new school building, and a newly organized Ladies' League for Democratic Action.

As Fisby and Sakini climb in their jeep to go to Tobiki, they find they are compelled to take a host of natives and animals, since not to do so would cause important people to lose face, and this loss would impede the American mission. Arriving in Tobiki, Fisby is ceremoniously given gifts by the natives, such as cricket cages with **no** crickets, chop sticks, turtle eggs and hand-made lacquered cups. He is then allowed to tell them of his plans to teach democracy, to build them a school shaped like the Pentagon, and to bestow upon them daily rations of rice. The natives then proceed to elect their representatives on very poetic bases—such as Mr. Seiko as Chief of Agriculture because of his lovely drawings of the golden wheat stalk. Mr. Sumata, upon leaving town, confers upon Fisby the gift of a geisha girl. Although it is against regulations for Fisby to keep her, he finds he must do so since she now has no home and to return her would be insulting. When Colonel calls on the telephone to discover how things are going, Fisby's report must be made through the interference of Lotus Blossom's dressing him for his evening's comfort.

ACT II (*four scenes*)

Fisby has many problems keeping the casual natives on the job and striving for the American objectives. He also has complaints: as League President, Miss Higa Jiga says Lotus Blossom receives favors denied to the other women; she wants this injustice corrected by having Fisby issue lipstick, cologne, and bobby pins to the general female populace and by having Lotus Blossom teach all the members of the League to be geisha girls. Fisby moralistically refuses. But when Sakini assures him that geisha girls are not prostitutes, as Americans consider them, but girls trained to listen to men's troubles and comfort them by singing, dancing, and preparing tea, Fisby relents. He hires Lotus Blossom as teacher. Upon Sakini's urging, he also agrees to build a teahouse instead of a school.

The teahouse is well on the way. Colonel, however, is dissatisfied with Fisby's reports because his progress is too slow. When Fisby reports that he is manufacturing getas (sandals) and cricket cages and wearing a kasa, Purdy sends him Captain McLean, the psychiatrist from a nearby island.

392

McLean arrives, disguising his true mission under the cover of making ethnological studies. At first, he is shocked by Fisby's costume and behavior; but when Fisby offers McLean, always a bug about agriculture, a chance to do some experimental farming, McLean is delighted. Thus when Purdy calls McLean to discuss Fisby's "condition," McLean talks only of farming. Purdy is then convinced that he must send someone to analyze McLean. Meanwhile, Fisby and McLean organize the Cooperative Brewing Company of Tobiki, to produce and market among the neighboring officers' clubs a wonderful sweet potato brandy. After the first few samples are distributed, the orders flow in prodigiously.

ACT III (*three scenes*)

Several weeks later, the villagers, Fisby, and McLean gather before the now completed Teahouse of the August Moon. Everyone is celebrating Fisby's birthday. There is an exciting wrestling match between the Chief of Police and the Chief of Agriculture. McLean and Fisby are leading the group in a spirited rendition of "Deep in the Heart of Texas" when Purdy walks in and screams: "What in the name of the Occupation is going on here?"

Now Fisby must explain to his colonel what progress he has made toward the objectives of Plan B. After ordering McLean back to his unit, Purdy hears Fisby tell of organizing the Ladies' League, but of building the teahouse instead of the school because Lotus Blossom needed it to teach the woman how to become geisha girls. To the colonel's query of the source of the great prosperity of the village, Fisby reports a great rise in the sale of mats, hats, and cricket cages. But Fisby is unlucky when Purdy answers the telephone and receives a call for an order of brandy. Purdy places Fisby under technical arrest and sends him to headquarters to await courtmartial. He orders Sergeant Gregorivich to destroy all the stills and the teahouse.

Using Sakini as interpreter, Fisby and Lotus Blossom discuss the future. Lotus Blossom asks Fisby to marry her, but Fisby tells her she would be disillusioned by his way of life in America. They promise always to remember each other. When Lotus Blossom asks if she should marry Mr. Seiko, Fisby tells her she must decide for herself.

Purdy is frantic. Upon his report to Washington, a senator thought Fisby's methods were excellent as a recovery program, a Congressional Committee is on its way out to study the methods, and a national magazine is sending photographers. To rescue the colonel from his mistake, Sakini shows that the villagers got Gregorovich drunk and he destroyed water barrels instead of stills. As for the teahouse, it was only disassembled; it is quickly reassembled. Sakini concludes the story, sending the "lovely ladies" and "kind gentleman" home to ponder.

394

96

FRANCES GOODRICH
ALBERT HACKETT (1900–   )

The Diary of Anne Frank (1955)

*Drama in two acts, based on
an actual diary kept for two years*

MAIN CHARACTER AND THEME: The problems and excitements of growing adolescence and of resistance to Nazism, as experienced by a high-spirited, intelligent Jewish girl, *Anne Frank*, born in Germany on July 12, 1929, and in hiding with her family in Amsterdam, Holland, from early July 1942 to August 4, 1944. Anne died in a Nazi concentration camp at Bergen-Belsen in March, 1945, but her diary was preserved.

OTHER CHARACTERS:

Mr. Frank, Anne's father, formerly an importer of spice and herbs in Germany

Miep, a Dutch girl of twenty-two, and *Mr. Kraler*, a kindly, dependable Dutchman, members of the Dutch underground who help the Franks establish and maintain their hiding place

Mr. Van Daan, a portly man in his late forties, whose family are in hiding with the Franks

Mrs. Van Daan, a pretty woman in her early forties

Peter Van Daan, a shy, awkward boy of sixteen

Mrs. Frank, Anne's mother

Margot, her sister

Mr. Dussel, a dentist, a meticulous, finicky man in his late fifties, also in hiding with the Franks

TIME: 1943 to 1945.

PLACE: Top floor of a warehouse and office building in Amsterdam.

MUSICAL HIGHLIGHTS: Carillon bells of the nearby Westertoren; drunken soldiers singing "Lili Marlene"; "Oh, Hanukkah!"; German military band playing Viennese waltz.

HISTORICAL NOTE: Drama of the tremendous disciplines the human being is capable of placing upon himself when determined to preserve his spiritual identity under the most severe pressures, and of the Jewish counter-resistance to the Hitlerian campaign for Semitic extermination. Although not set in America, nor involving any single American character, drama is American in a deep sense because it commands the spiritual allegiances of most Americans. First produced at Cort Theatre, New York, October 5, 1955, under the direction of Garson Kanin, with Joseph Schildkraut as Mr. Frank and Susan Strasberg as Anne. Initial run: 717 performances. Winner Antoinette Perry, Critics' Circle, and Pulitzer awards as outstanding American play for the 1955–1956 season.

ACT I (*five scenes*)

In the opening scene, in 1945, Mr. Frank is taking leave of Amsterdam in spite of Miep's insistence that he is needed there. He asks her to burn all papers. But when she shows him Anne's diary, he picks it up and begins to read it. As he reads, his voice is joined by Anne's. Then Mr. Frank's voice dies away, and Anne's carries on. Throughout the drama, it bridges the scenes.

The second scene reverts to July, 1942. The Van Daans are already in the hiding place worrying because the Franks have not come. When the Franks do arrive, with Miep and Mr. Kraler, Mr. Frank explains that they had a long walk around because of many Green Police in the streets. Everyone is introduced. Miep and Kraler begin arrangements for food. Mr. Frank explains to his fellow inmates that daytimes between eight and six, when men are working in the rooms below, there must be no unnecessary movement, everyone must walk in stockinged feet, must speak in whispers, must not run water in sink or water-closet. No trash may be thrown out; everything must be burned in the stove at night. After six, they can move about, work, and play. He shows them all their rooms and the common room. In meeting Peter and his cat Mouschi, Anne talks of school (where Peter admits he was a lone wolf), of her friends, and of not wanting to throw away her Star of

David. She decides to think of the hiding place as a very peculiar summer boarding house. Receiving a diary from her father, she starts to go down to get a pencil—since no one is in the building; her father tells her she must *never* go beyond the door. Now she feels the meaning of hiding: never to breathe fresh air; always to fear discovery.

Two months later, Anne is engaged in teasing Peter, who is still shy. She teaches him how to dance. Dressing herself in his clothes, she mocks him artistically. Her father is teaching her algebra and Latin. She is busy querying the Van Daans about their pre-marriage romance. Mr. Van Daan tries to get her to be quiet like her sister; but when she spills milk on Mrs. Van Daan's coat, Mrs. Van Daan is quite angry. Later, Anne helps to induct Mr. Dussel, a newcomer, into the mysteries of the apartment.

Months later, Anne wakes screaming from a nightmare, believing herself captured. The experience disturbs the whole group and calls attention to Anne's extreme preference for her father, which causes her mother to suffer. At this time, Anne also mentions the increase in the severity of air raids over the city.

For the Hanukkah celebration, Anne devises ingenious presents. To her mother, for example, she gives an IOU for ten hours of complete obedience; to Peter, a safety razor which Miep got for her; to her sister, a cross-word puzzle book she had previously done, but all rubbed out for starting anew. During the celebration, they are all horrified by a crash below. As Peter tries to turn out the lights for safety, he loses his balance and falls: the iron lamp shade crashes. Despite great worry that their discovery and capture is imminent, Anne leads the group in singing "Oh, Hanukkah!... the sweet ... celebration ...."

ACT II (*five scenes*)

For New Year's Day, Miep brings them all a cake, and there is trouble about dividing it. There is also fear because a man who works in the building below hinted to Mr. Kraler that he knew of Mr. Frank's hiding place and wanted more money on the job (gentle blackmail). But in spite of having less and less food, Anne is somewhat happier because Peter has expressed an appreciation for her.

Anne is visiting Peter in his room, and her mother is complaining. At nine o'clock, after a touching conversation, she leaves Peter and he dazes her by kissing her on the cheek.

Mr. Van Daan is caught stealing food from the common supply and Mrs. Frank is so angry that she wants the Van Daans put out. Anne begs that the Van Daans not be exposed to such danger; Mrs. Frank is willing to let them stay until Miep finds them a place. As they talk, Miep comes to tell them all that the Normandy invasion has begun. It is enough to cause Anne and her mother to speak very sweetly to each other.

Just before they are captured—the crash months ago represented a thief who eventually revealed that there were noises up above him—Anne describes the lovely day to Peter—the jonquils, the crocus, the violets that she sees up through the skylight.

97

MICHAEL VINCENTE GAZZO (1923–   )

A Hatful of Rain (1955)

Realistic drama in three acts

MAIN CHARACTER AND THEME: The private life of *Johnny Pope*, twenty-seven, a narcotics user—his marriage and expectant fatherhood, his career as son and brother, his relationship with the people who supply him, and his hope for happiness and escape; especially, the way in which his addiction summarily rearranges the lives of all those with whom he has close contact.

OTHER CHARACTERS:

John Pope, Sr., Johnny's father

Celia Pope, who for four years has been Johnny's wife

Polo Pope, Johnny's brother

Mother, a tall young man who wears dark glasses and peddles drugs

Apples, nineteen, Mother's "sidekick"

Chuch, Mother's strong-arm man

Man, another strong-arm man

Putski, a rich girl from Connecticut who uses narcotics

TIME: 1950's.

PLACE: Remodeled apartment on New York's lower East Side.

MUSICAL HIGHLIGHT: Street carousel.

HISTORICAL NOTE: One of the few successful dramas on the life of a narcotic addict, symbolizing a basic evil of present-day American society, especially as indicating the persistent need for boost and the subsequent distortion in the return to equilibrium. Though criticized for its tendency to place theatrical effect above the thorough pursuit of the clear problem it had posed, this drama aroused considerable discussion, dramatically and otherwise, during the 398 performances it played at the Lyceum Theatre, New York, after its opening on November 9, 1955. The acting of Shelley Winters as Celia, Ben Gazzara as Johnny, Anthony Franciosa as Polo, and Frank Silvera as Father was widely praised, as were designs by Mordecai Gorelik.

ACT I (two scenes)

Hoping to enter his own business with the $2500 Polo has saved, Father comes in from the South to discover the money gone. He and Johnny, nevertheless, renew old times: he speaks with pride of Johnny's heroic service in World War II and of his having gone to engineering school on his credits under the G.I. Bill. No one has yet told him that Johnny has lost four jobs in six months for reasons apparently related to his army wounds. When Father speaks of the vacuum-living they all seem to be doing, not believing in the future, Celia angrily opposes him.

Celia is still working as a secretary, although four months pregnant. She is much worried about Johnny's recent erratic behavior. When she gets him alone, she asks if there is another woman. He insists he loves her alone.

Johnny is called to the door, and in spite of Celia's inviting his company inside, he and his visitors confer beyond the closed door. The visitors are Mother, Apples, and Chuch, who have come to collect the seven hundred dollars Johnny owes them. It is revealed that Johnny must have drugs twice a day, costing twenty dollars each time: in short, he has "a forty dollar-a-day-habit." Mother makes Johnny promise to pay at least five hundred dollars by the next day—Mother does not care how he gets the money; he even leaves Johnny a gun. After Mother and Apples depart, Chuch tells Johnny how Willy de Carlo, who owes much less than Johnny, was terribly beaten.

Later that evening, Johnny prepares to go out alone, as he has often done recently. Celia tells him that she is love-starved to the extent of almost throwing herself at Johnny's brother. Johnny nevertheless goes, but not before Polo, who has come home intoxicated, has been put to bed by Johnny and Celia.

At about two o'clock in the morning, Johnny has not returned. Polo tells Celia how Johnny has always been the favored one. In the adoptive homes through which their father brought them up, Johnny was always getting adopted, Polo never. Celia tells Polo he must move because she knows he is in love with her, and she can stand the situation no longer. Despite his insistence, she will not say how she feels about him.

ACT II (*two scenes*)

As he has done two or three times a week for months, Johnny again is out all night. Celia was at Polo's door during the night, but could not go in. She tells Polo she is through loving Johnny since he cares nothing for her or for the baby they will soon have. To help her, Polo decides to stay home from work.

At ten in the morning, Johnny comes home. All night he has been looking for someone to give him an injection of drugs, but the police net is being drawn tightly, and the peddlers have gone into hiding. Chuch gave him enough heroin to carry him through the night, but he needs more. Since Ginnino has promised to hold him some drugs for fifteen minutes, he begs Polo for the necessary twenty dollars. Polo refuses, saying it is time he stopped putting his money into Johnny's arm. It is now disclosed that the entire $2500 Polo promised Father went to Johnny for his expensive habit. In despair, Johnny decides to wait until Mother comes for him, but Polo says they must leave at once.

Father arrives. He tells Johnny Celia was right about caring: now, he does care. Father is still trying to find out what Polo did with the $2500. Periodically in the conversation, he asks Johnny was Polo keeping an expensive apartment for some girl? was he gambling? did he pay $250 a week for board?

Recalling that he never had a family life, Johnny tells Father that the two of them and Polo do not know one another. Johnny tries to hint to Father what his trouble is—he reminds him of the heavy dosages of narcotics he got in the hospital—but Father does not catch the hint. After Polo gets rid of Father, Johnny begins to sweat, the first stage of his narcotic fit. When Mother and Apples appear for their money or for Johnny's punishment, Mother tells Polo that the only way he can save Johnny is to sell his car for eight hundred dollars and bring all the money to Mother. The additional money will cover the treatment Mother will give Johnny now to put him out of his pain.

By that evening, Johnny has cleaned up the house and spread flowers around. He seems well. Celia, however, tells him that she is leaving—she does not love him any more. He swears he does love her and persuades her to stay. At last he confesses his trouble. She promises to stand by him. When Father comes in, he tells a story of Johnny as a child digging to make money, and all he got was a hatful of rain. Father hears from Johnny the story of his trouble, and the result is a bitter quarrel which is broken up only when Johnny rushes out. In the tense atmosphere, Celia suffers an attack; Polo takes her to the hospital.

ACT III

Mother, Chuch, and Apples return for their money; seeing no one around, they wait. Under the influence of narcotics, Mother is "flying." With him is Putski who is going to take them all up to her place in Connecticut which is vacant because her parents are in Europe. When Johnny comes in, he is threatened by two of Mother's men. But Polo avoids disaster by paying Mother the eight hundred dollars, and Mother and his crowd leave. Father slaps Polo for paying for Johnny's habit, but later when Celia decides to call the police, Father objects. Having recovered from her attack, Celia is glad she will not lose her baby; but having talked with her doctor about Johnny, Celia now knows that his chance for recovery and cure is slim. She courageously decides to take the one chance and persuades Johnny. Sending Father and Polo out, she calls the police and reports the presence in her home of a dope addict.

98

JEROME LAWRENCE (1915–   )
ROBERT E. LEE (1918–   )

Inherit the Wind (1955)

Semihistorical drama in three acts

MAIN CHARACTER AND THEME: Of *Henry Drummond*, a public-spirited lawyer dedicated to the search for truth, and his adventures in a community swept by religious fundamentalism.

OTHER CHARACTERS:

Rachel Brown, twenty-two, in love with Cates

Meeker, bailiff

Bertram Cates, in jail for violating a new state law against teaching evolution

Mr. Goodfellow, storekeeper

Mrs. Krebs, housewife

Rev. Jeremiah Brown, religious leader of the community

Corkin, a workman

Bollinger and *Platt*, ordinary small-town citizens

Mr. Bannister, a respected citizen but one who cannot read

Howard, thirteen, and *Melinda*, twelve, schoolchildren

Mrs. Blair, Howard's mother

Mrs. McClain, who is selling fans for the Funeral Home

Mrs. Loomis, another housewife

Hot Dog Man

Elijah, "holy man" from the hills

E. K. Hornbeck, a cynical Baltimore newspaperman

Hurdy Gurdy Man

Timmy, a breathless youngster

The Mayor

Matthew Harrison Brady, sixty-five, three-times candidate for President of the United States, defender of the fundamentalist faith, special counsel for the prosecution

Mrs. *Sarah Brady*, his devoted, fashionably dressed wife

Tom Davenport, circuit district attorney

The Judge

Mr. Jesse Dunlap, farmer and cabinetmaker

Mr. George Sillers, who works at the feed store

A Reuter's Man

Harry Y. Esterbrook, the radio man

Townspeople, Hawkers, Reporters, Jurors, Spectators

TIME: Summer (probably July 1925).

PLACE: A small town named Hillsboro (probably Dayton, Tennessee).

MUSIC: "That Old Time Religion"; "Marching to Zion."

HISTORICAL NOTE: The authors say the drama could happen at any time; it undoubtedly stems from the famous Scopes trial of 1925 (Cates is Scopes); Drummond is based on Clarence Darrow (1857–1938), and Brady on William Jennings Bryan (1860–1925), and Hornbeck on H. L. Mencken (1880–1956). First performed professionally on April 21, 1955, at the National Theatre, New York, with Paul Muni as Drummond and Ed Begley as Brady, after staging by Margo Jones at Theatre 1955 in Dallas, Texas.

ACT I (*two scenes*)

On her visit to Cates, Rachel brings a suitcase of his clothes, tells him that Matthew Harrison Brady is coming down to help prosecute him, and further that he should be ashamed. Cates merely asks her to love him, and they are embracing when Meeker returns to sweep up. Rachel breaks away. Cates tells Meeker he does not not know who will defend him. Whipped up by Rachel's father, the Reverend Jeremiah Brown, the townspeople prepare with banners and placards (one blares "*Read Your Bible*", another, "*Where Will You Spend Eternity?*") to greet the mighty Brady. Hornbeck drifts through, sneering and speaking blank verse. Brady, sixty-five, appears with his wife, the Mayor, and Tom Davenport. To the throbbing crowd he announces that he has come to defend "the Living Truth of the Scriptures." Empowered by the Governor, the Mayor confers on him a commission as Honorary Colonel in the State Militia. At the picnic which follows, Brady eats too much. Hornbeck discloses that Cates will be defended by Drummond, a celebrated agnostic. This announcement creates a shock until Brady declares: "If St. George had slain a dragonfly, who would remember him?" When all have gone, Drummond appears. Melinda, the youngster, screams,

404

"It's the Devil." Hornbeck greets Drummond: "Hello, Devil. Welcome to Hell."

A few days later, the jury is being selected. Bannister is accepted when Drummond learns that he cannot read. Drummond rejects Dunlap because he believes in the Holy Word of God and Matthew Harrison Brady. Drummond's purple galluses appear when the Judge allows coats off. When Drummond objects to Brady's being called Colonel, the Judge and the Mayor join heads and make him one. The jury selected, the Judge announces a prayer meeting: Drummond promptly objects to "this commercial announcement." When Rachel begs Cates to back down, Drummond promises to give up if Cates tells him he knows he was wrong. Cates wavers, but holds to his conviction. Drummond warns both that they are dealing with thinking and ideas. Rachel says she may have to testify against Cates, but also that she does not trust her father; she only fears him.

ACT II (*two scenes*)

On the courthouse lawn, Brady holds a press conference, at which he says he does not hate Drummond, and genuinely appreciates the support Drummond gave him on the second of his three unsuccessful candidacies for president, in 1908. The prayer meeting is fervent. Brown, Rachel's father, reviews the seven separate days of creation. He cries for condign punishment upon Cates, and even upon his daughter for begging mercy for Cates. After the meeting, Brady asks Drummond why he has moved so far away from him; Drummond replies that perhaps Brady has moved—by standing still.

Two days later, the trial is in full swing. Howard, the youth, tells how Cates taught them evolution, but cannot (upon cross-examination) say that he has felt any harm. In the guise of trial examination, Brady delivers many explosive orations. Rachel is a damaging, though unwilling, witness against Cates. She is forced to tell that Cates left the church two years before because her father condemned to hellfire an 11-year-old boy who had never been baptized; and that Cates had said: "God created Man in his own image— and Man, being a gentleman, returned the compliment." The Judge will not allow Drummond to call his expert witnesses—famous professors from notable universities. Frustrated, Drummond puts Brady on the stand. He compels Brady to admit that one day in Creation might have elastic limits, and that, if a sponge "has the right to think," so has Man. Little by little, he steals a portion of the audience by making his opponent look silly. Eventually, Brady in a frenzy continues to recite the names of the books of the Bible even after the Court is adjourned. Brady tells his wife that "they're laughing at me, Mother" and that he cannot stand it. She rocks him to sleep, calling him "Baby . . . Baby . . . !"

ACT III

In the courtroom the following day, the people await the verdict. A man from radio station WGN sets up a wire to broadcast the news to the world. The Jury files back: Cates is guilty! The Judge is about to pass sentence when Drummond wins "last words" from him. These declare that he intends to oppose the law. On orders from higher up, Cates is fined one hundred dollars and let out on five hundred dollars bond. Brady vigorously protests. Drummond appeals, and is granted thirty days for the purpose. The Court adjourns sine die. In the midst of having his big victory speech cut off the radio, Brady freezes and topples over. Picked up, he is delirious, reciting an acceptance speech for the presidency of the United States. Drummond tells Cates that effectually he has won—he has opened an important door. The Baltimore *Herald* has promised to pay all of Cates's bills. Rachel returns. She tells Cates she has broken with her father and wants to go with him because bad or good, "the ideas have to come out—like children." She hands Cates his copy of Darwin. Hornbeck comes back to report that Brady is dead "of a busted stomach." When Drummond defends Brady, Hornbeck, contemptuously, calls him a religious man. Drummond extends the impression by quoting from Proverbs: "He that troubleth his own house shall inherit the wind: and the fool shall be servant to the wise in heart." Packing the Darwin and the Bible together, half-smiling, half-shrugging, Drummond climbs to the empty square on the street above.

99

ROD SERLING (1924–   )

Patterns (1955)

Television drama in three acts

MAIN CHARACTER AND THEME: The story of *Fred Staples*, a young, dynamic executive, and his fight to put sensitivity, decency, and ideals into his ascension to business heights.

OTHER CHARACTERS:

Fran, Fred's attractive wife, ambitious for her husband

Ramsey, tough, icy, predatory but honest corporation head, in his early sixties

Andy Sloane, sixty-six, who has given thirty years of service to the firm but seems to be outmoded on the job

Marge Fleming, Andy's secretary, very loyal to him

Miss Margaret Lanier, Ramsey's executive secretary

Secretaries of Ramsey and Company—

First Secretary, Miss Stevens, Miss Hill, Miss Evans

Executives of Ramsey and Company:—

Gordon, head of sales

Jameson, head of purchasing

Smith, comptroller

Vandeventer, chief engineer

Latham, head of service

Grannigan, record control

Portier, head of operations

Paul, Andy's son

Billy, Fred's assistant

Tommy, elevator starter

Elevator Operator

Telephone Operator

TIME: 1954.

PLACE: New York City—Grand Central area and residential section.

HISTORICAL NOTE: Serling became nationally famous with *Patterns*, winning all the major awards in television writing. His dramas, while lacking literary depth and inclined to cliché, are hard-hitting in the television medium. They also show a good psychological sense and carry forward the analysis of the internal struggle between ambition and ethics going on in the mind of the young American businessman, which has been extensively developed in literature since Theodore Dreiser. Television drama generally must adapt itself to its medium and must specialize in symbols (such as clocks), close-ups and spreading scenes, highly compressed action and dialogue (usually impressionistic rather than penetrative), a perpetual sense of immediacy instead of gradual development, and a tendency to have characters confess and dramatically describe things that in regular drama usually have to be demonstrated.

ACT I

A new office on the fortieth floor of Ramsey and Company, in the executive suite, has been prepared for Fred Staples, who is expected momentarily. The office is outfitted in early American, Fred's favorite furnishings, and is third down the hall from the president, an indication of its rank. But, as Miss Lanier tells the gossiping secretaries, Fred's true position will be determined only by Mr. Ramsey, who has not yet spoken on the subject. Fran accompanies Fred to the office entrance and sends him upstairs congratulating him on his great advance over his former job in Cincinnati. Fred and Andy, recognizing their possible rivalry for status, feel each other out, and Marge, Andy's regular secretary, is temporarily assigned to extra duty with Fred. In the first meeting of company executives, Ramsey, an obvious production genius but also a tyrant, taunts Andy for preferring to sympathize with two hundred jobless workers rather than to vote to save the company two hundred and fifty thousand dollars. On the other hand, Ramsey praises Fred for having no opinion when he is not fully acquainted with the facts. After the meeting, Fran brings Fred a two-hundred-and-thirty-eight-dollar watch as symbol of his present luxury position.

ACT II

Three months later, Fred is well entrenched. Speaking unofficially and not as a secretary, Marge tells Fred that Andy's ethical sense may lead to his elimination from the firm. Later, Andy praises Fred for the suggestions he contributed to Andy's annual report, saying he has incorporated the suggestions verbatim. Andy says that although Ramsey wants his resignation he will not give it: he cannot surrender the bait—the pattern of living in the upper brackets—in spite of two big bleeding ulcers, a bum heart, and a permanent cringe.

At Fran's party for the executives, Fran gives Ramsey the impression that the annual report is primarily Fred's work. Ramsey readily believes her, saying that Andy is through because, like Ramsey's father, he is too sentimental, and a big firm is not built on sentiment. Ramsey tells Fred he was brought in as Andy's replacement. When Ramsey has gone, Fred reproves his wife for leaving an untruthful impression about the report, but Fran markedly notes that Fred did not correct the impression. As he retires for the night, Fred experiences a struggle within himself over becoming a vice president over Andy's dead body. He anticipates becoming conscience-stricken about the next day's meeting.

ACT III

Ramsey draws a line through Andy's name on the report. Later, Marge reminds Fred that he and Andy are much alike and that although he is winning today, he will be in Andy's shoes in another ten years. On the way to the meeting, Andy will not accept Fred's "unburdening." At the meeting, Ramsey praises Fred's report, brushing aside Fred's effort to correct him. Andy protests briefly, but then his "guts cave in," and he concedes that a secretarial error put his name on the report. Ramsey asks each executive to examine the report thoroughly.

After the meeting, Andy falls sick and needs his heart pills; Ramsey calls an ambulance. Fred tells Fran that he cannot take Ramsey's type of brutality and insensitivity: he is prepared to resign. In the final scene, Fred tells Ramsey that he believes in the kind of ethics and conscience for which Andy stands, and that Andy has been Ramsey's conscience all along. Fred boldly accuses Ramsey of beating Andy to death. He tells the president he is "a washout"—an organizational marvel with no compassion. Before completing his speech, he indicates his readiness to resign at once. Ramsey asks him to stay on with the understanding that they will be good for each other—Fred to be Ramsey's conscience, Ramsey to develop Fred by challenging and testing him at every turn. Fred accepts.

100

ARCHIBALD MACLEISH (1892–   )

J. B. (1958)

*Verse drama and philosophical allegory
in prologue and eleven scenes*

MAIN CHARACTER AND THEME: The story of *J. B.*, a twentieth-century Job, in his middle or late thirties, a rich and successful businessman, told with contemporary and with universal implications.

OTHER CHARACTERS:

Mr. Zuss, who plays God

Nickles, who plays Satan

A Distant Voice (Voice of the Almighty)

Sarah, J.B.'s wife, a few years younger than he, with a New England background

J.B.'s Children:

David, thirteen

Mary, twelve

Jonathan, ten

Ruth, eight

Rebecca, six

Two Middle-aged Maids

Two Messengers

Girl

Chorus of Neighbors—*Mrs. Adams, Jolly Adams, Mrs. Lesure, Mrs. Murphy, Mrs. Botticelli*

Prophets—*Zophar, Eliphaz, Bildad*

TIME: Any time and always.

PLACE: Corner inside of an enormous circus tent—side show set up. On left, a wooden platform six or seven feet high, with wooden ladder leaning against it. Clothes strewn about resemble vestments of churches of many ages.

HISTORICAL NOTE: A rare successful attempt of modern American poetic drama to frame universal truth in the dynamic thought of the current generation. Opened in New York at the ANTA Theatre, December 29, 1958, with Pat Hingle as J. B., Christopher Plummer as Nickles, and Raymond Massey as Mr. Zuss.

THE PROLOGUE

Mr. Zuss and Nickles are two circus vendors (the former sells balloons, the latter popcorn) who as actors always try to control the stage. The bare stage records life on earth, the platform life in heaven. In a mask that is huge, white, blank, beautiful, expressionless, with eyes lidded like those in Michelangelo's "Night," Mr. Zuss is going to act God. Of God Nickles says: "If God is God He is not good, If God is good He is not God." Nickles, thinking Mr. Zuss wants him to play Job, is shocked to learn that he is to play the Father of Lies. Nickles' mask is dark and open-eyed, eyes wrinkled with laughter and staring, mouth drawn down in agonized disgust. After a while, Nickles prefers his mask to Mr. Zuss's. The two adjust their masks and begin to recite the Job words from the Bible, in the dark. After a great guffaw, Mr. Zuss demands lights. Nickles swears he did not make the guffaw, and further that the eyes of the mask can *see*, and further still that Hell is to *see*: seeing to Satan is absurd despair, ridiculous agony. When they try the scene again, a Voice interferes, speaking Mr. Zuss's lines. But they manage to get through the six lines beginning "Whence comest thou?"

Scene 1

At a conventional Thanksgiving table, J. B. and Sarah ask their children if they have thought of God thankfully. When Rebecca says that they take the bounty because it is good, Sarah wants to know of J. B. if even he is sufficiently grateful. From their conversation the thought emerges that when God is good to you, it is not luck. Sarah fears something in the thought because God, being just, punishes as much as He rewards.

Scene 2

Up on the platform, Nickles says, "A rich man's piety stinks." Mr. Zuss says God will show him what God is, but that Job will praise God no matter

411

what. Nickles says he will suffer *to learn*. Eventually they confront each other in their masks. Godmask agrees to have Job thoroughly tested, but adds: *"Only/Upon himself/Put not forth thy hand!"*

Scene 3

Two Messengers present themselves as David's friends. They talk and behave drunkenly, reviewing their war experiences with David. They express shock that the army has not told David's parents about him. Eventually they disclose the fact that David was destroyed in action right at the close of the war. Nickles leers at Mr. Zuss as Sarah, J.B.'s wife, reacts deeply.

Scene 4

In darkness, there is first silence, and then a loud crash, and then silence again. First Messenger again appears, this time with a news camera slung from his neck; Second Messenger follows with a notebook. At last comes a stylishly dressed girl, who holds the attention of J. B. and his wife while the other two chronicle their reactions to the news that J. B.'s son and daughter have been smashed and killed in a drunken-driving accident. J. B. curses the reporters as Sarah helplessly pronounces the names "Mary . . . Jonathan . . . ." Sarah begins to blame God, asking why He is doing all these things. When he was lucky, she reminds J. B., the credit went to God. J. B. protests her analogy. She replies: "Don't touch me!"

Scene 5

After Mr. Zuss and Nickles review the progress of events, First Messenger reappears wearing police sergeant's cap, with Second Messenger wearing patrolman's cap. Identified by her red parasol, Rebecca, J. B.'s youngest, has been found by the police after being raped and killed by a 19-year-old boy, "hopped to the eyes." Sarah is overwhelmed into silence. Touching the parasol, J. B. recites: "The Lord giveth . . . (*his voice breaks*) . . . the Lord taketh away!"

Scene 6

In steel helmets and brassards, Two Messengers bring in Sarah, crying for Ruth. Ruth, J. B.'s bank, and his other possessions worth millions,

412

have been blown away in an air raid. Telling Sarah that they still cannot despair, J. B. insists God is still there, even in their desperation. While Sarah condemns God as a killer, J. B. says: "Blessed be the name of the Lord."

Scene 7

For accepting all this, Nickles calls J. B. immoral, indecent. He says God always asks the proof of pain but forgets what a man can do when his body is loaded with pain. Satanmask and Godmask speculate on what will happen when Job is afflicted in bone and flesh.

Scene 8

By the light of a lantern, J. B. is seen lying on a propped-up table, naked except for a few rags of clothing. Nickles condemns Mr. Zuss for making too big a mess with his atomic explosion. As women walk slowly around J. B. and Sarah, J. B. begs to die. Sarah taunts him; says God is their enemy. The Chorus evaluates J. B. uncomplimentarily. J. B. wants to sleep. Sarah will not let him, saying that if God is just, their slaughtered children stank with sin. She finally says that she will not stay to hear him lie in God's defense; J. B. answers that we have no choice but to be guilty. Sarah says she will not love him, and since he has no choice, he should curse God and die. Learning that Sarah is gone, J. B. cries: *"Show me my guilt,* O God!" From above Nickles taunts him.

Scene 9

Alone in enormous loneliness, J. B. wishes he had not been born. The Comforters—Zophar, Eliphaz, Bildad—come: J. B. is too blind to see them. They argue with J. B. about God's justice, Eliphaz saying that it is a psycho-phenomenal situation—all men are victims of guilt, not guilty. Turning from them, J. B. asks God to show him his transgression. Commanding God to answer him, he cries violently, "Though he slay me, yet will I trust him." He also sends up the ancient human cry, "Oh, that I knew where I might find Him!" The Comforters grow cold and leave. At last J. B. says: "Mine eyes seeth thee! . . . wherefore I abhor myself . . . and repent . . . ."

Scene 10

Mr. Zuss and Nickles now argue violently over whether J. B. is a strong man or an accepting coward. Saying the play is not over, Mr. Zuss calls for lights. He tells Nickles J. B. will get his wife back, and in natural course, other children. Nickles says he wouldn't touch her. Mr. Zuss says he does though, and so does man every blessed generation. Nickles goes down to J. B. and makes him aware of what is going on. Although he sees J. B.'s skin healed, he is still sure J. B. will fling all this restoration in God's face. J. B. hears someone at the door.

Scene 11

The light through the canvas door presents Sarah showing J. B. the forsythia. She reminds him that he wanted justice when there was only love. At last she tells him—in darkness—to blow on the coal of her heart.

101

DORE SCHARY (1905–   )

Sunrise at Campobello (1958)

Biographical drama in three acts

MAIN CHARACTER AND THEME: How *Franklin D. Roosevelt*, previously invincible in body and mind, reacted to a devastating attack of disease and how he sought to capitalize upon golden opportunities despite his crippled state.

OTHER CHARACTERS:

Eleanor Roosevelt, Franklin's wife

Anna, his daughter

Franklin, Jr., James, and *John*, his sons

Edward, an American servant

Marie, a French servant

Mrs. Sara Delano Roosevelt, then in her sixties, Franklin's mother

Miss Marguerite (Missy) LeHand, Franklin's secretary

Louis McHenry Howe, his chief adviser and most enduring friend

Doctor Bennet, his physician

Franklin Calder, a Canadian friend

Three Canadian Stretcher-bearers

Mr. Brimmer, a business opportunist

Mr. Lassiter, who is circulating a bigoted petition

Alfred E. Smith, Governor of New York

Daly, Franklin's attendant

Policeman

Senator Walsh, a leading Democrat

A Speaker

TIME: August 10, 1921, to June 26, 1924.

415

PLACE: Campobello, New Brunswick, Canada; New York City—Town House on 65th Street and Madison Square Garden.

MUSICAL HIGHLIGHT: "Sidewalks of New York."

HISTORICAL NOTE: Accurate, kindly, and inspired picture of three crucial years in the life of a famous American; also, highly dramatic. First performed on the 76th anniversary of FDR's birth, January 30, 1958, at Cort Theatre, New York, with Ralph Bellamy as Franklin and Mary Fickett as Eleanor; later carried on a national tour. Schary's early reputation was based upon his production of motion pictures with more than ordinary enlightenment.

ACT I (*three scenes*)

At the FDR summer home in Campobello, the accent is on water sports although the family exuberance is displayed in many forms. Except for Eleanor, all the Roosevelts are in bathing suits, enjoying swimming in the lagoon and diving in the bay. Eleanor arranges the replenishment of household supplies. The spirit of Granny (Sara Roosevelt) is present, although she is far away, in reiteration of her love of Europe, her hatred for Louis Howe, and her determination to have everyone in the family speak French. To Eleanor's wonder that perhaps Franklin's Wall Street job, at five hundred dollars a week, is hurting his progressive ideas that are so much needed in the country, Franklin replies negatively—no more, he says, than his ideas were hurt by Tammany Hall, seven years in the Navy Department, and his mother's massive objections to his being in politics at all. Each receives his assignment for the reading, that night, of *Julius Caesar*, and the reading excitedly proceeds. At the end of the scene, Franklin successfully defends, against each son, his hand-wrestling championship. Following this, he stumbles and clutches his back. Though Eleanor is concerned, Franklin retires to bed with what he calls merely a touch of lumbago.

For three weeks, Franklin has been in bed: Louis has come to take care of him. Sara, Franklin's mother, also arrives, worried, from England. Franklin's disease has been variously diagnosed, but a Boston doctor calls it infantile paralysis and says his "wonderful legs" are in danger. Doctor Bennet expects Franklin to recover almost completely. Sara and Louis continue their warfare: Sara demanding that her son settle at Hyde Park and stay there; Louis, with equal stubbornness, urging that he follow his ordained destiny in politics.

416

"*Sunrise at Campobello*" (1958)

Two weeks later, Louis directs Franklin's "escape" from Campobello so as to throw the reporters off the trail—the other members of the family are used as decoys. Though in obvious pain, Franklin, in his stretcher, says: "By gosh—I feel like the Caliph of Bagdad."

ACT II (*two scenes*)

In his New York town house, Franklin shows the effects of his illness in an angry session with Miss LeHand concerning a letter to Cordell Hull. He tells Eleanor of his loneliness and fear, especially fear of being caught in a fire; he nevertheless expresses the belief that his legs will also improve as his back muscles have. He is still proud of his ship models and his stamps. Following his confession of his enduring faith and of his struggle to learn humility, he and Eleanor embrace. Later, Louis comes in proud of his maneuver in having a newspaper report Franklin as a good candidate for Governor of New York. Louis offers to take Eleanor to Mouguin's for snails and a much-deserved outing. He also insists that Franklin must give up some of his innumerable memberships in organizations. But while Eleanor reads to her children, she bursts out crying. Declining Louis' offer to go out, she promises herself never to break down again.

Wrestling simultaneously and victoriously with Elliott and Franklin, Jr., he makes them cry "Uncle-Hiram-Joshua-Lafcadio-Turntable." Because he had told the newspapers he liked Henley's "Invictus," he has now received fourteen copies of the poem, the last one printed and framed. Eleanor has made a successful speech to a woman's organization about the League of Nations, but Franklin has made another bad business investment. As they once more discuss his learning patience and overcoming the Rooseveltian haughtiness, they reiterate their love: he calls her, "Cousin—wife—dearest." When Anna comes in without knocking, her father sharply rebukes her, and Anna leaves in tears; later, Anna and her father have a tender scene by making up. Trying to be diplomatic with her son but determined to get him to live up to the traditions of the Dutch aristocracy to which they belong, Sara is hurt by Franklin's abrupt ending of their conversation. Eleanor smooths things over. Alone, Franklin tries to walk on crutches; he fails miserably; painfully he makes his way back to his chair; he is exhausted, and rests; then he laboriously reaches for the crutches again as the curtain falls.

ACT III (*three scenes*)

On May Day of 1924, Franklin sharply rebukes Lassiter who requests from him a letter condemning the candidacy of a Catholic for President of the United States. In a memorable scene, Al Smith asks Franklin to nominate him for President at the Democratic National Convention, and Franklin accepts. After Al leaves, Franklin plans how he will walk and stand at the Convention. Louis thinks his steps there will be the ten biggest steps he ever took.

In a small room of Madison Square Garden, at 11:30 P.M. on June 26, 1924, Franklin, James, Louis, and Sara await the zero hour. Eleanor is there, too, knitting quietly. Louis thinks Franklin should use Judge J. M. Proskauer's inspiration to call Al the "happy warrior"; at the moment, Franklin thinks not. Senator Walsh bangs for attention. He recognizes the Honorable Franklin Delano Roosevelt of the State of New York.

As the band plays "Sidewalks of New York," Franklin walks the ten steps and waves. Cheering continues through the curtain.

LORRAINE HANSBERRY (1930–   )

A Raisin in the Sun (1959)

Realistic drama in three acts

MAIN CHARACTER AND THEME: Trials of *Lena Younger* (Mama), a struggling Negro woman in her early sixties, in accommodating her deep-seated dreams of spiritual emancipation with the more sophisticated dreams of the other members of the family on the occasion of her receipt of a legacy.

OTHER CHARACTERS:

Ruth Younger, Walter's wife

Travis Younger, age ten, her son

Walter Lee Younger (Brother), Lena's son and chief hope

Beneatha Younger, Lena's daughter, who plans to go to medical school

Joseph Asagai, a Nigerian student in America

George Murchison, son of a well-to-do family, who dates Beneatha

Karl Lindner, chairman of the New Neighbors Orientation Committee of the Claybourne Park Improvement Association

Bobo, Walter's prospective partner in a business venture

Two Moving Men

TIME: Sometime between World War II and 1959.

PLACE: Apartment on Chicago's South Side.

MUSICAL HIGHLIGHTS: "Ocomogosiay," a Nigerian dance number; "Oh, Lord, I Don't Feel No Ways Tired!"

HISTORICAL NOTE: Though similar to *Native Son* (*q.v.*, #84) in locale and viewpoint, this play breaks new ground in the drama of an outstanding

419

American problem—equal racial opportunity—through co-ordinating social protest, interracial insights, and effective natural humor. After opening at the Ethel Barrymore Theatre, New York, on March 11, 1959, with Claudia McNeil as Mama and Sidney Poitier as Walter, it won the Critics' Circle Award for the 1958–1959 season.

ACT I (*two scenes*)

The strongest first impression of the drama is that the Youngers are tightly packed into their living quarters: Travis and his father must fight for occupancy of the bathroom with the Johnsons, and both run the risk of being late—Travis to school, his father to his job as chauffeur. Beneatha and Mama share the same room; a small breakfast room has been made over as quarters for Walter and Ruth; and Travis sleeps on the "living room" couch whenever Walter and his pals, Willy and Bobo, talk far into the night about their plans to get money for a liquor-store franchise. It is apparent, also, that the individual members of the family are concerned with the exact moment of arrival of a check for ten thousand dollars, the insurance payment to Mama for the death of her husband, Big Walter, whom Mama characterizes as a fine man who "just couldn't never catch up with his dreams." Walter is frantically determined to have the whole ten thousand dollars for his share in underwriting the liquor store. Although Mama tells Ruth that a part of the money must go for Beneatha's medical education and speaks musingly of devoting another part to "a little old two-story somewhere, with a yard where Travis could play . . . ", she is still far from decided about the whole thing. She is not undecided about home principles, however, because when Beneatha argues scientifically that "there simply is no blasted God," Mama compels Beneatha to repeat after her the phrase, "In my mother's house there is still God." Later, Ruth collapses as the result of a new pregnancy.

Next morning, Beneatha and Mama entertain Asagai in spite of Saturday cleaning. Asagai brings Beneatha a Nigerian costume and drapes it over her. The money arrives in the morning mail, making everyone nervous. Mama tells Walter point-blank that there will be no money for a liquor store, but Walter does not give up. Not knowing of Ruth's pregnancy, Walter refuses to attend when Ruth calls him aside; all along he shows a gradual loss of love for Ruth. Finally, Ruth confesses that she went out that morning to make a five-dollar payment to a woman who will get rid of her unborn child.

420

In spite of Mama's urging Walter to say to Ruth that they are a people who give children life, not destroy them, Walter is somehow unable to speak. Mama, telling Walter he is a disgrace to his father's memory, prepares to go out and do something decisive.

ACT II (*three scenes*)

Draped in her Nigerian costume, Beneatha plays on the phonograph a Nigerian record and dances a Nigerian dance. She is joined by Walter who gives to the dance words that suggest fighting for better things. In the midst of this colorful performance, George Murchison arrives to take Beneatha to the theatre. George persuades her to change her costume, but as she does, George and Walter belittle each other's social positions—waster college boy versus the working man full of quixotic ideas but going nowhere. That Walter has been drinking is demonstrated when he quarrels with Ruth about her failure to uphold him. As a result of the quarrel, however, they draw closer together. Mama returns to announce that, to the end of cementing her family together again, she has used about a third of the insurance money to put a down payment on a new home. Eventually she says the home is in Clybourne Park; her children tell her that she has bought a residential problem since there are no Negroes in that sector. Once Mama and Walter are alone, he accuses her of always encouraging her children to dream and of just having gone out "and butchered up" a dream of his.

A few weeks later, Walter comes home, drunker than ever, telling his family that he has not been to work for three days, giving vent instead to his frustration. Unable to stand his disintegration, Mama gives him the $6,500 remaining after the down payment and puts in his hands the guarding of the $3,000 for Beneathea's medical course and the spending of the rest of the money as he sees fit.

Ruth reports that Walter is a changed man—he is happy, and again her sweetheart. Karl Lindner comes in to try to get the Youngers not to move into a neighborhood where they are not wanted. The family (except Mama) let him make his diplomatic effort—he offers to give them more than their down payment—and then turn him away. When Mama returns, the family give her presents—garden tools and a big garden hat. In the midst of all their joy, Bobo comes to tell Walter that Willy has absconded with all the money Walter gave him, including Beneatha's tuition fund. Mama begs

God for strength, remembering the great struggle she and Big Walter went through, a struggle now utterly defeated through Walter's manipulations in a bad cause.

ACT III

An hour later, Asagai speaks brilliantly to Beneatha of his plans to live for true Nigerian independence and he draws from her her own story of ambition to remake broken bodies. Eventually, he asks her to marry him and practice medicine in Nigeria. Walter has invited Lindner to return so that he may receive the money previously promised; as a result, he has made Beneatha entirely disgusted with him. Though disagreeing with Walter, Mama reproves Beneatha for not sticking by her brother when she is most needed. The Moving Men and Lindner arrive at the same time. When Lindner comes in, Mama will not let Ruth dismiss Travis: she wants the little boy to hear his father tell the white man where the dreams of five generations of Youngers have gone to. After some eloquent hesitation in his speech, giving Lindner hope, Walter finally tells Lindner that the Youngers are determined to move into their home and do not want his money. Mama is proud of her son, who has at last seen the light; she picks up her plant, looks around the room for the last time, as though surveying the past, and leaves to join the movers and the moving family.

Appendixes

1. ALPHABETICAL LIST OF THE PLAYS

425

2. AUTHORS, LYRICISTS, AND COMPOSERS

(Artists listed here are authors unless otherwise indicated. Names of lyricists are designated [L], and of composers [C]. The numbers throughout the appendixes refer to those in the listing of plays.)

Aiken, George L. (1830–1876) 19

Alfriend, Edward M. (b. 1843) 32

Anderson, John Murray (1886–1954) 93

Anderson, Maxwell (1888–1959) 54, 70, 72

Anonymous 6

Arent, Arthur (1905?–   ) 76

Baker, Benjamin A. (1818–1890) 18

Baker, George Melville (1832–1890) 25

Barker, James Nelson (1784–1858) 8, 11

Barry, Philip (1896–1949) 60

Behrman, Samuel Nathaniel (1893–   ) 64

Belasco, David (1854–1931) 34, 36

Berney, William (1920–   ) 88

Bird, Robert Montgomery (1806–1854) 14

Boker, George Henry (1823–1890) 20

Boucicault, Dion (1820–1890) 21, 22

Brosius, Nancy Bancroft (?   –?   ) 53

Burke, Charles (1822–1854) 22

Connelly, Marc (1890–1964) 51, 62

Crouse, Russel (1893–   ) 78

Daly, Augustin (1838–1899) 23

Davies, John (?   –?   ) 12 (C)

Dunlap, William (1766–1839) 7

Fitch, Clyde (1865–1909) 35

Gazzo, Michael Vincente (1923–   ) 97

Gershwin, George (1898–1937) 63, 69 (C)

Gershwin, Ira (1896–   ) 63, 69, 82 (L)

Gillette, William (1855–1937) 33

Godfrey, Thomas (1736–1763) 2

Goodrich, Frances (189?–   ) 96

Green, Paul (1894–   ) 84

Hackett, Albert (1900–   ) 96

Haines, William Wister (1908–   ) 90

Hammerstein, Oscar II (1895–1960) 86 also (L)

Hansberry, Lorraine (1930–   ) 102

Harrigan, Edward (1845–1911) 26

Hart, Moss (1904–1961) 73, 82

Hecht, Ben (1894–1964) 58

Hellman, Lillian (1905–   ) 79, 85

Hendl, Walter (1917–   ) 88 (C)

Herbert, Victor (1859–1924) 42 (C)

Herne, James A. (1839–1901) 28

Heyward, Dorothy (1890–1961) 69

Heyward, Du Bose (1885–1940) 69

Howard, Bronson (1842–1908) 46

Howard, Sidney (1891–1939) 57

Howells, William Dean (1837–1920) 31

Appendixes

3. SONGS FROM THE PLAYS

430

431

Appendixes

4. DISTINGUISHED ACTORS AND OUTSTANDING ROLES IN THE PLAYS

George Abbott as Jim in *Processional*

Margaret Anglin as Ruth Jordan in *The Great Divide*

George Arliss as Sir Wilfrid Cates-Darby in *The New York Idea*

Fay Bainter as Topsy in *Uncle Tom's Cabin*

Tallulah Bankhead as Regina Hubbard in *The Little Foxes*

Lawrence Barrett as Lanciotto in *Francesca da Rimini*

Blanche Bates as Cho-Cho-San (Madame Butterfly) in *Madame Butterfly* and as The Girl (Minnie Falconer) in *The Girl of the Golden West*

Ed Begley as Matthew Harrison Brady in *Inherit the Wind*

Ralph Bellamy as Franklin D. Roosevelt in *Sunrise at Campobello*

Holbrook Blinn as Regan in *The Boss*

Humphrey Bogart as Duke Mantee in *The Petrified Forest*

Dion Boucicault as Wahnotee in *The Octoroon*

Anne Wiggins Brown as Bess in *Porgy and Bess*

Joseph Buloff as Ali Hakim in *Oklahoma!*

Mrs. Burke as Harriet in *The Forest Rose*

Macdonald Carey as Charley in *Lady in the Dark*

Ina Claire as Marion Froude in *Biography*

Robert Clary in a variety of roles in *New Faces of* 1952

Lee J. Cobb as Willy Loman in *Death of a Salesman*

George M. Cohan as Nat Miller in *Ah, Wilderness!*

Elisha Cook, Jr. as Richard in *Ah, Wilderness!*

Mr. Cooper as Bland in *André*

Frank Craven as Stage Manager in *Our Town*

Broderick Crawford as Lennie in *Of Mice and Men*

Laura Hope Crews as Mrs. Phelps in *The Silver Cord*

A. H. Davenport as George in *The Octoroon*

E. L. Davenport as Lanciotto in *Francesca da Rimini*

Bradford Dillman as Edmund in *Long Day's Journey into Night*

Alfred Drake as Curly McClain in *Oklahoma!*

Todd Duncan as Porgy in *Porgy and Bess*

Mildred Dunnock as Linda in *Death of a Salesman*

436

Florence Eldridge as Mary in *Long Day's Journey into Night*

Charles Ellis as Eben in *Desire under the Elms*

Mary Fickett as Eleanor in *Sunrise at Campobello*

Mrs. Fiske as Cynthia Karslake in *The New York Idea*

Edwin Forrest as Metamora in *Metamora* and as Spartacus in *The Gladiator*

Ben Gazzarra as Johnny Pope in *A Hatful of Rain*

William Gillette as Captain Thorne in *Secret Service*

Claude Gillingwater as Mr. Sharpless in *Madame Butterfly*

Mr. Hallam as Arsaces in *The Prince of Parthia* and as General (Washington) in *André*

Richard B. Harrison as God in *The Green Pastures*

Orville Harrold as Captain Dick in *Naughty Marietta*

Mr. Henry as Colonel Manly in *The Contrast*

Katherine Corcoran Herne as Margaret in *Margaret Fleming*

G. H. Hill as Jonathan Ploughboy in *The Forest Rose*

Pat Hingle as J. B. in *J. B.*

Celeste Holm as Ado Annie in *Oklahoma!*

Leslie Howard as Alan Squier in *The Petrified Forest*

Henry Hull as Jeeter Lester in *Tobacco Road*

Walter Huston as Ephraim in *Desire Under the Elms*

Joseph Jefferson as Scudder in *The Octoroon* and as Rip in *Rip Van Winkle*

Danny Kaye as Russell in *Lady in the Dark*

Arthur Kennedy as Biff in *Death of a Salesman*

Eartha Kitt in a variety of roles in *New Faces of* 1952

Gertrude Lawrence as Liza in *Lady in the Dark*

Marion Lea as Vida Phillimore in *The New York Idea*

Canada Lee as Bigger Thomas in *Native Son*

Gene Lockhart as Sid in *Ah, Wilderness!*

Pauline Lord as Anna in *Anna Christie*

Paul Lukas as Kurt Muller in *Watch on the Rhine*

Bert Lytell as Kendall in *Lady in the Dark*

Claudia McNeil as Mama in *A Raisin in the Sun*

Danforth Marble as Jonathan Ploughboy in *The Forest Rose*

Frederick March as Tyrone in *Long Day's Journey into Night*

Raymond Massey as Abe in *Abe Lincoln in Illinois* and as Mr. Zuss in *J. B.*

Victor Mature as Randy in *Lady in the Dark*

Frank Mayo as Davy in *Davy Crockett*

Burgess Meredith as Mio in *Winterset*

437

Henry Miller as Stephen Ghent in *The Great Divide*

Cameron Mitchell as Happy in *Death of a Salesman*

Paul Muni as Drummond in *Inherit the Wind*

Elaine Pendleton as Abbie in *Desire Under the Elms*

Christopher Plummer as Nickles in *J. B.*

Sidney Poitier as Walter in *A Raisin in the Sun*

Mme. Ponisi as Francesca in *Francesca da Rimini*

Marie Powers as Mme. Flora (Baba) in *The Medium*

Jason Robards, Jr. as James, Jr. in *Long Day's Journey into Night*

Joan Roberts as Laurey Williams in *Oklahoma!*

Agnes Robertson as Zoe in *The Octoroon*

Joseph Schildkraut as Mr. Frank in *The Diary of Anne Frank*

Martha Scott as Emily Webb in *Our Town*

Randolph Scott as Duncan in *So Red the Rose*

Mr. Silsbee as Jonathan Ploughboy in *The Forest Rose*

Howard da Silva as Jud Fry in *Oklahoma!*

Mr. Simpson as Jonathan Ploughboy in *The Forest Rose*

Otis Skinner as Lanciotto in *Francesca da Rimini* and as Uncle Tom in *Uncle Tom's Cabin*

Susan Strasberg as Anne in *The Diary of Anne Frank*

Margaret Sullavan as Vallette in *So Red the Rose*

Laurette Taylor as The Mother in *The Glass Menagerie* and as Peg in *Peg o' My Heart*

Denman Thompson as Joshua Whitcomb in *The Old Homestead*

Emma Trentini as Marietta in *Naughty Marietta*

June Walker as Sadie in *Processional*

Mrs. Wallack as Lydia in *The Forest Rose*

David Wayne as Sakini in *The Teahouse of the August Moon*

Mr. Wignell as Jonathan in *The Contrast*

Hope Williams as Linda in *Holiday*

Shelley Winters as Celia Pope in *A Hatful of Rain*

Louis Wolheim as Yank (Robert Smith) in *The Hairy Ape*

438

5. LITERARY ORIGINS OF THE PLAYS

(Specific information about the origin is given in the synopsis of each play. If a play is not listed, its source is presumed to be the private information or inspiration of the author. Many of the plays listed below also rely heavily upon such information and inspiration.)

HISTORY
   1, 3, 4, 7, 8, 9, 11, 13, 14, 23, 33, 36, 42, 54, 72, 76, 90, 98

NOVEL OR SHORT STORY
   6, 15, 19, 21, 22, 29, 34, 59, 62, 66, 69, 70, 71, 78, 84, 93, 95

POEM
   20

LEGENDS
   22, 24, 43, 88, 100

PLAY
   51, 86, 91

BIOGRAPHY OR BIOGRAPHICAL MATERIALS
   19, 47, 72, 75, 78, 83, 96, 100, 101

6. TYPES OF DRAMA REPRESENTED IN THE PLAYS

COMEDY
  manners 5, 16, 17, 39, 64
  musical 86, 91
  musical, satire 63
  specialized 45
  straight 65, 78
  with social emphasis 81

DRAMA
  agitprop (propaganda) 56, 71, 76
  Americanization 50
  analytical, with music 82
  biographical 75, 96, 101
  community entertainment 25
  expressionistic 49, 51, 71, 84, 85
  fantasy 22, 43, 51, 87, 88
  folk 5, 22, 52, 88
  frontier 36, 67
  high society 35, 46, 60
  historical 9, 33, 75, 98, 101
  impressionistic 44
  legendary 22, 24, 88
  motion picture 70
  naturalistic 41, 73, 92
  operatic 8
  poetry of living 80
  presentational 77
  problem 21
  realistic 28, 29, 38, 40, 46, 47, 57,
    58, 61, 68, 79, 83, 94, 99, 102
  sentimental comic 48
  symbolical 43, 100

television 99
vaudeville-type musical 56
war 33, 54, 90

DRAMATIC DIALOGUE 3

FABLE 62

FARCE
  literary 31
  radio 53
  realistic—allegorical 10
  sardonic—blank verse 4
  satirical 6

MELODRAMA
  crime 32
  farcical musical 30
  frontier 23, 24
  local 18
  moral domestic 15
  pure 37
  vaudeville-type 27

MUSICALS (plays ranging from any significant use of music to full musicals)
  8, 12, 19, 30, 42, 51, 56, 62, 63, 69,
  82, 86, 89, 91, 93

OPERA
  folk 69
  pastoral 12
  realistic 89

440

Appendixes

7. ACT AND SCENE STRUCTURE REPRESENTED IN THE PLAYS

(Numbers in parentheses represent the number of scenes or parts in a given play.)

SIX-ACT
    19, 32

FIVE-ACT
    1, 2, 5, 7, 11, 13, 14, 15, 16, 17, 20, 21, 23, 24, 79

FOUR-ACT
    22, 27, 28, 29, 33, 35, 36, 37, 39, 40, 41, 43, 44, 46, 47, 56, 57, 83

THREE-ACT
    8, 9, 10, 30, 38, 45, 48, 52, 54, 58, 59, 60, 61, 64, 65, 66, 68, 69, 72, 73, 74, 75, 77, 78, 79, 81, 85, 89, 94, 95, 97, 98, 99, 101, 102

TWO-ACT
    4, 6, 12, 18, 42, 63, 67, 76, 82, 86, 88, 89, 91, 92, 93, 96

ONE-ACT
    25, 26, 31, 34, 50, 53

SCENES
    49 (8), 71 (7), 76 (11), 84 (10), 87 (8), 100 (11)

REELS
    70 (9)

PARTS
    51 (2), 55 (3), 62 (2)

DRAMATIC DIALOGUE
    3

442

8. TIMES COVERED IN THE PLAYS

(The times referred to are not dates of authorship or production of the respective dramas but time limits of the action of the drama and therefore of the period of life covered in the drama.)

ANCIENT TIMES
> First century B.C. 2, 14

MEDIEVAL TIMES
> 1300 A.D. 20

SEVENTEENTH CENTURY
> Early settlement in America 8, 11, 13, 43

EIGHTEENTH CENTURY
> 1, 42
> Revolutionary period 3, 4, 7, 22
> Post-revolutionary period 5, 6, 22

1810's
> War of 1812 9, 10, 17, 24

1820's
> 12

1830's
> 75

1840's
> 15, 16, 18, 75
> Gold rush 36

1850's
> 19, 21, 55, 75

1860's
> 23, 75
> Civil War 33, 70

1870's
> 26, 29, 59

1880's
> 27, 78

1890's
> 28, 30, 31, 32, 38

1900's
> 34, 35, 37, 39, 40, 41, 45, 46, 65, 77, 79, 86

1910's
> 44, 77, 83
> World War I 54

1920's
> 47, 48, 49, 50, 51, 52, 53, 56, 57, 58, 60, 61, 69, 98, 101

1930's
> 63, 64, 66, 67, 68, 71, 72, 73, 74, 80, 81, 84, 87

9. THEMES REPRESENTED IN THE PLAYS

(Only themes which assume more than casual importance in a play are considered for this list, but a play may be listed under more than one theme.)

Adolescent upbringing 65, 68, 84, 93, 96, 98

Adventurous life and dream fulfillment 23, 36, 38, 42, 60, 64, 67, 74, 82

American wars and battles 1, 4, 7, 9, 13, 33, 54, 70, 90, 95, 96

American way, the 5, 16, 39, 49, 50, 52, 63, 75, 85

Artists and the artist life 41, 51, 64, 91, 93

Bigotry 11, 19, 48, 52, 56, 58, 71, 99

Business life 10, 35, 41, 44, 46, 48, 49, 51, 56, 60, 78, 79, 92, 98

Careers and occupations 58, 64, 82, 89, 95

City–county (urban–rural) contrast 12, 37, 86, 102

City life 5, 18, 30, 32, 35, 39, 41, 58, 61, 76, 78, 84, 97, 98, 102

College life 81

Criminal and shady activities 32, 35, 36, 37, 40, 41, 47, 56, 67, 69, 80, 89, 91, 97

Domestic conflict 22, 28, 39, 57, 61, 81, 91

Domestic triangle 20, 28, 34, 55, 57, 93

East–West contrast 23, 38, 67

Espionage 33

European–American contrast 5, 16, 17, 29, 32, 45, 54, 64, 85, 90, 93

Family conflict 55, 79, 83, 97, 102

Feminine aspiration 9, 28, 34, 36, 47, 55, 65, 94

Frontier development 23, 24, 36, 38, 59, 67, 86

Immigrant, the 18, 42, 45, 47, 50, 59, 61

Indian co-existence 8

Indian conflict 1, 13, 23

Inter-class conflict 16, 24, 31, 35, 45, 49, 56, 68, 71, 81, 84, 95

Justice 58, 72, 98, 100

Love and Duty
 (Asiatic setting) 2
 (European setting) 20
 (Southern United States) 70
 (Under Nazi oppression) 96

Marriage and divorce 16, 28, 34, 39, 57, 77, 81, 91, 93

Moral satire 6

Moral suasion 19, 32, 37, 40, 43, 100

Mentalism 40

10. OUTSTANDING PERSONALITIES FROM THE PLAYS

11. HONORS AND DISTINCTIONS WON BY THE PLAYS

Winner of Pulitzer Prize, Critics' Circle Award, and Antoinette Perry Award

The Diary of Anne Frank

Winners of Pulitzer Prize and Critics' Circle Award

The Time of Your Life
Watch on the Rhine
The Teahouse of the August Moon

Other Winners of Pulitzer Prizes

Anna Christie
Street Scene
Of Thee I Sing
Abe Lincoln in Illinois
Long Day's Journey into Night

Other Winner of Critics' Circle Award

A Raisin in the Sun

OTHER HONORS AND DISTINCTIONS

First drama by an American to be professionally produced

The Prince of Parthia

Second drama by an American to be professionally produced; first native American drama

The Contrast

448

Appendixes

Dramatization concerning first (or second) American novel published

Occurrences of the Times

Most powerful of the temperance dramas in the mid-nineteenth century; carried over the country by P. T. Barnum; became an olio in the 1930's, playing for nearly 7,000 consecutive performances to more than 2,000,000 spectators

The Drunkard; or, The Fallen Saved

Only drama written that has been performed millions of times

Uncle Tom's Cabin

Record holder for 28 years (1891–1919) for continuous performances in New York

A Trip to Chinatown

Played 5,987 performances, with eight companies, in three years

Peg O' My Heart

First radio play printed in America (1925)

Sue 'Em

First significant portrayal of the modern American newspaperman in American drama

The Front Page

Represented America on the cultural scene in many foreign countries, for several years in the 1950's

Porgy and Bess

Holds the record for consecutive performances of a drama in New York (3,216 performances)

Life with Father

Dramatization of an epoch-making novel by the first fully accepted American Negro novelist

Native Son

449

Holds the record for continuous performances of a musical drama on the American stage (2,248 performances on Broadway)

Oklahoma

12. FOR FURTHER PURSUIT

As stated in the Preface, it is highly desirable that the reader move from these synopses to the full texts of these plays and of others like them. It is not feasible, however, to include here a bibliography that would cover the field. Instead, there follow suggestions of significant sources, listed by name of author or compiler only. By reference to card catalogues in libraries and to standard reference works, the names of the necessary volumes for further pursuit can easily be found.

Suggestions are grouped below. Drama periodicals serve as sources and offer enlightening contemporary notes; special theater collections contain many standard plays and many original (often unique) playscripts and documents on American drama and American life.

Besides all these, the reader should consult works by the authors of plays in this volume and biographical and autobiographical material relating to actors, producers, and other stage personalities.

ANTHOLOGISTS, BIBLIOGRAPHERS, COLLECTORS, AND INDEXERS OF PLAYS

Blanch M. Baker, Daniel C. Blum, Jack Burton, Bennett Cerf and Van H. Cartmell, John Chapman, Barrett H. Clark (often with collaborators), Kathryn Coe and William H. Cordell, Richard A. Cordell, Thomas H. Dickinson, Alan Downer, Francis E. W. Drury, Charles Evans, Famous Plays, Ina Ten Eyck Firkins, John Gassner, Jack Gaver, Rosamund Gilder, Allan G. Halline, Phyllis Hartnoll, Harlan Hatcher, William H. Hildreth and Wilson R. Dumble, Frank Pierce Hill, Louis Kronenberger, Hannah Logasa (and collaborators), Burns Mantle, Walter J. Meserve, Montrose J. Moses, George Jean Nathan, John H. Ottemiller, John Parker, Arthur H. Quinn, Robert F. Roden, Robert L. Sherman, Garrison Sherwood, M. W. Steinberg, *Theater Arts* magazine (publishes a new text each month), Ruth G. Thomson, S. Marion Tucker, Robert Warnock, Oscar Wegelin, E. Bradlee Watson and Benefield Pressey, Charles Whitman.

HISTORIANS

T. Allston Brown, William W. Clapp, Barrett H. Clark, Harold Clurman, Oral S. Coad and Edwin Mims, Jr., Mary C. Crawford, Alan Downer, William Dunlap,

Hallie Flanagan, Marvin Felheim, Eleanor Flexner, George Freedley (and collaborators), Edmond M. Gagey, John Gassner, Norman Hapgood, Barnard W. Hewitt, Arthur Hornblow, Norris Houghton, Lynton Hudson, Glenn Hughes, Edith J. R. Isaacs, Reese D. James, Wisner P. Kinne, Joseph Wood Krutch, Margaret Mayorga, Joseph Mersand, Richard Moody, Montrose J. Moses, George Jean Nathan, George W. C. Odell, Arthur H. Quinn, George O. Seilhamer, Robert E. Spiller *et al* (also bibliography), Eugene Tompkins and Eugene Kilby, Moses Coit Tyler, Arthur Wilson.

CHIEF CRITICS AND INTERPRETERS
(See also Historians, Anthologists, and Collectors)

Brooks Atkinson, Eric Bentley, Frederic G. Cassidy, Thomas H. Dickinson, Walter Pritchard Eaton, Edmond M. Gagey, Rosamund Gilder *et al*, Isaac Goldberg, Laurence Hutton, Frank O'Hara, Oliver Sayler, Richard D. Skinner, Felix Sper, Thomas K. Whipple, Stark Young.

DRAMA PERIODICALS

New York Theatre Critics' Reviews, Quarterly Journal of Speech, Stage (1923–1939), *Theatre* (1900–1931), *Theatre Annual* (1942–1956), *Theatre Arts* and *Theatre Arts Magazine*; also drama pages in newspapers such as *The New York Times.*

SPECIAL THEATER COLLECTIONS

American Antiquarian Society, Worcester, Massachusetts; Boston Public Library; Brown University Library; Harvard University Library; Henry E. Huntington Library, San Marino, California; Howard University Library; The Library of Congress (especially the Rare Book Collection); New York Public Library (especially the Theater Collection); Players Club, New York; Princeton University Library; University of Chicago Library; University of Pennsylvania Library; Yale University Library.

DATE DUE

HIGHSMITH 45230